JEWS IN
BRITISH INDIA

JEWS IN BRITISH INDIA

IDENTITY IN A COLONIAL ERA

JOAN G. ROLAND

PUBLISHED FOR BRANDEIS UNIVERSITY PRESS BY
UNIVERSITY PRESS OF NEW ENGLAND
HANOVER AND LONDON

UNIVERSITY PRESS OF NEW ENGLAND

Brandeis University   Dartmouth College
Brown University   University of New Hampshire
Clark University   University of Rhode Island
University of Connecticut   Tufts University
University of Vermont

Printed in the United States of America

∞

LIBRARY OF CONGRESS CATALOGING IN PUBLICATION DATA
Roland, Joan G.
    Jews in British India.
    (The Tauber Institute for the Study of European
Jewry series ; 9)
    Bibliography: p.
    Includes index.
    1. Jews—India—History.   2. Bene-Israel—History.
3. India—Ethnic relations.   I. Title.   II. Series.
DS135.I6R65   1989   954'.004924   88–40113
ISBN 0–87451–457–6

For Alan,
Tika, and Ariel

The Tauber Institute for the Study of European Jewry, established by a gift to Brandeis University from Dr. Laszlo N. Tauber, is dedicated to the memory of the victims of Nazi persecutions between 1933 and 1945. The Institute seeks to study the history and culture of European Jewry in the modern period. The Institute has a special interest in studying the causes, nature, and consequences of the European Jewish catastrophe and seeks to explore them within the context of modern European diplomatic, intellectual, political, and social history. The Tauber Institute for the Study of European Jewry is organized on a multidisciplinary basis, with the participation of scholars in history, Judaic studies, political science, sociology, comparative literature, and other disciplines.

THE TAUBER INSTITUTE FOR THE STUDY OF EUROPEAN JEWRY SERIES
Jehuda Reinharz, General Editor

CONTENTS

Illustrations follow page 28

PREFACE

My interest in the Jews of India dates from my first visit to India in 1964, when I was introduced to the Bene Israel of Bombay by Samuel Daniel, a friend from New York who was a member of the community. Coincidentally, I was working at the time on a dissertation on the activities of the Alliance Israélite Universelle with the Jews of North Africa during the period that the French were consolidating their presence there. As I became more aware of the evolving identity of the Jews as a minority group in an imperial setting and some of the intracommunal struggles that were thus engendered, I gradually realized that there were parallels in the situation of the Jews in British India and of those in colonial North Africa. It was not, however, until 1977, after preliminary research in New York, that I was able to go back to India and spend close to a year collecting the materials, both written and oral, for this study.

This study simply could not have been done without the cooperation of the Jews of India. Their willingness to share their experiences and memories with me, to lend me materials in their possession and to guide me to others, was invaluable. Although the contributions of many will become evident in the text, there are a few to whom particular thanks are due. I owe a very special debt to the late Benjamin J. Israel, the Bene Israel scholar whose unfailing cooperation with and generosity toward many researchers have enriched and influenced the study of his community for the last thirty years. He served as my guide throughout this work, giving me free access to his collection of early twentieth-century Bene Israel materials, articles that he had not yet published, and files of his father's correspondence and documents. Most important, he shared his insights and analyses with me during my stays in India and through correspondence over a period of several years, and he read portions of the manuscript. I am also grateful to the late Isaiah Isaac Shapurkar, another Bene Israel who lent me volumes of archival materials that he had carefully preserved from a vast array of sources over many years. Others who provided access to either personal or institutional archival materials were Daniel Elijah Gadkar in Poona; Ezra Kolet in New Delhi; Sam Abraham, Joel Ezekiel, Moshe Sultoon, and Albert Elias in Bombay; and Dr. Sol Erulkar in Philadelphia.

Many people provided generous hospitality in India, but I would particularly like to mention Sam and Bension Abraham, and Sophie and Simon

Israel. Meher Patuck and Marge and Na'im Gubbay not only opened their homes to my family but provided immeasurable assistance in solving the problems of daily life during several stays in Bombay.

The personnel of numerous libraries and archival collections, such as the Jewish Division of the New York Public Library and the Jewish Theological Seminary in New York, the National Archives in New Delhi, the Maharastran Archives in Bombay, and the Central Zionist Archives in Jerusalem, rendered considerable assistance. I would particularly like to thank Roy Anderson of the Bombay University Library, Priya N. Athavale of the Mumbai Marathi Granthasangrahalaya in Bombay, and L. Cohn and Trudi Levy of the Mocatta Library in London, who were extremely helpful in locating materials and making arrangements to reproduce them. For translations, Professor G. H. Godbole and R. D. D'Silva assiduously rendered into English the relevant Marathi sections from nineteenth- and early twentieth-century Bene Israel periodicals. Ora Percus helped with some nineteenth-century Hebrew materials.

Conversations and correspondence with Shirley Isenberg of Jerusalem helped shape some of my thinking on the Bene Israel and led me to further sources. Comments by Myron Weiner on my paper on Zionism in India suggested new avenues of research. I am indebted to several people who have read parts or all of the manuscript. Thomas Timberg has encouraged me with suggestions at all stages of the research and on the final draft. I have benefited enormously from David Lelyveld's comments on an earlier version of the manuscript: discussions with him opened new perspectives that enabled me to place my material on the Jews in a broader Indian context. Nathan Katz added new insights and refinements. For preparation of the final manuscript, Jean McConochie's careful editing helped greatly. I must also thank Charles Backus of the University Press of New England, whose insistence that the study be presented as effectively as possible and whose efforts to help me in that direction were painful at times, but much appreciated. Joan Bothell's meticulous copyediting and the support of the Press staff have also helped to make this a better book.

Research in England, India, and Israel was made possible by a fellowship from the Fulbright-Hays Faculty Research Abroad Program. I would like to thank their staff in India, particularly C. S. Ramakrishnan in New Delhi and R. P. Sharma in Bombay for their help in gaining access to official archives and assistance with living arrangements. Additional financial support came from the Memorial Foundation for Jewish Culture. I am also grateful to the Scholarly Research Committee of Pace University, whose grants of funds and of released time from teaching over the years have enabled me to turn my research into a book. I especially wish to thank Dean Joseph E. Houle, vice-provost of Pace University and dean of its Dyson College of Arts and Sciences,

who provided a subvention to help defray the publication costs. Thomas
Timberg, editor of *Jews in India* (New York, 1986), has kindly granted me
permission to reproduce, in chapter 4 of the present work, material that
appeared in slightly different form in my contribution to his book. I am
grateful to the Tauber Institute, Brandeis University, for inclusion in this
series on the study of European Jewry.

And finally, thanks go to my husband, Alan, for his support (and sympathy)
throughout the many stages of this study, and to my children, Tika and Ariel,
who must at times have wondered if either of their parents would ever finish
"those books on India."

New York, New York   J.R.
April 1988

JEWS IN
BRITISH INDIA

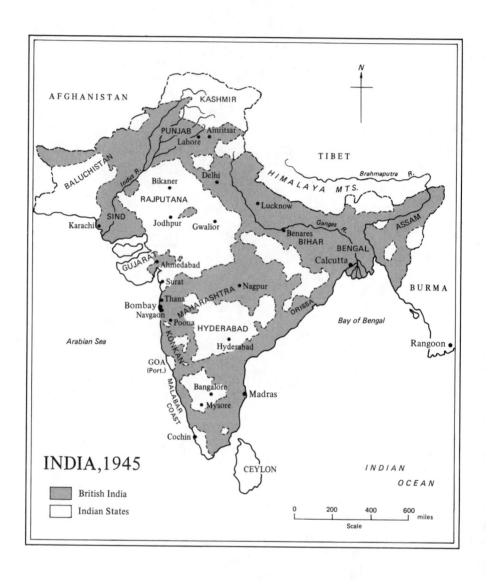

AFGHANISTAN

KASHMIR

PUNJAB •Amritsar
Lahore•

BALUCHISTAN

Indus R.

TIBET

Brahmaputra R.

HIMALAYA MTS.

Bikaner •Delhi

RAJPUTANA

•Lucknow

SIND

Karachi•

Jodhpur •Gwalior

Ganges R.

ASSAM

•Benares
BIHAR

BENGAL

Calcutta•

GUJARAT

•Ahmedabad

•Surat

•Thana

•Nagpur

MAHARASHTRA

Bombay•
Navgaon•

•Poona

HYDERABAD

BURMA

Arabian Sea

KONKAN

GOA
(Port.)

Hyderabad•

Bay of Bengal

Rangoon •

MALABAR
COAST

Bangalore•

•Mysore

•Madras

Cochin•

INDIA, 1945

███ British India

☐ Indian States

CEYLON

INDIAN

OCEAN

0	200	400	600

miles

Scale

INTRODUCTION

Although scholarly specialists and some laypeople have long been aware of the existence of Jews in India, it was ironically a noisy controversy in Israel that drew the attention of many to these relatively unfamiliar communities. Concerned about their observance of marriage laws, the Sephardic chief rabbi, Itzak Nissim, issued a directive in 1962 ordering rabbis in Israel to investigate the ancestry of the Bene Israel, one of the two main groups of Indian Jews who had recently emigrated to Israel, "as far back as it is possible" before officiating at any marriages between a member of this group and a Jew from any other community. Unless it could be proved that there were no infractions of Jewish marriage and divorce procedures, or unless he or she were marrying another Bene Israel individual, the person in question had to undergo formal ritual conversion before the ceremony could proceed.

Quickly this issue became a *cause célèbre*, as the Bene Israel and their supporters accused the rabbinate of "racism," arguing that reformed Jews from affluent Western countries were not subject to such an extensive investigation before being permitted to marry other Jews. After demonstrations in August 1964, Prime Minister Levi Eshkol persuaded a specially convened session of the Knesset to pass a resolution supporting the Bene Israel position and asking the rabbinate to remove "every factor producing a feeling of discrimination." Two weeks later, the Chief Rabbinate Council issued a statement deleting the words "Bene Israel" from the directive so that the extensive investigation would apply to all Jews whose status was doubtful.

Interestingly, the eruption of the controversy over the Bene Israel may have been the result of the export of group conflict from India to Israel. The Bene Israel charged that it was no mere coincidence that the chief rabbi, Itzak Nissim, was from the Baghdadi Jewish community of Iraq, a segment of which formed another principal group of Jews resident in India, and that his views may have been colored by Baghdadi attitudes toward Bene Israel that had long prevailed in India.[1]

Just who are these people, and what were their Indian origins? Although representing a microscopic segment of the Indian population, the three major Jewish communities there—the Cochin Jews of the Malabar Coast in the southwest, the Bene Israel of western India, and the Baghdadi (or Iraqi) Jews of Bombay and Calcutta—have always aroused curiosity because of the legendary long-term residence of the first two groups, the commercial and

1

philanthropic activities of the third, and the security enjoyed by all. Yet their reputation and importance always far exceeded their numbers. At its peak in 1951, the total Jewish population was no more than thirty thousand in a country that at the time contained over three hundred million people. And now, although India is perhaps the one country in the world where the Jews have maintained their identity without ever being exposed to anti-Semitism or other forms of religious persecution at the hands of their hosts, the Jewish communities there are gradually disintegrating. As materials disappear and elderly people and their memories die, it becomes imperative to make the published record of Jewish life in India as complete as possible.

Indian Jews themselves have endeavored for almost a century to write about their past for the benefit of both their own communities and the outside world. Some of their works have served as sources for pioneer studies by Western Jewish historians and social anthropologists. Specific aspects of Bene Israel and Cochin Jewish history in India and Israel have been the subjects of dissertations and articles. Many of these studies have been attempts to identify their origins and early history, often focusing on the question of whether they were originally Diaspora Jews or native converts. Indeed the dispute over the authenticity of the Bene Israel's "Jewishness," which is still alive in some quarters, dates back to the nineteenth century.[2]

Generally speaking, the development of Zionism over the last hundred years and the emergence of the State of Israel have given the question "Who are the Jews?" a significance that goes far beyond the limits of Jewish history proper. The modern concept of the Jewish people as a nation is essentially a European one, with its roots deeply embedded in nineteenth-century nationalist ideology. For non-European Jews, however, the constructs of community, ethnicity, and religious sect were more relevant in their efforts to maintain their identity. The diverse origins of the current Israeli population are often reflected in their divergent views on these matters.

Defining the Jews of India, in particular, has its own set of special problems. In India, a group-based society, the groups to which an individual belongs greatly determine his behavior. There are indeed two interrelated contexts in which the position of the Jews of India may be observed, both of which can serve as a focus for exploring identity and social change: caste and ethnic pluralism. Although caste was not necessarily the most significant aspect of the Indian Jewish environment, it was certainly a unique feature—as distinct from the experience of other Jewish communities in the world. Indeed, caste cannot be overlooked in any study of groups in India, even if one is writing about a non-Hindu minority. An individual Hindu is born into a caste: his caste is ascriptive and unchanging. Ideas of purity and pollution are extremely important concepts in the caste system, where pollution may refer to uncleanliness, defilement, impurity short of defilement, and indirectly even to sinfulness, while purity refers to cleanliness, spiritual merit and indirectly to holiness.

The structural distance between various castes is defined in terms of pollution and purity. A higher caste is always "pure" in relation to a lower caste, and in order to retain its higher status it should abstain from certain forms of contact with the lower. It may not ordinarily eat food cooked by them, or marry or have sex relations with them.[3]

When one speaks of mobility in the caste system, one really means group mobility, not individual mobility. This mobility comes about through a process that M. N. Srinivas has called Sanskritization, in which "a 'low' Hindu caste or tribal or other group, changes its customs, ritual, ideology, and way of life in the direction of a high, and frequently, 'twice-born' caste."[4] Generally, such changes are followed by a claim, made over a period of time, to a higher position in the caste hierarchy. The upward movement of a caste is marked by, among other things, the banning of divorce and widow remarriage. Thus, the tendency of caste groups that are low in the social hierarchy to imitate the style of life of higher castes introduces a degree of fluidity into the total hierarchy of castes. Yet the imitation of behavior of higher castes alone is not enough to bring about changes in caste status; other significant changes in economic activities or relations between the castes are necessary.[5]

Indian civilization is also marked by a form of absorption, of tolerance, of the acceptance of "unity in diversity." Under the caste system, people tend to feel that some institutions, ideas, beliefs, and practices are relevant to one's group while others are not; Hinduism is prepared to affirm, in a culturally pluralistic way, the truth of all religions. Indeed, many educated Hindus see evangelism by people who believe their own religion to be true and all others false as the manifestation of aggressive intolerance.[6]

One of the ways in which Hindu toleration of small minority communities has expressed itself has been through the almost castelike designation of varied groups. The caste system "made heresy-hunting unnecessary. A rebel sect or group in the course of time became a caste, which ensured its existence though at the cost of sealing it hermetically from the rest of the society."[7] Thus, although they were not rebels or heretics within the Hindu system, groups such as Christians, Jews, and Parsis in particular were thought to have certain traditions, roles, culture—so that a live-and-let-live policy could develop within a caste environment.[8]

In the eighteenth and nineteenth centuries, rural Bene Israel living in an area known as the Konkan, south of Bombay, were called *Shanwar Telis* (Saturday oil-pressers), a relatively low-caste designation, the name stemming from the fact that many practiced this occupation but abstained from work on the Sabbath. The Bene Israel in this period often refrained from widow remarriage and beef-eating—sometimes all meat-eating. Perhaps they were attempting to raise their position socially or to rise in public esteem by imitating the behavior of the higher castes (a form of Sanskritization) or perhaps they simply wished to show respect for their neighbors by not engaging in practices that the latter would find offensive. The occupation of oil-presser and the concept of pollution that determined the relations between the Bene Israel and Hindus made it difficult for the Bene Israel as a group, despite their adoption of higher caste practices, to raise their status in the caste hierarchy in the Konkan. Since the religious difference actually put the Bene Israel outside the caste hierarchy proper, theoretically they should have had the status of outcastes. But in practice, non-Hindus tended to have a social status higher than that which their occupations would give them if they were Hindus. Before the British came, the Konkan was dominated by Muslims much longer than by Hindus. During this period, the Bene Israel lived in very close harmony with the Muslims and shared their status. From the beginning of the twentieth century, however, "the Bene Israel derived their status not from their standing in Konkan society, but from their position in the cosmopolitan city of Bombay . . . [where] social status no longer derived from caste, but from class, which cut across caste or religious divisions."[9]

Even if one thinks of Indian Jews as a whole as a castelike group, one can also see the overtones of the caste system in the relationship within and between the Jewish communities themselves. The Cochin Jews had three endogamous castelike groups—"black," "white," and "brown" Jews—that did not interdine and intermarry. Bene Israel also distinguish between *Kala* (black) and *Gora* (white) Jews. In both cases, the questions of ancestry, or descent, were important. The so-called white Jews of each group considered the others "impure" because they were believed to descend from non-Jewish mothers or from those who had been converted. Although the concept of purity in this case is not the same as that in the true Indian caste sense, which refers to ritual purity and cleanliness, dietary restrictions were naturally maintained by the Jews also. *Kashruth*, the observance of Jewish ritual dietary laws, was important for all Indian Jews. Moreover, white Jews among both Cochinis and Bene Israel did not want black Jews near their cooking utensils. The Baghdadi Jews also adopted castelike attitudes toward the Bene Israel because of their lack of ritual orthodoxy and supposed "ancestral impurity." In some, but not all, of these instances of "caste" distinction, color played an important secondary role.[10]

Thus, in speaking of Jewish ethnic identity in India, one inevitably deals with caste. But superimposed on this traditional Indian structure was the British colonial presence, especially after 1857, when direct political rule over

India was transferred from the British East India Company to the British crown.[11] Jews in India now became British subjects.

It is commonly accepted that the phenomenon of imperialism is an important facet of European Jewish history. The establishment of colonial empires affected not only those Jews from the mother country—or other countries—who chose to migrate to newly acquired lands, but also indigenous Jews in territories that now became European colonies.

British India provides an excellent example of the experience of Jewish communities as minorities in an imperial setting. How did the British presence affect the way in which the Jewish communities related to each other and to other Indian groups, the extent to which they identified with other Indians or with the colonial rulers, their attitudes toward Indian political aspirations, and their eventual relationships with Zionism, a European ideology? What did it mean to be a Jew in British India? Did the position of the Jewish communities remain static or did it change? And, ultimately, because of the economic repercussions, what was the effect of the British departure from India on the decision of Jews to remain in or leave the country?

Further complicating the choices faced by the Jewish communities of India was the emergence, simultaneous with the development of Indian nationalism, of world Zionism. Although Cochin and Baghdadi Jews had always been conscious that they belonged to an international brotherhood of Jews, the awareness of the Jewish world beyond India and their connection with it developed only gradually among the Bene Israel, beginning primarily in the nineteenth century with the teachings of the Christian missionaries and the contact with British Jewry that the acquisition of English facilitated. Zionism was a whole new ideology that forced the communities to rethink their identity as Jews, within both an Indian context and an international one.

These three factors—the Indian setting, the rise and fall of the British presence there, and the emergence of Zionism and the State of Israel—provide the essential background and context for this study. The focus is limited primarily to the Bene Israel and Baghdadis in Bombay and, to a lesser extent, in Calcutta. The Cochin Jews are mentioned only in passing. Never numbering more than twenty-five hundred persons and therefore constituting a much smaller group than either the Bene Israel or the Baghdadis (about twenty thousand and five thousand respectively, at their maximum strength in 1951), the Cochin Jews have always been the best known of the Indian Jewish communities to the outside world. Because this group has been studied in depth and because Cochin was in any case an Indian state, not a part of the British raj, it is not a principal subject of this book.[12]

If the historical process of a Jewish community developing its identity is the focus of this book, an underlying theme is that of ethnic diversity in a plural society. Because the understanding of the Jewish experience in India can be enriched by comparisons with the experience of other minorities, a brief note about three of these groups seems in order. Although the Muslims are the largest of the minorities in India—over 11 percent of the population— the experiences of the Indian Christian, Anglo-Indian, and Parsi communities are more relevant for this study.

Although Christianity originally gained adherents in India from the upper castes—and there are pockets of Christians, particularly the Syrian Christians in Kerala, who have been in India for many centuries—most Indian Christians are descendants of low-caste Hindus and untouchables who converted in the nineteenth and twentieth centuries. Caste distinctions may still be found among Indian Christians: those who claimed more ancient and religiously pure descent considered themselves superior to Christians of more recent conversion. The census of 1981 showed the Christians to constitute about 2.4 percent of the Indian population, some 16.2 million people.[13]

One consequence of colonization in Asia has been racial mixture between European males and Asian females. In India, unions of British soldiers and traders with Indian women beginning in the late seventeenth century were the origins of the Eurasian, or Anglo-Indian, population. The Indian Constitution defines an Anglo-Indian as

> a person whose father or any of whose other male progenitors in the male line is or was of European descent but who is domiciled within the territory of India and is or was born within such territory of parents habitually resident therein and not established there for temporary purposes only.[14]

If the male parent was Indian and the female parent European, the person was simply considered Indian. Thus, the Anglo-Indians are the only Indian minority essentially definable in racial terms. It has been estimated that the present population does not exceed a hundred thousand. Although the Anglo-Indians' customs, family patterns, language, and religion—they are Christian through their ancestry, rather than through conversion—are more similar to those of the British than those of Indians, they often developed separate schools, clubs, and churches.[15]

The Parsis, Zoroastrians fleeing Persia (Iran) after the Muslim conquest, arrived in India in the early eighth century. From the seventeenth to the nineteenth centuries, they were able to take advantage of the new opportunities provided by the developing commerce and the growth of Indian ports, particularly Bombay, under the British. Although they had early on adopted Gujarati as their mother tongue, they were prepared to take advantage of Western education, and their command of English enabled them to serve as middlemen between the British and Hindus. Large Parsi fortunes, such as those of the Jijibhoys and Tatas, led to considerable philanthropy, similar, as we shall see, to that of the Baghdadi Sassoons. According to the 1971 census, there were more than ninety-one thousand Parsis, living chiefly in Maharastra and Gujarat.[16]

This study of the Jews of India is based on research in the National Archives in New Delhi, the Maharastran Archives in Bombay, Jewish institutional archives in Bombay and New Delhi, the Central Zionist Archives in Jerusalem, and the Mocatta Library in London. The Bene Israel community's own voice comes out most clearly in its nineteenth- and twentieth-century periodicals in English and Marathi (which were translated for me), located in the Marathi Mumbai Granthasangrahalaya in Bombay and in private collections. Twentieth-century Baghdadi periodicals were also a valuable source of information. Another important segment of my research consisted of a series of interviews I conducted with more than forty Bene Israel and Baghdadi Jews in India and with concerned individuals in Israel, all of whom were aware that their responses might be used in this publication. Some of these interviews and conversations lasted no more than an hour. Others represented a series of talks over a three-year period. These sources are naturally subjective—particularly when informants are talking from memory, perhaps reporting on events that occurred during their childhoods. At times it has been possible to corroborate (or correct) this material with written sources; at other times, however, this information has to be seen as the modern historical self-view of Indian Jews.

PART I
THE SETTING

CHAPTER 1

JEWS AND SOCIETY
IN PREMODERN INDIA

Origins and Early History of the Bene Israel

A lack of reliable evidence prevents us from determining the actual origin or direct lineage of the Bene Israel and the exact time that the group appeared in western India. Bene Israel traditions maintain that they are descendants of one of the Ten Tribes of Israel, but from that part of the population which was not deported after the Assyrians defeated the Kingdom of Israel in the eighth century B.C.[1] According to their legends, the ancestors of the Bene Israel left northern Palestine, possibly fleeing the persecutions of Antiochus Epiphanes around 175 B.C., or perhaps later, and were shipwrecked near the village of Navgaon on the Konkan Coast of western India, twenty-six miles south of Bombay. Only seven men and women survived; they buried the bodies of the others in large graves still to be found at the site.[2] Other scholars have proposed different theories of place and date of origin of this community: that the Bene Israel arrived in the reign of King Solomon in the tenth century B.C., before the Ten Tribes separated from the other two,[3] that they came from Yemen in the middle of the first millennium A.D.,[4] or that they were part of the dispersal that took place after the destruction of the Second Temple in A.D. 70. There may have been more than one immigration, including one from an Arab country in the fourth century A.D. as a result of the Sasanid Persian persecution. B. J. Israel, the most knowledgeable Bene Israel writing about the community in recent times, studied these various claims and seemed to favor a theory that the Bene Israel came to India in the fifth or sixth century A.D. from either southern Arabia or Persia (in both places there was trouble for the Jews at the time).[5]

But as there are no written records, inscriptions, or other evidence to confirm or disprove any of these conjectures, the origins of the Bene Israel remain shrouded in legend. A few individuals have even suggested that the Bene Israel descend from local inhabitants who were converted. In a letter

11

to the rabbis of Lunel written in 1199 or 1200, Moses Maimonides, the celebrated Jewish philosopher, theologian, and physician, wrote, "The Jews of India know nothing of the Torah and of the laws nothing save the Sabbath and Circumcision."[6] The only Jews in India that would have fit that description were the Bene Israel, although we have no evidence that that was the community to which he was referring. The earliest written reference to a permanent Jewish settlement in the Konkan region is a letter from J. A. Sartorious, a Danish Christian missionary, who in 1738 mentioned hearing about a community of Jews in "Surat and Rajapore" who called themselves Bene Israel, and who did not have the Bible or know Hebrew. The only prayer that they knew was the Shema, the most important prayer of the Jews. In the earliest Cochini reference to the community, the Cochin Jewish merchant Ezekiel Rahabi wrote a report to the Jews of Amsterdam in 1768, mentioning the role the Cochinis were playing in the instruction of the Bene Israel. Bene Israel tradition speaks of a David Rahabi who around A.D. 1000 came to the Konkan and "discovered" the Bene Israel, recognizing them as Jewish from some of their practices: observance of circumcision and the Sabbath, and the refusal of the women to cook fish without scales. Actually, Rahabi family records do show that a son of Ezekiel Rahabi, David, visited western India and encountered the Bene Israel in the mid eighteenth century, while serving as an agent of the Dutch East India Company. B. J. Israel suggests that the Bene Israel might have in their memory amalgamated the first "discovery" by Maimonides with the later visit of David Rahabi.[7]

Nor is it clear when or how the name *Bene Israel* (Children of Israel) was adopted. H. S. Kehimkar, a Bene Israel historian writing at the end of the nineteenth century, claimed that the community took the name from the Koran (*Banu Israel* of the Hijaz) so that its members would not suffer at the hands of Muslims as they might have had they been known as Jews, or *Yahudis*. B. J. Israel suggests that the Bene Israel might have originated in a country dominated by Islam or that they took their name in India while under Muslim rule.[8]

The early history of the Bene Israel is also obscure. From Navgaon they gradually dispersed throughout the coastal Konkan villages, living in small communities of perhaps no more than one hundred people. Intermarriage with native women probably occurred to some extent. Cut off for centuries from contact with the mainstream of Jewish life, the Bene Israel gradually forgot all but a few essential elements of the Jewish religion. They continued to observe dietary laws and circumcision and abstained from work on the Sabbath. They celebrated the festivals of the New Year, Day of Atonement, Passover, Purim, and Feast of Ingathering, reciting the Shema on these and other important occasions. Given their long isolation, the maintenance of these traditions seems remarkable. For the rest, they slowly assimilated into their surroundings. Having no Hebrew prayer books, Bible, or Talmud, they forgot most of their Hebrew language and prayers.[9] They adopted the regional dress as well as the local language, Marathi, as their mother tongue. Even their names began to show signs of assimilation. First names were Indianized: Samuel became Samaji; Ezekiel, Hassaji; Isaac, Issaji.

They developed traditional Marathi surnames by adding the suffix *kar* (inhabitant of) to the names of the villages where they originally resided, so that those who lived in Kehim became Kehimkars, those from Cheul, Cheulkars, residents of Talgaon, Talgaonkars. Nowadays, the Bene Israel have reverted to traditional biblical first names and also use biblical surnames, often patronyms. Although the village surnames are rarely used, most members of a community know the village names of others.[10]

The Bene Israel also adopted certain social customs from their Hindu and Muslim neighbors, such as laws of inheritance, ceremonial food offerings, and observance of certain marriage and funeral customs, but these did not affect Jewish ritual.[11] They engaged in agriculture and coconut oil-pressing, gradually becoming known as *Shanwar Telis* (Saturday oilmen). This castelike designation placed them at the lower end of the Konkan class structure, since farming and oil-pressing were not particularly prestigious occupations. Some Bene Israel who had moved considerably up the socioeconomic ladder later resented being called *telis* because of the lower-class implications.[12]

Many Bene Israel date an early revival of their Jewish heritage to somewhere between the eleventh and fifteenth centuries A.D., when David Rahabi recognized them as Jewish and began to teach them the Hebrew language, as well as the liturgy, scriptures, rituals, and ceremonies of Judaism that they had forgotten. If this individual is indeed the mid-eighteenth-century Rahabi who came from Cochin, it is likely that he is the one who taught them Hebrew and brought them into the mainstream of Judaism. He selected young men from three prominent families—the Jhiradkars, Shapurkars, and Rajpurkars—for special teaching. These families had already been providing the community with leaders or teachers called *kajis* (from the Arabic *kadi*, or judge), who traveled throughout the Konkan to officiate at ceremonies and to settle disputes.[13]

By the middle of the eighteenth century, the Bene Israel population of the Konkan probably did not exceed five thousand. At this time they began moving from the villages to the towns of Pen, Panvel, and Thana, and then to Bombay, which was developing under the British and needed carpenters, masons, mechanics, and skilled tradesmen and artisans of all kinds. Bombay offered educational opportunities as well as employment, and the British East India Company was still seeking to expand its native regiments there.[14] The first Bene Israel synagogue was completed in Bombay in 1796 and was known as Sha'ar ha-Rahamim (Gate of Mercy).[15] Until the establishment of this synagogue, Bene Israel had worshiped at the homes of prominent families.

By 1833, some two thousand Bene Israel, one-third of their total number, lived in Bombay. They enlisted in the regiments, took up skilled trades, became clerks in government service and with private firms, and eventually also found work in the mills of the Sassoons, Iraqi Jews.[16] As the Bombay community grew, the Bene Israel spread into several districts of the city, where they established additional synagogues and prayer halls. Military pensioners also retired to Poona, Ahmedabad, and Karachi, where they were instrumental in founding synagogues.[17]

A second religious renaissance began in the first decades of the nineteenth century. In 1826 and again in 1833, small groups of pious, idealistic Cochin Jews arrived in Bombay to teach the Bene Israel more Jewish ritual and ceremonials and to acquaint them with their heritage. Their efforts were augmented by those of the Arabic-speaking Jews from Iraq, who were also settling in Bombay at the time.[18] A most important role in this religious revival was played by Christian missionaries who, after the ban on missionary activity in India was lifted in 1813, exerted a vital influence, particularly through their educational endeavors, on the Bene Israel. The American Marathi Mission (Congregational) established a number of schools for Bene Israel children in Bombay and nearby Kolaba district, where Hebrew was taught and Bene Israel were often employed as teachers. In the 1830s, the Free Church of Scotland's mission was represented in Bombay by the outstanding archaeologist and linguist Dr. John Wilson, who took a special interest in the welfare of the Bene Israel and in their origin and history. By 1836, 250 Bene Israel children (perhaps one-quarter of the school-age Bene Israel in Bombay at the time), one-third of whom were girls, were attending the Reverend Dr. Wilson's schools. Six years later, 38 Bene Israel were registered in the college he had opened, where they could also study Hebrew.[19]

The missionaries were hopeful that the Bene Israel, already monotheists, could eventually be brought to accept Christ as the Messiah. To this end, they translated books of the Old Testament into Marathi and developed Hebrew grammars in Marathi so that the community could become more familiar with the religion and language of its ancestors. Absorbing the Protestant emphasis on the importance of the text of the Bible, the Bene Israel became less concerned about rabbinical teaching and the law than about the scriptures themselves. Missionaries also recorded early Bene Israel beliefs and practices as they were related to them by the community. But as responsive as the Bene Israel were to the missionaries' educational overtures, they rarely took the final step of conversion. They would reply to missionary arguments,

"We do not know the replies to your questions; our learned men elsewhere do; ask them."[20]

Missionary encouragement led to a rash of publishing and translation from Hebrew into Marathi undertaken by the Bene Israel themselves in the second half of the nineteenth century. But missionary activity also stimulated the spread of English among the Bene Israel, which enabled them to become acquainted with books of Jewish interest published in England and the United States. Soon, fewer translations of religious works into Marathi were necessary.[21] This access to English materials naturally increased the Bene Israel's sense of belonging to a larger Jewish community, gradually reducing their isolation and their dependence on other Jewish communities and missionaries in India for religious instruction and sustenance.

The Baghdadis Arrive

The port of Basra on the Persian Gulf had been a trading center of the British East India Company from 1760 on, and many Jews of that port and of Baghdad who had already played an important role in the English commerce in that part of the world gradually moved on to India. In the late seventeenth century, European Jewish merchants had taken up trade in the port of Surat, 165 miles north of Bombay on the west coast of India, to be joined in the following century by Arabic-speaking Jews from Aleppo, Baghdad, and Basra. They formed the Arabian Jewish Merchant Colony under the leadership of Shalom Obadiah ha-Cohen of Aleppo. Referring originally to Jews who came from the area between the Tigris and Euphrates rivers, for centuries a center of Jewish learning and culture, the term *Baghdadi* or *Iraqi* soon came to include as well Jews from Syria and other parts of the Ottoman Empire, Aden, and Yemen, all of whom were Arabic-speaking, and even Jews from Persia and Afghanistan, who were not. In Bombay, the term *Baghdadi* was most common for all these groups. At the end of the eighteenth century, Surat must have included at least ninety-five Jewish merchants and had a synagogue and Jewish cemetery. As the British presidencies of Calcutta and Bombay developed, however, Surat lost its preponderant position as a port, and the Jewish merchants began to look for new commercial opportunities.

Indians could take greater advantage of the growing trade and commerce of the eighteenth century in Bombay than they could in Calcutta, where the British monopolized the production and export trade to London of jute, tea, and indigo. Not until the twentieth century could Indians really enter these markets. But Indians could participate in Bombay's cotton and opium trade which, heading primarily east, was not affected by the British monopoly.[22]

Encouraged by the British to go to India to expand commerce, prominent
Baghdadi families such as the Sassoons, Ezras, Eliases, Gubbays, Kadouries,
and Abrahams became wealthy merchants or acted as middlemen for the
large cotton-, jute-, and tobacco-processing plants.[23]

The origin of the Baghdadi Jewish community in Bombay dates back to
about 1730, when Joseph Semah, who had settled in Surat, moved soon after
to Bombay. Toward the end of the century, Solomon Jacob, a successful
merchant, played a leading role in the economic and commercial affairs of
the city. The persecutions of Daud Pasha (governor of Baghdad, 1817–31)
and the forced conversion of the Meshed Jews in 1839 led to an increase of
Iraqi Jewish refugees arriving in India. In the early 1830s there were perhaps
twenty to thirty families of Arab Jews out of a total Bombay Jewish population
of 2,246.[24] They called themselves "Jewish Merchants of Arabia, Inhabitants
and Residents in Bombay." Religious services were held in a house rented
from Parsis. Solomon Jacob died in 1834, but the year before, there arrived
in Bombay a figure who was to found a great dynasty and a merchant house
known throughout the world: David Sassoon (1792–1864) of Baghdad. A
scion of a family that had long held the position of chief treasurer to the
governor of Baghdad, but whose political fortunes had waned, David Sassoon
had escaped the oppression of Daud Pasha. The economic empire that the
Sassoons eventually established, with centers in Bombay, Calcutta, Rangoon,
Hong Kong, Shanghai, Singapore, and elsewhere, and their great charitable
enterprises earned for them the title of "Rothschilds of the East." The history
of the Iraqi Jewish community in Bombay is closely connected with that of
the house of Sassoon.

David Sassoon entered the import-export arena of Bombay, then dominated by wealthy Parsis and English merchant houses. He began by exporting
English textiles to Persia, Iraq, and nearby lands, importing products and
textiles of these countries to be resold to the British in India. His familiarity
with local countries, conditions, and languages, his reliable Jewish corre-
spondents in all centers, and his firm's reputation for absolute integrity soon
made his business one of the largest operating in the region. By 1841, he was
recognized as the principal member of the local Arabian Jewish trading community. He gradually extended into central Asia and southern China, trading
in Bombay yarn, English piece-goods, and opium. By the next decade, he
had purchased much real estate. Sir Bartle Frere, the governor of Bombay,
described him as "the first of our non-European merchants in wealth and
respectability."[25] Like the Rothschilds, David Sassoon placed his many sons
as agents in various cities and countries. The family's fortunes rose during
the American Civil War, as they exported increased supplies of Indian yarn
to England. During this period, the Sassoons also established business operations in England.

David Sassoon was an observant Orthodox Jew. Initially, all the firm's accounts and correspondence were in Judaeo-Arabic (Arabic language in Hebrew script). Business stopped daily at the appropriate times for prayer. Offices, branches, and workshops closed on Saturday as well as on Sunday, the official day of rest. Every Saturday the heads of the Bombay Jewish community and any scholars present in the city met in David Sassoon's house to study and to chant traditional hymns. Out of these meetings emerged a group calling itself *Hebrath Beth David* (the Brotherhood of the House of David), which became a nucleus of a new organization of Baghdadi Jews, financially subsidized by Sassoon. In 1861, he built the Magen David Synagogue in the then fashionable neighborhood of Byculla. In the compound were housed a hostel for travelers, a ritual bath, and a Talmud Torah (a religious school).[26]

Word spread among the poor Jews in Baghdad and even in Aleppo and Damascus in Syria that employment was available in the firm of David Sassoon and Company in Bombay. To accommodate the new arrivals, Sassoon not only arranged food, housing, and medical care for them, but established the David Sassoon Benevolent Institution (now a public library) to educate their children. In addition to the languages and basic arithmetic they would need to hold jobs, the children also learned ritual slaughtering of animals so that they could eat meat if they were sent to places where there was no established Jewish community.[27]

David Sassoon's philanthropy extended to his coreligionists all over the Orient who requested funds for schools, prayerbooks, and even dowries. But he also contributed enormously to the development of Bombay, financing the Sassoon Reformatory and Industrial Institution for Juvenile Offenders, the Sassoon Mechanics Institute with its reading room and library, an illuminated clock-tower for the Victoria and Albert Museum, and a marble statue of the prince-consort, with a Hebrew inscription. In Poona (Pune), which became a summer resort for wealthy Bombay Jews, he had constructed a beautiful synagogue, which is still a town landmark, a school, an asylum for the relief of destitute invalids, and a large European-style general hospital open to all castes and creeds. This generosity paralleled that of the Parsis, whose philanthropy both within the Parsi community and for others grew enormously in the nineteenth century, with the establishment of engineering, liberal arts, and medical colleges, a school of art, libraries, and the Tata Institute of Social Sciences. Sir Bartle Frere, who was eager to get the backing of the rich merchantile community for all his projects, especially education, public buildings, and beautification of the city, wrote in 1862 of the Baghdadi Jews of Bombay: "They are, like the Parsees, a most valuable link between us and the natives—oriental in origin and appreciation—but English in their objects and associations, and, almost of necessity, loyal."[28]

After David Sassoon's death, his eldest son, Abdullah, who also called himself Albert, assumed the management of the firm and became a major force behind the development of the textile industry in Bombay. He opened a series of cotton mills that, along with Parsi enterprise, helped to revolutionize the weaving industry in India and to enable Bombay to grow, in the second half of the nineteenth century, into an important manufacturing city.[29] He promoted and financed the construction of the first wet dock in Bombay, still known as the Sassoon dock, which greatly stimulated the city's commercial growth. Following in his father's philanthropic footsteps, Albert-Abdullah contributed toward the reconstruction of Elphinstone High School and the erection of a large equestrian statue of the Prince of Wales to commemorate his visit to India in 1875. He financed many scholarships and became a close advisor to the government on educational and building projects. He also became a leading member of the Chamber of Commerce and a member of the Bombay Legislative Council from 1868 to 1872. Although Albert mixed with Indian nobility and received court emissaries from China and Persia, he also managed to permeate the exclusive English society in Bombay and Poona. His contacts with Persia and China were helpful to the British government, which was concerned with Russian ambitions in Persia and central Asia, and in 1872 Albert Sassoon was knighted.[30]

Jealous of the assumption of leadership by Albert-Abdullah, his next younger brother, Elias, resigned from the parent firm and established a rival company to be known as E. D. Sassoon and Company. The original firm, David Sassoon and Company, continued to act as general merchants; the new firm became involved mainly in banking and property and ultimately became more prosperous. By 1875 Albert had moved to England to manage his firm's operations from there, leaving the direction of affairs in Bombay to another younger brother, Solomon David Sassoon, who also took an active part in public life and in Jewish activities. When Solomon David died prematurely, his wife, Flora Sassoon, a noted scholar and Hebraist, took over the management of David Sassoon and Company. A famed landmark, Flora Fountain, is named for her.

At Elias Sassoon's death, the E. D. Sassoon firm was taken over by his son Jacob, who established new mills and further helped to expand the cotton industry. In the 1880s, Jacob Sassoon actively recruited workers from Baghdad, promising them the usual benefits and facilities, until at one point, the mills of his firm employed fifteen thousand people (only a small fraction of whom were Jews): "In the history of the cotton textile industry in western India, the name of Jacob Sassoon stands out more prominently than that of any other single individual, not excepting even his Parsee rival Jamsetji Tata."[31] He endowed cemeteries, funds for feeding poor, elderly, and disabled Jews, a dispensary, the Jacob Sassoon Free High School for Baghdadi children, and a new synagogue, Knesset Eliahu, in the now fashionable Fort section of Bombay, in memory of his father.[32] At Poona he established a European general hospital in the compound of the Sassoon hospital, providing kosher food for Jewish patients admitted to it. In recognition of his service to the development of India, Jacob Sassoon was also knighted, in 1909. It is understandable, in the light of all the Sassoon activity, that the economic, social, educational, and religious history of the Baghdadi Jewish community of Bombay should revolve around this family. Other leading Baghdadi families in Bombay and Calcutta such as the Musleahs, Gubbays, Ezras, and Abrahams intermarried with the Sassoons. In Calcutta, where, by the end of the nineteenth century, the Jewish community numbered over eighteen hundred, Jews had moved into the stock exchange and become large urban landowners. Like their European counterparts in that city, large Jewish firms such as those of B. N. Elias, S. Manasseh, E. Meyer, A. M. Shellim, and M. A. Sassoon developed international networks, engaged in shipping jute and cloth. The Ezras became the most important Jewish family in Calcutta, and much of the history of the Baghdadi Jewish community there revolves around the acceptance of or opposition to this dominance. Spiritually and religiously, the Baghdadi Jews in India remained attached to the teaching and tradition of Baghdad, seeking guidance from that city's *hahams* (wise men) in questions of ritual and law. They imported religious books from Europe and then lithographed others. Although many learned Hindustani for trade purposes, they tended not to learn the regional languages, Marathi and Bengali, very well. When they were ready to drop their Arabic, they went directly to English.[33]

Bene Israel-Baghdadi Relations: The Early Years

How would the arrival of the Baghdadi Jews in Bombay affect the Bene Israel and what would be the relationship between the two communities? The Jewish experience in the United States and England might suggest that those Jewish communities already established and, to some extent, assimilated would look down upon the newcomers, and even consider them a threat to their hard-won position. Thus, the German Jews in the United States were troubled by the influx of Eastern European Jewry after 1880 and even tried to stem the tide. Members of the old Sephardic community in England reacted similarly. The new arrivals in those countries met with tremendous pressure to assimilate and drop their foreign ways. India, however, had a different history: in fact, the process seemed to work in reverse. In broad historical terms, newcomers came in as conquerors and established their hegemony over the peoples already there, whether one refers to the Indo-

Europeans asserting supremacy over the Dravidian population, Muslims over Hindus, or British over Indians. One could almost trace a pattern: the later the arrival, the fairer the skin, the higher the status. Add to this pattern a colonial situation and the environment of caste, where relations between castes were invariably expressed in terms of pollution and purity, and where problems of commensality and marriage were extremely important, and the stage seemed be set for relationships among Jewish communities in India that were different from those in Western countries.[34]

When the Baghadis first arrived in Bombay, they were welcomed by the Bene Israel, who invited them to attend services in their synagogues and to bury their dead in the Bene Israel cemetery. The Bene Israel had just recently learned of many of the *halachic* (Jewish legal) rules and Jewish traditions. They were urbanized, some were educated and westernized, but they were less affluent than the Baghdadis. Those who were poor could not afford the two sets of eating and cooking utensils needed to keep kosher food regulations. If they had only one pot, they would kosher it by boiling water in it. If they could afford to eat meat at all, they ate only kosher meat. But the *hazans* (readers or cantors) from Cochin and the Baghdadi *Cohans* (descendants of priestly families) who officiated in Bene Israel synagogues would not eat in Bene Israel homes because they feared these households were not thoroughly kosher.[35] This reluctance, although common to ultra-orthodox Jews the world over, seems also to have had caste overtones in India. Nevertheless, the Baghdadis tried to help the Bene Israel in their efforts to return to orthodoxy, and leaders of both the Baghdadi and Bene Israel communities submitted joint petitions to the president and governor-in-council of Bombay in 1831 and 1833 concerning grievances connected with the Jewish cemetery. Soon after, however, a rift developed, the Baghdadis apparently deciding that the Bene Israel were very different from them after all. In 1836, David Sassoon and nine other Arab Jews sent a petition to the Bombay authorities requesting that a partition wall be erected in the cemetery to divide the two groups. They pointed out that there were two distinct tribes of Jews in Bombay, "one having the customs of the natives of India and the other faithful to their Arabian fathers." Both groups, they claimed, wanted the wall to divide the burial ground. The government did not grant the request.[36]

The growing rift between the Baghdadis and the Bene Israel was to manifest itself in many ways. The question of intermarriage emerged early, not because of the risk of ritual pollution in the Hindu sense but because of the fear of intermarriage with non-Jews. The Baghdadi communities of Bombay and Calcutta frequently referred to Sephardic rabbis and *hahams* in Baghdad and Jerusalem to ascertain whether intermarriage with the Bene Israel was permissible.[37]

It was during this period that a Jewish traveler, Israel Joseph Benjamin, visited India and published his book *Un An de Séjour aux Indes Orientales (1849–50)*. He mentioned that the race called Bene Israel was not recognized by the "Babylonian" Jews as belonging to "Mosaism," but he had no doubt that they did, and he gave his reasons for thinking that they descended from the Ten Lost Tribes. He noted that for some time the Iraqi Jews of Bombay had been sending *shohets* (ritual slaughterers) and "rabbis" to the Bene Israel villages to spread religious knowledge and teach them, but the Iraqis obstinately refused to ally themselves with the Bene Israel, comparing them (wrongly, thought Benjamin) to other sects who had borrowed certain Jewish rites. He felt that the Bene Israel energetically justified their title as Jews and tried to get closer to the Iraqis. They wanted to strengthen their religious union with the Baghdadis through intermarriage.[38]

It is not clear whether or not the Baghdadis in Bombay at this time felt the Bene Israel were actually non-Jewish. If they did, it may have been because of the Bene Israel's Hindu customs, the Baghdadis not seeing that the same could be said about their own adoption of external Islamic customs. Bene Israel complained that Jews in Muslim or Christian countries rarely saw as "un-Jewish" customs that they copied from their neighbors, but when they saw people living like Hindus, proscribing widow remarriage and meat-eating, they reacted differently.[39]

In 1859, a Rabbi Shmuel Abe of Safad who visited India remarked on the excellent influence upon and aid accorded to the Bene Israel by the Baghdadis. He noted that the "B'nai Yisroel" observed all the *mitzvot* (commandments) of the written and oral law and all the *halachic* ordinances of the Jewish people. In 1870, Sephardic and Ashkenazi *hahams* of Safad and Tiberius announced that it was a great *mitzvah* (good work) to be close to the Bene Israel, who were good Jews in every sense, and that one ought to be on good terms with them. They cautioned against those people who sought to set them apart. The letter stirred up considerable controversy when it was published in a Baghdadi newspaper in Bombay.[40]

Jewish Politics and Loyalty in Premodern India

As a microscopic community essentially minding its own affairs, the Bene Israel did not have a great deal of contact with the British government on a day-by-day basis, except on matters of employment, in both the military and the civilian branches. Military service provides us with the most notable early example of the Bene Israel's involvement with government. Their inclination toward and their success in this endeavor distinguish the Bene Israel from most modern Jewish communities until the establishment of the State of Israel. In the Konkan, in western India, where there were no permanent loyalties and frequent changes of rulers, the Bene Israel seem to have served in the army and navy of the Marathas and possibly in other armies as mercenaries. When the British East India Company began to recruit for the Bombay army in the mid eighteenth century, therefore, the Bene Israel may have enlisted because they traditionally served in the armies of the pre-British rulers. B. J. Israel points out that owing to their superior education and merit, the Bene Israel stood out and earned promotion to officer ranks out of all proportion to their numbers in the regiments. He believes, although this belief cannot be confirmed, that at one time about half the Indian officer strength of the Bombay army consisted of Bene Israel.[41] Other minorities were also active in the military. Up until 1786, the Anglo-Indians in the East India Company's troops were treated as equals to Europeans. Anglo-Indians who had received higher education in England frequently came back as officers in British regiments. After 1786, however, the directors of the East India Company and senior military officers feared that the Anglo-Indians were becoming numerically superior to the British. Aware that some of the leaders of the rebellion in Haiti were members of a racially mixed population, the British feared that the Anglo-Indians might ally themselves with Muslim or Hindu rulers to expel the colonial administration. Thus, for almost twenty-five years, they restricted Anglo-Indian employment in the civilian and military branches of the country until, in 1808, all Anglo-Indians were discharged from the regular British army. When the Anglo-Indians responded by enlisting in the ranks of the Maratha, Mysore, and other princes, enemies of the company, the company called them back into its military service and then summarily discharged them again.[42]

The Jews were not subjected to these swings of the pendulum. Throughout most of the nineteenth century, the Bene Israel served in many regiments of the army and their services were well recognized. They distinguished themselves in such campaigns as the Maratha wars, the Mysore wars, the Sind wars, the Punjab wars, and others, and won the respect and appreciation of their European superiors as well as the good will of the Indian rank and file.

The Bene Israel sepoys' loyalty to the British during the Mutiny of 1857 was never questioned. Although the Baghdadis were not in the military, David Sassoon offered to assemble and equip a Jewish legion in the event of civil war. To celebrate the end of the Mutiny, the Sassoons ordered every Jew in Bombay to light up his house and recite prayers and blessings for the royal family. When the East India Company officially ceded all its political powers to the crown, David Sassoon marked the occasion with a magnificent party at his home. The chief guest, the governor, Lord Mountstuart Elphinstone, proposed a toast to David Sassoon: "We must not forget that at the time of the Mutiny, when threatened with danger and whilst some were panic-stricken, Mr. Sassoon and his family were the first to come forward in support of the British Government." Although Calcutta Baghdadis seemed to take only a passive interest in the events, a service was held in the Bethel Synagogue for the success of the British and the continued rule of the queen's forces.[43]

Two changes in army policy, however, soon led to a decline in Bene Israel enlistment. The Bengal army's system of promotion by seniority replaced the Bombay army's policy of promotion by merit and, because of their small numbers, the rate of promotion of Bene Israel personnel declined sharply. Then, "growing caste consciousness within the regiments led the authorities to make the Bombay regiments predominantly Maratha or Rajput in character, virtually excluding smaller communities like the Bene Israel which were not numerous enough to man a whole regiment."[44] Thus there could only be one officer out of each one hundred caste members. With little chance of becoming officers, the Bene Israel did not want to remain in the lower ranks with the relatively low pay. By the third quarter of the century, their enlistment practically stopped.[45]

Reflecting on this situation, the *Bene Israelite,* a community newspaper, implied that an organized Jewish communal structure such as existed in Great Britain and the United States might be helpful:

> The recent caste rules and regulations passed and brought in force by the military authorities in India have deprived many a Bene Israel of the offices of commissioned officers in active regiments and particularly of the good chances of serving the British Government faithfully. . . . A Bene Israel joined an Indian regiment, though as a private, with the sure hope of rising to the rank of a commissioned officer, and many a time such hopes were fully realized. But according to the recent "caste" rules, a Bene Israel can never be made a commissioned officer in future and it is with much sorrow we are obliged to see the list of Bene Israel commissioned officers brought to an end. The Bene Israel soldiers have thus been deprived of the means of showing to the anti-Semites that Jews are in no way cowards and a non-fighting race. A representation ought to have been made to the military authorities giving the names of the persons who fought the various battles for the British Government in days past and thus assuring them of the fighting element possessed by the Bene Israel. We have neither a Board of Deputies nor that of Guardians to undertake the cause of our people in India. . . . Will not anyone think of representing the prospects of our people in the regiment marred by the recent caste rules and setting everything arights?[46]

By the end of the century, very few senior Bene Israel officers remained in active service. The small numbers are indicated by an annual return showing the class composition of the armed forces of India as of 1 January 1906. Of a total of 222,402 in the Indian army, Imperial Service, military police, and militia, there were thirty-seven Jews: four native officers, fourteen noncommissioned officers, two musicians, and seventeen privates.[47]

No longer finding the military attractive, the Bene Israel turned their attention to the ancillary services such as supply, works, accounts, education, and medicine, which required a higher level of education and a good knowledge of English, and had higher status than military services in the ranks.[48] This shift was to lead to a new sort of dependency on the British.

Social Change in British India

The reorganization of the army regiments according to caste reflects an aspect of British analysis of Indian society that was to have a profound impact not only on the Bene Israel but on the very nature of group identity in India.

The classic description of Indian society is that of Louis Dumont in *Homo Hierarchicus*. Dumont, in discussing the caste system, talks about an ordered hierarchy in traditional India. He distinguishes between legitimacy derived from ritual status, which is hierarchical, and material success and power in the world, which is political. Ritual superiority does not mean secular or economic dominance. While emphasizing hierarchy instead of the isolation and separation of the castes from one another, Dumont points out that the ideology of the caste system is directly contradictory to Western egalitarian theory.[49] Thus castes were groups in society whose identity had been based on a fluid interaction with each other with "an overarching concept of hierarchy." The castes were ranked but not counted. In traditional society, they were in flux, not competing. Dumont also argues that the ideology of hierarchy "encompasses" the politico-economic domain of life.[50]

In traditional India, the mobility characteristic of caste led not to structural changes but only to positional changes for particular castes or sections of castes. Individual castes might move up or down, but the structure remained the same. Because each caste had its own occupation, customs, ritual, traditions, and ideas, the caste system provided an institutional basis for tolerance and cultural pluralism.[51]

The fluidity of the political system throughout pre-British India was an important source of social mobility for some strategically situated individuals and groups. Once a caste attained political power, it had to Sanskritize its ritual and style of life. Although the high-caste status depended on several factors, especially in Kerala, the maharaja of Cochin had the power to influence caste-rankings in his kingdom.[52]

Bernard Cohn has discussed how the British, through a different analysis of Indian society, transformed these hierarchically ranked castes into competitive groups. By the early nineteenth century, as the British became increasingly aware of the variety of peoples, histories, political forms, systems of land tenure, and religious practices in India, they began to do statistical surveys of various aspects of Indian society.[53] These surveys led to a continuing effort undertaken by the British in India to collect, collate and publish for official as well as scholarly use detailed information about all aspects—physical, cultural and sociological—of every district in India, which reached its high peak with the Imperial Gazeteer of India, published in the twentieth century. . . . With the publication for the first time of the census of India on a systematic and all-India basis in 1872, a whole new body of material on Indian society became available.[54]

The British method of collecting information about the caste system partly determined the "official" view of caste (and of Indian society). The British saw caste as a concrete and measurable entity with "definable characteristics—endogamy, commensality rules, fixed occupation, common ritual practices." The information collected was quantified for reports and surveys. "India was seen as a collection of castes: the particular picture was different in any given time and place, but India was a sum of its parts, and the parts were castes," which could be counted and classified. In 1901, an official effort was made to establish an ethnographic survey of India as part of the census of that year. In the census of 1901, castes were classified and ranked on the basis of "social precedence as recognized by native public opinion." Various ambitious castes now quickly perceived the chances of raising their status. They held conferences and formed councils to see that their status was recorded in a way they thought was honorable to them.[55]

As David Lelyveld has put it, "The fluid, interactional nature of group identity and ranking . . . was replaced by a concept of bounded corporate groups that one could count and rank in a fixed linear arrangement."[56] These bounded descent groups now became considered the active units of society. The center of identity in classical India had been centrifugal, not bounded. The bounding came from the naming and counting.

The British not only made and counted categories of people, but used these categories for the allocation of patronage. The British assumed that as educational resources and government employment became available, the various groups had equal rights to compete. Thus the castes were no longer ranked, as in traditional India, but competing. They also became the basis of political competition as representative institutions were introduced and as proportional representation developed in legislatures and offices.[57] In keeping with their theories of Indian society, the British introduced new governmental and economic institutions that provided a new framework for individuals and groups to compete and form interest groups. A transformation in group identity through a greater integration of social networks and more sharply defined boundaries between groups resulted.[58]

This British analysis of society was relevant not only to Hindu castes but to the non-Hindu minorities as well. Muslims, Christians, Anglo-Indians, Parsis, and Jews would eventually also be classified and counted, and these numbers (as well as other factors) were taken into consideration when it came to patronage. For the minorities as well as the castes, Lelyveld's statement holds true: "Major political and economic institutions, founded on principles of equality, have replaced the model of hierarchy with open competition and transformed the internal structure of groups as well as their relation to each other and to society as a whole."[59]

One of the results of the British proclivity for naming and counting groups of people may have been the development throughout India in the late nineteenth century of voluntary caste associations or *sabhas*. Although they retained occupationally or ritually defined caste names, these associations represented new combinations of diverse groups. Reflecting British census categories, they tried to obtain government recognition of higher status and patronage in official employment.[60]

There were numerous caste *sabhas* in several areas in 1911, and by the time of the next census, they were an all-Indian phenomenon. The caste associations articulated as well as organized the new push for mobility. They held meetings and often published newspapers and periodicals, focusing on issues of concern to the group, and collected funds for scholarships and hostels for their students. Eventually some created cooperatives, banks, and even maternity homes and hospitals. They promoted a "caste consciousness" and tried to serve the general interest of the caste and its status in the hierarchy. The *sabhas* also altered the style of life of their castes in the direction of Sanskritization. This process often involved giving up meat and liquor, although sometimes its social reforms, such as raising the age of marriage, were in opposition to what a higher caste was doing. The associations lobbied with the government and took cases to court when it looked like governmental or private actions threatened the status of the caste.[61]

Hindu castes were not alone in organizing. Ethnic groups throughout India, not least of all the Jews, formed associations. A number of organizations for communal improvement, such as the Bene Israel Association, the Bene Israel Benevolent Society, the Association for the Right Guidance of the People, and the Society for the Protection of the Jewish Religion, emerged by the end of the nineteenth century. This period also witnessed the publication of several Bene Israel periodicals in Marathi, some with English columns, such as *Satya Prakash* (Light of Truth), *Friend of Israel, Lamp of Judaism, Israel Dharmadeep,* and the *Bene Israelite.* Though most of these publications were rather short-lived and a lively rivalry ensued among them, their reporting of domestic functions and communal events and their articles on religious topics and Bene Israel affairs suggest an awakening of communal consciousness. But despite the emerging group consciousness, continual disputes, often over the management of synagogues, marred this period and frequently led to litigation, with an unfortunate, concomitant waste of communal financial resources.[62]

Among Baghdadi Jews, the need to found schools and synagogues in both Bombay and Calcutta led to the formation of communal associations to manage and maintain them. A short-lived Judaeo-Arabic press emerged in Calcutta.[63] Factionalism prevailed here too, although in Bombay in particular communal affairs tended to be dominated by the Sassoons and a few other families—often related by marriage—rather than managed through a more democratic communal association.

Not all voluntary associations were caste-oriented. Landholders' associations, organizations for social reform, and literary and scholarly societies that cut across ethnic boundaries were also formed, although they were small and sometimes short-lived. Parliamentary procedure was followed, resolutions were passed, and reports were published. The experience in these voluntary associations was later carried over into the nationalist movement.[64]

Until the middle of the nineteenth century British domination had little direct effect on Indian social, economic, and cultural life. The British rulers carried out some essential reforms, laid the foundations of the political, administrative, and legal integration of India, and started English-language schools and colleges, open theoretically to people of all religions and castes. Through the study of Western literature, history, political thought, and law the Indian elite absorbed new values, such as equality before the law and the importance of civil rights. Humanitarianism underlay many of the reforms introduced by the British in the first half of the nineteenth century, and mission-run institutions also played a role in the social reforms.[65]

The Mutiny of 1857 forced the British to rethink their policy toward India. Just as they abandoned the reform of Indian institutions and customs, members of a new, increasingly strong, westernized elite took up the task of reforming society, and realized that they needed political power to do so. By the late 1860s, a westernized intelligentsia had emerged to become the "torch bearers of a new and modern India."[66]

Thus, the British conquest brought about changes in power that affected all groups. Muslims, who for centuries had had the upper hand, lost practically all their means of livelihood along with political power, while Hindu merchants were promoted to a powerful position. Among Hindus, the access to higher education and the resulting availability of prestigious positions increased the social and economic distances between the higher and lower castes. When a lower caste became wealthy or achieved secular power, it usually tried to Sanskritize its style of life, customs, ritual, and ideas, and it usually claimed to be a high caste, but it could not so easily westernize. Along with upper-caste Hindus, the Parsis, Jains, and Jews were also able to profit from the expanded opportunities of urbanization under British rule.[67]

The period from approximately 1870 to 1918, when Gandhi emerged on the scene, was a very important one from many perspectives. It marked the beginning and early development of the nationalistic movement and the changing British responses to it. In 1865, the appointed British and Indian justices of the peace in Bombay had been united into a town council (municipal corporation), which was responsible for authorizing taxes. The corporation was reorganized in 1872, permitting the election of half its members by a restricted electoral roll of fewer than four thousand taxpayers, constituting 0.6 percent of the city's inhabitants.[68] In 1882, Lord George Ripon, the viceroy, in order to introduce a measure of local self-government, established municipal and district government boards, of which at least two-thirds of the members were to be elected local nonofficials. Although the municipal corporations and the local boards had limited power, as Lelyveld suggests, they "summoned up virtually all the issues about communal representation that were to dominate the Indian political scene until partition."[69] Not only various Hindu castes, but also all the minority groups, including the Jews, would now have to compete. In the political and cultural field, westernization had given birth not only to nationalism but also to revivalism and communalism, and had heightened linguistic and caste consciousness and regionalism. The introduction of electoral politics now politicized the caste *sabhas*. These voluntary associations now helped their own members to contest elections and to develop political skills that could be used in the broader arena.[70] It is to this period that we must now turn.

Figure 1. David Sassoon (1792–1864) in formal Baghdadi dress. From the private archives of the family of Rabbi Solomon Sassoon.

Figure 2. David Sassoon with three of his sons, Elias, Abdullah (Albert), and Sassoon David, the first of the family to wear western dress (c. 1857). From the private archives of the family of Rabbi Solomon Sassoon.

Figure 3. Subedar Joseph Ezekiel Kolatkar, Bene Israel officer, Bombay Army, late nineteenth century. From H. S. Kehimkar, *The History of the Bene Israel of India*.

Figure 4. Sirdar Bahadur Solomon Isaac Zawlikar, Bene Israel officer, Bombay Army, late nineteenth century. From H. S. Kehimkar, *The History of the Bene Israel of India*.

Figure 5. Bene Israel woman with her children. Her sari and the boy's cap show Maratha influence, late nineteenth century. From H. S. Kehimkar, *The History of the Bene Israel of India*.

Figure 6. The Jhirad family (c. 1890). A well-to-do Bene Israel family, the Jhirads owned coffee estates in Bangalore. Note the variety of male dress. Courtesy of Elijah Jhirad.

Figure 7. Khan Bahadurs Shalom B. Israel (left) and Jacob B. Israel (right) with their sisters. The saris are worn in the Maratha style. The long coat is similar to that used by Muslims and Parsis; the hat shows Muslim influence (c. 1892). From Benjamin J. Israel, *Khan Bahadur Jacob Bapuji Israel: A Personal Sketch.*

Figure 8. Khan Bahadur Jacob Bapuji Israel and his wife (1893). From Benjamin J. Israel, *Khan Bahadur Jacob Bapuji Israel: A Personal Sketch.*

Figure 9. Cartoon from the weekly *Sandesha* (The Message) supplement, 2 December 1917. The legend reads: "Mr. Jacob Bapuji, Shalom Israel and Dr. Erulkar and other leaders of the Bene Israel community have declared that we do not want caste-wise representation at all." Courtesy of Benjamin J. Israel.

Figure 10. Conference of the All-India Israelite League, 1918. Jacob B. Israel is in second row, ninth from left; Abraham S. Erulkar is in third row, tenth from left; David S. Erulkar is in third row, twelfth from left. Courtesy of Benjamin J. Israel.

Figure 11. The blowing
of the shofar (1930s).
From H. S. Kehimkar, *The
History of the Bene Israel of
India.*

Figure 12. Interior view of a synagogue.

PART II
CHANGING RELATIONSHIPS
1870-1918

CHAPTER 2

THE EMERGENCE
OF INDIAN NATIONALISM

The Challenge

By the middle of the nineteenth century, Western religious ideas and modes of thought had started to affect certain Indian leaders in some cities. Although they resented European attacks on Hinduism, the Hindu elite began to take a critical view of their own religion, resulting in a serious effort to reform religious and related social practices. Bengal, under the influence of Ram Mohan Roy, the leader of the "Hindu renaissance," Dedendranath Tagore, and others, played a central role in this movement. This impulse toward reform of Indian society intensified until the last quarter of the nineteenth century, when it was overshadowed by a new interest, that of nationalism.[1]

The urge toward Indian independence had already been given indigenous expression in a number of ways. Landlords, orthodox religious groups, and old ruling elites in North India had opposed the government during the Mutiny. The Arya Samaj, founded by Swami Dayananda Saraswati, who seemed to suggest that the revival of Hindu power could be brought about by the cultivation of discipline and patriotism, "met . . . the need for a national consciousness to be rooted in a self-confident assertion of its own virtues."[2] The development of a new vitality in regional languages, which expressed itself in literature and newspapers, also contributed to a heightened sense of Indian identity. But as economic, educational, and social changes got under way, new rumblings, "fed by the study of European history and English literature, and by the liberal strand—visible from very early in British rule—in British policy toward India,"[3] and spurred on by the frustration of the increasing numbers of graduates of Indian universities, were heard. In the 1860s, the government opened the elite Indian Civil Service, previously staffed only by the British, to Indians, but as the admissions examinations were held only in England, very few Indians, no matter how well qualified, could take advantage of the new opportunity. Similarly, Indians who had been educated in England found themselves shut out from higher academic ranks in Indian universities because the chairs were reserved for the British. And inexperienced junior British officials were given preference over experienced and well-trained Indian assistant magistrates and collectors in the local districts, "for the youngest and newest British recruit to the Indian Civil Service in effect outranked any member of the lower civil services, composed of Indians."[4]

Indian resentment at the discrimination in higher ranks of the administration and the army was further fueled by the growing racial discrimination by the British. Hannah Arendt, who has discussed the emergence of "race-thinking" in all Western countries during the nineteenth century, sees racism as a powerful ideology of imperialistic policies from the beginning of the twentieth century. In England it originated among middle-class writers, not the nobility. Ironically, the English statesman who emphasized a belief in races and race superiority as a determining factor of history and politics was a man of Jewish ancestry, Benjamin Disraeli (prime minister, 1868, 1874–80). Regarding India as the cornerstone of the empire, Disraeli made the queen of England the empress of India. As the crown took over direct rule from the East India Company, India was to have a carefully planned administration that would lead to a permanent government, managed by "an exclusive caste in a foreign country whose only function was rule and not colonization." For this concept to be realized, "racism would . . . be an indispensable tool. It foreshadowed the menacing transformation of the people from a nation [England] into an 'unmixed race of a first-rate organization' that felt itself to be 'the aristocracy of nature'—to repeat in Disraeli's own words."[5]

In India, a heightened sense of racism emerged after the Mutiny. India was regarded as a conquered country and its people as a subject race: official opinion believed that no one but an Englishman could do anything. The British became religiously and intellectually arrogant toward Indians, and exclusive. A president of the Ethnological Society argued that Indians were inferior as a race. The British tendency to treat all castes alike angered the higher Hindu castes and upper-class Muslims.[6] After 1840, British officials began to develop an admiration for the peasant and a contempt for the educated urban middle-class Indian. British businessmen, meanwhile, regarded all Indians as natural inferiors, no matter how educated they might be. Certainly, by the second half of the nineteenth century, color distinctions blotted out others, and the racism was directed against both Indians and Anglo-Indians.[7] At first, the latter were too small a group to constitute a threat, and so the British accepted them as equals. But as notions of supremacy and exclusiveness replaced the concept of equality, the Anglo-Indians, as a mixed group, were assigned a new and intermediate position:

> Subject to race prejudice and social ostracism from the British, Anglo-Indians were able to relieve their feelings of frustration by passing on the imputation of racial inferiority to Indians whom they now saw as beneath them. This heightened enmity of Indians toward the mixed population and built up a reservoir of ill-will that came out later.[8]

As British attitudes of racial superiority became more pronounced and policies discriminated increasingly against the westernized elites, the English-educated Indians, who had initially supported and collaborated with the British, now viewed their rulers more and more as colonial exploiters and finally took a more positive view of themselves.[9] In 1876, Sir Surendranath Banerjee, a leading Bengali, founded the Indian Association, an organization through which the new elite would make direct appeals to the people and try to rouse public opinion. The controversy over the Ilbert Bill in 1883 served as a turning point. Until then, Indian judges were not permitted to try European British subjects. When the Ilbert Bill proposed to remove this distinction, the strong display of racism on the part of British residents in India who opposed the bill helped trigger the formation of the Indian National Congress in 1885. In its early years, Congress asked for increased Indian representation on the central and provincial legislative councils, for easier access for Indians to the Indian Civil Service through examinations held in India, and for officers' commissions for Indians in the army. It also criticized Britain's economic policies, which inhibited Indian industrial development. Congress's long-term goals were to educate the people politically and to secure a form of responsible government.[10]

A profound disagreement developed, however, over which should have priority: reform of society or demand for freedom. A group of "moderates," represented by G. K. Gokhale and M. G. Ranade, stressed the former. The so-called extremists, led by Lokamanya B. G. Tilak, insisted on freedom first.

Gopal Krishna Gokhale, an admirer of the West, believed in reason, in liberal principles, in cooperation and gradual reform. He and other moderates, such as Banerjee and Pherozeshah Mehta, thought that "only through social regeneration could the new Indian nation become strong enough to take over the reigns of power." Gokhale envisaged a self-governing India along Western lines and, expressing his faith in the British sense of justice, believed that constitutional agitation would lead to political reforms. He was friendly to the British but not afraid to make requests. Western-oriented Indians approved of his conciliatory attitudes, his speeches, and his parliamentary manner. Lokamanya Bal Gangadur Tilak, on the other hand, like Gokhale a Chitpavan Brahmin, considered British rule disastrous to India, wanted the foreigners out, and felt that revolutionary action, not moderation, was the only way to achieve the goal.[11] Tilak's more radical methods involved approaching the masses by using traditional Hindu symbols and heroes and calling for a strong Hindu reaction against foreign rule. He appealed to the Marathas in their own language with his writing and speeches, which looked back to past Maratha and Hindu glory. This Hindu revivalist approach alienated many Muslims, who felt they would be disadvantaged in a Hindu state. Thus, although Tilak's advocacy of religious revivalism was directed against the British, it led to communal antagonism.[12]

Earlier, Sir Sayyid Ahmad Khan (1817–98), a founder of the movement toward westernization among Muslims, had preached cooperation with the British to avoid being overshadowed and assimilated by the Hindus. When the Congress was founded in 1885, he had advised Muslims not to participate because, in an independent India, the majority would rule and the Hindus outnumbered the Muslims by three to one.[13] Religious, political, and economic differences eventually combined in 1906 to motivate members of the Muslim upper classes to form the Muslim League, which insisted that Muslims constituted a separate nationality. The Indian National Congress did include some Muslims, some of whom were quite westernized, but it was largely the traditionalist Muslims who supported the Indian nationalist movement.[14] How this Hindu-Muslim struggle affected Jewish interests in the 1930s will be taken up in later chapters.

The initial split in ideology, goals, and means of the early nationalists ended in a temporary victory for the extremists, especially when the attitudes and policies of Lord Curzon (viceroy, 1898–1905), particularly on the partition of Bengal, increased antigovernment feelings. The Indian National Congress adopted, in 1906, the goal of the "system of self-government obtaining in the self-governing colonies." But this approach produced an open split the following year, at the Surat sessions of the Congress, in which the extremists were expelled. In 1908, Tilak, after justifying a bombing incident, was arrested and accused of incitement to violence and "sedition." He was tried, convicted, and imprisoned for six years.[15] The British believed that the nationalists represented only a tiny segment of the society, a conspiracy furthering their own interests, rather than an expression of legitimate Indian strivings for self-government.[16]

In order to encourage Indian cooperation, the British passed the Indian Councils Act of 1909, known as the Morely-Minto Reforms, which met many of the demands of the Indian National Congress. The act increased Indian representation on the government legislative councils and established the principle of election, specific groups and organizations being given the vote. The Muslim League was placated by the introduction of what came to be known as communalism in Indian politics: Muslims were granted special constituencies that guaranteed them places in the central and provincial legislative councils. The Indian National Congress soon objected to this principle of special representation for Muslims as detrimental to the concept of Indian nationhood.[17]

The Bene Israel Response

The Awakening of Bene Israel Political Consciousness

As opportunities for Indians to advance increased toward the end of the nineteenth century, Bene Israel journals recorded with pride the achievements of members of that community. In this period, the British conferred certain honorary titles upon Indians as recognition of their accomplishments and services: *khan sahib* and *khan bahadur* were titles reserved for Muslims, Parsis, and Jews, while *rao sahib* and *rao bahadur* were designated for Hindus. The first Bene Israel to receive a *khan* title was a Haeem Solomon for his services in the construction of railroads. Dr. Joseph David Borgawkar was made *khan bahadur* in 1894. Shalom Bapujee Israel, the deputy collector of Janjeera, was also designated *khan bahadur*, while Ezra Reuben, a subjudge of the Bahuri district, was a *khan sahib*. While noting these occasional honors, the contemporary Bene Israel press also voiced concern at the lack of Bene Israel advancement in the independent professions as well as in high government positions. It seemed that other communities were moving faster than the Bene Israel and there "were no Bene Israel who could be reckoned among the great and influential men of India," even though members of other communities could be. The journals were staunch advocates of communal improvement and promoted efforts to rise up from the poverty that held the community back. Interestingly enough, the census of 1881 reported a 62 percent literacy rate among Jewish school-age boys in Bombay Presidency, a rate exceeded only by the Parsis and upper-class Christians.[18]

Although the Bene Israel press in this period did not seem to pay a great deal of attention to general politics, now and then it criticized the government, as in 1881, when the salt tax had raised the price of salt so high that a woman in Karachi was imprisoned by the police for trying to collect salt by heating saltwater. More often, the press would mention how pleased the Bene Israel were under the just and educated administration of the British government, pointing out that people in other countries were not so happy.[19]

The Bene Israel frequently expressed their loyalty to the British crown. Queen Victoria's Fiftieth Jubilee, celebrated on 16 February 1887, provided such an opportunity for various Indian communities, including the Baghdadi Jews and Bene Israel. The Bene Israel illuminated their synagogues and used a Hebrew prayer prepared and translated into English and Marathi by Joseph Ezekiel Rajpurkar, their leading literary figure at the time:

It is a duty of every person to be very grateful for the happiness and pleasures we are able to enjoy in this Kingdom of the Queen Victoria. We should show our loyalty to her for it. We should indicate our gratefulness and praise the Lord for that. In fact, this is our primary duty.[20]

Copies of the Bene Israel prayers for the queen were forwarded to England, where they reportedly were well received by Chief Rabbi Dr. Herman Adler and others. A copy was also sent to the Anglo-Jewish Historical Exhibition in April 1887.[21]

The Bombay Bene Israel community also prepared an address to be forwarded to Queen Victoria; it included this sentence: "If the Government of Queen Victoria had not been in India, then even the remnant of the Israelite community would not have been left." A Brahmin journalist, the editor of *Vaibhava* of Poona, took offense at the statement, which he interpreted to imply that the kings of India were eager to uproot the Bene Israel. He censured the community, calling it wretched, wicked, and ungrateful. The Bene Israel editor of *Curiosities of Judaism* tried to defend the statement, arguing, "If we understand this sentence literally, it appears to be a great exaggeration. But if we glance at social conditions, then it is true. The great calamities and tortures that are being experienced by the members of our community in other nations are indescribable." He pointed out that under Hindu and Muslim kings in India, the Bene Israel, although recruited in the military, were never given any honorable jobs or say in the administration, nor were they offered sufficient protection, whereas under the British, some Bene Israel were appointed as judges and government officers. Before the arrival of the British, he argued, the Bene Israel had changed their customs, manners, and even names in order to assimilate to the natives. They might have been amalgamated with the local people or even converted to Islam, had it not been for the British and the accompanying missionaries, who enlightened the Bene Israel about their religious beliefs and scriptures. Thus, the Bene Israel were grateful to the British government for enabling them to have a more complete knowledge of their religion.[22]

The incident attracted the editorial attention of *Dyanoda*, a journal published by the American Marathi Mission, which reacted in a strongly worded editorial of support for the Bene Israel on 24 March 1887.[23] Considering that appreciation for the order Great Britain had brought as well as for the benefits of Western education had previously been expressed by outstanding Indian leaders such as Raja Ram Mohan Roy, G. K. Gokhale, and Dadabhai Naoroji, and was also a main theme, along with loyalty to the British crown, of the early years of the Indian National Congress, *Vaibhava*'s attack does seem excessive.[24]

Additional celebrations were held ten years later in commemoration of the Diamond Jubilee of Queen Victoria's reign. The Bene Israel gave a fund-raising dinner for the Bene Israel Benevolent Association, the first function of its kind among the community. For this jubilee, Dr. Herman Adler prepared a special prayer and forwarded it to all the Jewish congregations of the British Empire; he requested that the Bombay Jews offer this same prayer. Although the *Bene Israelite* suggested that following the plan would save money (separate prayers for different congregations would not need to be printed), money that could be used to relieve the poor and needy on Jubilee Day (which would please the queen), there seems to have been some friction between the two Bene Israel synagogues in Bombay: one preferred to use a new prayer written by Joseph Ezekiel Rajpurkar. An additional address was sent by the Ahmedabad Bene Israel to the queen on 9 June 1897:

> We, the undersigned members of the small but loyal Bene Israel community, which is proud of having supplied the most loyal soldiers to your Victorious Majesty's Bombay Army, and which has received manifold blessings during your noble Majesty's benign and beneficent rule of sixty years, which have been marked by security and comfort, peace and plenty, health and happiness, and advancement in learning to our community in common with your Gracious Majesty's all other Indian subjects beg, on behalf of its members at Ahmedabad . . . to [express] feelings of deep loyalty, . . . [to England] which is unsurpassed for its even-handed administration of justice to all [its] Indian subjects of every taste and creed.[25]

The loyalty of the Bene Israel was often recognized by outsiders whom, in the late 1890s, the Bene Israel Benevolent Association usually invited to preside over and address their annual meetings. At the forty-third annual meeting, for example, S. M. Moses, a successful Baghdadi businessman, praised them for their loyalty and valuable services during the Mutiny. He also referred to the excellent work done by Bene Israel serving in the Subordinate Department of the Indian Medical Service as physicians and hospital assistants, and by Bene Israel justices and special constables during the plague, hoping that they would be recognized by the government. The following year, a Lieutenant Colonel Waters of the Indian Medical Service acknowledged that because they were willing to take part in "all that pertains to good citizenship, the native army had always had a large proportion of Bene Israel." He added, "Indeed, I can say without hesitation, that our most gracious sovereign has no more loyal subjects than the Bene Israel community of Bombay. Their lot hitherto has been hard, but let us hope that brighter things are in store for them in the near future."[26]

Bene Israel Identification with Indians

Although their loyalty to Great Britain seemed unquestioned, the issue of the degree to which the Bene Israel should identify with Indians culturally and politically while at the same time trying to maintain their Jewish identity loomed large. Toward the end of the nineteenth century, the Bene Israel periodicals often dealt with these matters. The problem of acculturation was raised as some Bene Israel had adopted the prohibitions of widow remarriage and meat-eating. Although it was argued that they had done this not so much to assimilate to Hinduism as to show respect for the Hindus, the line was thin. There is no accurate way of knowing how the Bene Israel really felt about their adaptation to the Hindu environment before the Baghdadis arrived because there is nothing on record to indicate to what extent the Bene Israel felt they were different from the Hindus. For example, in an earlier period, when it was common for the Bene Israel to have idols in their homes, did the idols represent an acceptance of Hinduism or rather, as B. J. Israel suggests, an acceptance of magic—the copying of superstitions from their neighbors? The Bene Israel had assimilated in so many ways to Hindus that when their quarrels were taken to court, local (sometimes Hindu, sometimes Muslim) law was applied to them, and they often suffered a great loss. In two cases of adoption that had reached the High Court, however, they had been governed by British law; the Bene Israel journal *Israel Dharmadeep* wondered whether the British law of inheritance was applicable to them. The editor suggested that it would be helpful if the law commission or law council would publish a small booklet of the laws that would govern the community in order to remove all doubts.[27]

The ambivalence was evident. In 1895, *Israel Dharmadeep* noted that the community had been moving toward higher standards of modern civilization and showing an increased interest in "higher education, literature, science and the fine arts, which was leading to better appointments and higher positions." But the journal also noticed a distinct, if gradual drawing away of the community from the natives of the country among whom they had been living: "The time seems not far distant when . . . [the Bene Israel] will entirely throw off their manners, customs, dress and language. We have too long mixed with and become, as it were, one with the gentiles. And today, we hear the voice saying, 'come out of her, oh my people, and be separate.' "[28] In order to foster Jewish identity, the periodicals tried to present portraits of outstanding Jewish, particularly Anglo-Jewish, personalities. These articles often appeared in the Marathi columns and featured sketches of, for example, Dr. Herman Adler or the chief justice, Sir John Simon, "because we want to hold forth the subject of our illustration to the younger generation of the Israelite community as a bright model of how Sir John Simon on account of his vast learning and legal acumen has been an honor to English Jews."[29]

The Bene Israel might have been distinguishing themselves culturally, but their response to the issue of political reforms in this period must also be considered when we discuss their identification with Indians. Interestingly enough, no mention of the Indian National Congress appears in these early

Bene Israel periodicals. In 1895, *Israel Dharmadeep* reported that it had received a copy of a weekly paper just launched in Bombay by "influential gentlemen whose primary object was to bring matters of vital importance affecting the country's good before the public, to organize and introduce certain reforms, to guard the interest and promote the welfare of the people of the land and to represent matters regarding India and her people before the rulers in a proper light."[30] The Bene Israel journal wished this new publication well. Similarly, the editor of the *Friend of Israel*, in discussing a lecture entitled "Revival and Reform" given by Justice M. G. Ranade, a distinguished Brahmin judge of the Bombay High Court and a leading social reformer, acknowledged that although Ranade had dealt with the subject from the Hindu point of view, many of his remarks were of considerable interest to the Bene Israel:

> Jews though we are, by nationality we are Indians and . . . our domicile in this country for about twenty centuries, if not more, has had a considerable influence in the shaping of our life, our character, and our destiny. There are many things in our social, moral and religious life which require to be eradicated or given a new turn in a different direction to accord with the new spirit, and the light which Justice Ranade's remarks throw upon such questions as we are concerned with will prove of such great help, if we wish, as we ought, to take our destiny in our own hands instead of drifting wherever circumstances might lead us.[31]

Representation in the Public Services

The British not only named and counted castes and other groups, but treated them differently in regards to employment. Distinctions were made between Indians and Europeans and among Indians themselves. On the whole, the Bene Israel in the services were treated like Indians, but there were occasions when they were accorded other status. Between 1877 and 1886, for instance, the Bene Israel were allowed to draw rations for traveling allowances on the scale for Europeans and Eurasians (or Anglo-Indians) because their mode of living and habits closely agreed with those of Europeans. Parsis, however, were classed as natives.[32]

In the late nineteenth century, the British formed the Volunteer Corps, an auxiliary force open only to Europeans and Anglo-Indians. At first, the Bene Israel complained that they were not allowed to join; it is not clear why they wanted to—perhaps to express their loyalty to Great Britain, or simply because it was a mark of European status. In actual fact, Christians and Jews were admitted to the Volunteer Corps. If a person called himself a Bene Israel, the authorities might not understand and might not take him, but if he called himself a Jew, he would be accepted, no distinction being made between Bene Israel and Baghdadis. A number of young Bene Israel from Bombay, Poona, and Karachi did join the Volunteer Corps, and a periodical dated 1887 says, "We're thankful to the British Government for including them [the Bene Israel] in this Volunteer Corps. It was primarily due to our loyalty, innocence and intelligence and because we are foreigners."[33] The writer does not explain what he meant by "foreigners."

The privilege entailed some vulnerability. In 1897 during riots in Calcutta a Baghdadi Jewish youth, a Mr. Cohen, ascended the roof of a house and cut the telephone wires in order to cut off communications in the town. Because Cohen had been a member of the Volunteer Corps in that city, some anti-Semites attacked the Jews for disloyalty to the government. The *Saturday Journal* of Calcutta answered the accusers:

> It is necessary to show strictest precaution in enrollment of volunteers, but to debar all Jews from volunteering would be an act of the greatest injustice. Cohen was cut off from Jews and had allied himself with the low natives of the town. . . . As for the Jews, they are, and must always be, in the same boat with Christians in the event of a Hindoo or Mohamedan disturbance. They suffered as cruelly in the Mutiny as any European.[34]

Echoing the view that the Jews were not responsible for Cohen's actions as they had already excommunicated him, the *Bene Israelite* felt that in such cases, the synagogue authorities ought to inform the government of the real circumstances of a man who had been excommunicated so that the Jewish community as a whole would not be blamed.

Later the Indian Territorial Volunteer Force, which accepted Indians, was formed, but Anglo-Indians and Europeans still had a separate corps. Jews and Christians continued to join the European corps, although Parsis were not admitted. Though the Bene Israel continued to join the European Volunteer Corps from about 1910 to 1930, a period when the social rift between them and the Baghdadis was at its height, fewer did so after 1930. The educated Bene Israel in particular identified increasingly with the Hindus, Parsis, and others whom they met in schools and colleges rather than with the Anglo-Indians; they did not want to be recognized as different from ordinary Indians.[36]

In the lower ranks of certain public services, such as posts and telegraphs, police, and railways, quotas were reserved for Anglo-Indians, who received higher salaries than Indians when performing the same jobs. These services were partly connected with internal security, and the British wished not only to reward the Anglo-Indians for their total loyalty during the Mutiny, but also to encourage them, with their fluency in English, to enter these positions. Indeed, until 1878, Anglo-Indians and domiciled Europeans practically monopolized the telegraph services, and until 1920, customs. After the turn of the century, however, Indian nationalists pressured Britain to admit more Indians to the railway and telegraph services. In other services where there were uniform scales of pay, the Anglo-Indians were permitted to have lower qualifications. In the secretariat, for instance, Anglo-Indians and domiciled Europeans merely had to have school-leaving certificates, whereas others, including Bene Israel, had to be college graduates. Indian Christians, also with a high literacy rate in English, were similarly encouraged to enter these public services.[37]

The few Baghdadis who entered the lower services were treated like Anglo-Indians. Those Bene Israel who enrolled as Jews were also given Anglo-Indian rates of pay; others received the Indian scale. Classification depended on the idiosyncracy of the recruiting officer. If an applicant gave a traditional Marathi surname, such as Divekar, he would be taken as an Indian, but if he used Jacob or Samson, for instance, and spoke English, he would be given Anglo-Indian status. Many Indian Christians, including some Portuguese-Indians with Goan names, also passed as Anglo-Indians. Those Jews who did pass as Anglo-Indians enjoyed the privileges without suffering the prejudices: Anglo-Indians, being a mixed people, were looked down upon by both the British and the Indians. Although Benjamin Reuben, giving the presidential address at the Fifth Annual Bene Israel Conference in 1921, claimed that since the Bene Israel standard of living approximated that of Europeans, they should be classed as Europeans in the public services, most Bene Israel did not try to be recognized as non-Indian and were satisfied to be treated like Indians in the services. They could be loyal to Britain and still be proud to be Indians. Many Bene Israel resented the Baghdadis because the latter denied the Bene Israel's Jewishness, not because they considered the community Indian.[38]

During the first two decades of the twentieth century, the Bene Israel community in Bombay was divided into two parties, commonly known as the "Samson party" and "Dr. Elijah's party" after the principal leaders on the two sides. D. J. Samson, an engineer who worked as an assistant land manager in the Bombay Improvement Trust, included among leading members of his faction his brother I. J. Samson, a solicitor; Khan Bahadur Jacob B. Israel, retired chief administrator of the Indian State of Aundh, and his brother Shalom Israel, a deputy collector of Janjeera State; David Erulkar, a young barrister, and his brother, Dr. Abraham Erulkar, both educated in England. The key followers of the physician Dr. Elijah Moses were Solomon Moses and Jacob I. Apteker, both solicitors, and, acting more behind the scenes, David Abraham Tarankhopkar, an assistant commissioner of income tax.[39]

These factions developed partly as a result of personality clashes, but primarily because of differences of opinion regarding the management of the two most important communal institutions, the Israelite School and the oldest Bene Israel synagogue, Sha'ar ha-Rahamim. The parties alternated in power controlling these institutions. The conflict between the two groups intensified during the period 1913–16, when D. J. Samson was involved in litigation in a bribery case concerning the Bombay Improvement Trust. Although the case terminated with Samson's acquittal in October 1916, he acquiesced when the board of the Bombay Improvement Trust requested his resignation. As the litigation was coming to a close, Dr. E. Moses' party launched a journal entitled the *Friend of Israel,* whose chief raison d'être seemed to be to express its founders' views in the Samson case and to attack Samson, if often through innuendo. The Samson party continued to support its leader, resisting the *Friend of Israel*'s suggestion that he ought to resign from Bene Israel communal affairs.[40]

Seemingly to counter the accusations of the *Friend of Israel,* the Samson party started a journal of its own, the *Israelite,* in January 1917. In 1925 the *Bene Israel Review* succeeded the *Friend of Israel,* which had ceased publication in 1922. For about a decade the community enjoyed an active period of journalism unmatched in later years. Appearing monthly, bimonthly or sometimes quarterly, the periodicals contained English and Marathi sections. The English columns dealt with political topics (including Zionism), communal affairs, news of Jewish communities elsewhere, and religious commentaries. Aimed at a slightly lower class, the Marathi sections contained some similar material, but also stories and poems, religious homilies, advice about practical domestic affairs, and communal announcements. Most of the Bene Israel could read both the English and the Marathi sections of the journals, but some young educated people could not read the Marathi, while not all of the working class could read the English.[41] The existence of these journals enables one to write a more detailed history of this period than of others, a history that must be reviewed in the light of the personality clashes and conflicts over the management of communal institutions and the parties to which they gave rise.

The Marathi Issue and Bene Israel Identity

Within the broader cultural context, the "Indianness" of the Bene Israel was manifest in many ways. In the area of dress, for example, although the men in Bombay in this period were beginning to wear Western clothes (as were men of other communities), Bene Israel women continued to wear saris. Baghdadi women, however, when, beginning in the late nineteenth century, they abandoned the long Arab-style dresses, adopted Western dress. Bene Israel foods were very Indian. Those Bene Israel who could obtain kosher chicken, but not meat, often abstained from eating meat, making their diets closer to those of their Hindu neighbors, who leaned toward vegetarianism. Baghdadis tended to prepare food in the Arab style, although they also adopted curries.

The role of a common language in developing a national consciousness, so vital (and in some cases, simple) a factor for most emerging nations, was extremely complex for India. We cannot here go into the many ramifications of the debate over the use of English or some form of Hindi as a way of overcoming the diversity of regional languages—a problem still plaguing India today.[42] But this issue did raise a dilemma in terms of the Jews' identification. The Baghdadis were less conflicted: they moved from Arabic to English without really adopting an Indian language. For the Bene Israel, however, who had already adopted Marathi as their mother tongue, the situation was more complicated.

In the pre-British period, the Marathi of the Bene Israel was similar to that of other uneducated and illiterate people of the Konkan. Except for those in the military who mingled with higher-class Hindu society, and thus spoke a better Marathi, Bene Israel did not often come into contact with those who spoke the language well. With the introduction of education under the British, some Bene Israel men were able to pursue higher education and improve their Marathi, writing articles and poems in the language. But the women's continued use of the less-educated Marathi prevented the language of the entire community from becoming a pure or mature dialect. As the Bene Israel began to learn English, Marathi receded. When Jacob Sassoon referred to the Bene Israel as "Hindis," this description encouraged the shame over Marathi; Bene Israel who encountered Europeans, Eurasians, or Baghdadis at the office, at a party, or at a railroad station spoke English. Some women who did not know English preferred to speak a poor Hindustani rather than Marathi.[43]

As English became even more attractive and useful as a key to higher posts in government service and the professions, parents in all communities wanted to raise their children with English as a mother tongue and to educate them in the European schools that used it as a medium of instruction. Non-Christians, especially Parsis and upper-class Hindus, rushed to the proliferating Christian schools, staffed in the early nineteenth century mainly by Anglo-Indians and retired soldiers. A very high percentage of Parsis then enrolled in Elphinstone and St. Xavier's colleges in Bombay.[44] Muslims lagged behind under the influence of religious leaders who disapproved of Western education.[45] Bene Israel parents felt that not only was the education superior in the English-speaking schools, although they neglected Marathi and the other Indian languages, but the children came from a higher social milieu and the discipline was better. Boys were often sent to Anglo-Indian schools, where English was used from the beginning, although girls might still be enrolled in Anglo-vernacular schools, where they were instructed in the native language for the first few grades, after which English became the medium of instruction.[46]

In April 1917, the *Friend of Israel* published an article signed by "verbum

sap" (abbreviation for *verbum sapienti sat est* [a word to the wise is enough])
entitled "A Plea for the Study of Marathi," which argued that the rising
generation was being denied the benefits of vernacular education:

> We live and have our being among the Marathi speaking public, and it
> is very necessary that our children should know their mother-tongue prop-
> erly and be conversant with its literature. But many educated people can
> scarcely write or speak a few sentences of Marathi correctly.[47]

The author castigated those parents who believed that Marathi was of little
use in practical life and that sending children to English-medium schools
would give them special advantages:

> Many boys going to English teaching schools pick up the manners of
> the Eurasian or Eurasianized boys with whom they come in contact and
> begin to look down upon their Indian fellow brethren and even go to the
> length of calling them "niggers." The only worldly advantage they derive
> is that they are taken up in Railroads and Telegraphs on the same scale of
> salary as Europeans and Eurasians. But any gain they secure from this
> position is almost nullified by their trying to live extravagantly as *Sahibs*
> and aping western ways, without any attempt at the assimilation of what is
> really good in them. Thus by teaching children to despise their mother-
> tongue, we teach them indirectly to despise the race to which they belong,
> the country that has nurtured them, and the faith of their fathers.[48]

"Verbum sap" maintained that children should begin their education at vernacular schools, where they could develop sympathies for other Indians and
where the study of Marathi literature would teach them something of the
philosophy, theology, mythology, and folklore of their neighbors. It was dis-
graceful to be a stranger in one's own country.[49] Similarly, if girls went to
English schools, they would reject the dress and simple and unsophisticated
modes of living of their mothers and sisters and would want to become "*Mem
Sahibs*" and "dolls of the living room." He concluded:

> The salvation of the Bene Israels in matters social or otherwise would
> be achieved by their persisting to retain the Marathi language as their
> mother tongue and having "plain living and high moral thinking" as their
> motto, even after studying Western literature and imbibing Western cul-
> ture.[50]

The article was clearly controversial and elicited considerable response.
One concurring reader pointed out that the Israelite school was teaching
Marathi just enough to satisfy the government regulations, which prescribed
its study up to the third Anglo-vernacular standard (grade). On the other
side, a correspondent asked *why* Bene Israel children had to learn the theology, mythology, and folklore of "those of another creed and blood." He
argued instead that the Bene Israel had enough Marathi at home to develop
sympathies for their Indian brethren. Why waste several years on a language

that served no practical purpose and on which Hindus themselves often wasted little or no time? The Bene Israel did not have to pick up the manners of Eurasians.[51]

An important editorial entitled "Marathi: Its Place in the Bene-Israel Polity," which appeared in the *Friend of Israel,* supported "verbum sap" and raised another issue: the tendency of modern educated Bene Israel toward complete Anglicization. Although it might be unwise and impracticable to try to stem this current, the editor admitted, it had to be guided into safe channels if the Bene Israel wanted to prevent a catastrophe. The neglect of Marathi was a centrifugal and disintegrating force within the Bene Israel community itself. English could not filter to the masses of artisans, oil-pressers, carpenters, and farmers (or perhaps to older people or women) to become the medium of daily intercourse for them. Nor was it likely to become the "home language" of all for generations. If the educated classes neglected Marathi, they would become totally alienated from the masses of the Bene Israel and look down upon them. The Marathi speakers in turn would become suspicious of the English speakers. If the community was to remain unified and to progress, the educated classes would have to lead it and must be able to communicate with people in Marathi. The writer further argued:

> The Bene Israel has always been a very self-contained community sufficient into itself, neither giving nor receiving anything from its neighbours. This has had the effect of narrowing their mental horizon, confining them and their interests to communal matters. They find sufficient intellectual food in discussing petty communal jealousies and communal bickerings. Great national events leave them unmoved, great national activities are unknown to them. They are indifferent to anything but communal affairs. This narrow outlook on life has hampered their progress and has left them far behind in the race of civilization. . . . Neglect of Marathi will serve to enhance the isolation of the Bene Israel from their neighbours. For no degree of perfection attained in English will bring them into any closer relations with Europeans in India, while ignorance of Marathi will effectually cut them off from Indians in whose midst they have been living for the last ten centuries or so.[52]

The editorial concluded by arguing that materially, anyone who wanted to succeed in any walk of life or profession in India must know one of the vernaculars.[53]

All of the articles and correspondence referred to so far were in English; in 1918, however, the *Friend of Israel* published an editorial on the topic in the Marathi section of the journal. Here the editor noted that although the progress in women's education in the previous thirty years had improved the standard of Marathi of the community, Bene Israel students were at a disadvantage in studying this language because they lacked a basic knowledge of Hindu philosophy, customs, and manners. The Marathi courses contained many selections from the *Mahabarata* and the *Ramayana,* so that Hindu students who had the background in the legends had to concentrate only on the language. The editor urged that the Jewish school hire properly trained teachers for Marathi who would have higher expectations of the Bene Israel children. He felt that the Bene Israel were regarded as a backward community because of the low standard of Marathi in their schools.[54]

The conflict over language reflected divergent thinking within the Bene Israel community. Although those who favored moving ahead with English were probably motivated less by political considerations (i.e., identification with the British) than by economic ones, those who insisted on strengthening Marathi seemed particularly conscious of the need to maintain ties with other Indians and to promote cohesiveness within the Bene Israel community itself. Interestingly enough, the staff of the *Friend of Israel,* who felt so positively about the importance of Marathi, with its implications for the future of the Jews in India, were also strong Zionist sympathizers.

World War I: Politics and Communal Conferences

The concern about Marathi was not the only indication that the Bene Israel were sensitive to their position and role in a changing India. By 1914, Indian nationalism had been developing steadily for thirty years. With the coming of war, however, the movement shifted into lower gear because the British government in India, in seeking the cooperation of the nationalists, implied that with the successful completion of the war, many of their demands would be met.[55] In order to secure help in the war, the government, early in 1917, passed the Defence of India Force Act, which opened voluntary military service to all communities of India. For those Indians (including many Bene Israel) who were already members of the Volunteer Corps, military service now became compulsory. The Bene Israel journals urged other members of the community to enlist. The *Friend of Israel* wrote in an editorial:

> The passing of the Indian Defence Force Act may be said to be an epoch in the history of British India. The privilege it gives to Indians to come forward to defend their country and thus relieve the militia for active services is no small concession at the present state of their political evolution. The Act has been welcomed in all quarters. . . . The Bene Israel has played an unostentatious, but by no means an insignificant part in the establishment of British rule in India and we would ask our young men to respect their noble traditions by "doing their bit." Young women . . . can help to crush German militarism by participating in the humanitarian work of the Women's Branch of the War Relief Fund.[56]

The editorial also urged all who could to subscribe to the war loan, pointing out that although the war bonds or loans might be too expensive, the post office cash certificates were especially suited to a poor community like the Bene Israel.[57]

The recruitment of Indians as soldiers led the British, in 1917, to an initial accommodation to a nationalist demand by making Indians eligible for commissions as lieutenants. But the repeated calls for sacrifice and the delays in granting reforms soon exasperated many Indians. The mood of the political activists changed during World War I from loyalty and eagerness to help to an expectation of change. Gokhale, who had forged the Imperial Council into an advocate for moderate nationalism, had died in 1915, while Tilak, who had returned from prison in Mandalay before the war, became popular again. Mrs. Annie Besant, the theosophist, now turned her attention to nationalist politics. Although she was a moderate who believed in constitutional gradualism, she and Tilak now raised the cry for home rule, or self-government for India within the empire. Because the home rule leagues were not radical, did not demand British withdrawal, and were well-received by the public, the Indian National Congress moderate leaders took Tilak back into their counsels. At the same time, Mrs. Besant and Tilak worked for a rapprochement with the Muslim League.[58]

The Muslim League's early loyalty to the British disintegrated during World War I, when Turkey, toward whom Indian Muslims had looked for Islamic leadership, entered the war on the side of the central powers. Under the guidance of Abdul Kalam Azad, Indian Muslims who were now ready to join forces with Hindus against the British promoted a joint meeting of the Indian National Congress and the Muslim League in Lucknow in 1916. Compromise was the order of the day: Muslims would support Congress's demand for representative self-government in return for Congress's recognition of the need for separate Muslim constituencies. The two organizations agreed to a plan of constitutional reform that would enable India to join the other self-governing dominions of the British Empire.[59]

In the decade following 1916, many imperial, national, and provincial conferences were held to discuss political, industrial, economic, and social advances. These meetings were paralleled by communal conferences organized by various caste associations and other Indian groups who, encouraged by the government's intention to safeguard the political interests of the minorities by creating separate electorates as expressed in the 1909 reforms, now experienced a growth of communal self-awareness and political consciousness. Communities such as the Parsis, Kayasthas, Muslims, Jains, Patidars, Marathas, and Bhandaris held conferences to talk about communal problems and uplift, especially educational improvement. Soon the Bene Israel caught the spirit.[60]

Writing in the *Israelite* in June 1917, David Erulkar suggested the holding of a Bene Israel conference. In the past, he said, the Bene Israel were few in number, living together in a limited area, with a simple mode of life and few problems. But the increase in numbers, the migration all over India, the spread of education, and the introduction of "artificialities of Western Civilization" had brought them face to face with complex problems and changed conditions:

> We have developed factions and have no central body to link units, to deliberate over communal problems, recommend abolition of evil customs, to encourage the introduction of reforms and above all to keep us a homogeneous unit. . . . At present we are an obscure community little known in our country and hence often neglected and forgotten. An annual conference of our people would be the surest way of enlightening other people of our existence and of our activities in communal regeneration.[61]

The Israelite League, a communal organization, appointed a provisional committee composed of leaders of both the Samson and Dr. E. Moses factions to plan the "convening of a Bene Israel Conference to consider various communal questions of vital importance." When the group met on 4 November 1917, the members were divided on the advisability of incorporating a clause regarding politics in the definition of the goals of the conference. The Samson party wanted to include those political topics that touched on Bene Israel concerns, realizing that certain matters relating to communal advancement or rights might require approaching the government for special legislation. Although they claimed that they did not intend to include in their deliberations general politics (issues relating to the general administration of India), as doing so would serve no national or communal purpose and "a Conference would not survive the shock of political controversies," Dr. E. Moses' party feared that that was their aim. The Moses faction was probably concerned that the Erulkar brothers, who had come under the influence of Tilak while studying in England, might drag the community into broader politics, especially the agitational kind favored by the lokamanya. Tilak's trial for incitement to violence and "sedition" had been held at around the time David Erulkar returned from England to Bombay to begin his law practice, and Erulkar became a junior counselor for the lokamanya (the senior counsel for the defense being Muhammad Ali Jinnah, the Muslim nationalist who became president of the Muslim League and, eventually, the first prime minister of Pakistan). The Erulkars insisted that although they wanted to be free to participate in general politics themselves, they would not involve the Bene Israel community.[62]

Since many Bene Israel felt that it was all right to ask for more jobs or improvements in actual conditions, but were afraid to identify themselves with the demands of greater self-government or greater devolution of power by the British, David Erulkar suggested that the proposed conference should not identify itself with any political party in the country and should "exclude general politics not peculiar to the Community." This proposal was rejected, the majority voting instead to accept Solomon Moses' compromise wording that the "object should be to deliberate upon questions relating to the social, educational and religious condition of the community and such other questions (not of a purely political nature) affecting the community."[63]

At a public meeting held on 11 November 1917, J. B. Israel admitted the blessings that British rule had brought to the Bene Israel community but dwelt on the necessity of legitimate political agitation, arguing that the government was not opposed to such action and that no one would suffer thereby.[64] D. J. Samson maintained that the whole community would have to express its opinions to ask for special legislation and that the resolutions reached at a conference would bind all the synagogues. The opposing side pointed out the difficulty that would arise in defining "pure politics" and argued that the Bene Israel community enjoyed special privileges at the hands of the government and had no grievances. In order that a large number of government employees not hesitate to take part in the conference, it was necessary to expressly exclude politics altogether. At the end of the meeting, an amendment proposed by Jacob I. Apteker (of the E. Moses faction), stating that "a conference of the Bene Israel community be called to deliberate upon social, religious, educational and economic conditions of this community and such other questions (not of a political nature) affecting the community," was passed by a large majority. Thus the phrase "not of a purely political nature," accepted by the provisional committee a week earlier, had been altered.[65] A new committee was then appointed to make arrangements for convening the conference.

The Samson faction now accused its opponents of bad faith. The accepted definition of the objectives would deprive the conference of any right to express its opinion on some vital questions for the community that came within the definition of the word *politics,* inasmuch as they involved approaching the government for legislative changes, in such matters as the disabilities of the Bene Israel in the army, the desire of many Bene Israel to have polygamy prohibited by law, and their wish to have the divorce law reformed. Dr. E. Moses' party replied that it considered these topics nonpolitical and would be willing to discuss them. Nevertheless, the Samson party felt that if the others were so worried that general politics would be included, the clause excluding "pure politics," as in the compromise resolution, would have solved the problem.

The two factions took their quarrel to the broader public. In a letter addressed to the Bene Israel community, members of the Samson faction complained that the extreme politicophobia of the others was not a compliment to the intelligence and moral courage of the community or to the government. They warned the community:

> If you are afraid to put before the authorities even your communal grievances, if you dread approaching them for legislation to eradicate some of our social evils, . . . what impression will the other Indian people get of the *brave* Bene Israel? What contributions or co-operation are they or the Government to expect from you, if you dread anything that savours of politics even if it be peculiar to our Community? What wonder if we lose the goodwill of our countrymen, who gave us shelter and allowed us to live in peace without persecution for centuries. That goodwill. . . . means much to us; it is our greatest stake in the country. To lose it would be to sow the seeds of our future sorrow.[66]

In a separate public letter, J. B. Israel spoke of people who realized the necessity of reforms but who smothered them, not out of loyalty to the British government, but out of fear raised by the misconceived idea about the British government and its policy. "There is no greater danger to the country than such suppressed discontent," he wrote. To believe that government employees would experience repercussions if they participated in a conference that dealt with political issues was a perverted view of the policy of the government and its officers, he argued. This perception charged the government with "possessing no genuine desire for reform and its officers with possessing a desire to throttle their loyal servants for pursuing communal objects admittedly legitimate and extremely necessary to create unity and strengthen the hands of the Government in its present difficult situation."[67]

Serious efforts to reconcile the two groups under the auspices of Moses Elijah of Simla and Abraham Reuben, the acknowledged leader of the Bene Israel community in Karachi, proved abortive.[68] Thus the factionalism that had earlier expressed itself in the rivalry for control over synagogue and school management now came to the fore in the efforts at communal organization and would seriously hamper these efforts throughout the period.

The Representation to Montagu

In July 1917, Edwin Montagu, a Liberal who happened to be Jewish, was appointed secretary of state for India. The *Israelite* was delighted with the choice:

> The fact that the heavy responsibility has been entrusted to one of our co-religionists, especially at a time when the Indian question involves difficult and complex issues, is an event in the history of our race. Never before has one of our faith held such a responsible post connected with the Government of this country.[69]

In response to the increased nationalist agitation and India's help in the war effort, Montagu, on 20 August 1917, made a famous declaration of postwar policy to the House of Commons:

> The policy of His Majesty's Government, with which the Government of India are in complete accord, is that of the increasing association of Indians in every branch of the administration, and the gradual development of self-governing institutions, with a view to the progressive realization of responsible government in India as an integral part of the British Empire.[70]

If the British felt that this policy was radical, envisioning a kind of dominion status, similar to that of Canada, Australia, South Africa, and New Zealand, many Indians now thought it was too little. No date was set for the achievement of dominion status, and the statement really promised "responsible government" more explicitly than "self-government."[71] In preparation for the reforms that he and Lord Frederick Chelmsford, the new viceroy, were about to introduce, Montagu toured India in 1917–18.

The Morely-Minto Reforms of 1909 had enlarged the powers of the provincial councils and had granted separate electorates and reserved seats for Muslims, introducing the principle of communal electorates. The first decade in the twentieth century had seen a sharp increase in Hindu caste-consciousness as well as nationalism all over India. Leaders of the non-Brahmin movement were afraid that Brahmins might seize any power transferred to Indian hands, and therefore, to prevent an oppressive Brahmin oligarchy, insisted upon communal representation.[72] As mentioned above, Congress and the Muslim League had agreed at Lucknow in 1916 that there should be separate representation for Muslims, but not for other communities. But in 1917 a number of smaller communities pressed for separate constituencies. Communal leaders stressed the wide gaps existing between various castes and classes in India and the lack of education; they partially impressed Montagu with their arguments that the country was not ready for democracy.[73]

The term *communalism*, an Indian contribution to the English language, has been defined as "that ideology which emphasizes as the social, political and economic unit the group of adherents of each religion, and emphasizes the distinction, even the antagonism, between such groups."[74] Srinivas has pointed out that in a country segmented along the lines of religion, caste, language, and region, heightened national self-awareness necessarily implied heightened self-awareness at every level of the social structure, from the highest to the lowest. In the case of sects and religions, self-awareness has resulted in the reinterpretation of traditions, communalism, and even revivalism.[75] Dumont has maintained that communalism is thus the affirmation of the religious community as a political group: "A community's consciousness of being different from others, . . . and its will to live united as against others as well as its capacity . . . to reflect itself in a given territory, makes communalism resemble nationalism. . . . At the same time the adherence to group-religion distinguishes it sharply."[76]

Despite this general trend, in November 1917 the Samsons, Erulkars, Israels, and four other Bene Israel submitted an address to Montagu, expressing their agreement with the aims of the Indian National Congress and the All India Muslim League, and their intention not to seek separate communal representation for the approximately twenty thousand Jews of India. It is worthwhile to reproduce this statement in its entirety.

1. We, the undersigned, members of the Bene-Israel community, beg to submit, in the interests of our community, the following representation in connection with the constitutional changes in the administration of the country at present under consideration of the Government of India and the British Cabinet.

2. The scheme of reforms adopted by the Indian National Congress and the All India Muslim League has been before the country for some time past. This scheme has our entire approval and hearty support.

3. We would urge the granting of these reforms at an early date. We also pray that the same be granted liberally and generously, not as a reward for services rendered by our country, but as a recognition of our country-men's fitness for a responsible share in the Government of this country after over a century of British rule, and also as a faithful fulfilment of promises made by British Sovereigns and Statesmen.

4. In connection with the questions of communal representation, though we belong to a microscopically small community, the past history of our community in India, extending over the long period of two thousand years, has convinced us of the spirit of tolerance and fairness practiced by those Indian communities who command the majority towards their numerically insignificant sister communities; and hence we are of the opinion that the interests of small communities will not suffer in any way by a general representation as distinct from communal representations.

5. For a large community such as the Mohamedans, a separate representation may be necessary for a time, but we feel that smaller communities stand to lose by communal representation, inasmuch as they are marked out, and whatever special representation they may get, can never be very effective. The Jews in England are a minority, and yet they have never suffered for the want of communal representation. We are, therefore, of the opinion that the principle of communal representation, if applied at all, should be limited to Mohamedans only.

6. On the other hand, if the principle of communal representation be extended to smaller communities, we beg to submit, that there should not be separate communal electorates. In place of communal electorates or Government nominations, we would recommend that communal representatives be co-opted by the representatives of the general electorate, which must then necessarily include all the persons with franchise irrespective of caste or community.

7. By giving a separate electorate to a community, the racial feeling is accentuated and the interest of the community is narrowed down to its own activities. Such communal elections do not foster the development of the

Indian nation; they rather retard it. In our opinion these disadvantages of communal electorates can be overcome and communal representation be secured, if considered necessary, by some plan as we have submitted to you.

8. We feel sure, that a nation which has sacrificed so much for the liberty and freedom of small nations cannot but uphold the same principle in the case of a large nation.

9. We also feel that you, sir, whose co-religionists have suffered for centuries in many Western countries, disabilities based on race and creed, cannot but sympathize with the just and legitimate aspirations of three hundred millions of your fellow subjects, whose disabilities are mainly based on creed, colour and race.[77]

There seems to have been no effort to enlist Baghdadi participation in this representation. Perhaps the authors knew that the Baghdadis did not identify sufficiently with Indians to be sympathetic. The address was accorded a great deal of favorable publicity in the Indian press, being reproduced in whole or in part in the *Times of India* on November 29, in the *Bombay Chronicle*, and elsewhere. An unidentified paper reproduced an extract in its December 5 issue, commenting:

The members of the Bene Israel community have submitted to Mr. Montagu a very sensible representation on the subject of constitutional reforms. The representation is, indeed, an oasis in the desert of bewildering, silly and stupid clamour for representation on the basis of class, creed and caste, which self-seeking elements in some of the most advanced communities, like the Parsis and Anglo-Indians, have chosen to claim. We would commend the Bene Israel representation to the careful study of people like Sir Jamsetji Jijeebhoy and the "Anglo-Indian" fraternity, who shamelessly attempt to gamble for advantages to themselves at the expense of the commonweal of the nation.[78]

The weekly *Sandesha* (The Message) supplement published a cartoon on 2 December 1917, expressing its approval of the Bene Israel representation. The cartoon depicts a dog, who symbolizes the demand for caste-wise representation, with the members of various minorities driving him—all except the Bene Israel. The legend reads: "Mr. Jacob Bapuji [Israel], Shalom Israel and Dr. Erulkar and other leaders of the Bene Israel community have declared that we do not want caste-wise representation at all."[79]

This representation to Montagu, supporting Congress as it did, could not be construed as a sign of disloyalty to Britain because Congress had not yet committed itself to an antigovernment attitude. Congress was still moderate; the Liberals did not withdraw to form their own confederation until 1918–19. As might have been expected, however, the members of the Dr. E. Moses faction would not allow the signers to get away with such a step and sent a counterresolution to the government, signed by Dr. E. Moses, Solomon Moses, J. I. Apteker, and their followers. Unfortunately, it was never published and no copy of this statement is available. Even most of the community members seemed unaware of its contents.[80] Rather than dealing with the substantive question of communal representation, this counterrepresentation most likely argued that the signers of the original address lacked authority to represent the community. The "counter" writers probably did not make any suggestions about how the reforms should take place or whether there should even be any reforms at all. These surmises are drawn from an editorial entitled "An Unauthorized Representation" published in the *Friend of Israel*, the organ of Dr. Moses' party. The editorial argued that the signatories of the document should have made clear that this representation was their personal act and that the community whose interests it was intended to safeguard had not been consulted about it. Instead, the signatories seemed to be trying to obtain for their unauthorized action an *ex post facto* sanction from the community by distribution of printed copies of the "Address to Montagu." The *Friend of Israel* exhorted the community to protest the sending of the representation, as silence would be seen as approval of the signatories' views.[81] The Moses faction seemed to be insisting on its apolitical stance here. The signatories responded that they had drafted the address "in the interests of" and not "on behalf of" the community, and that they therefore did not have to consult, and indeed, had the right to express their opinion.[82] It is worth noting that with all this communal and political activity occurring in November 1917, little attention seems to have been paid in the meetings to the Balfour Declaration, which had been issued on 2 November 1917.

The anticipated governmental reforms were spelled out in the Montagu-Chelmsford Report in July 1918. More authority was given to the provinces, where the principle of dyarchy, or divided responsibility, was introduced. Some branches of the provincial administration would remain under the direct control of the governor, a British appointee, and some under the control of ministers responsible to elected legislatures. The legislative councils were enlarged, with the majority of the members to be elected. The granting of the franchise for the elections highlighted the communal problem. Although the Montagu-Chelmsford Reforms recognized "that communal electorates perpetuated and deepened class divisions" and "that to give a minority representation because it was weak was a positive encouragement for it to stay weak so that it would not lose privilege," there was no alternative that would satisfy the Muslims. Special constituencies were therefore created not only for Muslims, but also for Indian Christians, Sikhs, Anglo-Indians, Europeans, landlords, universities, and chambers of commerce. Hindus voted in the general constituencies. Race and religion as well as property qualifications now determined the right to vote, which varied according to the strength of minority groups in each province, for the provincial and central legislative councils. Not receiving special representation (because of the size of their community), the Jews voted in the general constituencies, which had, of course, a Hindu majority. The reforms were finally incorporated in the Government of India Act of 1919, which provided for the appointment of a statutory commission every ten years to inquire into Indian conditions and recommend further constitutional reforms to be introduced toward the goal of fully responsible government.[83]

The debate over the wisdom of discussing politics did not subside. Late in 1917 Samuel S. Mazgaonker, another member of the Samson faction, published a pamphlet in which he argued against those who encouraged the Bene Israel to identify with Europeans and Anglo-Indians in their opposition to Muslim and Hindu efforts at reform. It was the Bene Israel's primary duty to cooperate with the Indians when they were fighting for independence, he stated. He reminded them that Jews in England were not afraid to put before the British government their demands, even those concerning Zionism. And yet Montagu and Simon were not removed from their posts because of these Jewish demands.[84]

The First Bene Israel Conference was finally held in Bombay on 25–27 December 1917. Chaired by Dr. Joseph Benjamin Bamnolker, a prominent physician from Ahmedabad, it was boycotted by the Samson group. Following the pattern of the early Indian National Congress, the resolutions of the Bene Israel Conference (and later, those of the All-India Israelite League) always commenced with expressions of loyalty to the British rule and the king-emperor, prayed for victory in the war, and welcomed important British officials visiting India, in this case Lord Chelmsford and Edwin Montagu. The latter was congratulated for being the first secretary of state for India of the Jewish faith.

The conference also passed a resolution asking the government to grant some of the new royal commissions in the military intended for Indians "to some deserving educated Bene Israel in consideration of the services rendered by their forefathers in the military line and as an incentive to young men to render similar services."[85] The Samson party now argued that the organizers of the conference, after having tabooed politics of all sorts, having alienated some of the most prominent members of the community by claiming they intended to introduce general politics, and having convinced some government employees and students to come to the conference by promising to exclude politics, had now discussed and passed resolutions of a political nature.[86]

The *Friend of Israel*, which as the journal of Dr. E. Moses' party now became the organ of the Bene Israel Conference, argued that these resolutions did not truly deal with political issues: the qualifications for the officers' posts that had been created were already established.[87] In reality, one cannot help but conclude that the Samson party took this opportunity to attack its opponents by focusing on the *principle* of the matter, because the members probably agreed with the *content* of the resolutions. It seemed to be the very sort of issue they had in mind when they themselves demanded that politics not be excluded from the conference because some requests to government might have to be made.

The Samson party now launched a rival organization, the All-India Israelite League, founded—unlike the Bene Israel Conference, its members claimed—"along constitutional lines" with the stated purpose "to organize the Bene Israel community in India and Burma, to work for its welfare and advancement."[88] If Bombay remained the center of conference support, the league had a greater following in Karachi and Poona. One joined the conference or league according to which group one supported in the management of the Israelite School and the Sha'ar ha-rahamim Synagogue.[89]

At its second annual meeting, in 1918, the Bene Israel Conference laid down a new version of its objectives:

> The object of the Bene Israel Conference shall be to promote the progress of the Bene Israel community by deliberating upon social, religious, educational and economic questions relating to the well-being of the community and taking steps to carry out the resolutions passed by the Conference from time to time.[90]

Political subjects were still excluded, not by express exclusion as in the original objectives, but rather by clear omission. This change was meant to provide an opening for the leaguers to join the conference, if the words indeed had been the real obstacle.[91]

Political developments on the international and home scenes attracted the attention of both the All-India Israelite League and the Bene Israel Conference in 1919. Both passed resolutions welcoming the Reform Bill (the Government of India Act of 1919), urging the community to "play its part in the New Era dawning for India," in cooperation with "their other Indian brethren for the welfare of India, which had been their Motherland." A league resolution expressed the conviction that the grant of constitutional reforms would smother the bitter feelings in the country and work for peace, progress, and prosperity. Both organizations also appealed to the British government to intervene to prevent further pogroms and similar outbursts of anti-Semitism in eastern Europe.[92]

The Baghdadi Response

Politics and Identity

Having arrived in India toward the end of the eighteenth century, the Baghdadi Jews did not consider themselves "natives" nor did they intend to assimilate or to identify with the indigenous population. When they discarded their traditional Middle Eastern clothing, they adopted the dress of Europeans, not Indians.[93] They gradually shed Arabic in favor of English as a mother tongue; there was no debate over the use of an Indian vernacular, as had occurred among the Bene Israel. When Albert Sassoon was appointed to the Order of the Star of India in 1866, he "celebrated with an elaborate supper and ball. . . . The *Bombay Gazette* reported with approval that no 'natives' were among the three hundred guests and solemnly congratulated Mr. Sassoon and his family on their evident wish to ally themselves with English society in Bombay."[94] The struggle to escape their marginal status and to be considered fully European constitutes a main theme of the Baghdadis' sojourn in India; their relationships with government and their political affiliations and attitudes must be examined in this context.

Although Baghdadi Jews were not active in politics, a few participated in public life. In Calcutta, they were named as honorary magistrates and voted in municipal elections from at least 1882. Leading members of the community were invited to the viceroy's levees and celebrations, helping to organize some of the latter. In 1879, Elia David Joseph was appointed sheriff of Calcutta, an honor later conferred upon his two sons. His eldest son, Joseph, served as municipal councillor from 1886 to 1896. Other municipal councillors included E. M. D. Cohen (1897–1918), David Jacob Cohen (1906 until after Indian independence), and the latter's brother, Immanuel J. Cohen (1903–24 and 1930–49).[95] In Bombay, in addition to serving as honorary magistrates, Jews played an even larger role. The government of Bombay offered David Sassoon many public appointments, but he accepted only that of justice of the peace, in which capacity he arbitrated disputes between Jews. When Sassoon died in 1864, the *Times of India* wrote, "Bombay has lost one of its most energetic, wealthy, public-spirited and benevolent citizens. . . . In personal appearance, private character and public life most remarkable."[96] David Sassoon's son, Albert-Abdullah, had been a member of the Bombay Legislative Council from 1868 to 1872. After his term there were apparently no Jews on the council, for in 1896 the *Bombay Gazette* suggested that since there were nearly ten thousand Jews in India and they were influential, an Israelite should be appointed to fill a vacancy in the Legislative Council. The *Gazette* proposed the name of Mrs. Solomon David (Flora) Sassoon, who, if appointed, would have been the second Jew and the first woman in the history of the Bombay Presidency Legislative Council. There is no indication that she was appointed, and in any case, she moved to London in 1902. Sir Sassoon J. David had served on the Council of the Governor-General of India, on the Imperial Legislative Council (the predecessor of the Legislative Assembly), and on the Bombay Municipal Corporation for twenty years, becoming its head in 1921–22.[97]

Until 1885, Baghdadi Jews, perhaps because of their late arrival in India, their fairer skin, and their assimilation of European standards of dress, language, social habits, and education, were classified by the government as "Europeans." The Jewish Girls' School, which opened in Calcutta in 1881 to counter missionary efforts among the poor, used English as the medium of instruction; by 1884 it was subject to the European Inspectorate.[98] The Defence Association, organized in the days of the Ilbert Bill in the interests of the Europeans in India, considered the Jews as "British." It is not surprising, therefore, that Baghdadi Jews sought to be classified as Europeans for political purposes. They regarded their way of life as closer to that of the British, identified their interests with theirs, and continued to express their loyalty to Britain. The Baghdadis also believed that their prosperity was a direct result of British rule. Thus the community in Calcutta was disturbed when, in 1885, it was declared "non-European," although the Armenians continued to enjoy European status. Musleah suggests that this reclassification might have happened because most Indian Jews—that is, the Bene Israel and Cochinis—having lived in India for centuries, physically resembled other Indians. But the Baghdadi Jews continued to consider themselves "British-oriented" and "European." They did not question racism; they just wanted to be on the privileged side. Many Parsis felt the same way: they saw themselves as a "purely white race," did not want to be called "natives," and sought a close connection with the British, who refused to accept them as "their own kind."[99]

A year later, an interesting case related to the status of the Jews was raised by the Jewish community of Aden, which had been taken over in 1839 by the British East India Company and annexed to British India. In 1886, the Jews of Aden, numbering about thirty-five hundred by their estimate (fewer in the estimates of others),[100] petitioned the government of India to pass a law making Jewish law and custom in relation to inheritance and succession applicable to the community in Aden and exempting it from the operation of the Indian Succession Act of 1865. That act was based on English law, whereby when a man dies, his property and assets are divided between his wife and children, daughters inheriting along with sons. According to Jewish law, however, a married daughter does not receive a share of her father's property at his death because she is given her share at the time of her marriage, and thus has a claim for further maintenance against her husband only. Provision at death is made only for the widow, unmarried daughters, and minors. The rest of the property is divided equally between the sons or, if there are no sons, the daughters, including the married ones. The Aden Jews claimed that the bulk of their community was of foreign extraction, similar to the Jews of Arabia, and unacquainted with the principles and practices of Indian law, nor were they aware that their own customs and law had been superseded by the Indian Succession Act of 1865. They pointed out that in non-European lands, particularly in "Oriental lands," Jews were usually governed by their own laws and customs, and not the general law of the country in which they resided.

The Indian government reacted sympathetically. Its members consulted encyclopedias and other books on Jews in Asia and Arabia to ascertain whether the Jews in Aden were as close to those of Arabia as they claimed, and decided that they were. They were prepared to exempt them from the succession act, realizing that the courts would then, in most cases relating to succession among Jews, probably apply principles of Jewish law. The government's main concern, however, was that this exemption should not become a precedent and that the Jewish communities of Bombay and Calcutta not demand the same treatment. At first, the government even wondered why the Sassoons, Ezras, and the like did not object to the succession act, but accepted their claim that in lands where "civilization" had extended, Jews were content to live under the general law of the country. The government acknowledged that the Jews of India did not seem dissatisfied with the laws of succession. The Aden Jews managed to persuade a visiting Calcutta Baghdadi to intercede with Bombay and Calcutta Jews to agree to the provision. The Baghdadi Jews of India gave the required guarantees to the government. Twenty-one prominent Jews of Bombay and twenty-seven from Calcutta wrote, in the summer of 1886:

> The Jewish community at Aden is entirely distinct from the Jewish communities in India. We consider that having regard to the various circumstances, geographical and otherwise, connected with the Israelite community at Aden, their request is only reasonable; and we pledge ourselves that the granting of their present application shall constitute no precedent for a similar application on the part of the Jewish community at Calcutta [or Bombay].[101]

David Sassoon and Company of London and India also supported the wishes of the Aden Jews. The governor-general in council therefore granted the petition and the Jews of Aden were exempted from the operation of the entire Succession Act. Indian Jews also believed that the Jews in Aden were victims of social and civil discrimination at the hands of their Muslim fellow citizens, and the editor of *Paerah*, a Calcutta periodical, advised them to bring their grievances to the British resident.[102] In supporting their coreligionists in Aden while not demanding similar privileges themselves, the Baghdadi Jews of India seemed to be acknowledging their satisfaction with British law. Perhaps again, they wanted to reassert their status as Europeans. They did not want to be singled out, as Jews, for special treatment.

The classification of "European" or "non-European" had important ramifications in the area of education, partly because European education was subsidized by the government. Immediately after the 1885 exclusion of the Jews as Europeans, the inspector for European schools ceased his visits to the Jewish Girls' School in Calcutta. The community then submitted a petition to Sir Rivers Thompson, the governor of Bengal; in 1886, he agreed that the Jewish school should still be visited, mainly because of its high standard of English education, but warned that Jewish students attending other schools would not be considered Europeans.[103]

The issue could have implications for higher education too. In 1908, a D. Sassoon of Calcutta inquired of the Home Department whether Jews were eligible for the state scholarships tenable in Europe by Europeans and Eurasians domiciled in India. One official stated that an applicant of European Jewish extraction would be eligible, but an Asiatic Jew, such as Sassoon— an "Armenian Jew"—would probably not be. Another official believed that, as some Jews were natives of England by statute, and some served the government of India and were practically Europeans as the term was used in connection with the scholarship scheme, one could not exclude them entirely. Home Department officials finally decided that a domiciled Jew, such as Mr. Sassoon, probably came within the spirit although not the letter of the resolution, and so they sent his letter to the government of Bengal for disposition.[104]

Around 1914, the classification of Baghdadis in Calcutta as non-Europeans created more serious educational problems for them. Christians schools operating under the European Code in that city could not admit non-European children as more than 15 percent of their enrollment. "Non-European" included all Jews, whether born in Europe or India, Parsis, native Christians, and others. The graduates of the Jewish Girls' School, which had been recognized as a European school and supported by the government since 1904 because it prepared for the Junior Cambridge Examinations,[105] thus faced an admissions quota if they wanted to enter a Christian school for the Senior Cambridge. If they were accepted, they were classed as non-Europeans and lost their scholarships. I. A. Isaac, a Bene Israel journalist, lecturer, and crusader for educational and religious reforms resident in Calcutta, blamed the situation on a certain inspector of European schools, a Mr. Hallward, who was considered to be anti-Semitic and who feared Jewish students would win all the scholarships through merit examinations. He tried to have all Jewish children barred from participating in scholarship examinations and urged the heads of European schools in Calcutta to charge Jewish children double fees. Infuriated, Jewish leaders submitted a memorial to Sir Edward Baker, director of public instruction in Bengal, praying for a removal of the restrictions and disabilities, but received only a vague reply. As there was no clear definition of the rights of Jews to full educational privileges, the Education Department did not see any reason to relax Hallward's rigid interpretation.

Isaac felt that the only solution was for Jews to found their own separate Jewish senior schools, noting that school authorities actually suggested this remedy.[106] Isaac also argued in a letter to the *Statesman*, Calcutta's leading English newspaper, that Jews throughout the British Empire were recognized as Europeans and there was no reason why they should be treated as nondescripts in India. In 1917, the European Code was amended to read "that all Jews, Armenians and Parsees living European lives, or approximating their ways of living, be considered as Europeans for the purposes of the Education Code." But the breach of the amendment by the European schools practically kept their doors closed to Jewish children. As late as 1922, the Jewish Association of Calcutta was still asking the government to remove the 15 percent clause.[107] Despite these educational problems, Musleah felt that after 1900,

> the Jewish community [of Calcutta] came to accept its politically nebulous position because for the most part, the discriminatory measure existed only on paper. There was free social intercourse between statutory Europeans and Jews who were admitted to membership of the exclusive European institutions such as the fashionable clubs, a privilege to which prominent Indians could not aspire.[108]

Bombay Jews were not always so fortunate. Although Baghdadi Jewish firms were admitted to the Bombay Chamber of Commerce, whereas Indian firms, even Parsi, were not, the Baghdadis were not always admitted to the exclusive European clubs. When they were, they might be sneered at behind their backs. B. J. Israel suggests that many British probably thought the Baghdadis were crude and "pushy." Teachers and administrators at Cathedral School, the leading school in Bombay, thought Baghdadis were trying to pass as "whites," although they were Asiatics. The Armenians, who were Christians, were more readily accepted by the British. Here too, the Baghdadis seem to have encountered a certain amount of British anti-Jewish racism, since they never tried to conceal their Jewishness. Israel feels that British Jews in India, however, went out of their way to hide their heritage, except for a very few, like Sir Godfrey Davis, an Indian Civil Service judge, and Sir Jeremy Raisman, finance minister of the viceroy's council. Many English Jews in the bureaucracy never admitted their Jewishness and would have been embarrassed, he feels, to extend themselves to local Jews. They did not observe their Judaism and did not want it emphasized.[109]

Baghdadi Identity during World War I

If the main concerns of the Bene Israel during the war years—aside from their communal conference—were how they could best serve the British war effort and the effects on the community of the 1917 law that opened military commissions to Indians, for the Baghdadi Jews the issues were quite different.[110] The question of national identity became particularly troublesome during the war because of British anxiety about the surveillance of Ottoman Turkish subjects in India. Most of the Baghdadi Jews were officially Turkish, and yet, before hostilities had broken out with the Ottoman Empire, they were generally exempt from the Registration of Foreigners Act because they were considered Asiatics. According to the Home Department, on 1 September 1914 there were 3,197 Turkish subjects in all of India—the bulk being in Bombay—including 2,600 Baghdadis.[111] The outbreak of war posed a problem for the government. Should the British require registration of all Ottoman subjects, regardless of religion? They feared that if they interned those of military age, as they were doing with nationals of other hostile nations, they would offend Muslims in India. Perhaps deporting all Ottoman citizens quickly would be less likely to excite Muslims. But what should they do about nominal Turkish subjects, such as Arabs of "Lower Mesopotamia," Baghdadi Jews, and Shi'ites, all of whom were probably anti-Turkish and would require special and careful treatment? The government finally decided to intern and remove all "Turks proper," that is, European Turks, but "European Jewish Turks" would not be deported. It was not clear how they were defining "European"—perhaps simply geographically. All non-European or Asiatic Turks, including Arabs and Baghdadi Jews, would also be allowed to remain. The government decided that the Bombay government could handle matters as it saw fit and needed to intern only dangerous and suspicious Baghdadis and Arabs.[112]

Once that decision had been made, the question arose whether to allow Ottoman subjects who were Greeks, Armenians, or Jews to travel around within India for business purposes. The government of Bengal felt that its almost two hundred Ottoman subjects (186 Jews, 3 Greeks, and 6 Armenians) in these categories were harmless, did not sympathize with Muslim and Turkish military success, and should be permitted to travel. Indeed, the government of Calcutta had received several petitions from Jewish subjects for permission to travel outside the Presidency of Bengal for trade, claiming they would be destitute if they could not. The home, army, foreign, and political departments as well as the director of criminal intelligence all agreed, however, that only Turkish subjects of Armenian and Greek origin could get licenses to travel if they needed them to earn a living, and that in general, Calcutta was a big enough place for petty traders. It is not clear why Jews were excluded unless, perhaps, because they were far more numerous. There does seem to have been some fear that since the Jews were anti-Russian, they might be pro-German. When, a few months later, the Bombay government asked whether the Turkish Baghdadi Jews could be given travel permits, the central government still adhered to its negative decision. Baghdadi Jews were considered to be foreigners for the purpose of the Foreigners Act.[113]

A related debate developed over the prohibition on granting certificates of naturalization to Austrian, German, and Ottoman subjects during the war. As special concessions had been granted to some Germans and Austrians, and many Baghdadi Jews applied to the government of Bombay for similar privileges, Bombay felt that it would be wise to grant these certificates to those who were entirely loyal, and also to Greeks and other non-Muslim Ottomans who had long been resident in the city. The central government, apparently more worried about establishing precedent than were the provincial governments, who thought mainly in terms of the interests of their own populations, refused:

> The proposal to extend the privileges of naturalization opens the door to a host of claimants who for the present had better remain in their status of disability. We may say that we have no reason to suppose that the naturalization of Baghdadi Jews would assist our general policy in regard to Turkey.[114]

Although exceptions could always be made for special cases, to grant certificates for all would be too wide a departure from the general policy of refusing naturalization to alien subjects of hostile powers while the war lasted. When the war finally ended, British principles stated that ordinarily all enemy subjects had to wait for ten years after the conclusion of peace for naturalization, unless they were members of a race or community known to be opposed to the late enemy government. But as these principles had no legal force in India, Baghdadi Jewish cases could be treated on individual merits, without particular reference to the question of whether the Jewish community in whole or in part was opposed to enemy governments. In any case, the British rule in Iraq after World War I made officials in India even more aware of the sympathies of the Baghdadi Jews, whose security increased with the British influence.[115]

Conclusion

In assessing their experience during this initial period of change under the British, one observes the Jews of India struggling to define their identity in an increasingly competitive environment where communal identity is becoming a significant factor. The germs of conflict in the Bene Israel position are there: having emerged in the late nineteenth century with a heightened consciousness of themselves as Jews, they now had to deal with the question of their "Indianness," an identity that would take on a political coloration. If the British were going to extend rights and political representation, where did the Bene Israel fit in? Did they need separate reservations, as other communities were demanding? Where did they stand on the language issue? And how did they feel about the burgeoning nationalist movement? Would it be dangerous to take a strong political stance? Did they benefit more from an Indian or a British connection? These were the questions they debated in their journals and communal organizations. The fears of those who felt that the Bene Israel's economic dependency required them to be politically neutral clashed with the intuition of those who felt that Indian nationalism promised to dominate the future and that the community ought to be part of it. As it turned out, the Bene Israel Conference attracted most of the educated communal leaders and a larger mass following. The handful who served as the main movers of the All-India Israelite League were perhaps the more elite, visionary intellectuals. They were more politically conscious, saw beyond parochial Bene Israel interests and had a broader approach to communal and Indian problems. They identified strongly with the cause of Indian nationalism.[116]

For the Baghdadis, the situation generated less ambivalence. Aware of British racism and unsympathetic to Indian nationalism, they stood even more firmly in the British camp. It is hard to conceive of any Baghdadis signing a memorandum to the secretary of state for India in 1917 expressing their willingness to be included with all other Indians for the purposes of electoral representation. Whatever requests Baghdadi Jews were signing in those years voiced their desire to be considered Europeans and to be given the concomitant privileges. Access to educational opportunities was a major issue, as was their status during World War I, at least for those who were still Ottoman nationals. How would their increasing need to identify with the British affect their relationship with the Bene Israel, their darker, more "Indian" brethren?

Toward the end of this period, the emergence of Zionism threatened to complicate the issues. To what extent did these Jews in India see themselves as members of yet a wider group? What would be the political implications of such an identification once the British were also in Palestine and were in a position to facilitate or impede the Zionist cause? The British presence in both India and Palestine was certainly to affect the attitudes of Indian Muslims. Would it affect those of the Indian Jews as well? It is to these questions of intracommunal relationships and Zionism that we must now turn.

CHAPTER 3

A STATE OF
COMPLEX IDENTITIES

The Impact of Nationalism
on Baghdadi–Bene Israel Relations

If certain aspects of the "Indianness"—customs, dress, and color—of the
Bene Israel had contributed to the Baghdadis' doubts about them, the attitudes adopted by the two Jewish groups toward identification with Indians,
nationalism, and the British presence would also affect the relationship between them. The process of identity formation—or transformation—was
more complex for the Bene Israel, who had been part and parcel of the
Indian environment for many centuries, than for the Baghdadis, who ada-
mantly resisted being considered Indian. As the growth of Indian nationalism
pushed the Baghdadis to embrace ever more firmly a pro-British stance, their
relationship with the Bene Israel became more troubled.

Especially after 1870, serious cleavages between the Baghdadis and the
Bene Israel appeared. As they became more prosperous and better known,
the fair-skinned Baghdadis, eager to be considered Europeans, shed their
Arabic customs and became Anglicized. Indeed, between 1865 and 1870, the
Sassoons moved to England where they were accepted in British society. In
India, the rapidly westernizing Baghdadis had to show that they were not
connected with any indigenous community. They were embarrassed over the
Bene Israel, whose presence, they felt, hindered their assimilation with
whites, and therefore the Baghdadis tried to establish a distinction between
themselves and their "native" coreligionists. The timing of this growing rift
was possibly related to the general idea of keeping Indians in their place,
which emerged after the Mutiny. Real racial antagonism between the British
and the Indians increased as the Indians demanded more equal treatment,
insisted on admission to the higher services, and organized political parties
or political action. In the 1870s and 1880s, the racial arrogance of the British
began to show itself openly, thus creating the context in which the separation
between the Bene Israel and the Baghdadis really took root.[1] By 1881, the

census distinguished between "Jews proper" (2,264) and "Beni Israel" (1,057) in Bombay.[2]

Perhaps the Baghdadis simply needed to say: "There are Jews of different origins. We are white Jews, they are brown and black Jews. We identify with European Jews, these people are Asian Jews. All we have in common is our religion. The cultures are different."[3] The Baghdadis' willingness to accept the differential treatment accorded to the Aden Jews over the law of succession is an example of how this might have been done. Yet instead, the Bombay Baghdadis attempted to accentuate the distinctions even further. They tended to view the Bene Israel as impure Jews, alleging that throughout the centuries the men had married Hindu women without properly converting them, so that the offspring were not fully Jewish. The Bene Israel defended themselves against this charge by arguing that they themselves distinguished between the descendants of such mixed marriages, who were referred to as *Kala* (black) Bene Israel, and the pure Bene Israel, who were known as *Gora* (white) Bene Israel. Until the mid twentieth century, perhaps, *Gora* and *Kala* did not intermarry or interdine. They used the same synagogues, but *Kala* were not permitted to wear the *tallith*—a ritual prayer shawl. The number of *Kala* was never large. Strizower, doing fieldwork in the 1950s, was able to distinguish about fourteen *Kala* families, although some *Gora* claimed there were more. There does not seem to have been any economic or occupational distinction, however.[4]

Starting in the 1870s, the dispute reached the columns of the *Jewish Chronicle* of London, which had begun to take an interest in the Indian Jewish communities and had asked British Jews to help them in their efforts at communal uplift and improvement. The *Jewish Chronicle* printed correspondence from both groups, including letters discussing controversies within the Bene Israel community and those airing problems between Bene Israel and Baghdadis. Local Bene Israel journals sent copies of their papers to the *Jewish Chronicle* even though most of the writing was in Marathi.[5] When a *Jewish Chronicle* article tried to defend the Bene Israel, arguing that even though some original Jewish settlers had married Hindu women, there was no ground for still maintaining the social barrier against their remote descendants, a *Bene Israelite* article replied that the Bene Israel tradition was not that the shipwrecked ancestors had married Hindu women, but that a few centuries afterward some Bene Israel had married heathen women and then were separated as *Kala*. The whole Bene Israel community could not be said to have descended of heathen women, the *Bene Israelite* insisted, adding that the Baghdadi Jews themselves might have originated the tradition of shipwrecked ancestors marrying Hindus: "These Baghdadi Jews can raise any rumour whatsoever, and being rather rich, consider themselves superior to the Bene Israel."[6]

Indeed, toward the late nineteenth century, the Bene Israel themselves were quite preoccupied over the question of "caste," or "black" and "white." The Bene Israel considered a black Jew to be the progeny of a marriage between a white Jewish male and a woman from another community, or else a person from another community who had accepted the Jewish religion.[7] There is some indication that in this period, the Bene Israel distinguished between "white" and "black" Baghdadis, seeing "black" Baghdadis as the offspring of Baghdadi Jewish men and non-Jewish women. Baghdadis have not heard of the term "black" Baghdadis and claim such people would be few because although Baghdadi Jewish women occasionally married non-Jewish men, Baghdadi men rarely married non-Jewish women.[8]

The Bene Israel concern with purity of caste is revealed by a letter sent in 1899 by the wardens of the Bene Israel Synagogue at Revdanda to an elder of the white Jewish community of Cochin, in which they inquired whether a certain Moses Elia Madai, who had passed himself off as a white Jew from Cochin and had been engaged as a *hazan* (cantor) and *shohet* in the synagogue of Alibag, was perhaps a black Jew. They feared that if he were a black Jew, all of the ceremonies performed by him were irreligious. They wanted to know what distinction the white Jews of Cochin kept between themselves and the black Jews: did they call upon them to read the Torah in their own synagogue and did they appoint them to be *hazans* and *shohets*? Did black and white Jews ever intermarry? The *Gora* Bene Israel observed that they had not allowed Cochin black Jews to be *hazans* and *shohets* for many years. They did not want to assimilate to black Jews. The letter revealed that these *Gora* Bene Israel were equating, wrongly, the Bene Israel *Kala* subgroup with the so-called black Jews of Cochin. The first Cochini teachers of the Bene Israel had been white Cochin Jews who may have discredited the black Cochin Jews together with the *Kala* Bene Israel.[9]

In any case, the Baghdadis were not inclined to recognize the fine distinction between *Gora* and *Kala* that the Bene Israel made about themselves. Some Baghdadis even thought that all Bene Israel were originally Indians who converted to Judaism.

In addition to questioning their "purity," the Baghdadis also expressed very genuine doubts about the religious orthodoxy of the Bene Israel. The remnants of Judaism practiced by the latter were limited indeed until the religious renaissance fostered by the Cochin Jews, the Scottish and American missionaries, and the Baghdadis themselves. But even after the revival, major points remained at issue concerning marriage and divorce laws. The Bene Israel did not follow Orthodox Jewish tradition and divorce wives who were separated from their husbands; thus, if the wives remarried, the children might be bastards. Nor did they observe the biblical injunction of *yibboom*, whereby a man was required to marry the widow of his deceased brother if the brother had died childless, or of *halitza,* whereby the surviving brother could formally refuse to marry his sister-in-law, thus setting her free to marry again according to her own choice (Deuteronomy 25:5–10). And yet, B. J. Israel writes, "if there had ever been departures from accepted Jewish practice in respect of marriage and divorce owing to ignorance, they had almost vanished by 1870; whatever infractions may have occurred thereafter were clandestine and unauthorized."[10]

Around 1887, Joseph Ezekiel Rajpurkar, a Bene Israel who was a fellow of the Bombay University and a headmaster of the Sassoon School, sent a letter to the Calcutta Baghdadi Congregation, possibly in response to questions they had posed, in which he tried to justify Bene Israel practices and prove their acceptability. Among other points, he argued that most Bene Israel observed the Sabbath and, unlike the "Arab Jews," did not count nonobservers in the *minyan* (quorum of ten required to begin services) for prayers. *Hahams* from Jerusalem prayed with the Bene Israel and permitted them to read from the Torah at synagogues.[11] The Bene Israel had *mikvehs* (baths for ritual purification) attached to their synagogues and kept the dietary laws. Although their marriages and circumcisions could be performed in Baghdadi Jewish synagogues in Bombay and Poona, they did not regularly attend these synagogues, he explained, because they had their own. Marriages between Bene Israel and Baghdadis had taken place.[12]

This letter was reprinted some twenty years later by I. A. Isaac, the Bene Israel editor of *The Hebrew and the Voice of Sinai,* a Jewish journal published in Calcutta. Hoping to change Baghdadi Jewish attitudes toward the Bene Israel, which by then had apparently deteriorated, Isaac commented,

> We give publication to the above letter for the enlightenment of the uncultured Jews, as there exists some ignorance and prejudice among them regarding this noble race, their origins, customs, rituals and ceremonies, etc. We are in possession of their full history and would be glad to meet any inquiry on the subject.[13]

In the next issue, the journal reprinted from a Calcutta newspaper, *The Statesman,* an article on the history and present position of the Bene Israel; it stated as fact their arrival two thousand years ago and discussed their military record with the British, their professional and educated members, and their institutions.

The problem of intermarriage preoccupied the Baghdadi and Bene Israel communities during this period. In 1895, the *Bene Israelite* wrote:

> Though no intermarriages till now, with the exception of a few couples, have taken place between the two colonies, yet it is known to all that the richest families of the Jewish [Baghdadi] colony had offered to intermarry with the rich Bene Israels, who for certain reasons refused to be intermingled with the Jewish colony.[14]

B. J. Israel felt that from about 1900–1910, a large number of Bene Israel young people tried to assimilate with the Baghdadis. A few young men in particular, who would never have used Marathi or even identified with Anglo-Indians, looked up to the more sophisticated and more Anglicized Baghdadis. During this period a number of marriages between Bene Israel and Baghdadis took place. Most Baghdadis were reluctant, but some Baghdadi girls, especially the poorer ones, married out anyway: several married Muslims or Christians and a few married Bene Israel. Marriages between the educated Bene Israel men and lower-class Baghdadi girls, however, were considered a disgrace to the Bene Israel themselves. No matter how poor the Bene Israel family might be, it would not accept the Baghdadi girl. Ironically, these intermarriages occurred just when the cleavage between the two groups was growing. There may have been a connection: many Baghdadis, alarmed by the assimilation and these intermarriages, which were taking place at a time when British prejudices against Indians were becoming sharper, probably wanted to make the division between themselves and the Bene Israel even stronger.[15]

The Baghdadis continued to refer questions of intermarriage to their rabbis. In 1914, the *hahams* of Baghdad and Jerusalem, answering a question that came from the *hazan* and *gubbai* (treasurer) of a synagogue in Bombay, forbade Baghdadi marriage with the Bene Israel but were not able to accompany this answer with an investigation of the facts or *responsa* previously rendered in this matter. Although the ruling was indefinite, the Baghdadis treated it as an absolute ban. By 1937, however, S. D. Aaron, president of the Fourteenth Bene Israel Conference, suggested that the *Stree Mandal* (Women's Association) "record their emphatic protest against the suicidal ways of our young men finding their wives in the *Yehudi* [Baghdadi] fold, neglecting our marriageable and deserving daughters."[16]

Mutual Ambivalence in the Late Nineteenth Century

By the end of the nineteenth century the ambiguity of the relations between the Bene Israel and the Baghdadis was reflected in Bene Israel periodicals. There were frequent references to the benevolence of the Baghdadis. Certainly, the Sassoons were endowing Bombay with so many benevolent institutions, such as museums, libraries, training institutes, and medical facilities open to all classes and creeds, that the Bene Israel could not help noticing them. The Sassoons sometimes invited the editor of *Satya Prakash* to inaugural functions. Particular attention was paid, of course, to Baghdadi charity toward the Bene Israel community, such as when David Sassoon donated 150 rupees for a new Bene Israel synagogue at Thana. The press lamented the death of outstanding Baghdadis who helped the Bene Israel. When Lady Hannah Sassoon died in 1895, the editor of the Bene Israel paper *Israel*

Dharmadeep called her a woman of high enlightenment and wide sympathies, attributing her noble qualities to heredity. "She was one of the most large-hearted and influential Jewesses of western India," it wrote, "and her memory will have an important place in the history of her community." The papers noted that Jacob E. D. Sassoon had given money to provide food for the Bene Israel community in Revdanda and also a Sepher Torah (biblical scroll) for its synagogue. The *Bene Israelite*, reporting that Sir Jacob had contributed 1,000 rupees toward building a compound wall for the new Jewish burial ground at Poona, wrote: "The Sassoons here are the Indian Rothschilds and are doing everything in their power to alleviate the sufferings of our poorly afflicted brethren in Bombay and Poona." The paper mentioned the charity funds started for Cochin and Baghdadi Jews in Bombay, named the schools and synagogues that had been supported by the Sassoons, and indicated that Jews from all areas had been engaged in the Sassoon offices and mills.[17]

Bene Israel journals also manifested a general interest in the Baghdadi community and commented particularly on educational matters. They observed, for example, that although Bene Israel outnumbered Baghdadis in higher education, an increasing number of Baghdadis were turning their attention to it. Or they wished success to the first Baghdadi to pass the medical examination or to a well-known Baghdadi on his being appointed a fellow of the University of Bombay.[18]

Not all Bene Israel press comment was favorable, of course. An article in *Satya Prakash* about Jews in Baghdad mentioned that the population numbered about thirty thousand but that the women were very backward. They kissed the tombs to conceive children and practiced many other superstitions to keep the evil eye away from their children. Commenting on a report that Bene Israel had helped with the funeral of a Baghdadi Jew who had died at Karachi, an editor noted that Bene Israel had often helped Baghdadis at times of difficulty but Baghdadis did not return the favors. They just pretended to like the Bene Israel, and when they were well-established, they considered the Bene Israel a backward or scheduled caste. The forefathers of the present Baghdadis were more helpful to the Bene Israel, he complained, and considered them a good community, but the poorer ones considered them hopeless: "Thus, when they're brought down to our level, they consider they're superior. When they're rich, they must pretend we are good."[19]

Yet there were some instances of cooperation. In the mid nineteenth century, the Christian missionaries reduced their efforts in primary education, which was costly and was not producing the hoped-for results in conversions. The Bene Israel now had to assume the responsibility for primary education. H. S. Kehimkar and other philanthropic men formed an association called the Bene Israel Benevolent Society for Promoting Education, which opened a small primary school in 1875. With time, the Anglo-Jewish Association of

London responded to Bene Israel appeals for aid, and its subsidy, combined with a government grant, synagogue contributions, and other aid, enabled the school to expand into an Anglo-vernacular institution (with both English and Marathi as the media of instruction), known as the Israelite School by 1881. The Bene Israel also formed a branch of the Anglo-Jewish Association in Bombay, which, for the first few years, consisted only of Bene Israel. In the 1880s, however, the headquarters in London prevailed upon the Sassoons to play an active role in the Bombay branch and to contribute to the Bene Israel school. By 1882, London had promoted an entente between the two communities. Solomon David Sassoon, the most prominent member of the Baghdadi community, presided over the prize distribution ceremony of the Israelite School. After London sent out David Schloss to reorganize the Bombay branch of the Anglo-Jewish Association, the honorary officers, other than H. S. Kehimkar, the former president of the Bene Israel branch, consisted entirely of "pure" (Baghdadi) Jews, according to the *Jewish Chronicle*. The *Jewish Chronicle* stressed that the differences in the vernaculars (Arabic versus Marathi) would for some years prevent intimacy between the two groups but hoped that, as both learned English, the difficulty would be removed. "There is no reason why the Bene-Israel and the Arab Jews could not be merged into one important and extensive community," it wrote.[20]

The efforts of the Baghdadis to dissociate themselves from the Bene Israel were evident in the matter of separate cemeteries and, more painful for the Bene Israel, in the issue of participation in synagogue services. References to the burial-ground problem occurred frequently in the Bene Israel periodicals. After the Sassoons had bought new land and consecrated it as a Baghdadi and Cochin cemetery, the old cemetery continued to be used by the Bene Israel alone. But it quickly filled up, and the Baghdadi Jews did not offer the Bene Israel the opportunity to bury their dead in the new Baghdadi cemetery while waiting to procure a new burial ground of their own. "This speaks for itself and any animadversions on the subject are unnecessary," wrote the *Bene Israelite*.[21]

Nevertheless, even toward the very end of the nineteenth century, relations between the two groups over synagogue participation were not yet strained. Bene Israel were still counted in the ten persons required to make up the *minyan* and were called up to read the prescribed portions of the Torah. Although the Poona cemetery was already divided into a separate Bene Israel and Baghdadi section, and by 1877 a Bene Israel prayer hall had been opened in that city, Bene Israel still attended Ohel David, the Baghdadi synagogue, were allowed full rights, and were allowed to marry there.[22] In 1882–84, when Elia David J. Ezra was building a synagogue in Calcutta, he wrote to a *haham* in Baghdad to know if Bene Israel could be seated anywhere or just in back. The response was that they could be seated anywhere. E. M. Musleah claims that in Calcutta they were always called up to read the prescribed portions of the Torah, not just extra ones, and that Bene Israel and Baghdadis intermarried. But the treatment in death was different: the Calcutta cemetery was divided between Baghdadis, Bene Israel, Cochin, and Western Jews.[23]

Soon after, although the exact date cannot be pinpointed, Bene Israel were no longer being counted in the *minyan* and were not being permitted to read the prescribed passages of the Torah in the Baghdadi synagogues in Bombay. E. D. Moses, a Baghdadi who served as the beadle in the Baghdadi synagogue (Magen David) in Byculla from 1909 to 1916 or 1917, said that some Bene Israel did come to that synagogue during that period but that they were never called to read the Torah from the pulpit. If they were married in the synagogue, they had to pay a fee of twenty-five rupees for the prayers.[24]

The distinctions between the two communities were clearly reflected in the clauses of the charity trusts established around the turn of the century by Sir Jacob Sassoon. Bene Israel were expressly excluded from the benefits of the charity fund, burial ground, and dispensary established for the Jews of Bombay. These trusts would seem to confirm the thinking of some Bene Israel that, in general, the trouble started with Sir Jacob, and not with David Sassoon, who lived in an earlier period when the cleavages were less pronounced.[25] The trust deed of the Jacob Sassoon Bombay Jewish Charity Fund, dated 13 February 1899, stated:

> The income of the Said Funds shall be devoted to the following objects, Viz: for the benefit of all poor Jews and Jewesses resident in Bombay (not being Beni Israel Jews or Black Jews from Cochin who are hereby expressly excepted) who are widows, orphans, aged, crippled, sick, deaf, dumb, blind, lunatic, weak intellect or unable to earn a livelihood on account of some physical or "bodily" defect or infirmity.[26]

The trust deed of the Bombay Jewish Burial Ground refers to the repairs and upkeep of the burial ground and to land that is to be used as a burial ground for members of the Jewish community excepting members of the "Beni-Israelite" community. The trust deed of the Lady Rachel Sassoon Dispensary established a facility to provide free outdoor medical relief to poor Jews, except "Bene Israelites," residing in Bombay. The trust deed of the Sir Jacob Sassoon Passover Food Trust Fund, dedicated to the provision of food for the Jewish poor, however, provides *matzas*, rice, meat, and raisins during the eight days of Passover and does not exclude the Bene Israel.[27]

Religious and Social Tensions after 1909

The years immediately following 1909 witnessed a high point of friction between the Bene Israel and the Baghdadis. Europeanization had progressed considerably among the Baghdadis, while the Indian identity of the Bene Israel had also increased. The Indian conditions of caste, color, and, especially in this period, community may have become more important than the Baghdadis' concerns over religious observances, since even they had grown more lax in that area, though religious objections were still raised.

The conflict between the two communities and the resentment of the Bene Israel toward Sir Jacob Sassoon again reached the columns of the *Jewish Chronicle* of London and the *Times of India*. In an interview in the *Jewish Chronicle*, Sir Jacob accused the Bene Israel of having drifted away from Judaism and having assimilated with the Hindus, claiming that his grandfather, David Sassoon, had facilitated their return to Judaism. The white Jews (Baghdadis) regard themselves as a superior "caste" to the Bene Israel, he noted. Bene Israel responded by asking Sir Jacob how many English Jews had managed to "keep themselves free" from English ways and habits. Once again they defended Bene Israel orthodoxy and tried to clarify the difference between *Gora* and *Kala* Jews.[28]

During this period, a number of Bene Israel writers tried to justify some of their community's practices and to defend it against Baghdadi accusations. In a pamphlet entitled "Our Synagogues and Their Functions: An Address to the Bene Israel," Solomon Moses Vakrulkar argued that the Bene Israel had lacked synagogues and certain rituals until recently because their forefathers had separated from the main body of Jews during the Babylonian Captivity, and thus their religious growth had stopped. He felt, however, that the previous generation of Bene Israel were more familiar with Judaism than the current one, and he railed against those Bene Israel who, in searching for "things spiritual," had turned to the theosophy preached by Madame Blavatsky and Annie Besant, and even to Yoga.[29]

The Baghdadis now accused the Bene Israel of not observing the Sabbath, to which the Bene Israel replied that they were very poor and would not get jobs if they refused to work on Saturdays. They repeatedly pointed out that although the Sassoon mills used to close on the Sabbath, the late Jacob Sassoon had canceled this practice because he realized that the Baghdadis simply went off (in taxis) to the races. Thus the Baghdadis now had to work on Saturdays also. Because of the need to work, Bene Israel synagogues held early, shorter morning services on Saturdays.[30]

The controversy over the Sabbath prompted the Reverend Isaac E. Sargon, a white Jew from Cochin who was serving as a *hazan* in a Bene Israel synagogue in Bombay, to write in 1911 to Chief Rabbi Dr. Moses Gaster, head of the Sephardic Jews in England, for guidance. Sargon explained:

> There are in Bombay a congregation of Jews named Benai Israel (you are already aware of them.) These people are very religious and observe the Mosaic laws as our co-religionists do, but unfortunately most of them cannot observe the Sabbath as they are poor and they are forced to earn their daily bread by working on Saturday. They have got synagogues and prayer halls,

in which they attend to prayers. They have appointed me as their *Chazan*
and I therefore request you to kindly let me know, if our law permits to
count those Jews working on Sabbath for *minyon* and *Kedusha*[31]

Dr. Gaster replied that although one must not sanction Sabbath breaking,
it was a fairly universal phenomenon, and if the Bene Israel were excluded
from all religious services, a *minyan* would be difficult to obtain unless they
formed a very small minority. Instead, they should be given full rights so
that they would not be driven away. He added, "I know the Benai Israel very
well, and I know they are very religious and good Jews. I have often taken
up their cause, and I have personally declared them to be identical with the
rest of the House of Israel."[32] Gaster's response was frequently referred to
years later by Sargon's sons, who edited a Jewish newspaper and who championed the cause of the Bene Israel. In any case, Gaster's statement must not
have been very convincing to the Baghdadis, if indeed they were aware of it,
because, as indicated above, in 1914 they were still making requests to their
hahams about marriage with the Bene Israel.

Jacob B. Israel was particularly concerned about the racial issues. In a
pamphlet entitled "The Purity of the Bene Israel," published in 1918, he
suggested that it was the writings of a Christian missionary in Bombay, the
Reverend J. Henry Lord (*The Jews in India and the Far East*, 1907), that
had put ideas into the heads of the Baghdadis and sowed dissension within
the ranks of the Jewish community. Lord had questioned the purity of the
Bene Israel, suggesting that they were half-caste Jews. In a separate article,
J. B. Israel argued that at about the same time the Baghdadis realized there
was a specific advantage in India in passing as Europeans. Their color helped,
but they saw the Bene Israel as the greatest obstacle and thus, rather than
acknowledging them as brothers, they tried to cast them outside the pale of
Judaism. The reasons alleged, according to Israel, were that the Bene Israel
were not following certain customs "which would be considered barbarous
these days in India and which were not followed by Jews in other countries."
The writer thought it remarkable that the Baghdadis should "close the door
of the House of God against the Bene Israel when they accepted the hospitality
and charity of the Bene Israel and worshipped in their synagogues when they
first came." He hoped that Jews in other parts of the world would recognize
the underlying motives of the Baghdadi attempts to cast out the Bene Israel
and would not deny them the status of genuine Jews.[33]

Israel's son, Benjamin J. Israel, suggested that his father's attack on the
Reverend Mr. Lord may have been unfair, as Lord was only saying what
most people believed, that total absence of admixture over the centuries was
inconceivable. There may have been some concubines, if not irregular marriage. But in any case, any admixture that would taint the Judaism of the
Bene Israel, in addition to raising questions of purity of descent, would be

troublesome. The Bene Israel were particularly sensitive on the question of purity because they did not want to be considered half-caste.[34]

In a caste environment, the desire for ritual equality loomed large. In the same period that the Bene Israel were examining and defining their identity as Indians, they also had to defend their identity as Jews. In the decade following 1917, Bene Israel periodicals often included Marathi and English articles that took on the religious objections of the Baghdadis. They defended the Bene Israel community's Jewish purity, justifying its nonobservance of certain traditions concerning *tebilah* (the ritual bath), divorce and marriage, and so forth on the grounds that these practices were obscurantist.[35]

On the problem of *tebilah*, the Bene Israel writers suggested that since the Baghdadis came from Arab countries, where water was scarce, they perhaps had to construct a *tebilah* near the temple to store water so that the women could be pure. But the Bene Israel felt that the water was filthy, and there was nothing holy about it; their women preferred to clean themselves daily from tap water, rather than in that "cesspool." One writer claimed that the few Bene Israel who did go to the *mikvehs* in the synagogue had them emptied, cleaned, and refilled with clean water before using them.[36]

The Bene Israel also insisted that many of the advanced communities in the West had abandoned the practices of *yibboom* and *halitza* and that there was no reason to adopt them in order to please the Baghdadis. Although levirate marriage and *halitza* do not seem to have existed among the Bene Israel, they did have a custom by which a man intending to marry a childless widow had to pay a small sum to the synagogue authorities, which could be claimed by the surviving brother if he so desired. He rarely did. The Bene Israel pointed out that although there was reference to *yibboom* in the Bible, there was none to *halitza*.

The Baghdadi accusations that the Bene Israel were not real Jews because they did not follow these customs were so disturbing to a few educated Bene Israel that they supported the Bene Israel New Synagogue's proposal to introduce *halitza*. Others, like I. J. Samson, a well-known solicitor, suggested that it would be better to adopt the views of European Jews, especially regarding polygamous marriages, which a few Bene Israel were still contracting. If all the Bene Israel synagogues in India would refuse to perform polygamous marriages, the practice would die out. If it did not, the Bene Israel should ask the government to declare polygamy illegal, as the Parsis had done.[37]

Divorce had always been recognized among the Bene Israel, although it was very rare. A *get*, a religious divorce certificate, written in English or the vernacular, was drawn up before witnesses, signed by the husband, and attested by the witnesses. The Baghdadis claimed that the Bene Israel were not real Jews because the *get* was not written in Hebrew and did not follow rabbinical procedure, but the Bene Israel countered that since not many of their community understood Hebrew, it was better to have the document written in a language easily understood by both parties. It did not matter how the bill of divorce was drawn up as long as the divorced wife had clear proof of divorce and was free to marry another man.[38]

The issue of the *get* was alive as late as 1936, for in that year, A. Benjamin, the president of the Bene Israel Tiffereth Israel Synagogue, wrote to *Haham* Gaster asking whether a *get* made out in any language other than Hebrew was illegal according to Jewish law. Gaster wrote back that such a *get* was invalid as no translation could take the place of the definite and detailed prescriptions formulated down to the most minute particle. The presiding rabbi should make it clear in the popular language to both parties what the document contained and what it meant.[39] Benjamin then replied:

> There is no qualified Rabbi here, and very few well-versed in the Hebrew language. When questions of Jewish law arise in Courts of Law or Hebrew translation of Documents are required, two or three Bene Israel gentlemen who are Hebrew scholars are requisitioned in the Court Case, even between Baghdadi Jews. But they don't even undertake to write *Gets*. Although some Baghdadi Jews do write them—for heavy fees—as they speak neither English nor the vernacular, they cannot question the parties or explain the document to the Bene Israel. How can we abide by the law? We need a substitute—an English translation.[40]

Gaster replied:

> You depict there a very sad and deplorable condition of your communal life . . . you must have a man endowed with rabbinical knowledge . . . capable of teaching and guiding religious and spiritual life . . . Poverty is no excuse. No community is too poor to dispense with a religious guide. But don't elect any man coming from Europe. You wouldn't understand one another. Get one from Syria, Iraq, Persia, or above all, from Palestine if possible. Join hands with the Bene Israel if necessary and do not hold aloof out of prejudice. No concession can be made on the *Get*.[41]

Gaster apparently did not realize that Benjamin himself was a Bene Israel.

In 1917, I. A. Isaac, the Bene Israel journalist residing in Calcutta, reflected the view of many when he noted that the *get, halitza,* and *tebilah* were not among the fundamental principles of Judaism and suggested that "these have nothing to do with their [Baghdadi] aloofness; the true reason being the colour prejudice, the garments of the Bene Israel and their poverty." He too suspected that Arab Jews feared that by mixing with their dark coreligionists, their claim for European rights and privileges in India would be very much depreciated. Isaac observed, "Colour and money cover a multitude of sins. A nonobservant European Jew will command a deal of deference because the colour and dress prejudice do not exist. Had Bene Israel been wealthy, all objections would have disappeared long ago." He advised the Bene Israel to continue along liberal lines to uplift the community and not to pay attention to the Baghdadis' "worthless objections" or try to bring about a closer union between the two communities.[42]

The lack of trained rabbis for their synagogues and the reliance on *hazans* disturbed both Bene Israel and Baghdadis. Periodically, they talked about finding a trained rabbi in Europe, particularly for the synagogues in Bombay. The Bene Israel had a few *hazans* of their own, but often used both Baghdadi and Cochin *hazans*. After a while, the Cochin white Jews stopped coming, and only the brown or black Jews served, often only for the low salary the Bene Israel synagogues paid for reading prayers and teaching Hebrew reading. As the years went on, some Bene Israel decried their dependence on the Baghdadis for ritual observances. They relied on Baghdadis to serve as *hazans* and *mohels* (ritual circumcisers), to blow the *shofar* (ram's horn) on Rosh Hashana, and to correct their *Sepher Torahs*. Some Bene Israel felt that although the Baghdadi *hazans* knew how to read certain prayers and sing the hymns, their religious knowledge was very limited. Bene Israel *hazans* would be preferable because they knew the tunes in the Cochin style, with which the Bene Israel were familiar, whereas the Baghdadi and Yemenite *hazans* recited in Arabic or Persian fashion in a prosaic manner and the members of the congregation lost interest in the prayer. Nevertheless, there were things to be learned from the Baghdadis: the *Israelite* recommended that the Bene Israel visit the Magen David Synagogue in Byculla to see how the Baghdadis conducted the service on Simhat Torah, shortening the prayers and songs for every circuit, and follow that custom. The editor was against the suggestion, made by others, of inviting *hazans* from Europe or the Hebrew Union College of Cincinnati to help the community advance, because of the language problem and the standard of living and practices in the Bene Israel community. He feared that outsiders would criticize the Bene Israel and ridicule them, especially for the dress of the women, and would tell the world that they had originated from Hindus. Instead, he recommended that the community select bright boys, teach them Hebrew and have them study it as a second language in high school, and then send them to England to study in Jews College. The boys would have to give a bond that after returning they would work in the synagogue for a specific payment and teach in the Hebrew school.[43]

The Bene Israel were perhaps unwise not to take the religious doubts, some of which might have been legitimate, of the Baghdadis very seriously.[44] It is clear, however, that some Baghdadis used these doubts as a rationalization for their dissociation from the Bene Israel, a dissociation based more on racial, social, and economic considerations than on religious concerns. While condemning Bene Israel assimilation to Indian customs, dress, and language, they ignored their own adoption of Arabic customs and language.

Although the Baghdadi elite often referred to the Bene Israel as poor and uneducated, a great many Baghdadis actually lived in these same circumstances. Bene Israel often complained of the vices of the Baghdadis: begging, gambling, and prostitution. Numerous Bene Israel informants remember Baghdadis (often Afghan Jews, but included in the Baghdadi community) coming around regularly to beg, even though the Bene Israel were poorer, and the Sassoon doles were supposed to take care of the poor Baghdadis.[45] Gambling, particularly at cards and the races, was a favorite pastime of the Baghdadis, but prostitution was usually a result of poverty. From about the 1880s to the 1920s or so, many very poor Baghdadis came to Bombay seeking employment and perhaps help from the Sassoon trusts, about which they had heard. Between 1880 and perhaps 1910 or 1915, young Baghdadi girls who needed to earn a dowry before marrying took up prostitution. It was not a regular profession but was acceptable for a lower-class girl in financial straits. There is no doubt that the upper-class Baghdadis must have been ashamed of this practice. By about 1930, the drift from Baghdad had ceased, probably because Turkish rule in Iraq had ended and the position of the Jews there improved for a while with the British presence.[46]

Despite the continuing resentment, Bene Israel periodicals still took note in the teens and early 1920s of Baghdadi events, sometimes sympathetically. The death of Jacob Sassoon on 22 October 1916, was reported by the *Friend of Israel*:

> The East has lost a great philanthropist and a pioneer of commerce and industry by the death of Sir Jacob Sassoon. . . . It is needless to enumerate Sir Jacob's princely public benefactions. The first among the list stands his magnificent gift of rupees ten *lakhs* for the establishment of the Royal Institute of Science. Sir Jacob was keenly alive to the interests of his own community and he has amply provided for the feeding of the poor, the relief of the ailing and the burial of the needy Baghdadi Jews. He has built and richly endowed a free school for the poor boys and girls of his own community. He also built a synagogue in Hong Kong.[47]

Not a word about the fact that the trust deeds of his charities excluded Bene Israel!

And yet the Bene Israel did not lose sight of their difficulties. Over the High Holidays in September 1917, they invited some European Jews serving in the army to meet some members of their community in the garden of the Israelite School. One of the guests deprecated the ignorance of Jews in England about the Bene Israel, of whom several of the soldiers had never even heard while in England. In turn, Jacob B. Israel asked the European Jews not to be carried away by what they heard about the Bene Israel from people (the Baghdadis) "in whose interest it was to malign them, but to see things and judge for themselves and convey to their brethren their true impressions about the Bene Israel."[48]

The challenge posed by Indian nationalism, the need to compete for representation and patronage, and the struggle to work out "intracaste" problems affected non-Hindu communities as well as Hindu castes. Muslims, Christians, and Jews, however, also had relationships with their coreligionists outside of India—relationships that might influence not only their attitudes but also the attitudes of other Indian groups toward them.[49] It was the connection with world Jewry—becoming increasingly important—that complicated the question of identity for all three Jewish communities within India and ultimately decided their destiny. It is in this context that the Indian Jews' developing interest in Zionism, another nationalism that emerged, ironically, about the same time as Indian nationalism, must be examined.

Zionism in India: The Initial Phase

Early Contacts with the Holy Land

The custom of *shlichim* (singular *shaliach*), or emissaries who traveled from the Holy Land (Eretz Israel) to Jewish communities in the Diaspora to collect funds for their communities or educational or religious institutions, to search for the Ten Lost Tribes of Israel, and to give spiritual direction and legal advice, dated back to the first century A.D.[50] Many of the *shlichim* sent to India spoke Arabic but most were Ashkenazim, or Europeans, and could converse with Indian Jews only in Hebrew. Often, Indian Jews were willing to give to Sephardic *shlichim*, but not to Ashkenazi ones.[51]

Although commercial contacts between India and Palestine date from ancient times, the earliest documented visit of an emissary to India occurred in 1740, when a *shaliach* was sent to the Cochin Jews. The earliest documented proof of contact between Bene Israel and Palestine Jews is apparently a tombstone in a Bene Israel cemetery in Navgaon inscribed with the name of a *shaliach* from Safed who was buried there in 1824. Other early visitors to the Bene Israel included Rabbi David d'Beth Hillel in 1829 and Rabbi Eben Saphir in 1859. An indication of the results of these visits could be seen at the well of Rachel's tomb near Bethlehem, where an inscription reads:

> This well was made possible through a donation from our esteemed brothers, the Bene Israel, who dwell in the city of Bombay, may the Lord Bless that place. In honor of the whole congregation of Israel who come to worship at the gravestone of the tomb of our matriarch Rachel, may her memory rest in peace. Amen (Year 5625–1864).[52]

Some of the emissaries who visited the Bene Israel, such as Rabbi Abraham Haim Abo in 1869, became involved in the disputes between them and the

Baghdadis; others, such as Rabbi Asher Abraham Halevi and Rabbi Abraham Shraga Ashkenazi, in 1882 became involved in *Gora-Kala* disputes among the Bene Israel themselves.[53]

At times the requests became too demanding for the Bene Israel, who in 1896 reported in their newspaper that they were constantly receiving appeals from charitable institutions and congregations in the Holy City and asked pardon of those concerned for not opening separate funds for them in their columns, as requested by the presidents of the institutions and the chief rabbi of Jerusalem, but "the Bene Israel were so poor that they were conducting their own charity institutions with great difficulty."[54] The Bene Israel were also worried about false *shlichim*, especially the occasional itinerant Baghdadi Jews who collected monies supposedly for institutions in Jerusalem, Palestine, or Mesopotamia but were often fraudulently soliciting on their own behalf. Bene Israel leaders urged their community not to waste money by giving it to such individuals, who could easily trick and coerce the people in the *mofussil* (countryside). The country folk thought these collectors were pious Jews and they feared their curses if they refused charity. One writer said that he did not want to suggest that all Baghdadis were cheats, but he thought that certainly most of those who went around begging funds in the name of others were. He advised his community to be really sure that the recipients were genuine cases of charity.[55]

Although the contacts with the Holy Land existed mainly through the *shlichim's* visits, occasionally Indian Jews made pilgrimages to Palestine in the nineteenth century. The first Bene Israel pilgrims, Isaac Solomon Ghosalkhar and Dr. Joel Samuel Shapurkar (Shirkolkar?), spent twenty-one days in Jerusalem in the spring of 1880; when they returned, Ghosalkhar reported on their journey in a public meeting and, in 1887, published a book about it. In 1894, Jacob Ezekiel Pingle spent a month and a half in Jerusalem with his family, having received helpful letters of introduction to Palestinian Jews from Bene Israel scholars such as Joseph Ezekiel Rajpurkar, then headmaster of the David Sassoon Schools, and from Sassoon Gubbay, a Baghdadi. He also received a letter of recommendation to the English consul at Jerusalem from the Reverend John Wilson, then in Bombay. Pingle published an illustrated book entitled *Pilgrimage* about his travels to Jerusalem.[56]

Early Responses to Zionism

When invitations went out to the First Zionist Congress to be held in Basel in 1897, the Bene Israel received one. The community convened a meeting at which well-educated individuals discussed whether or not to send a representative to Basel. The Bene Israel were aware that the Lovers of Zion in England and many rabbis in America had refused to participate in the congress. They themselves felt that "Jews in India were an orthodox community and looked upon the fulfillment of the restoration of the Jewish Kingdom by the Divine Hand and would undertake nothing that would give even the smallest chance or opportunity to anti-Semites to rise against the Jews."[57] Thus, they refused to send a delegate. After the congress had met, Heinrich Loewe, an early German Zionist leader and a friend of Theodor Herzl's, sent a report to the *Bene Israelite*, stating in his covering letter, "It would be most desirable and important for Jewish affairs and the cause of Judaism if the Bene Israels send delegates to the Zionist Congress next year, after having founded before hand Zionist associations in towns and villages of India."[58] Bene Israel views were reiterated by Kehimkar, who, at around the same time, wrote:

> The Bene-Israel, and the Jews in general have no ambition to gain even an inch of ground anywhere except in Palestine, the possession of which they expect to acquire by some miraculous agency. Their predilection, therefore, lies in the direction of that country, and the dream of their life is the reconstruction of Jerusalem and the country of which it forms the natural Capital. . . .
> Happy, therefore, shall be the day for the Jews and the Bene Israel when the proud dream of theirs is realised, and glorious will be the condition of Palestine when Jerusalem is rebuilt by the chosen people of God. But until this desired event is brought to pass, the Bene Israel, as well as all the Jews on the face of the Earth, loyally regard the country in which they are living as their fatherland, and consequently they are entitled to have every disability under which they labour, entirely removed.[59]

The Jews of Cochin also had some early contacts with the Zionist movement. Herzl's audience with Sultan Abdul Hamid II in Constantinople in May 1901 seems to have inspired N. E. Roby, a prominent member of the white Jewish community in Cochin, to write to the Zionist leader a few months later:

> The Zionist movement created by you has put your coreligionists throughout India into great excitement especially after your interview with the Sultan of Turkey. Now you can draw enormous sum [*sic*] from India in the aid of the movement if you inform the Jews of India of your aim.[60]

Roby went on to suggest that Herzl authorize him to collect money from the Cochin congregations and other leading Jews of India, whose names and addresses he provided, to raise funds for the movement.[61] On the same date, 15 October 1901, Roby sent a letter to *Die Welt*, the Zionist newspaper in Vienna, announcing that the Zionist idea had made "its victorious entrance also into Cochin" and that it had many enthusiastic friends in India. He hoped shortly to be able to report on the formal establishment of Zionist branches in many cities and on the consolidation of these branches into a subfederation of the "English Zionist Federation"; he also indicated that he was already collecting *shekels* (membership fees) and shares. Indeed, in 1903 the Cochin Zionists founded their first organization and sent *shekels* to the Zionist Federation in London; as they could not delegate a representative of their own, they appointed Israel Zangwill, a leading British Zionist, as their representative to the next Zionist congress. A Zionist group was also started in Rangoon, Burma, at this time.[62]

In these first years, the rank and file of the Jewish community in Calcutta seems to have been unaffected. The local Jewish paper, *Maggid Mesharim*, published until 1900, made no mention of the First Zionist Congress in Basel in 1897 or of subsequent ones. The initial effort to found a Zionist organization in Calcutta seems to have resulted from a visit of Julius Steinberg to that city in August 1913. Some Calcutta Jews, including the Bene Israel journalist I. A. Isaac, responded positively to Zionism and corresponded with the Central Zionist Organisation officials, who sent them reports about the activities of the organization and newsletters. The head office suggested that they subscribe to a Zionist periodical and forward fortnightly reports of the latest events of the new branch. Although the attempt proved abortive, the Central Zionist Organisation nevertheless asked the Calcutta Jews to collect funds to found new Hebrew schools in Palestine.[63]

Although most politically aware Bene Israel in Bombay seemed preoccupied with nationalist and communal problems in 1917, the *Friend of Israel*, at least, manifested some interest in Zionism. That May it reprinted, without commentary, an article in favor of the Jews going to Palestine. This article was followed a month later, on the occasion of the news of the encampment of the British expeditionary force near Gaza (beginning the conquest of Palestine from the Ottomans), by an editorial entitled "England and Palestine," in which the writer recalled the historical links between England and Palestine. He added:

> With due respects to the pious wishes of those of our coreligionists who ardently hope that England will convert Palestine into an independent Jewish state, we cannot help expressing our doubts as to whether England will so readily make a free gift of Palestine to the Jews after having made such enormous sacrifices. Besides, the politicians of Europe will think twice before allowing England to take the risk of creating a new state which will have sympathisers all the world over, and thus adding to the difficulties and uncertainties of the world politics. We shall, however, be glad if our fears in this respect are falsified and Palestine is handed over to the Jews after the successful termination of the present war.[64]

Meanwhile, the *Times of India*, which had devoted much coverage to the Palestine campaign, first mentioned the Balfour Declaration on 13 November 1917. An editorial on Zionism noted two obstacles to the aims expressed in the Balfour Declaration: that liberal and "cultural" Jews had no desire to resettle in Palestine and preferred assimilation to their countries of residence, and that it would take work to develop Palestine with Jewish labor. The *Times* doubted that Jewish settlers intended to recreate the country by the sweat of their brows. If the allies found themselves, after the war, in a position to offer Palestine to the Jews, there would be no guarantee that the Jews' interest in making money would not prove stronger than their traditional attachment to the land of their origin. Even the Jews in the Rothschild colonies, added the writer, used Arab labor. This skepticism elicited a response from an "S. J.," who agreed that there were serious difficulties in accomplishing Zionism, but argued that they were not the two noted by the editorial. Rather he cited the opposition of the Turkish government to the colonization of Palestine by foreign Jews (a problem that would be eliminated once the Turks were no longer in control) and the objection of most Jews to Zionism because of the biblical prophecy of divine intervention. "S. J." added that Jews also made money with the sweat of their brows, not without it; Jews would work and still make money.[65]

A few days later, Donald Munro of the Young Men's Christian Association also took issue with the *Times*, maintaining that liberal and "cultural" Jews, even those who wanted to assimilate elsewhere, also had a keen desire to take part in the resettlement of Palestine and supported the Zionist movement. Munro, a Christian who had lived in Palestine for five years and had observed the Jews working much harder than the Arabs, the Jewish colonies flourishing, and the Jewish population increasing greatly, attacked the *Times* writer for his jibe about Jews and moneymaking.[66]

Soon after, another *Friend of Israel* editorial, entitled "The Fall of Jerusalem," talked about the invasion of Palestine by the Allied armies and how the Balfour Declaration had given rise to Jewish hopes the world over that Palestine would be made into a free Jewish state at the end of the war. Zionism was not often mentioned in the Jewish periodicals of Bombay during 1918, except for an article, again in the *Friend of Israel*, in the fall of that year, that discussed the movement and the support the Balfour Declaration had been given. The enthusiasm with which the Weizmann Commission (a Zionist commission that visited Palestine in 1918 to make plans for the future) was welcomed by Jews and Arabs alike was also noted by the journal. Although Musleah claims that the Balfour Declaration went almost unnoticed by the Jews in Calcutta, Ezra reports that E. M. D. Cohen's announcement of the news of the Balfour Declaration at the Sabbath service in Magen David Synagogue on 3 November 1917 was enthusiastically received by the congregation.[67]

There was, however, another group that was quite aware of what was going on in Palestine and that, by the end of 1918, felt it necessary to comment on the situation: the All-India Muslim League. Indian Muslims had been angered by the Treaty of Sèvres, which had attempted to dismember Turkey;

Dr. M. A. Ansari, the Ali brothers (Muhammed and Shaukat), and others now launched the Khilafat movement to protest the division of the Ottoman Empire and the weakening of the authority of the caliphate. Opposed to the demands of Sherif Husayn and the Hashemites to establish an Arab caliphate at Mecca, the Khilafat insisted that the Ottoman sultan-caliph be permitted to retain his empire with both temporal and spiritual authority in order to defend Islam and protect the Muslim holy places. The movement argued that the geographical center of Islam, an area embracing Arabia, Mesopotamia, Syria, and Palestine, must remain under Muslim rule.[68] At the eleventh session of the All-India Muslim League, meeting in December 1918, Dr. M. A. Ansari, in his welcoming address, discussed the Khilafat movement and the need to protect the holy places, which he listed, ranking Jerusalem's Al-Aqsa Mosque as the second "House of God in Islam" after the Kaaba in Mecca. Expressing his deep concern about Britian's intention of turning Palestine over to the Zionists, whose claim he felt was illegitimate, Ansari said:

> It has given a great deal of pain and much resentment has been created among the Musalmans of India to see that the attitude of their own Government, in connection with this matter, has been diametrically opposed to their wishes and sentiments.[69]

This attitude of the Indian Muslims was to have far-reaching ramifications in India and Palestine and would also affect the thrust of Zionism in India.

Conclusion

Given the Indian context of the second half of the nineteenth century, in which the British-Indian relationship was that of superior-inferior, the identification of the Baghdadi community with the Europeans was bound to result in a social rift between the Baghdadis and the Bene Israel. Doubts as to the "purity" of descent and religious observances of the Bene Israel would probably not alone have caused the Baghdadis to dissociate themselves from their Indian coreligionists, although they weakened Jewish fraternal ties and explained, in part, the ethnic and color distinctions that had such unfortunate results.[70] While the Bene Israel may have had to accept the inferior position imposed upon them by their white rulers, they resented the attitudes of the Baghdadis, a resentment not assuaged by Baghdadi provisions of employment and financial assistance to their schools. Perhaps it was the mounting rejection by the Baghdadis in the first two decades of the twentieth century that eventually prompted some Bene Israel to seek to strengthen their ties to the Jewish world beyond India by becoming involved in the growing Zionist movement. It is ironic, therefore, that the British colonial environment, superimposed

on the underlying Indian themes of caste and color, promoted conflicts between the two Jewish communities in India, the consequences of which would
finally be felt in the State of Israel almost a century later.

In the period following World War I, as Gandhi emerged as the leader of
a growing nationalist movement, many of the themes of these last two chapters—Indian nationalism, Bene Israel-Baghdadi relations, and Zionism—
were to develop and become even more intertwined.

PART III
JEWISH OPTIONS IN THE INTERWAR YEARS, 1919-39

CHAPTER 4

INDIANS, JEWS, OR EUROPEANS?

By 1918, most Indians were convinced that independence was more important than the reform of their society. The nationalist movement had intensified during the war, and at its conclusion, many Indians expected some sort of responsible government for India as a reward for their cooperation. Indeed, the 1919 Government of India Act, which implemented the Montagu-Chelmsford findings, did provide a nominal measure of representation to Indians. At this point, however, a totally new element emerged on the nationalist scene: the influence of Mohandas K. Gandhi, who was respected by Indians and British because of his work in South Africa. Returning to India in 1914 after years abroad, Gandhi traveled throughout his homeland, becoming acquainted with the situation and the nationalist leadership and responding particularly to the grievances of the peasants and workers, which had been aggravated by the wartime economic dislocation. When, in 1917, he began to move into a position of nationalist movement leadership, he recruited many who were to become prominent in the freedom struggle, including the Nehrus and Sardar Patel. Though a disciple of Gokhale, Gandhi was less friendly toward the British and believed in *satyagraha,* or nonviolent action. But few thought of him as a national leader before 1919–20; he was considered "too mild, moral and impractical."[1]

For Gandhi as for others, the Amritsar Massacre of 1919 proved to be a turning point. Gandhi's influence and his commitment to nonviolence at first prevented large-scale outbreaks of violence in response to the killing of several hundred protesters by British troops led by General Reginald Dyer, but when the House of Lords voted in favor of General Dyer and England raised a heavily subscribed fund in appreciation of his services, Gandhi proclaimed that "cooperation in any shape or form with this satanic government is sinful."[2] In September 1920 he launched his first noncooperation movement against the British, urging Indians to resign from government office, withdraw from government schools and colleges, and boycott law courts, foreign goods, and the forthcoming elections to the legislative councils. Gandhi's proposal was too radical for the moderates, who now split off to form the Liberal Federation. Despite Gandhi's pleas, few officials resigned. Schools and colleges were disrupted only briefly as substitute "national" institutions developed, then collapsed. Only a third of the voters participated in the elections, however, so the elected councils were dominated by the Liberals. Although the noncooperation program was eventually revoked, it set the stage for further opposition. Gandhi's movement had also won the support of the Muslims, and thus became an all-India phenomenon. When Muslims launched the Khilafat movement, Gandhi seized upon the opportunity to support it as a way of promoting Hindu-Muslim unity.[3]

Post–World War I Politics: The Bene Israel Response

The Erulkars and Jacob B. Israel, who were mostly responsible for publishing the *Israelite* in the early years, tried to keep politics out of the journal to avoid embarrassment to the community, but there were occasional lapses. When B. G. Tilak died in August 1920, D. S. Erulkar, who had been the junior counsel at Tilak's defense and a great admirer of the lokamanya, wrote an editorial commending the great leader's nonpolitical activities and services, "without distinction of caste or creed."[4]

A month later, the *Israelite* referred to "an incident of Jewish interest at the Indian National Congress" in Calcutta, where one of the speakers, Jitendranath Bannerjee, made a remark that might have been construed as an aspersion on the Jewish faith of the secretary of state, Edwin Montagu. He was immediately reprimanded by President Lala Lajput Raj. When the Bombay papers publicized the incident, David Erulkar sent a telegram of protest to the president: "Indian Israelites, legitimate sharers in Motherland's vicissitudes, resent J. B.s aspersions to Montagu's religious creed as highly reprehensible and mischievous. Public apology indispensable to assure minorities of religious tolerance and fair treatment." In a personal letter to Erulkar, telling him he had referred to the incident and telegram in his closing address and had apologized to the Hebrew community, Lala Lajput Raj wrote:

> During my residence abroad I have learned to respect the Hebrew community and the valuable service they have rendered to the cause of culture and humanity. No one with any knowledge of the great literature of the world can for a moment forget that the Hebrew community has produced some of the greatest writers and thinkers of the world, besides having produced a galaxy of great artisans, singers, composers, poets, etc.[5]

The Bene Israel ambivalence vis-à-vis politics was revealed at the third annual meeting of the All-India Israelite League in December 1920. I. J. Samson, the chairman of the reception committee, stated that although the community had so far scrupulously avoided politics, the time was now ripe for its members to declare their views as a community. The British had recently given to the Indians a reformed constitution and an extended electorate, and he exhorted the Bene Israel to understand thoroughly their political situation in order to exercise their votes to the best advantage of the community. Samson was afraid to pursue the subject further, as it had always been a red flag to the community. However, the president of the meeting, K. M. Elijah, advised the community to keep clear of all political movements as there was "chaos and darkness in their own house which required their immediate attention."[6]

In November 1921 noncooperators boycotted the visit of the Prince of Wales to Bombay, using, in some places, intimidation and force. This action led to serious riots in Bombay, Madras, and elsewhere, those in Bombay resulting in much loss of life and destruction of property. The Bene Israel community did not suffer, but the Baghdadis were accused in the press of having participated in the riots, a charge that created some confusion in the public mind over whether the Bene Israel were also among the street rioters. Gandhi made special inquiries about the Bene Israel and was anxious to know if any member of the community was harmed in any way. He apparently was much relieved to learn that Bene Israel had neither participated in the riots on either side nor had suffered from the rioters. At the fifth annual meeting of the Bene Israel Conference in December of that year, Dr. Benjamin Reuben, the president, commented on the royal visit:

> As a community, we participated in the loyal welcome accorded to His Royal Highness . . . prayed to God that messages of peace and goodwill which His Royal Highness brought to their country might bear fruit and might lead to the strengthening of the feelings of loyalty and affection which are entertained by the millions in this country towards the person of His Majesty the King-Emperor and the members of the Royal family.[8]

Lord Reading's Administration

Edwin Montagu, the secretary of state for India, was not the only British Jew who helped guide the destinies of India. In 1921, Rufus Daniel Isaacs, Lord Reading, who had been lord chief justice of England (1913–21), was named to succeed Lord Chelmsford as viceroy of India, a post he was to hold until 1926. The Bene Israel newspapers naturally brimmed with pride at Lord Reading's appointment. Dr. A. S. Erulkar's short piece in the *Israelite* summarizing Lord Reading's career and contributions challenged his own community to become politically active by ending with the query: "Have the Bene Israel nothing to contribute to the making of the Indian nation?"[9] The *Friend of Israel* offered congratulations to Lord Reading, adding:

> His appointment has been hailed with delight as the most appropriate one in all quarters and we have every reason to hope that he will prove successful in his mission of giving justice to Indians and that his administration will tend to strengthen the ties that bind India to the Empire.[10]

At the end of that year, the two major Bene Israel organizations also commented on Lord Reading's appointment. President Benjamin Reuben, in his opening speech at the Fifth Bene Israel Conference, affirmed:

> The [Bene Israel] rejoiced that in its determination to deal with Indian aspirations justly and fairly, the British Cabinet had chosen Lord Reading. . . . a leading light of English politics, and the first Jewish Viceroy in India. The British people and cabinet had therefore shown its capacity to rise above considerations of nationality and religion where merit was concerned. The task of Lord Reading is very difficult.[11]

Similarly, the fourth annual meeting of the All-India Israelite League praised the sentiments that Lord Reading had expressed regarding equality of treatment for all the subjects of his majesty the king-emperor in India, and hoped that his regime would abolish racial distinction and ensure peace and prosperity to the country. But the selection of Lord Reading, coming soon after the Montagu appointment, had angered some of the British. The *Morning Post* of London, an anti-Semitic and anti-Indian newspaper, demanded the recall of the new viceroy.[12]

At this time, H. M. Fraser of Calcutta, a lieutenant commander of the Royal Navy who was known to be very anti-Indian and racist, circulated anti-Semitic pamphlets about Lord Reading to let the public know "how the British Raj has for a good many years become less British and more of a Jewish Raj." He accused Reading and Montagu of seeking to discredit and weaken the British connection under the guise of forwarding Indian nationalism, to make Jewish control and dominion more complete. "Swaraj [self-government] before Indians are fit for it," he wrote, "merely means Jew Raj." Fraser also called Montagu's scheme for justice to India an attempt to "organize Asia's mute millions into a human avalanche to overwhelm Western civilization and thus Christianity." A. S. Erulkar felt that the anti-Semitism of Fraser and some of the English press had its origin in their anti-Indian sentiments and their fear that the appointment of two Jews to the head of the Indian administration would result in more rights and better justice for the oppressed Indian people. Writing in the *Israelite,* Erulkar reassured his community:

> Jews in India have found for twenty centuries, peace and prosperity at the hands of their Indian compatriots and they need fear nothing from such trash as the so called "Truth" pamphlets of Fraser, whatever the effect of such literature on the European community in India.[13]

Some of the English press came to Reading's defense. The *Statesman* of Calcutta wrote:

> The choice which the British Government have made must be looked upon as most fortunate and most timely. The Viceroy has gained his illus-

trious position by sheer force of his abilities and practical capacity. . . . The objection which has been taken to his appointment on the score of his race is singularly ill-founded. The Jew has always maintained his communications with the past, and what he has kept of his Eastern origin assists him in his comprehension of Eastern peoples.[14]

The *Bombay Chronicle,* the mouthpiece of Indian nationalism in western India, and the *Bengalee* of Calcutta also expressed their disgust at Fraser's pamphlets.[15]

Years later, in 1937, the Jewish faith of Lord Reading again became an issue as a result of a book published by Professor Arthur Berriedale Keith, a highly respected Sanksritist and Indologist, considered an authority on the Indian Constitution and imperialism. In *The King and the Imperial Crown,* Keith, referring to Lord Reading's appointment to the viceroyalty, remarked snidely that

> much courage was needed in holding that Lord Reading was a suitable selection in 1921, for he had risen to high rank from humble origins and was not a Christian, but a Jew, a religion held in no high honour in India.[16]

The Baghdadi *Jewish Tribune* indignantly challenged this statement in an editorial:

> The lack of honour for the Jews in India is only a figment of Professor Keith's imagination. Indians in all walks of life have repeatedly given utterance of their esteem for the Jews and have never been known to have shown discrimination in any form against the Jews. . . . Perhaps the Professor still remembers the name of the Jew, . . . the late Edwin Montagu . . . [T]he Indian people . . . hold him in high veneration and have . . . [shown] their appreciation of his services, which honour has been given to very few Secretaries of State for India.[17]

The *Indian Social Reformer,* a well-known and popular weekly published in English, also criticized Professor Keith in an editorial:

> [W]e need only say that . . . [Judaism] is held in as much honour [in India] as any other religion, certainly not less in honour than Christianity. We assure Professor Keith that the appointment of a Jew who rose from humble origins . . . was considered by Indians as a signal instance of British respect for merit rather than for birth or status. When on taking an oath as Governor-General at the Bombay University, Lord Reading kept his hat on and, declining the Bible that was presented to him, called for an Old Testament . . . those who witnessed the ceremony were impressed by the loyalty of the man to his ancestral faith, though he knew that it is held "in no high honour" by his Christian fellow countrymen.[18]

Early in his administration, Lord Reading granted a long-standing nationalist request, the Indianization of the officers' cadres in the army. It occurred to S. S. Mazgaonker, a prominent All-India Israelite League member and author, that perhaps the Bene Israel should use the opportunity to reenter the military. In an unsigned Marathi article in the *Israelite*, Mazgaonker suggested that the community launch a staunch protest against the caste regulations then prevailing in the army by holding meetings and passing resolutions that they could forward to Lord Reading. "Although we are too small to have our own battalions," he argued, "it is necessary for the Bene Israel to enter the military, which will inculcate discipline, which is the pass to progress." He pointed out that the Prince of Wales Royal Military College had recently opened at Dehradun and there were thirty-six students of different castes being educated there, as well as fifteen Indian Jews, but he did not know if they were Bene Israel or not. He exhorted the younger generation to seek admission into this college, receive military training, and earn important positions in the military on merit. Mazgaonker also urged young Bene Israel to enter the police department. Believing that India would receive independence very soon, he feared there could be chaos and confusion in the military and police departments if the British were to leave India suddenly and there were not enough qualified Indians to replace them. It was up to the nationalists to try to push Indians into the military and police. Otherwise there was no point in a movement of noncooperation.[19]

With Lord Reading's accession, politics began to appear more and more in the columns of the *Israelite*. In 1922, the journal reprinted an article entitled "Passover and India—the Great Festival of Freedom," which a Bene Israel had published in a recent issue of the *Bombay Chronicle*. The *Israelite* commented that "the lessons of our 'festival of freedom' ought to inspire Indian Jews always to contribute their little mite towards the emancipation of our Indian Nation." The article stated:

> The Jews should ever be foremost in the cause of freedom, of justice and of charity. Will our Viceroy remember these words when he celebrates the festival? Will he do his utmost to remedy the wrong done by Britain to India? During his stay of one year in India surely he must have found out for himself that India has been grievously wronged. Does he feel indignant at it and will he be foremost in helping to give freedom to India, and thus do an act of justice and charity? . . .
> The Almighty . . . will surely hear the cries of millions of his creatures and send a deliverer. Perhaps one has already come in the presence of Mahatma Gandhi and it is only a question of time. Perhaps the Almighty is trying the heart of the British as he did that of Pharaoh and freedom will come at an unexpected moment. Let us wait in hope and expectation, doing to the best of our abilities all that our great leader requires of us.[20]

It is doubtful that a Bene Israel paper would have published such views two or three years earlier. Even now, not all members of the All-India Israelite League agreed with those sentiments. At the fifth annual meeting of the league in December 1922, the chairman, Khan Sahib Mordecai Joseph, advised the Bene Israel to keep aloof from politics:

> If it does affect our community in any way, do by all means approach the government through constitutional means, keeping on the right side of the Government and bearing in mind that we Jews are peaceful and loyal subjects of the community and Government which gives us shelter and protection.[21]

From 1922 to 1924, M. D. Borgawkar annually assessed in the *Israelite* Lord Reading's accomplishments as viceroy. In justifying the first article, Borgawkar assured readers that he intended not to discuss political questions as such, but rather to present the most important events occurring during the first year of Lord Reading's administration. Nevertheless, in reviewing the political situation prevailing when the new viceroy arrived in India in April 1921, Borgawkar discussed the administration of Lord Chelmsford, as well as Amritsar and the subsequent imposition of martial law in the Punjab. In explaining Indians' dissatisfaction with the inadequate Montagu-Chelmsford reforms and the demand that government be made more responsible to the people, the author seemed to be expressing pronationalist views. He argued that the government had not tried seriously to redress the legitimate grievances of the people, which revolved around the Punjab events, the Khilafat movement, and the *swaraj* question, and had led to Gandhi's noncooperation movement. Turning to Lord Reading, Borgawkar admitted that the new viceroy's release of some martial law prisoners in the Punjab had not gone far enough in the eyes of some. His efforts to satisfy Indian Muslims had not been received sympathetically by the home government: as a result, the Khilafat movement had become stronger. As for *swaraj*, Reading had advised people to work out the reforms, thereby showing their capacity for managing representative institutions, before demanding more. Borgawkar described the government's more repressive policy after the riots over the visit by the Prince of Wales, the resulting resolution on civil disobedience passed by the Indian National Congress at Ahmedabad, and the heated debate in Parliament on Indian affairs, in which a member moved to censure Montagu and some members demanded the recall of the viceroy. Borgawkar's final assessment of Lord Reading's first year was positive, however, with praise for the viceroy's concern for Indian public opinion and his repeal of repressive laws.[22]

In assessing Reading's second year, Borgawkar became more critical. Although Gandhi had suspended the civil disobedience campaign, he had been imprisoned on charges of preaching disaffection to the government, and Borgawkar objected to his incarceration at a time when other prominent nationalists were also in jail. Borgawkar also criticized the viceroy's passing of the doubled salt tax after the Central Legislative Assembly had rejected it:

"This autocratic action . . . has shaken the faith of even the Moderates in the sincerity of the Reforms . . . Lord Reading has committed a great political blunder, the consequences of which will be seen in the course of time."[23] However, Borgawkar praised the government of India for supporting the Indian view in the question of Kenyan Indian immigration and for increasing the Indianization of the public services and the army. He concluded again on a positive note, asserting that Reading, in the last two years, had been "thriving at his work," and that his patience and tact had calmed a very serious situation during the first year. During the second year, the political atmosphere had been brighter and more hopeful. Borgawkar hoped that Lord Reading would continue to remember his first words in landing in the country: "The British reputation for justice must never be impaired during my tenure of office."[24] In his analysis of the third year of the viceroy's administration, Borgawkar expressed his pleasure at Gandhi's release from prison and hoped that Lord Reading would be able to handle the *swaraj* problem justly.[25]

Bene Israel concern about political developments appeared in programs organized for the Bene Israelite Boy Scout Troop. In 1923, for example, lectures entitled "The History of Non-Cooperation," "The Swadeshi Movement,"[26] and "Mr. Montagu's Constitutional Reform" were presented. The speakers tried to give the facts as impartially as possible so that the boys could draw their own conclusions.[27]

The years from 1917 to 1923, then, the period encompassing the preparation of the Montagu-Chelmsford reforms, their implementation in the Government of India Act, and the developments during Lord Reading's administration, saw an increasing awareness of general political issues on the part of the Bene Israel. Although perhaps only a few wrote about these events and most Bene Israel did not participate actively in the growing nationalist movement, most were keenly interested in the changes taking place and concerned with how their community would be affected.

The Nationalist Movement: Bene Israel Involvement

By 1924, Ataturk's abolition of the caliphate in Turkey had led to the collapse of the Khilafat movement. Indian Muslims felt isolated and once again feared Hindu domination. As Hindu-Muslim relations disintegrated into communal riots, Muhammad Ali Jinnah revitalized the Muslim League as a political force. The most successful Hindu political agitators, Tilak and Gandhi, had effectively injected religion, which permeates everything in India, into politics.[28]

Dumont has suggested that the British policy, in response to demands, of separate electorates, special representation, and compensatory privileges stirred a new life into minorities and underprivileged classes throughout the country and contributed to separatist and divisive group consciousness. While Gandhi did not oppose a separate electorate for Muslims, the liberals in the Congress Party, such as Motilal Nehru (father of Jawaharlal), opposed communalism.[29]

Dr. Jacob Solomon, one of the signers of the Bene Israel address to Montagu in 1917, became a municipal councillor in Ahmedabad in 1921. Active in the theosophical movement, where he had come under the moderate nationalist influence of Annie Besant, he became secretary of the National Home Rule League branch in that city. Mrs. Besant, having fallen out with Congress over the issue of *satyagraha* (noncooperation), supported constitutional methods of agitation. In 1921, Dr. Solomon delivered a public lecture, under the Home Rule League's auspices, on the aims, development, and decay of noncooperation.[30]

Three years later, Mrs. Besant forwarded to the national convention of the Home Rule League a thoughtful memorandum by Solomon entitled "The Problem of the Minor Communities." In it, Solomon maintained that reserving seats in the provincial councils or the assembly for the minor communities, or even for the Muslims alone, was detrimental to the interests of India. Even mixed elections, with candidates for reserved seats canvassing among voters of several communities, were suspect, Solomon said, because the percolation of the communal principle through all the lower strata of state life would introduce an element of "separativeness." He realized that it was in Britain's interests to support communal rights in the spirit of "divide and rule," but he hoped that the Indian and British leaders truly interested in the welfare of India and the commonwealth would try to prevent separativeness in the Commonwealth of India Act, which was shortly to be framed. Appealing to Muslims to rise above their communal interest and think foremost of what would be best for India as a nation, he insisted: "We are Indians first, and Muslims or Jews or Parsees afterwards." Special treatment might be needed to provide special opportunities for primary and higher education for the smallest of the minority communities, he argued, but not for filling posts in the services. Communal representation was required only to safeguard religious interests, which could perhaps be dealt with by an all-India religious board or committee in a national assembly or council of state. In order to place the ideal of a united Indian nationhood before the people, Solomon also suggested that the official language of India for interprovincial correspondence be Hindustani in Devnagara characters, and that it be studied compulsorily as a second language.[31]

Solomon apparently also had a lofty vision of the Bene Israel as mediators between East and West and "apostles of justice and righteousness." In a public lecture entitled "The Mission of the Bene Israelites," which he gave in Bombay in 1925, Solomon suggested that, as Indians felt that a European judge provided the best justice in a court case, a Bene Israel judge could take over that function with home rule because, as in 1857, the Bene Israel would maintain a link with Great Britain. (He did not mention that other groups had remained loyal to Great Britain at that time as well.) In Solomon's view, the loyal Bene Israel community believed that God's plan was that India and England must be together so that what was good in the East might blend with what was good in the West, "while the evil of both would be cast off."[32]

This moderation (some might call it fence-sitting) seemed typical of many Bene Israel, as they commented on the role of the community in the new atmosphere of the mid 1920s. Sometimes, in fact, the position of the two main Bene Israel organizations almost seemed reversed. At the Ninth Bene Israel Conference session, President Solomon Moses called attention to the intense communal consciousness in which each community scrambled to get whatever it could from the government: municipal jobs, political preferment, trade and other facilities. He argued:

> A minor community like ours can have no chance, therefore, unless we have merits out of the ordinary or can at least stand as high as the best in other communities. We should emulate the highest in the land in education, trade, professions, politics and character . . . forgetting we are Bene Israel and remembering only that we are Indians. We are part of the vast Indian Nation. We have to participate as Indians in the progress and development of this country. The needs of the country should, therefore, be our needs and our efforts as a community should be directed towards supplying those needs, so that not only should we be able to hold our own with other communities, but also to cooperate on the onward march of the country.[33]

This statement expressed a stronger identification with Indians—possibly because Solomon Moses himself felt very Indian—than the conference faction usually voiced.

For others, however, the increasing communal consciousness aroused more anxiety about Jewish representation. In "Notes and News," the *Israelite* warned: "Every community is now rising and claiming a voice in the rule of India. We Jews must awaken or else our voice will not be heard and in the midst of self-rule we will be a subject race."[34] The *Israelite* recommended a federation of all Jews in India, whatever their origins, to guard the political rights of the community and to see that Jews were fully represented in the administration of India, independently or along with other minorities. The article was not signed, but it was clearly the work of Jacob B. Israel, the editor. The rival *Bene Israel Review* seemed to approve of his views, but wondered why Israel, who had signed the petition to Montagu nine years earlier, had now reversed his stand to preach communal representation.[35]

Support for nationalist causes could have repercussions, however, as the I. J. Samson case was to prove. When Samson had set up his law practice in Bombay around the turn of the century, the community felt that it would be nearly impossible for a Bene Israel advocate to succeed, as the legal profession in that city was dominated by Parsis and Hindus, and a Bene Israel could have no commercial backing. Nevertheless, Samson soon built up a small but lucrative practice in the small causes court, earning a reputation for ethical professional conduct. In 1926, he was appointed acting additional judge of the Bombay Court of Small Causes, the first Bene Israel to be elevated to the Bombay bench, to replace a judge who was on a six-month leave. It was a high honor for the Bene Israel community, which hoped that the appointment might become permanent.[36]

Although the other judge returned on schedule, Samson was appointed acting judge once again in 1927, and the following year finally got an appointment as a permanent judge.[37] But he was never able to take his seat; his nationalism interfered.

In the beginning I. J. Samson had wavered between Gokhale's liberalism and Tilak's extremism. His son, Arthur Samson, described his father as a "brown sahib"—a term of derision for a middle-class Indian who aped British ways and customs[38]—because he wore formal Western clothes until around 1924. At that point, partly under the influence of his nephew, Dr. Jacob Solomon of Ahmedabad, he joined the theosophical movement and became a vegetarian, a follower of Gandhi, and an advocate of the *swadeshi* ("buy Indian") movement. He insisted that his family boycott not only British clothes but all apparel from abroad, even Japanese clothing, which also competed with Indian products. His brother D. J. Samson was less of an idealist than I. J.: D. J.'s pragmatism led him to believe that a gradual acquisition of power, even if it took years, would work better than immediate independence for India.[39]

Although the Government of India Act of 1919 had included a provision for parliamentary review after ten years, the Conservative Baldwin government decided on an early review as a gesture of good will and to preclude the inquiry being held under the auspices of a Labour government, which would be more sympathetic to granting self-government to India.[40] To this end, the government, in 1927, appointed the Royal Commission on the Indian Constitution, headed by Sir John Simon, with an all-British membership. In acknowledging the arrival of the Simon Commission, as it was popularly known, Jacob Apteker, president of the Eleventh Bene Israel Conference in 1927, affirmed:

> Though we form a small section of the scattered race, yet as Indian subjects we are affected by and concerned about all the movements which are taking place in and about India. We gratefully enjoy the blessings which

British Rule has conferred on India. We are hopefully looking forward to greater boons which the British Government has pledged itself to confer on India by progressive stages. The . . . Commission . . . which is shortly visiting this country . . . with a view to enlarge the scope of the present legislature is sure to take into consideration the interest of the minor communities in India.[41]

Apteker appealed to the Bene Israel to extend a cordial welcome to the commission, but the country as a whole was indignant that foreigners alone would decide the fate of India. All the political parties, except some Liberals and the Muslims, boycotted it, and Congress organized hostile demonstrations and protests wherever the commission appeared.

Nationalism had already invaded the Court of Small Causes, and I. J. Samson now organized a successful *hartal*—a traditional Indian protest by cessation of all activity for a day.[42] The bar was deserted. When the time came, therefore, for Samson's permanent appointment as judge to take effect, a lawyer who was promoting another candidate informed the government that Samson was a Congressite. Asked by the government if he were, Samson answered, "I am, but if I am appointed a judge, I certainly will have nothing more to do with politics until I come down." Nevertheless, the appointment was cancelled and given to the other candidate.[43] The incident showed that even minimal participation in the nationalist movement could have rather strong repercussions, and the lesson was surely not lost on many Bene Israel.

A few months before the publication of the Simon Commission report, however, the viceroy, Lord Edward Irwin, announced that "the natural issue of India's constitutional progress is the attainment of Dominion Status," and that a Round Table Conference of representatives of British India, the Indian states, and the British government would discuss the next step. The Congress leaders, concerned about timing, accepted Irwin's declaration but only on the condition that the proposed conference would meet "not to discuss when Dominion Status is to be established," but rather to discuss its implementation. When Irwin could not give that assurance, however, the Congress, at its annual session at Lahore in December 1929, declared its goal to be complete independence for India. The Congress, under the presidency of Jawaharlal Nehru, resolved to boycott the Round Table Conference and to launch a civil disobedience movement. In March 1930, Gandhi began his famous "salt march" to the seacoast at Dandi, where salt was manufactured from seawater.

The Simon Commission report, published in May 1930, recommended that the constitution of India be federal so as to include the Indian states as well as British India, and that the federation grow out of developing self-government in the provinces. The commission recommended that while full responsibility should be given to the provincial ministries immediately, the governor should retain a limited right to intervene: the central government must remain strong. In India the report caused great agitation on both sides: the Liberals wanted to accept it, while the Congressites said no, although the commission had recognized Congress as the one force that might be able to overcome the cleavages in Indian society.[44] Congress did boycott the First Round Table Conference (November 1930 to January 1931), but all other Indian parties, including the princes, were present. They agreed that the new constitution should be federal, with the Indian representatives favoring dominion status and a parliamentary form of government. They believed that Britain would transfer full power to Indian hands in less than a decade.[45]

At the time, I. J. Samson's sons, Arthur and Joseph, were sitting for the Senior Cambridge Examinations at the Christ Church School, a so-called European institution with an Anglo-Indian headmaster. Arthur remembers that they were asked by a teacher to write an essay on the Simon Commission report. Imbued with nationalistic feelings, and prompted by their father and by articles written by I. A. Ezekiel, a Bene Israel journalist working for Congress, the Samson boys strongly criticized the report. The teacher was very disturbed, called them communists, and insisted that they be expelled from the school. They were prepared to leave, but the headmaster, Charles Bigwood, was a man of broader principles. He told them that he admired and appreciated their courage, but that since they were in school on a government grant, they could not be "politicized." He told the teacher never to give political subjects for examinations again and asked the Samson brothers to promise not to reply even if she tried to goad them.[46]

I. J. Samson was not, of course, the only Bene Israel nationalist. In the early 1920s, David Erulkar, feeling that his defense of Tilak had compromised his career as a lawyer, left Bombay for Calcutta, where he joined the Scindia Steamship Company. His brother, Dr. Abraham S. Erulkar, also a close associate of Tilak in the early days, had returned to India from England with his medical degree and threw himself into the home rule movement, becoming vice-president of the Home Rule League. During the Gandhian era, he approved of the noncooperation movement and, along with other nationalist doctors, was instrumental in starting the National Medical College to accommodate medical students who were participating in the 1920–21 boycott of government schools and colleges. From 1918 to 1921 and again from 1930 to 1932, Dr. Erulkar (a noted gastroenterologist) received many abusive letters about his politics, some signed, and some with anonymous or bogus signatures. He also attended Gandhi during his twenty-one day fast in July 1933— not as Gandhi's personal physician, but as president of the Indian Medical Council. In the 1930s, he came under the influence of the Marxist M. N. Roy, who stood for a broad humanism, the freedom of the working classes and peasantry from exploitation, and the abolition of all caste, religious, and other barriers.[47] As for his own sense of identity, when a Bene Israel asked Dr. Erulkar, "Are we Indians?" he reportedly answered, "Look at your skin, and go look in the mirror. You'll soon see what you are."[48]

The Erulkars and the Samsons were highly placed professionals with Indian clients; according to some informants, their positions explained their attitude of "we are Indians first, second, and last." Since they were self-employed, they had little to lose and could afford to express their views, unlike those sympathizers who were either Government employees or middle-level professionals like Jacob Apteker, a lawyer and the editor of the *Friend of Israel*, and Dr. E. Moses, a general practitioner.[49]

The Erulkars, along with Jacob B. Solomon, ultimately became disillusioned, not with Gandhi's objectives, but with his methods of noncooperation. Dr. Solomon gave up his nationalist activities and became involved in social work, for which he received the Kaiser-i-Hind medal from the government. Another Bene Israel sometime-nationalist was the journalist I. A. Ezekiel, who worked for B. G. Horniman, the British socialist editor of the nationalist *Bombay Chronicle*, and later editor of the *Indian National Standard*. Ezekiel's political views seem to have run the gamut from communism (embraced in 1921) to anti-Gandhian nationalism (he wrote an anti-Gandhi book entitled *Swaraj and Surrender*) to mysticism. When he became disillusioned with communism by 1939, he took up a post in the government until 1945.[50]

The political views of Jacob B. Israel were perhaps the most complex of all. He had been a great admirer of Gokhale and strongly disapproved of Tilak. Although he was a close friend (and brother-in-law) of David Erulkar, he was angry at the Erulkars for being such staunch followers of the lokamanya.[51] Israel was anti-Congress and anti-Gandhi, believing that Congress represented only the upper-class Brahmins and other higher castes, who would exploit the common people and the lower classes. Until the broad masses were ready to take control, he felt, the British presence was necessary in India. (Jawarhalal Nehru shared some of this fear about exploitation and class struggle; he wished to replace imperialism with socialism.) Israel did not trust Gandhi on the uplift of the lower classes, feeling that the Mahatma's primary aim was to abolish British rule. Nor did he believe that Tilak had ever really represented the interests of the Indian masses. J. B. Israel actually joined a non-Brahmin party when one was formed in 1930 or so, but he did not take an active part in it, although he participated in the deputation that waited on the governor of Bombay.[52] He was loyal to Britain, in some ways, identifying with the British in the interests of India.[53]

Israel was also a frequent correspondent to the Indian press, especially to the *Times of India*. Although he wrote on a number of subjects, including agriculture, history, and language, in many columns he aired his views on Gandhi and Congress, emphasizing that Gandhi did not represent the entire

Indian nation and that most of the non-Brahminical classes did not follow him and did not wish to lose the protection of the British crown. Gandhi's movement had caused untold misery through the depression of trade and business and the dislocation of society, Israel insisted, and he hoped that non-Brahmin Hindus and non-Hindus would combine to tell Gandhi to quit. He was against *satyagraha,* which he felt had led to the killing of men, women, and children by starvation and imprisonment.[54]

Israel also criticized the detractors of the Simon Commission report, for he placed great faith in the ability of the Round Table Conference to find some reconciliation. He had, however, noticed that the words "Jews in India" were totally missing from the Simon Commission report, and he wrote to the *Times of India:*

> Perhaps the Commission, which was thoroughly English, did not even know that there were Jews settled in India. We are therefore likely to be totally forgotten for a voice at the Round Table Conference. . . . I saw a couple of letters in your columns suggesting a claim for Indian Jewish represen- tation, but no action seems to have been taken. . . . It is high time all Jewish congregations in Bombay should . . . have a representation sent to the Viceroy for Indian Jewish representation at the Conference. We have been an important community in India. What we did in opening the eyes of Europe towards the trade with India apart, we have been the best friends of Britain during the establishment of the British Empire in India and especially during the appalling calamity of the mutiny. . . . The Old Gen- erals who fought for peace and order in India and who used to know and love us are dead and forgotten. Let us revive the memory of our glorious ancestors.[55]

On the question of separate electorates, Israel felt that the leading commu- nities would take care of themselves, while advanced minorities could be grouped together, and backward and jungle tribes could secure representation by nomination of (preferably) their own suitable members or of other Indians who were in sympathy with their causes.[56]

The Jewish Nationalist Party

Because Congress was generally seen in India as a purely Hindu organi- zation, Gandhi's strategy was to form special parties for those communities that were reluctant to join it. For example, a nationalist muslim party was organized in connection with Congress to counteract the Muslim League, which in the early 1930s expanded enormously and began to talk of an independent Muslim state.[57] But Gandhi realized that many members of smaller minority communities, such as Christians and Jews, were also a little hesitant about openly joining Congress. They were not prepared to accept the call for civil disobedience or noncooperation, though they generally gave their support and could be considered fellow travelers. Gandhi advised these groups, who were dependent on the British government for jobs, not to endanger their positions by taking part in such political activities as breaking the law and going to jail. A small Christian party was formed, but very few Christians joined it except in the south, and it was not nearly as active as the Muslim nationalist party, for most Christians were very pro-British.[58]

The only extant document referring to the formation of a Jewish Nationalist party is a long article in the *Bombay Chronicle* of 21 July 1930, entitled "Jews Can't Stand Aside." According to this article, I. J. Solomon[59] convened a meeting that was attended by about seventy-five Jews, mostly Bene Israel. Dr. A. S. Erulkar presided. Solomon explained that considering the government repression, Jews could no longer stand aside and be mere spectators. He strongly believed that India would get *swaraj* (home rule) within five years and that it was the duty of the Jews to sympathize with the present national movement and join hands with other Indian communities who were fighting India's battle. Jews should take up the *swadeshi* (production and use of home manufactures) and boycott program of the Congress, he urged, and devote special attention to the temperance movement. Other Bene Israel suggested that they should form a party and persuade other members of the community to join it. Shalom Abraham, a leading Bene Israel educator, said that as suffering was the badge of the Jews, they must join the nonviolent *satyagraha* movement, which meant suffering quietly for a cause that one held sacred. The Jews had been treated like brothers by both Hindus and Muslims, he argued, and it would be ungrateful not to stand by their side at a time when the two great communities of India were fighting freedom's battle. A young Baghdadi Jew, H. Y. Horward, speaking in support of the idea, said that many of his friends sympathized with the movement but could not attend the meeting because they were employed in the E. D. Sassoon Mills.[60]

Dr. Erulkar claimed that although he did not like to join any institution conducted on communal lines, as the proposed party was meant for the political education of the Jewish community and its object was national service, he was glad to offer his services. He described the harrowing effect of brutal police lathi charges on unarmed people, some of whom he had treated at the Congress Hospital. Voicing pride that a Jew, Eli Abraham Naogaonker, had been sentenced for picketing in Bombay, Erulkar appealed for the boycott of British goods, declaring that except during a short recent stay in England, he had not purchased anything British for himself since 1916. The physician deprecated the idea of sending a Jewish representative to the Round Table Conference, arguing that a microscopic community like the Jews did not need special representation, and that even if they succeeded in getting it, they should participate in the Round Table Conference only if Gandhi and the Congress did also.

The meeting ultimately passed resolutions condemning the repressive policy of the government, congratulating Bene Israel *satyagrahis* for their sacrifice for the national cause, and appealing to the Jews to take a pledge to use *swadeshi* and to boycott British goods. Other resolutions established the Jewish Nationalist party and mandated a provisional committee, consisting of Dr. Erulkar as president, I. J. Samson and S. M. Benjamin as joint secretaries, and a half-dozen other members, to convene a public meeting of Jewish sympathizers of the national movement.[61]

Although the organizers were longtime associates of his, J. B. Israel was not pleased to hear about a proposed meeting in which a group might announce that the Jews of India were in sympathy with the *satyagraha* movement and its aim of driving the British out of India. Without waiting to see what the meeting would do, he wrote to the *Times of India* stating that if the group put forward such an endorsement, he would strongly object to its being called an all-India Jewish creed. He pointed out that there were many groups of Jews in the Indian Empire and that unless the group had gotten the sanction of every Jew in India, its action was

> unauthorized, illegal and treacherous to the race in general. As far as I know the general mass of the Jews in India is not at the back of this small group. . . . I venture to convey a timely word of warning to brother Jews in India, that if this tiny group of Israelites is allowed to have its own way about the Jewish population in India it will mean the loss of the status and situation it has attained during British rule in India and what is lost once will never be regained. Moreover, alienating British sympathy from us in India means the loss of the sympathy of our Jewish brethren in India and America.[62]

A letter of response by a B. Jacobs pointed out that J. B. Israel did not have the right to speak for the community either, that he was a retired deputy collector drawing a handsome government pension, and that it was well known that government employees were unable to take part in the national movement even if they were in sympathy with it.[63] One wonders if J. B. Israel had forgotten that some thirteen years earlier, he himself had been accused by members of the Jewish community of an unsanctioned action, the representation to Montagu.

There is no further published reference to the Jewish Nationalist party, but Arthur Samson recalls that small meetings did take place, that his father was president, Dr. Erulkar vice-president, and I. A. Ezekiel treasurer, and that apparently there were not many members. B. J. Israel suggests that Dr. Jacob Ezekiel, the nephew of I. J. Samson, and Jacob Solomon of Ahmedabad may have been members. David Erulkar was in Calcutta at the time. The party does not seem to have been very active, nor are any publications extant. Perhaps the members signed some manifestos of a general character or issued statements to the press supporting the demands of Congress. Perhaps they wanted to put the Jews on the nationalist map but realized that too active a role for the Jewish Nationalist party could hurt the community, which relied on preference in employment in the government's lower ranks. Few Baghdadis joined the Jewish Nationalist party, according to Percy Gourgey, a Baghdadi Jewish writer, not because they were anti-Indian, but because Gandhi had advised the small Jewish community to stand aside "lest it be crushed between the giant conflicting forces of British imperialism, Congress nationalism and Muslim League separatism." Gourgey maintains that individual members of the Baghdadi community nevertheless did join in the freedom movement. Arthur Samson seems to think that his older brother Joseph influenced the Baghdadi journalist Maurice Japheth to join the party. Arthur also thinks that the Jewish Nationalist party disintegrated shortly after his father's death, because by then Dr. Erulkar had pulled away, switching his loyalty from Gandhi to M. N. Roy, the only major nationalist leader to support Britain in World War II.[64]

Meanwhile, in January 1931, the working committee of the Congress passed a resolution guaranteeing fair treatment to the Anglo-Indian community in an independent India, stating that the Congress

> has always stood for religious and cultural liberty, equality of opportunity in the matter of education and public employment and freedom to pursue any trade or calling for all children of the motherland, irrespective of whatever creed or community to which they may belong.[65]

As a result of the truce between Gandhi and Lord Irwin in March 1931, Congress called off civil disobedience and agreed to attend the next session of the Round Table Conference, while the government released all political prisoners except those convicted of violence. But the truce collapsed: there were still many conflicting communal claims for electoral seats in the councils. Prior to Gandhi's departure for England for the talks, Dr. A. S. Erulkar headed a deputation of Bene Israel to speak with the Mahatma about the minority questions in India's new government.

On March 10, at a meeting held in Bombay, for the first time members of all Jewish communities in the city met on one platform to discuss the impending changes in the Indian Constitution. Bene Israel had been told that the meeting was convened under the auspices of the managing committee of the Sha'ar ha-Rahamin Synagogue, and some questioned whether a synagogue managing committee should be involved in such political activities. The Marathi handbill addressed to the Bene Israel stated that the purpose of the meeting was to discuss whether the government should be asked to protect the interests of the Jews (who at that point numbered 22,923 throughout India) and to reserve seats for them at the provincial and central legislatures. Meyer Nissim, a Baghdadi, presided over the meeting, but all of the speakers except two were Bene Israel.[66]

A resolution offered by Solomon Moses, the Bene Israel advocate, that the government should allow Indian Jewry to have a representative both in the provincial legislatures and in the Central Legislative Assembly, was seconded by E. A. Sargon, a Baghdadi advocate at the High Court, and supported by B. J. H. Somake, another Baghdadi, whose arguments, unfortunately, were not recorded. Jacob Ezekiel, a Bene Israel, proposed a counterresolution, congratulating Lord Irwin and Congress on the recent agreement and expressing the hope that in the new constitution that was to be drawn up, the interests of the Jews would be protected. This latter resolution was supported by the Bene Israel I. A. Ezekiel, Solomon Ezekiel, I. J. Samson, and Dr. A. S. Erulkar, all of whom still believed that elections should not be held along communal lines. Dr. Erulkar argued that Jews in other parts of the world had come to the forefront, not through special seats being reserved for them as Jews but merely through sheer brain power and capability. Even in India, he pointed out, Jews were elected to the municipal corporations and other public bodies without any special reservations for them as Jews. The ratio of Jews to non-Jews in India was one to ten thousand; thus if the Jews had a single representative on the basis of their race, the legislature would have to have ten thousand members. Even if this absurd ratio were not observed, what could a single representative do in an assembly of nearly three hundred? B. I. Sargon, a Cochini lawyer who was identified with the Baghdadis, agreed that a Jewish representation to the government would have little effect, adding that since the community had no recognized leader in communal affairs, it would be difficult to select a representative. In the end, Jacob Ezekiel's resolution not to ask for special representation was carried by an overwhelming vote.[67]

B. J. Israel, J. B. Israel's son, suggested that identifying oneself as an Indian did not necessarily mean taking the extremist position. Many Indians, including non-Brahmins and Parsis, were generally moderates in their political outlook, or even sympathetic to the British. And yet, it seemed to B. J. Israel, by 1930 most Parsis had changed and identified completely with Indian aspirations. They regarded themselves as Indian, to a greater extent and earlier, he thought, than did the Bene Israel. Because of their higher-class status, Parsis could participate in the political movements in the national Congress and public life to an extent that the Bene Israel could not. Because they struggled so for a living, Bene Israel could rarely devote the attention to public life that many Parsis did. There were not nearly as many lawyers at the top of their profession among the Bene Israel as among the Parsis.[68]

Thus it was possible for the Bene Israel to identify with Indians, to assimilate to the Indians, and yet not to want the British to leave. At first, many

Bene Israel may have thought that they were a little inferior to whites, that the British were "top dogs" because of their superior qualities and virtues. In this respect, they were no different from other Indians who had on one level or another internalized British racial arrogance.[69]

A sense of pride at being Indian developed slowly among the Bene Israel. B. J. Israel tells about the turning point in his own attitude in the early 1930s. The section in the Home Department of the Secretariat that dealt with intelligence reports on political agitation had only five or six men, and at first only Anglo-Indians were hired. Later, when fewer Anglo-Indians were attracted to the Secretariat, this section began hiring Indian Christians and Jews. (Only in 1937, when the Congress party came into power, did it begin to take Hindus.) B. J. Israel was hired in this department in 1932, the year that Gandhi came back disappointed from the second London Round Table Conference. The Mahatma restarted the civil disobedience movement and was jailed. Dr. B. R. Ambedkar, a Maharastrian leader who had developed a movement to free all Hindu untouchables from their disabilities, had complicated the communal problem at the Round Table Conference by demanding a separate electorate for the untouchables, or "depressed classes."[70] The decision was left up to the prime minister, Ramsay MacDonald, who in August 1932 announced his "communal award." The Muslims would continue to have separate electorates and also a certain percentage of seats reserved in central and provincial legislatures. The untouchables were also to have a separate electorate, a decision that Gandhi strongly opposed, believing that they should be included with the Hindu community by reserving extra seats for them in the legislature. In protest he started his "fast unto death" on 20 September.[71] Anglo-Indians in B. J. Israel's department rejoiced at Gandhi's weakening and hoped he might die so that the troubles of the British would end. Israel was shocked at their attitudes and realized then what it meant to be Indian. He experienced great anxiety over Gandhi's fast and felt that all his instincts were different from those of the Anglo-Indians.[72] He had always believed in the moderate school of politics, aiming at gradual changes. But now, with his Indian pride aroused, he began to think that perhaps the nationalists might be right in forcing the issue. He also felt that the less-educated Bene Israel might even have been more progressive than their educated brethren in their political attitudes and in their relationship to Indian opinion. Excluding the Erulkars, the Samsons, and I. A. Ezekiel, most educated people probably felt that their interests lay with the British. The individuals named were unusual not only in that they were activist but in that they strongly supported Indian nationalism to begin with.

B. J. Israel also illustrated the changing views in that period with an anecdote about his sister. She had passed the Senior Cambridge Examination with the highest score for girls in the Bombay Presidency in 1932, and her school wanted her to accept a large college scholarship reserved for the Anglo-Indian girl who stood number one on the examination. (The government was eager to encourage Anglo-Indian girls to attend college, as they rarely did so.) The school principal called Jacob B. Israel and said, "Just say you're a Jew; why do you insist on saying you're Indian?" Israel replied, "It's just for the scholarship. I'm not going to say it. We are Indians and we will remain Indians." The girl did not take the scholarship. B. J. Israel thinks that many Bene Israel would have done the same, that most would not have tried to claim privileges that were not available to Indians. And yet this incident occurred at the very time that the Baghdadis were insisting that they were Europeans and should be treated that way.[73]

Other informants confirm that while they felt that they were Indians first, then Jews, nevertheless they were not nationalists. They were loyal to the British who ran the country well, were civilized, and had discipline. Many Bene Israel did not identify with Gandhi, referring to the biblical injunction that one should always be loyal to the rulers of the country of residence. Another informant said that he could never have followed Gandhi because the Mahatma was not sufficiently concerned with the age of technology and science or prepared to adapt to it.[74]

But throughout the 1930s, as political interest centered on the slow preparation of the Government of India Act of 1935 and the issue of communal representation, the Bene Israel remained alert. To celebrate the inauguration of the newly built Magen Abraham Synagogue in Ahmedabad, the Bene Israel community of that city invited Lord Brabourne, the governor of Bombay, to visit the building and receive an address. The community gave a brief synopsis of its history and expressed its loyal sentiments, but it also requested separate elective representation to the Ahmedabad municipality and the legislative council. The governor replied that he could not grant the request as Ahmedabad had much larger minority communities that did not have separate representation for either body.[75]

Communal Representation in the Services

The controversy over communalism, which ultimately was to lead to the partition of India, usually focused on the issues of special constituencies and legislative representation for minorities. Yet another aspect of communalism, one that perhaps affected the Bene Israel even more, was representation in the public services. Here the British propensity to name and count castes as a method of allocating patronage had significant economic implications and thus influenced the political sympathies and sense of national identity of the Bene Israel. The Baghdadis, who preferred business and jobs in the mills to government service, were less affected.

The government of India, to prevent the preponderance of any one class or community in the public services and thus ensure a fair chance to all communities to secure government employment, eventually reserved some places for Muslims and also for "other minority communities"—a classification that included Anglo-Indians (including Domiciled Europeans), Indian Christians, Sikhs, and Parsis. Jews, along with Armenians, however, being smaller groups, were classified simply as "other communities," for purposes of communal representation in the services, and no places were reserved for them, although unreserved vacancies were open to everyone on the basis of merit.[76]

While the central government laid down its definition of minority communities, various provincial governments had different standards for minority communal representation in the services. The governments of Madras and the Punjab, by the late 1920s, had not established any classification for majority and minority communities. The government of Burma did not find it necessary to regard any group as a minority community. In the Central Provinces, Jews were actually classified as a minority community, along with Muslims, Indian Christians, Anglo-Indians, Parsis, Sikhs, and Buddhists, for purposes of recruitment. For appointment to the Bombay civil services, preference was given to non-Brahmins and Muslims in Bombay and to Muslims in Sind. But the Bombay government said that by 1923, the distinction was often not between minority and majority communities, but rather between educationally *advanced* and *backward* classes, with certain communities and also certain sects being recognized as backward, and certain percentages of recruitment vacancies being reserved for them. In some services under Bombay's control, preference was given only to specified communities, which varied with the different districts.[77]

Thus, if the positions reserved for the minority groups provided opportunities for non-Hindu communities, the concessions and privileges granted to "backward classes" permitted those sections of Hindu society, which historically had been overshadowed by Brahmins and other higher castes, to obtain their share of the patronage. Clearly, the backward classes were concerned not only with political reservations but also with access to education and jobs, roads to social mobility.[78]

For many years the Bene Israel were considered a backward class in English education in the Bombay Presidency. As early as 1917, a correspondent to the *Friend of Israel* suggested that although this status had enabled Bene Israel youngsters to take advantage of middle and high school scholarships reserved for "backward classes," the community had been making very rapid progress, and it would not be consistent with self-respect to allow themselves to be classed along with the Kunbis and other backward communities. He suggested that the community should ask the director of public instruction to remove the name of the Bene Israel from this classification.[79] Nothing seems to have been done.

Dr. Benjamin Reuben, president of the Fifth Bene Israel Conference, raised the issue again in December 1921, when a revision of the community classifications was being considered by the Bombay government. He felt that there ought to be a test by which a community could be judged before it was labeled backward. Reuben urged the conference to cooperate with the minister of education to remove the stigma. A committee was appointed to request that the Bene Israel be classified among the advanced classes, since the percentage of literacy was high among them. When the committee did not act, the sixth conference (1922) passed a resolution that it should do so. Finally, in 1924, the government stigma was removed. According to a notification of 10 October 1924, the Bene Israel were included under the general name "Jews" and were classified under the heading of advanced communities. Abigail Moses suggested that the Conference Education Fund would have to provide for the education of Bene Israel children in the *mofussil* (countryside surrounding Bombay) who would no longer enjoy the reserved scholarships.[80]

Although they were now classified as "advanced" for education, from 1926 to 1937 the Bene Israel were still classified as "intermediate" for recruitment. Certain preferences were given for intermediate communities, but for such a small community as the Bene Israel, the classification did not help very much, because the number of places reserved was comparatively small. The government made an effort to pick out backward classes for the lowest services, such as peons, but not even the uneducated or working-class Bene Israel were interested in these jobs. People who benefited most from the intermediate classification were Muslims and non-Brahmin Hindus such as Marathas and related classes. The Bombay government recognized the Standing Committee of the Bene Israel Conference, at its request, as a communal committee for the purpose of recruiting Bene Israel for government jobs. The assistant collector of customs in Bombay, for example, asked the Standing Committee to furnish him with a list of suitable candidates for employment in the Bombay Customs House. The Bene Israel Conference urged Bene Israel young men with suitable qualifications to forward their applications to the Standing Committee.[81] After 1937, classifications were changed: "intermediate" was abolished, and groups became either "backward" or "advanced." Now the Bene Israel were designated "advanced" for purposes of recruitment as well as education.

It seemed to B. J. Israel that the British officers had a natural preference for the Bene Israel, who seemed more loyal than Hindus. Showing a family connection with the government services was always helpful for a Bene Israel. So many members of the community had served in the army, the railroads, posts and telegraphs, and customs—services in which a disproportionately large number of intermediate grades were taken from minorities—that a Bene Israel could usually demonstrate a family connection. In many of these services, the Bene Israel were very well represented even by 1936, probably holding positions, at least in the lower services, out of proportion to their percentage in the population without needing any reserved places. Although one cannot say whether this high level of representation was because their fathers and grandfathers had worked in the army or services or whether it was because of their own merit, the Bene Israel in any case were considered to be hard-working and reliable.[82]

Nevertheless, the National Archives at New Delhi contain letters and representations from Bene Israel groups, especially in Poona, requesting that the central government specifically recognize the Bene Israel as a minority community for recruitment. In August 1935, A. Isaac, the secretary of the Association for the Welfare of the Bene Israel Community in Poona, wrote to the Home Department, expressing his group's "amazement" at not finding the Bene Israel included in the "minor communities" mentioned in a *Times of India* article regarding the apportionment of Superior and Subordinate Service appointments among the different communities. He was particularly surprised that the Parsi community, "which numbers many thousands in India, which is most influential in commerce, is rich and highly advanced in education and holds very high appointments in different branches of Government Service," should be considered a "minor community," eligible for reserved places, whereas the much smaller, less influential Bene Israel community was not. Isaac asked the government to consider the valuable services rendered by the community in the military and its great allegiance.

Having checked the figures of the Jewish community in India, the Establishments Department confirmed that it was too small to be recognized for the purposes of communal representation in the services. J. W. McElkinning, the home assistant secretary, argued that those few Jews who sought to enter government service in Bombay did not need any special protection as they were the "kind of people who can hold their own in open competition and obtain unreserved vacancies." He realized, however, that although Jewish candidates were not barred from nomination to any all-India or central service, such a nomination was unlikely if candidates belonging to any of the numerically more important minorities were available. Another official added that the Indian Jewish numbers were so small and their literacy figures so low—only 3,605 Jewish males of all ages being literate in English—that it would not be practical politics to recognize them as a minority community. The home secretary commented that while the small numbers precluded the Jews from being treated as a minority community, the low literacy figures did not support the presumption that they could hold their own in open competition.[83] The secretary wondered why, when most Parsis were in Bombay, with only a few thousand elsewhere, they had been singled out as a minority and suggested that perhaps the Parsis should have been recognized as a minority only for local recruitment for the central services in Bombay and Sind. The Home Department wrote to the Bene Israel group that it could not accommodate them. Isaac protested:

> most communities who have succeeded and are succeeding in getting themselves recognized have powerful organizations to voice their grievances through the press, the platform, the assembly, and the Council . . . but alas, we are so small, our resources are so limited, our organizations are so circumscribed, that we have only to depend on Government's good graces to see our wants and remedy them. . . . Even today in all the seething agitation against Government that is rampant in India, the Bene Israel are conspicuous by their absence and have remained loyal to the Crown and the duly constituted Government of India. But in spite of these facts the youth of our community have only to face disappointment wherever they try to get an entrance in Government Service . . . we have not been recruited at all in certain areas: Indian Audits and Accounts, the Central Legislature and other branches of the Government of India.[84]

But the government decision stood.

Occasionally, a Jew who had a European male ancestor tried to take advantage of the Anglo-Indian reservations. Members of one Bene Israel family in Karachi called themselves Anglo-Indian Jews. Some Baghdadis in Calcutta tried to get themselves recognized as Anglo-Indians. Bene Israel believed that while the British knew these individuals were Jews, not Anglo-Indians, they looked the other way because at least they were not Indians. In one instance, a Bene Israel who applied for a job with the police was told that there were reservations for Anglo-Indians, and that if he would falsely claim to be one, he could have the job. He refused.[85]

Government definitions could be fuzzy. In 1939 Joshua S. Joshua, a Jew, applied for a job as an apprentice in the Mechanical Engineering and Transportation Department in the state railroads. Of six vacancies, one was reserved for a member of the "other minority communities" (i.e., not a Muslim) and the Public Service Commission recommended Joshua for it. But since Jews were classified under "other communities," the railroads held that he could not fill the reserved vacancy. Joshua claimed that while he was Jewish by religion, he belonged to the Anglo-Indian community, which was recognized as an "other minority community," and was thus eligible for that reservation. Although two Muslim officials in the Establishments Department said a Jew could not be classified as an Anglo-Indian, other officials in the Home Department decided that if he met the accepted definition of an Anglo-Indian as laid down in the Government of India Act ("a person whose father or any of whose other male progenitors in the male line is or was of European descent, but who is a native of India"), he could be treated as an Anglo-Indian. Yet another official contended that that definition of an Anglo-Indian was meant for franchise purposes only and it would cause difficulties if applied in other spheres. In India, he maintained, religion identified a community as much as race, and because followers of Judaism were identified as a separate community in the census, they should never be included among Anglo-Indians. The Home Department finally decided, however, that a European Jew who satisfied the definition of the term Anglo-Indian should be treated as one, while the descendant of an Asiatic Jew should not be regarded as an Anglo-Indian. They advised the Railroad Department to decide Joshua's case in those terms.[86]

In 1945 the posts and telegraphs services asked if Jews could be included in "other minorities" for the purposes of local recruitment in Bombay, where there were more Jews than Sikhs. They argued strongly that the Jews should substitute for Sikhs in this category because Buddhists could be counted in Bengal, and Sikhs and Parsis all over, although they lacked an all-India character. The Home Department considered the request seriously and checked statistics but ultimately confirmed its original decision that Jews could not be considered one of the "other minorities."[87]

If Jews were preferred in the lower ranks in certain services, it was hard for the Bene Israel, partly because the community was so small, to enter the higher positions, which were generally dominated by high-caste Hindus. Indeed, I. J. Samson and Jacob Apteker were the only two Bene Israel legal practitioners in the Court of Small Causes at one time in the 1920s and 1930s. In the case of higher appointments, no preference was given, except perhaps for Muslims, of whom there was always at least one on the High Court.[88] Few Jews got commissions in the army before 1939. The Bene Israel had stopped enlisting in the army because few Indians were given direct commissions, and the Baghdadis were not generally attracted to the military. After 1939, many received emergency commissions, with no restrictions.[89]

Thus, if a sense of identity with Indians led some Bene Israel to be pronationalist, the question of status in the public services led many others, afraid to participate in nationalist activities and fearful of losing their advantage if the British left, to be pro-British. The question of representation in the services did not affect the Baghdadis, who, on the whole, did not seek out these jobs.

Baghdadi Politics and Identity

If the Bene Israel felt a certain ambivalence about their status as Indians and their stand on nationalist and communal issues after World War I, the Baghdadis had no such doubts. Their sympathies for Britain were only enhanced by the British liberation of Iraq from the Ottoman Empire. During the reign of King Faisal I (1921–33), and with a strong British presence, the position of the Jews became more secure. The approximately thirty thousand Jews of Baghdad comprised perhaps one-third of the city's population and an important segment of the business community. Jewish emigration from Iraq actually declined.[90]

The efforts of Baghdadis in India to establish their status as Europeans intensified right after the war. Their first request was for exemption from the operation of the Indian Arms Act of 1878, which prohibited Indians from carrying arms. Clause 13 exempted Europeans, East Indians, Armenians, and Americans—that is, non-Indian minority communities. Seventy-seven members of the Calcutta community, under the leadership of David Ezra, sent a "memorial" to the government in June 1919, claiming that they fell under this classification. The Baghdadis stressed their loyalty to the government and British rule in India and their aloofness from the political agitation there. They felt that they should not be forced to submit to legislation intended for Indians when their lifestyle, habits, customs, traditions, and aspirations were foreign to India. Contending that racially their claims were as strong as, if not stronger than, those of Armenians, who came from Iran, the Baghdadis stressed their Sephardic origins and complained that they were being

> deprived by law of a right common to all . . . [non-Indian] communities . . . of possessing arms . . . if you give us arms it will be a help to law and order in times of unrest. . . . our status should be established in equality with the status of Jewish subjects in other parts of the British Empire, and all natural-born [British] subjects of the Jewish community domiciled in British India should be included in the exemptions.[91]

The memorial made no specific mention of other Jews in India, either Bene Israel or Cochinis, but one can assume that the authors did not mean to include these groups in their pleas for equality with Europeans. The word "Jews" was not commonly used by Baghdadis to refer to Bene Israel, few of whom lived in Calcutta, and the memorialists apparently felt no need to emphasize the distinction. (It is possible that had such a memorial been sent by members of the Bombay Baghdadi community, they might have distinguished between the groups.) Two months earlier, however, the Home Department had passed a resolution to abolish all exemptions based on racial grounds and, in view of this policy, rejected the memorialists' request.[92]

Baghdadi Jews had a fine opportunity to display their loyalty to Britain in November 1921, during the visit of the Prince of Wales to Bombay. They could be particularly proud because one of their number, Sir Sassoon J. David, happened to be the president of the Bombay Municipal Corporation (the equivalent of mayor) at the time, and thus officially welcomed His Royal Highness at the Gateway of India. Sir Sassoon had donated forty thousand rupees to the reception fund and had given another large donation to charity in honor of the visit. Many prominent Jews were present for the major events in the amphitheater and others attended other functions that the prince graced during his five-day visit in Bombay. Sassoon J. David gave a garden party for the prince at Malabar Hill, to which he invited more than one thousand guests. *Zion's Messenger*, the organ of the Baghdadi Jewish community, wrote:

> Indeed, the extraordinary enthusiasm shown by our small community here is enough to tell how much we appreciate and how grateful we are for the inestimable boon conferred on us and on the vast populations of India by their gracious majesties, King George and Queen Mother Mary, by sending the Prince among us so that we may have the honour to see him and love him. . . . Have not many Jews laid down their lives for the Glorious British Empire on the battlefield in the Great War? The Prince has left behind him the Jewish community loyal to the British Throne and staunch friends of his and his House.[93]

But, as indicated earlier, not all Indians were so pleased with the visit of the prince; indeed, Gandhi had recommended a boycott of the event. Some of those who rioted to protest the visit and the British presence that it symbolized vented their rage not only on the thousands who had come out to greet the prince but also on passersby. The military opened fire to disperse the crowd and the riots spread quickly, with participants from all communities. The Indian press criticized the rioters and some accused Jews of being among them. *Zion's Messenger* tried to clarify the role of the Jews, claiming that they were either on their way home from the welcome or were mere passersby who had been accosted and roughly handled by the rioters. Several children from the Sir Jacob Sassoon School who were among the returning crowds were injured by stones. The military authorities intervened to protect the Jewish quarter in the vicinity of Parsi Statue, Byculla, when some rioters entered the houses of Jewish residents, including Bene Israel, in that locale.[94]

Baghdadi Electoral Representation in Calcutta: 1929–35

Implementing the Government of India Act of 1919, which had provided for legislation by communal groupings in both the central and provincial governments, the Electoral Rules of Bengal established four general constituencies for elected members: European, Anglo-Indian, Mohammedan (a term that was offensive to Muslims because it implied that they worshipped Muhammad as Christians worshipped Christ), and non-Mohammedan. The European group was not confined to pure Britons but embraced all the "white races" domiciled in British India. The Jews, not classified with any of the first three groups, by implication fell into the non-Mohammedan category, which was by far the largest and was primarily Hindu. The Jewish community of Calcutta became particularly concerned about these arrangements between 1927 and 1929, when the Simon Commission conducted its inquiry, as Indian leaders demanded a constitution granting immediate full responsible government on the model of the self-governing dominions.[95]

The revisions of the Central Legislative Assembly and the Bengal Legislative Council electoral rolls prompted D. J. Cohen, vice-president of the Calcutta Jewish Association and honorary secretary of the Beth-El Synagogue, to write to the secretary of the government of India through the chief secretary of the government of Bengal. His letter, revealing where many Baghdadi Jews stood on political issues in this period, deserves attention.

Cohen mentioned that the growing Jewish [Baghdadi] community domiciled in British India, composed mainly of Sephardim, dated its formation about a century back. Politically classified in the non-Mohammedan roll, which was composed mainly of Hindus and a few Indian Christians, with just a sprinkling of Jews and Armenians, the Jews were at a disadvantage in exercising their rights as citizens. They had to vote for Indian candidates who, no matter which party they belonged to, possessed a political vision that in many respects did not accord with the European view, shared by the Jewish community. Thus, he contended, the Jewish community could not take an intelligent interest in the elections. On one occasion, a Jewish candidate had been elected to the Bengal Legislative Council from a Calcutta non-Mohammedan constituency, but at a time when voters were "activated not by national feelings but by the legitimate consideration of merit," a consideration that no longer existed. Cohen therefore urged the government to include the Jewish community within the exceptions in the European roll. Even if the Jewish community could not elect one of its own members to the Legislative Council, its members would at least have the privilege of voting for candidates whose political views they shared. The community felt it was entitled to this privilege in view of its inherent loyalty to the British throne. Cohen also requested the government to consider nominating, in the absence of any elected member, a member of the Jewish community to the central legislature to watch over, safeguard, and press forward the particular claims of the community. He added that "although numerically small, my community are recognized both by Europeans and Indians as an important one who contribute largely towards Provincial and Municipal revenues."[96]

In forwarding Cohen's letter to the government of India, W. S. Hopkyns, of the Bengal government, noted that the 1921 census reported the Jewish community in Calcutta as numbering 1,820, out of a total Indian Jewish population of 22,000, most of whom were in Bombay. His total figures obviously included Bene Israel. The governor-in-council believed, therefore, that it would be impossible to include the Jewish community as such with any particular constituency. If a Jew satisfied the definition of a European or an Anglo-Indian, he should be recognized in the appropriate electorate. The only electorate that was based purely on religion was the Mohammedan one, he argued; for other categories there were other tests, and any alteration in the existing definition to meet the wishes of the Calcutta Jewish Association would be impossible without altering the whole character of the constituencies. The government observed that D. J. Cohen himself had been elected to the Bengal Legislative Council in 1921 from the Calcutta south central non-Mohammedan constituency. Although he was defeated in 1923, he was then nominated to the council by the governor in 1923 and 1926. Thus the Jews did not appear to have any legitimate complaint.[97]

Indeed, one note in the files suggested that as far as the Bengal Legislative Council was concerned, it was too late to consider the question of including the Jews among the European voters. The elections in Bengal were over, and so all that could be done now for the Jews, if anything was to be done, was to nominate one of them to the Legislative Council, a matter that was within the discretion of the governor of Bengal. The question of including the community in the European electoral rolls could not be considered until they were next revised. The government noted that the memorial seemed to speak only on behalf of the Jews of Bengal; Jews in other parts of the country had not been vocal even to this small extent.

As noted earlier, although the Bene Israel were debating the question of separate communal representation at this time, they never tried to get themselves included in European electoral rolls. They might see themselves as Jews, but not as Europeans. The government of India also considered that there was no case for a separate representation of the Jewish community in the Central Legislative Assembly. Apart from the fact that the community, except in Bombay and to a lesser extent in Calcutta, was very small, there were only fourteen nominated nonofficial seats in the assembly and it would be impossible to provide for all the minority communities. Nor was the central government inclined to overrule the Bengal government on the inclusion of the Jews within the European electoral roll.[98]

The Calcutta Jewish Association's attempts having been frustrated, Sir David Ezra, in August 1929, forwarded a copy of a second petition, addressed to the government of Bengal and signed by 114 Baghdadi elders and leaders, to Sir John Simon and members of the Indian Statutory Commission, asking that it be submitted to Lord Irwin, the viceroy. The content echoes that of the memorial drafted ten years earlier on the Indian Arms Act issue. The petitioners now explained that their community, which was Sephardic and different from that of the Bene Israel, was itself composed of two sections: one mostly foreign born, who had retained their foreign habits and not yet adopted British standards of living, and the other natural-born British subjects, who for several generations had been educated and lived in the British style. They had always kept aloof from political agitation in India, they explained, because of their "unswerving loyalty to the British Crown, their keen appreciation of the blessings of an enlightened and liberal Government, and their respect for law and constituted authority." But now feeling it necessary to participate in Indian politics, both to support the government and for self-protection, they felt frustrated at being included in the non-Mohammedan constituency in Bengal. Although they constituted a minority in the country, they represented considerable interests in landholding, commerce, trades, and professions in India. The petitioners contended that all natural-born British subjects of the Calcutta Jewish community living in the European style and domiciled in Bengal should have the same civic status and rights as the rest of British Jewry in the British Empire and as European groups in India.[99]

The government of Bengal felt that the Calcutta Jews wanted a new definition of the term *European* to suit their purpose. Since it was unclear what shape the new constitution and electoral rules would take, it seemed pointless to take up the question again; the government reiterated its refusal. After that rejection, the Calcutta Jews persuaded the Bombay Baghdadis to support their request by sending a memorial to Lord Irwin. Using the same language as that of the Calcutta petition, the Bombay request was signed by thirty-seven Baghdadi Jews. Unlike the Bengal government, however, the Bombay government said nothing about the extent to which Jews had been represented on the local legislative council either by nomination or by election. The government of India forwarded the Bombay memorial to the Indian Statutory Commission, reminding it that a similar document from the Jews of Calcutta had already been submitted.[100] Dissatisifed with the response of the Bengal government, David Ezra wrote to it again:

> The British section of the Jewish community considers it imperative that its political status be equitably established by the Government on a racial basis and that its race entitles it to be politically attached to the "European" group despite the fact that its descent is not "European."[101]

Ezra asked Bengal to convey to the government of India the expectation that the necessary action "to grant their prayer" might be taken "at the earliest possible opportunity after the Indian Statutory Commission had ceased to function." The petitioners also sent a copy of the memorial to Lord Reading, though he was no longer in office, hoping that as a coreligionist, he would be sympathetic to their claims. They asked him to use his influence to have their request granted. The Bengal government did submit the petition to Lord Irwin, who, preoccupied with the civil disobedience movement, passed the matter on to the Indian Office in London, where it was shelved for four years, despite further pressure by David Ezra in April 1932.[102]

Since the 1930–32 round table discussions being held in London between British and Indian representatives agitated the Baghdadis and the Bene Israel over the implications for their communities of possible changes in India, the struggle continued. In July 1933, the Calcutta Jews tried to define Jews "living in the European style" as including "all natural-born British subjects of the Jewish community speaking the English language and dressed in European style." They argued that the three Jewish schools in Calcutta were included in the scheme of European schools in Bengal and received from the government the prescribed "European grant."[103]

Edward Judah, a leading Calcutta Jew residing in London, tried to enlist prominent Britons to assist the cause. At Judah's request, Lord Reading did communicate with Sir Samuel Hoare (Viscount Templewood), the secretary of state for India, but to no avail. Barnett Janner, a Labour member of Parliment (and a Jew), promised support, but Sir Philip Sassoon felt that his own position as a member of the government (he was undersecretary of state for air) precluded his involvement. Judah did manage to persuade the Jewish Board of Deputies and the Anglo-Jewish Association in London to address letters to the undersecretary of state for India, but the lack of an acceptable definition of the phrase *Sephardic Jewish community* impeded the discussions in London. It seemed impractical to include the entire community because many of its members did not speak English or dress in the English style; however, there was no Indian counterpart to the chief rabbi in England who could certify the eligibility of doubtful cases. Afraid of becoming involved in local controversies, the secretary of state recommended reference to the government of Bengal. Edward Judah then had an interview with Sir John Anderson, governor of Bengal, to convince him to accept the principle of a non-European community joining a European group. He explained in a follow-up letter that local Jewish leaders had not approached the European community for official assistance because they felt their case was based on "racial rights," not on favors, and no other component units of the "European" group had been required to obtain permission to be included.[104] When the Bengal government asked the Bengal Chamber of Commerce and the European Association for their views in 1934, the association's executive committee (at Judah's suggestion) adopted the following definition of Jewish eligibility for European classification:

> British subjects of the Sephardic Jewish community including British subjects of mixed European and Sephardic Jewish descent, but excluding Ben-Israelites [*sic*], Black Cochin Jews and persons of Indian or mixed Jewish and non-European descent."[105]

The Bengal Chamber of Commerce supported this interpretation. Judah further proposed that the revised status of the Jews be incorporated in the forthcoming India Act as an all-India measure, with a provision that it would apply initially only to Bengal. The government of India would reserve the right to apply it to other provinces.[106]

The government of India and British officials had been preparing a new constitution ever since the inconclusive end of the Second Round Table Conference. Finally, in January 1935, the government of India introduced into Parliament a bill with the latest British proposals for Indian self-government. When the question of communal groupings for Indian legislative purposes came up for discussion in the committee stage in the House of Commons, one of the first issues addressed was the ambiguous definition of Anglo-Indians. To distinguish them from native Christians in terms of privileges in appointments and franchises, a clearer definition was needed; this definition depended on the definition of the term *European*. The government was prepared to accept an amendment stating that "a 'European' means a person whose father and any of whose other male progenitors in the male line is of European race and who is not a native of India as defined in Section Six of the Government of India Act, 1870." The discussion then turned to whether one should use the term *race*, disliked by some committee members, or *descent*, a term that had been used since 1919 and was also open to interpretation. What was meant by race—could one speak of a European race or races, or a white race? Should one talk of "European culture?" Or did the definition of European versus non-European relate to the birthplace and domicile of grandfathers?[107] No decision was reached, but eventually, the term *descent* was used.

As no mention of the Jewish community's request for European classification had been made in the proposals, Colonel Walter Smiles then moved an amendment that "British subjects of the Sephardic Jewish community, including British subjects of mixed European and Sephardic Jewish descent, but excluding Ben-Israelites, Black Cochin Jews and persons of mixed Jewish and non-European descent shall be entitled to vote as Europeans." He had thus accepted the European Association's definition. Smiles pointed out that the Sephardic Jews, numbering about two thousand and mainly in Calcutta (no mention was made of Bombay), were entirely different from other Jews in India since the Sephardim belonged to European clubs, were respected everywhere as Europeans, and had interests identical with those of the European community.[108]

The reaction of the committee members reflected the range of British opinion on the matter. Major James Milner remarked that although the Sephardic Jews were not European, they were ethnologically of the white race and recognized by the European community as part of it, being admitted to all their institutions. Thus they claimed that they were racially entitled to the political status of Europeans. He felt that they had been badly treated by the government, their memorials having been ignored for years. Milner commented that the European and Jewish associations in Calcutta and elsewhere supported the community's application to vote with the Europeans. But Earl Winterton argued that the principle of the amendment conflicted with the contention of the Jews in Palestine that they were a united people. He feared that giving special status to Sephardic Jews would wound those Jews in India described as non-Europeans. Colonel Josiah Wedgwood countered that no Jewish party opposed the amendment, and that the British community, which wanted to strengthen the European element by adding these big businessmen, approved it. Anyone who desired the British to remain in India ought to wish to increase their number and the power of their vote. He was anxious that Jews in Palestine should become British citizens and he wanted exactly the same thing in India, in the interest of the British Empire. Wedgwood, incidentally, had always opposed the idea of placing the Parsis on a separate communal roll, although their community was not dissimilar to the Jewish community in India.[109]

Barnett Janner, the only Jewish member of Parliament to take part in the discussion, and a man whom Calcutta Jews had thought would be helpful, declined to take a stand on the amendment but reminded the other M.P.s that drawing distinctions between Jews and non-Jews was not only vicious but led to undesirable misunderstandings, though he believed that the community had a strong case that should be considered. William Ormsby-Gore, first commissioner of works, considered pro-Jewish and a supporter of Jewish causes, said that the government felt it was impossible to single out one Jewish community. He opened up a discussion of the differences between Sephardic and Ashkenazi Jews. To allow two thousand Calcutta Jews to vote in a European constituency while all other Jews in India voted in a general constituency, with Armenians and Syrians, seemed to the government to be *prima facie* impracticable. Moreover, in response to Jewish wishes, Britain's whole effort in Palestine was to make no distinction between Jews, no matter whence they came. The government surely could not treat certain Jews in a high social position differently from all the other Jews. Ormsby-Gore's views carried the day and the amendment was withdrawn.[110]

Desperate, the Sephardic Jews, in pressing their case at the India Office, were now willing to include other sections of the Jewish community in India if a new amendment were drawn up.[111] The *Jewish Chronicle* of London seems to have had mixed views on the issue. At one point it wrote:

> there is no question but that any discrimination between Jew and Jew, especially when sponsored by Jews themselves, would be utterly repellent to the feelings of the race in whatever country they may be. It would merely be a repetition of the Nazi distinction between Ost Juden and the German Jews. . . . The amendment, we gathered, provoked strong disapproval in

authoritative Jewish quarters in this country. The difficulty in connection with the non-Sephardic Jews is, however, a very real one, and one can only hope that some acceptable formula will be thrashed out which will do justice to all interests concerned.[112]

A week later, however, the *Jewish Chronicle,* in speaking of a deputation received by Richard Butler, undersecretary of state for India, which consisted of Thomas Levy, M.P., Edward Judah, and Edward Eliot, wrote:

> There is every hope that the justice of the claims put forward will be officially recognized in the same spirit as they have been by European opinion in India, thereby placing the Indian Sephardi community on an equal political footing with Europeans.[113]

The defeat of the amendment elicited a strong reaction from the *Jewish Tribune* of Bombay, which commented in an editorial:

> Reading an account of the proceedings, it will be noticed that reference was made throughout the debate to the 2000 (?) Sephardi Jews of Calcutta, as if there were no other Sephardi Communities in other parts of India. We feel that if united action by the different Jewish communities in India was taken in the matter and the amendment had the backing of the entire community, satisfactory results would have been attained. Since the whole question has been postponed for discussion to some future date, it is not too late for those who have taken the initiative in Calcutta in this matter to get into touch with Bombay, Rangoon and Cochin Jewries. It is highly desirable that Sephardi Jews in India be allowed to vote as Europeans as they stand a better chance of being elected and further, their political outlook and interests are the same as those of the European community.[114]

This stance is surprising because Joseph Sargon, the editor, who was generally sympathetic to the Bene Israel, now seemed to be making distinctions. There is no indication as to what extent the presence of European Jewish refugees in Bombay might have influenced Sargon.

S. S. Koder, Jr., the head of the Cochin community, objected to these approaches on the grounds that any move to separate the communities into different political units would only embitter the already strained relations between the Baghdadi Jews and the Bene Israel in British India and between the white and black Jews in Cochin State, "which every Jew worthy of the name should avoid." Koder wondered what the sponsors of the scheme meant by Sephardic Jews. Was the distinction phonetic? Then Bene Israel and black Jews were Sephardic. He suggested that it would be more noble for all of the groups to vote as Jews and to send in a Jew to represent Jews. "Is it too late to fight for a Jewish seat now?" he asked.[115]

In the middle of all these negotiations, the Calcutta Jews were careful to send a congratulatory message to King George V for his Silver Jubilee. The message ended: "Today, more than even before, we Jews appreciate the privilege of being the subjects of so noble and rightly beloved a ruler, within whose dominions we enjoy equality, tranquility and justice."[116]

Nevertheless, six years of effort on the part of the Calcutta Baghdadis to get themselves included in the European electorate had come to nothing.[117] When it came to a question of identity, the British chose to define the Sephardic Jews of Calcutta not by their culture or "color" but by their religion, and a policy of dividing the Jews was out of the question. This position was to be reaffirmed by the government soon after in the J. J. Hospital and Rangoon Synagogue Cases.

The Bombay Baghdadis

The Government of India Act of 1935 envisaged federation, but this plan was never implemented. The act made no specific mention of either dominion status or independence as future goals, and the ultimate authority of the British crown was maintained. Nevertheless, greater ministerial responsibility now replaced dyarchy in the provinces while dyarchy was introduced into the central administration. The franchise was awarded to about 27 percent of the adult population, but the electorate was fragmented because of the communal question. There were general constituencies as well as those in which only specific racial, religious, cultural, or economic groups had the right to vote. For example, of the 175 seats in Bombay's Legislative Assembly, 114 were reserved for the general population, essentially the Hindus, with 15 of the 114 set aside for representatives of the Harijans (depressed classes) and other culturally and economically "backward" Hindu groups. The Muslims received 29 of the 175 seats, and 32 seats were divided among tribal peoples, Anglo-Indians, Europeans, Indian Christians, and representatives of industry, landowners, universities, labor, and women. As there were no special reservations for Jews, they were subsumed in the 114 seats for the general population and were obviously vastly outnumbered by Hindus—the same situation that the Calcutta Baghdadis had complained of. Although the British felt that they had safeguarded the rights of the minorities, particularly Muslims, while meeting the reasonable demands of the nationalists, many Indians were disappointed, feeling that the communal electorates undermined Indian nationality. The Indian National Congress denounced the new constitution but ultimately allowed Congressmen who had entered the elections and won seats to take office.[118]

Unfortunately, the attitude of the Bombay Baghdadis toward incorporation in the European electoral roll seems to be undocumented, except for the 1929 memorial supporting the petition of their Calcutta brethren. There are no communal records on this matter, and the community newspapers of the early 1930s say very little. Possibly the existence of the large Bene Israel community in Bombay made it awkward for the Baghdadis in that city to take a strong stand. Indeed, in 1931 Baghdadis and Bene Israel meeting together in Bombay voted not to request even separate Jewish representation.

It is hard to say whether the seeming lack of concern was related to the active role one Baghdadi, Meyer Nissim, was taking in Bombay politics at the time, but his career seems worth looking at here. A successful business-man, Nissim had been general manager of David Sassoon and Company for many years, as well as president of the Bank of Bombay. He was also an honorary magistrate and a member of the Bombay Municipal Corporation for more than twenty-five years after 1915. He was nominated to serve as a member of the Bombay Legislative Council during its consideration of the bill to transfer powers and duties from the Bombay Improvement Trust to the Municipal Corporation of Bombay, having been chairman of the Im-provement Trust for two years and a trustee of the Bombay Port Trust for several. In 1929, Nissim was elected president of the Municipal Corporation (the equivalent of being mayor of Bombay).[119]

The elections to the presidency went by communal rotation—first a Hindu, then a Parsi, then a Muslim, then a member from another com-munity: a domiciled European, a Christian, or a Jew (which for the Municipal Corporation meant Bene Israel and Baghdadi). Through this system Sassoon J. David was elected president of the Municipal Corporation in 1921, Meyer Nissim in 1929, and Elijah Moses, a Bene Israel, in 1937. The pres-idency was a ceremonial post for the most part and individual communities did not reap any harvest when their person was the incumbent. But without these reservations, Muslims and Hindus would have shared the top posts, and members of other communities might not have risen to such prominence. Congress, however, was against communal rotation and, soon after Dr. Moses' term, the system ended.[120]

Nissim was successful in his candidacy for the Bombay Municipal Cor-poration because he received the Jewish vote and most of the European vote in "A" Ward, the Fort area, which was the most thinly populated district and included many Europeans as well as Baghdadi Jews. In 1932 he even defeated two European candidates who had gotten a great deal of publicity in the Anglo-Indian press and had campaigned heavily. At the time, the *Jewish Advocate* lamented Nissim's unwillingness to give more of his time to the problems of his own people, feeling that if he took an active and personal interest in the welfare of his community, he could really help it reorganize. In 1939 Nissim was again reelected for a three-year term on the Municipal Corporation, but this election was the stiffest in his experience, as the elec-torate had already doubled and this election was the first municipal one to be fought under the Congress government. The European Association also put up a candidate and many electors who had backed Nissim in former years felt divided in their allegiance. The *Jewish Tribune* expressed gratitude that Jews of Bombay had at least one representative in the corporation who could look after their interests.[121]

Another Bombay Baghdadi, who, unlike most of his community, was active in politics during this period, was Michael I. David, a scion of the family of Sir Sassoon J. David. Michael David was one of the few Baghdadis who favored dominion status for India when this issue became crucial in the late 1920s and early 1930s.[122] In 1931 he took the lead in forming a new league for the "promotion of good will between Indians and Europeans." Frowned upon by European elders, the Progressive League was to "provide a common platform for those Europeans and Indians who stand for the speedy realization of Dominion Status by India with responsible government at the centre, also to promote the political and economic interest of India generally." Variously known as the "Welfare of India League Scheme" or the "Good Will Movement," the idea seems to have been accepted by the president of the Bombay Municipal Corporation as well as the local press. Meyer Nissim, at David's request, called a well-attended meeting at Municipal Council Hall, and a committee was formed, representative of the Indian and European communities, "of distinguished members of both sexes," to maintain and promote cordial relations between the two communities, to safeguard against communal trouble, and to restore intercommunal peace when necessary. Jewish members of the committee included Albert Raymond, Meyer Nissim, Michael David himself, and Dr. E. Moses (the only Bene Israel). David's main interest was to maintain communal peace in India; he was not concerned with politics (although he maintained close contacts with Gandhi, particularly on the question of better treatment for pronationalist political prisoners) and he received praise, including a congratulatory letter from Gandhi, for originating the movement and doing the initial work.[123]

Conclusion

The period between the Government of India Act of 1919 and the Government of India Act of 1935 constituted the blossoming years of the Indian nationalist movement and Jewish development within it. The nationalists had escalated their demands for dominion status and further autonomy. Gandhi had taken over the leadership and had introduced new techniques, drawing in the masses. Communalism—competition for political position and patronage—had grown increasingly important during this period. Although Bene Israel leaders in their petition to Mongtagu in 1917 renounced any demand for separate electorates, by the end of the period, some began to wonder if this decision had been wise. Even more problematic for the Bene Israel was their position in the changing India. Should they link up with and identify with the nationalists—was the future of India in their hands? Or should they continue to support the British, under whom they had benefited so much? The fence-sitting was reflected in the controversy over whether or not to discuss politics in their conferences. The political neutrality adopted by most Bene Israel reflected a tacit support of the British.[124]

The Baghdadi Jews, particularly those in Calcutta, meanwhile, had a much clearer path, never wavering in their attempts to be considered European, whether for educational purposes, for exemption from the Indian Arms Act, or, at the end of the period, for electoral purposes. Their arguments were always the same: they were different from other Indians, and from other Indian Jews as well, and they shared European culture and customs. Their sense of identification with Jews beyond India (from where, after all, they had more recently come) was perhaps greater than that of the Bene Israel. They wanted to be treated like Jews elsewhere in the British Empire, not like Indians. The British acted consistently, refusing to distinguish between Baghdadi and other Indian Jews for purposes of electoral rolls and, as the next chapter will show, not permitting the Baghdadi Jews to make such distinctions in their institutions.

How would the changing constitutional structure in India and its implications for Jewish identity affect the relationship between the Baghdadis and the Bene Israel? Would the need to define further what it meant to be a Jew bring them closer together or widen the rift? And what role, if any, would the growing Zionist movement in this period play in shaping the sense of identity in these communities? These questions must now be examined.

CHAPTER 5

INTRACOMMUNAL STRUGGLES
AND ZIONISM

Bene Israel–Baghdadi Relations

In 1931 Bene Israel and Baghdadis in Bombay convened a joint public meeting to consider whether Jews of India needed to have seats reserved for them in the provincial and central legislatures. Such a meeting could surely not have taken place fifteen years earlier, for the tensions between the two communities were so marked then that it probably never even occurred to the Bene Israel drafters of the representation to Montagu to consult with any Baghdadis, most of whom did not see the Bene Israel as "full Jews" anyway. Would the need to protect Jewish interests in a changing India now draw the two groups together?

Some of the conflicts between the two communities, so evident in the period from about 1909 to 1920, had already begun to subside. *Zion's Messenger*, the Baghdadi paper, had reported favorably on the Bene Israel Conference held in December 1921, stressing the loyalty resolutions and the Bene Israel pride in the selection of Lord Reading as viceroy of India. The following year *Zion's Messenger* again summarized the achievements of the Bene Israel Conference, singling out the resolutions offering to help build the Jewish National Home and expressing loyalty to the king-emperor. "It is with satisfaction that we note the progress that this community is making in India, and thereby adding its laurels to those of other Jewish communities all over the world," wrote the editor. The paper also thanked two Bene Israel, Elijah Joseph and David Benjamin Bhonker (Bombay and Poona), for helping in the appeal for cooperation in the relief work for Jewish victims in the Ukraine.[1]

As indicated above, it is difficult to date the exact period during which the Bene Israel were excluded from the *minyans* in Baghdadi synagogues, but it may have been from approximately 1909 to 1927. In the early 1920s, the Bene Israel of Poona built their own synagogue, Succoth Shlomo, because they were not permitted to read from the Torah in Ohel David, the Baghdadi synagogue. In 1923 the Bene Israel paper the *Israelite* argued that the Bene

Israel in Bombay needed a bigger synagogue because the Baghdadis would not allow them to use the large space in Magen David Synagogue for weddings, as they had in the past. After 1927, however, Baghdadi synagogues apparently admitted Bene Israel to make up the *minyan* and to come up for Torah readings.[2]

Ironically, it was a Baghdadi from Iraq, not India, who became a major benefactor of the Bene Israel school, the Israelite School, located in the Mazgaon section of Bombay. Since 1892 the school had been functioning as a high school, preparing students to take the university entrance examinations. Although a number of the wealthier families continued to send their children to private Christian-run schools, a large percentage of Bene Israel children received both a secular and a religious education at the Israelite School, where Hebrew was taught. Sir Elly Kadourie, a wealthy Jew from Iraq, contributed to many educational establishments all over the East, trying especially to help the lesser-known Jewish communities. In the late 1920s, when Sir Elly met Rebecca Reuben, the head of the Bombay Bene Israel school, in London, she prevailed upon him to donate 150,000 rupees to construct a new building to replace the old dilapidated structure that then housed the school. In return, the Bene Israel, in 1932, renamed the school the Sir Elly Kadourie High School. When Sir Elly Kadourie passed through Bombay in 1934, the Bene Israel presented him with an address and invited distinguished non-Jews to attend the prize distribution. The presiding officer, V. N. Chandavarkar, vice-chancellor of the University of Bombay and former mayor of the city, used the occasion to respond to Nazi propaganda and tried to explode the myth that the Jewish financiers of the world were engaged in a plot to control international finance. He mentioned how much Bombay owed to Jewish financiers, naming the contributions that Jews (mainly Baghdadis) had made to Bombay.[3]

In 1930 the three sons of Isaac Sargon, the Cochin Jew who had served as the *hazan* to the Bene Israel and had elicited the letter from *Haham* Gaster recognizing the Bene Israel community's Jewishness, began publishing a monthly newspaper. It was initially known as the *Jewish Bulletin* (through 1930), then as the *Jewish Advocate* (until March 1933), and finally, for most of its life, as the *Jewish Tribune*. Under its various names, this paper was a much more sophisticated and professional affair than *Zion's Messenger* (of which it considered itself the successor) or the Bene Israel papers, all of which had ceased publication by 1927. The Sargons were nephews of N. E. B. Ezra, editor of Shanghai's *Israel's Messenger*, and had learned some of their journalism from him. In addition to local news, feature stories, and items of Jewish interest, editorials and articles covered international events relating to Jews. The editor subscribed to many other Jewish papers and the Jewish Telegraphic Service—indeed, Joseph Sargon became the Bombay correspondent of the telegraphic service. The *Jewish Advocate (Tribune)* consisted of thirty pages, buoyed by the support of many subscribers and advertisers. Read mainly by the Baghdadi community (but also by some educated Bene Israel), it was during this period the only Jewish paper in India, Burma, Aden, and Iraq, and was also read in Shanghai, the Dutch East Indies, and England. The New York Public Library wanted to be on the complimentary mailing list.

Following in their father's footsteps, the Sargon brothers were staunch supporters of the Bene Israel, although they themselves were considered members of the Baghdadi community because their mother had been a Baghdadi. Their newspaper carried items about Bene Israel activities, achievements, and deaths, and published correspondence from Bene Israel. The Sargons also solicited contributions about the community's history from Bene Israel authors such as Jacob B. Israel, I. J. Samson, and I. A. Isaac.[4] Issues of the *Jewish Tribune* from the mid 1930s offer a glimpse of the efforts made in Bombay to bring about a rapprochement of the two communities. In 1932 Bene Israel contributed to a Baghdadi community fund on behalf of destitute Jews of Aden. On this occasion, the paper (then called the *Jewish Advocate*) wrote:

> We would like to see more co-operation between the two communities, if the solidarity of Bombay Jewry is going to be established. In the past there has been no general co-operation and consequently no important steps have been taken by us in a forward direction. Let's bring the two communities closer together now.[5]

The following year, in reprinting an extract from the London *Jewish Chronicle* of 10 February 1883, which discussed the relations between the Bene Israel and the Baghdadis at that time, the Sargons commented that the article

> shows the state of affairs which with slight alterations, still exists in our midst. The discrimination that one notices calls for comment and it is imperative that the gulf of discrimination that exists between the two people should be reduced to a minimum—nay, entirely removed. Is not Kol Yisrael one? What difference does it make whether we are Bene-Israelites, Ashkenazi or Sephardi? Are we not all Jews?[6]

In the same issue, these views were echoed in an article entitled "Indian Jewry," in which Jacob B. Israel maintained that it was unfortunate that Jews in India who hailed from different parts of the world kept apart from one another. He urged mutual cooperation and the formation of an "All India Jewish Society" for watching and caring for the welfare of all the Jews in India. Israel also suggested that a small committee of Jews from different sections in Bombay be formed to communicate with all other Jews in India through the *Jewish Tribune*. He voiced a hope for an annual Jewish gathering:

"Then alone can we prove the existence of a real Jewry with a voice in the new National India at present in embryo."[7]

Sometimes the Bene Israel were even held up as an example for the Baghdadis to follow. An article by "Observer" in the *Jewish Tribune* bewailed the lack of leadership in the Baghdadi community and the lack of community control of its own institutions, which were administered by the Sassoon trustees. The author was impressed that the Bene Israel in Bombay had the right of franchise in electing officeholders of their communal institutions. He also cited the "admirable" case of the Bene Israel in Ahmedabad, who, in spite of their comparative poverty, had successfully worked for a synagogue needed by the growing community.[8]

Provisions for Religious Observances

Special requests to the government about religious observances required cooperation between the two communities. Official accommodation to religious needs had long been evident. For example, Jews serving in the Indian army in the 1880s were granted leave for Passover in any part of India. A British judge postponed a case that would have required the presence in court on the Sabbath of Elia D. J. Ezra, then serving as a sheriff in Calcutta. Also during the 1880s, Silas Moses, a Baghdadi businessman, was appointed as a juror in a sessions court in Bombay; because he could not travel by carriage to the court on the Sabbath, the judge postponed a hearing until Monday. The editor of the Bene Israel newspaper *Israel Dharmadeep* commented:

> We are very happy to find this arrangement being made by the court. It is not desirable to force the Jews and the Christians to work on the day of the Sabbath except in military, medical and police departments. We only hope that the other officers and the industrialists will follow in the footsteps of the high court judge.[9]

On the other hand, government services did not permit absences from work on Saturdays, unless a department with regular working hours on Sundays chose to grant leave to people on Saturday instead of Sunday. This policy affected Seventh-Day Adventists as well as Jews. Muslims were permitted to absent themselves for an hour or so to attend *Juma* prayers on Friday but were not given a whole holiday every Friday. The government did allow a maximum of six communal holidays a year to all employees.[10]

A perennial problem for the Jews, especially in the 1920s and 1930s, was having to sit for university examinations that fell on the Sabbath, when they could not write, or on the Holy Days. The Cochin Jews were fairly successful in persuading the Cochin University to make exceptions; in 1928, for example, S. S. Koder and three other Jews were allowed to write their examinations after sunset when the tests fell on Saturday. Later, a university commission visiting Cochin expressed its willingness to avoid Jewish holidays and the Sabbath if they got early enough notice of a Jewish candidate. In 1927, however, when the Bene Israel community had asked Bombay University for a similar privilege, they were given exemptions only for Yom Kippur: if there were Jewish candidates, the exams would not be held on that day.[11] Unfortunately, matriculation and school final examinations often fell during Passover. In 1931, when some students refused to sit for exams rather than profane the Holy Days, Baghdadi Jews renewed the petitions and representations to Bombay University to avoid exams on the holidays, but to no avail: the university argued that the number of Jews constituted barely 1 percent of the candidates and that several such requests made by larger communities had not been granted.

In 1934, Albert Manasseh, the secretary of the Bombay branch of the World Sabbath Observance League, wrote to the government about his organization's goal of improving the legal situation of the Sabbath: exemption of Jewish children from all school and college attendance and university examinations on Saturdays and Jewish holidays and leaves for Jewish civil servants, government employees, soldiers, and sailors on holidays. To aid the central office at Amsterdam in compiling information on laws, regulations, and practices in various countries, the Bombay branch requested appropriate information on India. The government simply reiterated the position stated above. A year later, the *Jewish Tribune* pointed out that there was a deep "religious significance attached to the Sabbath and that work on that day would involve a transgression of the fourth commandment," although that was not the case for Jewish feast days. By then, Calcutta and Rangoon universities were exempting Jews from examinations on Saturday. But in Bombay, the problem was not solved. The desire to observe the Sabbath caused many well-to-do and middle-class Jewish parents to seek admission for their children at the Cathedral School, which was not only in a good location (the Fort area) but also was closed on Saturday.[12]

Problems involving ritual ceremonies were more easily resolved. In 1939, when a deputation consisting of Meyer Nissim, Dr. E. Moses, and Solomon Judah asked the health minister of the Bombay government for an exception to the prohibition laws, the government issued a resolution saying that the Jews could use wine on the Sabbath, on holy days, and for marriages and circumcisions, both in private house ceremonies and in synagogues. A similar situation occurred during Passover 1943, when wheat rationing as a result of the war made it impossible for the Jews to have *matza* for the holidays. Repeated requests to the authorities to release extra wheat or at least to allow the Jews to draw adequate rations ahead of time were met with refusals. As a last resort, E. E. Sassoon presented a memorial signed by 350 persons to the governor of Bombay, explaining the significance of Passover to the Jews and asking that a small supply of wheat be granted. At Sassoon's urging, the viceroy suggested that the government of Bombay reserve the required number of bags of wheat and hand them over to some organization on behalf of the Jewish community. With this sanction (or pressure?) the government of Bombay did grant the wheat to both the Baghdadi and Bene Israel sections of the community.[13]

Bene Israel in Baghdadi Institutions: Schools and Mills

Other facets of the interaction between the two Jewish communities in Bombay can be understood by examining the relationship of the Bene Israel to Baghdadi institutions such as the schools and the Sassoon mills, although the mills might not ordinarily be considered an institution.

The Sir Jacob Sassoon Free School, founded in 1903, was an English medium school that taught up to the matriculation (college entrance) standard. Children who passed the matriculation were offered employment in the firm of E. D. Sassoon and in other local firms. The trust deed did not specifically exclude Bene Israel children from the school (although Albert Elias, the head trustee in the late 1970s, thought that was the case), but it has always been considered a Baghdadi school.[14] Ironically, the school frequently had a Bene Israel headmaster because there were few Baghdadis suitable for the position. E. M. Ezekiel had started out as principal in the school's forerunner institution in 1887, and then served as headmaster of the Sassoon school until he retired in 1921.[15] The statement of the Baghdadi journal, *Zion's Messenger*, that the Sassoon school was "the only educational institution for the Jews in the Bombay Presidency," irritated the Bene Israel journal, the *Israelite*, which retorted:

> We have to enlighten our contemporary that there is another and much older educational institution for Jews in the Bombay Presidency utilized by the Bene Israel who are as much Jews and as good Jews as any and far better in education and culture than many others who cannot bear to own them as Jews because of their brown colour.[16]

In 1925, Mrs. E. Joseph, a Baghdadi, became headmistress of the Sir Jacob Sassoon Free School. Seen in the early years as a charitable institution for poor and destitute Jews, the school seems to have improved under Mrs. Joseph's tenure. Between 1926 and 1930 attendance rose from 246 to 410. Children from more affluent families began to attend (probably having a beneficial influence on the less fortunate children), examination results improved, and the educational inspection reports were good. Prominent Baghdadis such as Meyer Nissim and Albert Raymond took a deep interest in the school. By the 1930s the school had to refuse admission to children because of lack of room; some two hundred children were on a waiting list.[17]

The Sassoon school was attractive to some Bene Israel because it was an English medium school that taught Hebrew and observed the Jewish holidays. But even though the trust deed did not exclude Bene Israel, so many Bagh-dadis sought admission that there was little room for the Bene Israel. Ac-cording to the school register, only forty-five Bene Israel were admitted between 1922 and 1945. These were mainly older pupils, ages fourteen to twenty (most of them between seventeen and twenty), who were accepted into the higher standards to prepare for matriculation. It is difficult to tell how these children were selected. Possibly the extent to which they could benefit from education in English played a role. (Did they speak English at home? Did the child know enough?) The decision seems to have been up to the principal. In the 1930s a Bene Israel, Shalom Abraham, began to teach at the school and eventually became the headmaster. The Bene Israel com-munity differs over how much Abraham did to foster the admission of Bene Israel children. He says that he spoke to the board of trustees about it, but some Bene Israel felt that because he was dependent on the Baghdadi au-thorities, he did not push very hard.[18]

Sophie Corley, the Bene Israel head of the ORT School for Girls in the late 1970s, recalled that her brothers had gone to the Sassoon school in the 1930s because her father wanted them to have Hebrew, and that people had asked him why he was sending the boys to a free school, as most wealthy parents were too proud to do that. She claimed that more Bene Israel could have gotten into the Sassoon school, but they did not want to attend a free school. Some Bene Israel, however, felt that if the Baghdadis wanted to have nothing to do with them, they would return the compliment; thus, some of the pupils who attended the Bene Israel Elly Kadourie School, also free, would not have gone to the Sassoon school. Another Bene Israel, a Mrs. Malyanker, who as an adult taught at the Sassoon school, had been admitted as a student, along with her brothers, in the 1940s. She remembered that the few Bene Israel children there at the time did very well, winning all the prizes and scholarships because they were more interested in education than the Baghdadis, especially the boys. In the school, the two groups of children mixed well.[19]

An important factor in the relationship between the Bene Israel and the Baghdadis was the dependence of both communities on employment in the Sas-soon mills. The establishment of the mills and the other facilities that the Sassoons provided attracted many Iraqi Jews to Bombay. Throughout the first half of the twentieth century, Baghdadis assumed as a fact of life that any Baghdadi boy who dropped out of school before finishing could find employment in the Sassoon mills.

In the 1920s a nephew of Jacob Sassoon, Sir Victor Sassoon, assumed the chairmanship of E. D. Sassoon and Company and became an important figure in Indian industry. He served for several years as a member of the Indian Legislative Assembly, representing the Bombay Millowners Association and defending Bombay mill interests against those of Manchester; in 1929 he was a member of the Royal Commission for the Investigation of Labour Conditions in the Dominion. The growth of Indian nationalism, to which Sir Victor was not particularly sympathetic, coupled with troublesome labor conditions eventually induced the Sassoon firms to reduce their Indian commitments and concentrate more on their interests in China and England. In the 1930s, however, E. D. Sassoon and Company had the largest textile operation in India: eleven mills employed twenty-five thousand workers and produced more cloth than any other group of mills in the country. David Sassoon and Company had three or four mills. By 1939 wages were far higher in the Sassoon group of mills than in any other; employment in the textile industry seemed secure. The mills provided night schools, libraries, reading rooms, sports clubs, and even a babies' creche—an on-the-job day-care center for mothers working in the mills.[20]

Unfortunately, the role of the Sassoon mills in Jewish employment has never been seriously investigated, and it is doubtful that statistics could now be found. Not only the Baghdadis but also the Bene Israel turned to these mills for jobs. How extensively the latter relied on the Sassoon mills is unclear. B. J. Israel felt that only a small portion of the Bene Israel worked in the Sassoon mills and that they did not earn any more or do any better there than in other mills, receiving some preference in hiring, but not much in promotion. Only the Manchester Mill, Israel felt, went out of its way to employ Bene Israel and Baghdadi workers. Another Bene Israel observer, Isaiah Shapurkar, thought that in the 1930s about 60 percent of the employees in the E. D. Sassoon mills were Bene Israel. Without statistical evidence on the proportion of Bombay Bene Israel employed in the mills, and in the Sassoon mills in particular, it is difficult to verify the Sassoons' claim that they greatly aided the Bene Israel by providing employment. In the Sassoon operations, Bene Israel worked mainly in the mills, only occasionally as office clerks. Perhaps in marginal cases an influential Bene Israel who knew an influential Baghdadi could obtain a clerkship with the Sassoons for a Bene Israel.[21]

Certainly by 1916 the greater portion of Jacob Sassoon's office staff was composed of Jews, and he had a reputation for pushing Jews forward in all departments of his business. Such preferences could occasionally backfire. In 1922, with the collapse of the post–World War I boom, the Bombay textile industry faced a major crisis caused by increasingly vigorous competition from up-country and Japanese mills. The interwar years required a contraction of the labor force and wages: between 1922 and 1941 unemployment was a critical problem.[22] In 1923 the E. D. Sassoon mills dismissed sixty-seven employees, of whom twenty-one were Jews. The employees were apparently compensated fairly and were permitted to open accounts in the E. D. Sassoon firm that received 5 percent annual interest. But the community resented the retention of some well-paid, superfluous heads of departments who had been recruited from England; the salary of such an individual might be greater than the combined salaries of many of the dismissed employees. Furthermore, *Zion's Messenger* published a letter suggesting that several local firms refused to employ Jewish workmen on the ground that wealthy Jewish firms in Bombay presumably gave preference to "their own kind" in employment—although a few non-Jewish firms had made exceptions in favor of Jewish employees. The writer also complained that the Jewish firms did not employ enough Jewish youths as apprentices in the mills. He concluded that if the Sassoon mills had to dismiss employees, they should dismiss non-Jewish ones. He included Bene Israel as Jewish.[23]

One of the most successful careers of a Bene Israel in the Sassoon organization was that of M. A. Moses, who worked with the E. D. Sassoon mills from 1921 to 1956. He worked as secretary first to A. J. Raymond, the organization's director, whom most regarded as quite difficult, and then to Albert Raymond, his nephew, replacing J. N. Reuben, another Bene Israel in that position.[24] Moses served as a mill manager for a few years and then returned to the head office. The Shepperd reforms of 1933–34 required that all mills have labor officers; Moses was the second person (the first Jew) to hold that post for the Sassoons, and he kept it for many years, becoming responsible for all aspects of personnel work: recruitment, testing, employment, workers' welfare, settling disputes. M. A. Moses echoed B. J. Israel's observation that E. D. Sassoon's policy had been to give preference to Jews in initial employment, but not necessarily in promotion. Moses, whenever he could, gave preference to qualified Baghdadis and Bene Israel, and, given the choice between the two, all other things being equal, he selected the Bene Israel. Indeed, at one point (in the late 1930s, according to his son), M. A. Moses was accused of favoring Bene Israel. When he was asked to report to Sir Victor Sassoon, Moses was nevertheless able to show statistically that he was not giving preference to the Bene Israel and easing Baghdadis out.[25]

M. A. Moses felt that the Sassoons had a definite preference for European managers, often bringing them in from England and elsewhere. It was harder for Jews or other Indians to rise to these positions, although A. J. Raymond used to tell Sir Victor Sassoon, "Keep all your [English] captains and majors. I don't want them. I prefer my Indian staff."[26] In 1925, Jews occupied some twenty out of the fifty-seven directorial positions in nine Jewish-owned cotton mills for which data are available. However, these figures seem to reflect the multiple positions held by six or seven individual Jews such as Sir Sassoon David, A. J. Raymond, Albert Raymond, and Sir Victor Sassoon.[27]

Moses often encouraged Bene Israel to enter a technical line as they could move up more rapidly than they could in the clerical line. There were few clerks in the mills themselves, and within the head office, competition was even greater. As the Baghdadis preferred clerical or accounting positions to the technical areas, they were unlikely to become spinning and weaving masters.[28] The few Bene Israel clerks, however, seem to have done better and risen faster because they were more educated than the Baghdadis, who often dropped out of the Sir Jacob Sassoon Free School at an early stage.

J. N. Reuben always worked in the front and head offices and helped many Bene Israel get jobs. According to informants, other Bene Israel who advanced included Joseph Mordechai, who became a mill manager, and a Mr. Daniel, who was a weaving master in the Edward Mill. Sam Halegua, a Cochin Jew in Bombay, was a cotton-spinning master in the Jacob Sassoon Mill, the first non-European to become a spinning master.

Advancing to a higher position in the mill was one thing: socializing, evidently, was another. Moses recalled that, in general, Baghdadi and Bene Israel workers and clerks seemed to get along very well, but as he did not have very much contact with them, he did not know whether they talked about religious matters or about their differences. Shalom Abraham observed that the two groups said prayers separately but that otherwise there were no tensions between them. Isaiah Shapurkar reported that Bene Israel mill workers used to attend the Baghdadi synagogue, Magen David, in Byculla. At the managerial level, M. A. Moses felt that relationships between Baghdadis and Bene Israel were close professionally but not personally. When he invited one of the Sassoons to his son's circumcision, the man did not attend but sent a gift. Occasionally Bene Israel and Baghdadis might have invited one another to weddings, but Moses does not recall being invited to a Sassoon wedding. By the time his own children were married, the Sassoon mills had already been sold. Nor were there reciprocal invitations to dinner parties. Nevertheless, a few Bene Israel seem to have had a different experience. J. N. Reuben, Albert Raymond's personal secretary, and his wife did socialize with the Raymonds and other Baghdadis. They attended Sassoon marriages and circumcisions and invited them in return. When the Reubens had gotten married in 1923, however, J. N. Reuben refused to marry in Magen David, although most wealthy and "important" Bene Israel wanted to have their weddings there. He simply felt that if the Baghdadis would not accept Bene Israel in the *minyan* or call them up to read the Torah, he wanted to marry someplace else, even in a large hall, if necessary. Rachel Daniel said that her husband, the weaving master, socialized with the Baghdadis, but only because he was the "boss." Similarly, Sophie Corley reported that her father, who worked in the Sassoon mills for thirty-seven years as a mill manager, with many Baghdadis under him, socialized easily with them.[29]

Even when Sir Victor Sassoon no longer lived in Bombay, he made short, periodic trips to the city, where he still had large commercial interests. Whenever he appeared, the Baghdadi Jewish community focused its attention on him, hoping he would do something to solve the community's problems. As one of the lay heads of Indian Jewry, he helped to create a refuge for Jews escaping from Germany after 1933, but Sir Victor was never as actively involved in Jewish affairs as his ancestors had been. He felt that the community never did enough to help itself. In the late 1930s, when employment at the mills became a controversial issue, the editors of the *Jewish Tribune* called his attention to the community's serious unemployment problem. Sir Victor replied that the keynote of his system of employment was efficiency, and that if a Jew was efficient, he was given a job; however, in a community of three thousand Jews (the Baghdadi community), he could not accommodate everyone. Mill superintendents trained and employed all who were "real workers" and other things being equal, gave preference to the Jew, he explained, but he found quite a number of Jews were lazy and wanted easy jobs. "We lost lakhs through opportunities given to Jews," said Sir Victor. "This is not a charitable institution. But I'm always prepared to take care of promising lads."[30]

Many Baghdadi Jews took offense at his remarks and wanted clarification. Had Jews been given proper opportunities and failed to make good? If they showed ability, to what positions could they ultimately aspire and how many had risen from the ranks? An editorial in the *Jewish Tribune* contended that very few local Jews had been given positions of importance, in contrast to conditions in previous years. Was it lack of ambition or enterprise that made so many of them remain apprentices and clerks, or rather the lack of opportunities to distinguish themselves? How had the company lost lakhs because of Jews, and were local Jews or others responsible? Had Jews abused confidence placed in them, or had they simply made mistakes through lack of business acumen and experience?[31] Other writers complained that Sir Victor had not paid tribute to the many worthy Jews employed by the Sassoons since the foundation of the mills, Jews who had helped enhance the firm's wealth. One pointed out that practically until the retirement of A. J. Raymond, the heads of the departments and establishments were all local Jews, most of whom were educated at the Sir Jacob Sassoon Free School. He named Baghdadi Jews who had increased the number of cotton mills owned by the firm. A columnist wrote:

> How about the many Jews from Bombay who were sent to Hong Kong and Shanghai in pioneering days of the House, and due to whose services

Sassoon occupies so large a part in the China trade? Although some money may have been lost . . . on the whole, the House of Sassoon has benefitted considerably by giving Jews opportunities. The Sassoons have lost lacs on other enterprises as well. Perhaps more Jews don't want to be apprentices because they don't have much opportunity for advancement. . . . why can't capable ones be given opportunities as heads of departments and managers, as was previously done?[32]

In 1942–43, when it seemed probable that India would become independent after the war, Sir Victor began private, slow negotiations to sell off the cotton textile mills; by 1944, India United had purchased all twelve. J. N. Reuben and other Jewish managers stayed on, quadrupling their salaries. M. A. Moses, who had retired to become a government labor consultant, was recalled by India United in 1946–47 to solve some problems, and he remained there for fifteen years trying to straighten out matters. Although Sir Victor tried to insure that the new owners would protect Jews, it became harder for many Jewish boys to get jobs immediately in the mills if they dropped out of school.[33] Some have suggested that the closing of the Sassoon mills in the mid 1940s ultimately contributed to Jewish emigration. The security no longer existed.

Bene Israel versus Baghdadis: Government Intervention

Despite the signs of rapprochement and cooperation between the two communities in Bombay, there was a darker side to the Bene Israel-Baghdadi question in the 1930s. Two disputes attracted widespread attention and eventually required government intervention. It is probably no coincidence that these disputes occurred at the same time that the Calcutta Baghdadis were waging their struggle for political recognition as Europeans.

A case involving the Musmeah Yeshua Synagogue in Rangoon, Burma (at that time administered by India), aroused considerable interest in Jewish circles in both countries. The Jewish community of Rangoon numbered about thirteen hundred, with perhaps sixty Bene Israel and the rest mainly Baghdadi or of other Middle Eastern origin. Since 1926 the Bene Israel had participated in the election of the Musmeah Yeshua Synagogue's trustees, but they were not allowed to stand for election. On the eve of new elections in 1934, the retiring trustees not only refused the request of some Bene Israel to be listed among those eligible for election but also withdrew the Bene Israel franchise on the grounds that they did not observe the Jewish laws of divorce, *yibboom*, and *halitza* and therefore were not good Jews. Certain Bene Israel instituted legal proceedings against the trustees.

The question at issue was whether those Bene Israel who fulfilled the age and residence criteria for the list of voters and candidates could be disqualified for not being "good Jews." There was also some unsubstantiated suspicion that one of the trustees had really decided to withdraw the Bene Israel voting rights because they were backing his opponent.[34] The Bene Israel plaintiffs and their witnesses, including two Baghdadis, testified that the Bene Israel were Orthodox Jews in all respects. Baghdadi witnesses for the defendants said that they were not. The matter of Sabbath observance elicited much discussion, the Bene Israel arguing that, since many of them were employed as government civil servants (railway employees and jailers), they had to work on the Sabbath.

Testimony also differed on whether the Bene Israel had been or should be called to read the seven prescribed portions of the Torah and counted in the *minyan*. In fact, the Bene Israel seemed more concerned with these problems of their status as Jews than with the question of voting rights *per se*.

M. R. Daniel, a Bene Israel witness, said that he had read the obligatory portions of the Torah in the Musmeah Yeshua Synagogue in 1909. In 1913 rules formulated to govern the observances in the synagogue had excluded Bene Israel from going up to the pulpit except for extra readings. (During this same period there was heightened tension between the Bene Israel and Baghdadis in Bombay, where the Bene Israel were excluded from Torah readings in the Baghdadi synagogues.) In 1915, when the Rangoon Bene Israel Subedar Daniel raised the question of exclusion from the Musmeah Yeshua pulpit, the trustees resolved that they saw no reason to depart from the "old custom" of not calling the Bene Israel up except for extra readings. After 1916 a Bene Israel was usually denied a first reading because his work obliged him to break the Sabbath; after 1924 his nonobservance of divorce, *yibboom*, and *halitza* was held against him. In 1926 the trustees had permitted one Bene Israel to do a first reading because he signed a statement that he would follow the Jewish law in regard to those practices. The trustees were prepared to allow full voting rights and participation in the services to other Bene Israel if they gave a similar written undertaking, but the Bene Israel refused, on the ground that such a promise, if required of them and not of other Jews, implied that they were not originally Orthodox. The Bene Israel testified that they observed all laws and produced receipts showing that they had paid for privileges in the synagogue connected with prayers, ceremonies, and burials.[35]

Because of overcrowding in Musmeah Yeshua, a new synagogue, Bethel, was opened in 1932. Here Bene Israel were treated exactly like other Jews: they could read the prescribed portions of the Torah from the pulpit. Only two or three Bene Israel attended the Bethel Synagogue during its earliest years—constituting 2 to 3 percent of its congregation. Of the five trustees, none was a Bene Israel.[36]

When the dispute over Musmeah Yeshua's rules was submitted to the High Court, both parties solicited opinions from various rabbis and authorities in Iraq, Palestine, and the British Empire. In fact, the High Court wanted a decision from the Religious Court (Beth Din) in London. Rabbi Dr. J. H. Hertz, chief rabbi of the British Empire and the London Beth Din, had said that equal privileges and rights, including being counted in the *minyan*, might be extended to the Bene Israel when they promised to abide by and carry out all the Jewish laws and practices. Dr. Moses Gaster, however, reiterated the support that he had given the Bene Israel almost twenty-five years earlier, stating that they were full-fledged Israelites.[37] In the course of the proceedings, Judge Alfred Leach, the presiding magistrate, after studying Jewish tradition and Bene Israel history and practices, declared that most Jews in Rangoon no longer observed the traditions of divorce, *yibboom*, and *halitza*. Since the Bene Israel did not differ from other Jews in observance of these laws, he ruled, they came within the definition accepted by the defendants and thus were eligible for appointments as trustees and entitled to vote. Costs of the litigation were to be borne by the Synagogue Trust Fund.[38]

The defendants appealed, contending that the Bene Israel had separated from other Jews and, whether or not they professed Judaism or conformed to Jewish practices, they were a community distinct from the Baghdadis. (The Calcutta Baghdadis might have been pleased with the arguments.) J. M. Ezekiel, one of the plaintiffs, then asked *Haham* Gaster to confirm his decision by referring the matter to the Beth Din of London. Gaster felt it would be unwise since the Beth Din belonged to the Ashkenazi community and, knowing nothing of the Sephardic traditions, might be more in sympathy with the views of the so-called white Jews. His position was just as valid as that of the Ashkenazi chief rabbi and of the Beth Din, which served as that rabbi's adjunct.[39] Also, applying to the Beth Din would have implied a recognition of its authority in matters Sephardic. The High Court appellate division finally dismissed the appeal on 8 January 1936, stating that the appellants could not raise the question of separate communities for the first time in the appeal.

This test case was an important victory for the Bene Israel throughout India; they now felt that they had been vindicated and could claim to have legal status as Jews. The *Jewish Tribune*, sympathetic as always to the Bene Israel, gave extensive coverage to the affair. It chastised the synagogue trustees for wasting substantial funds in litigation when there were so many poor Jews in the community, and deplored taking the question outside communal walls to a court of law. "There are no Jewish 'untouchables' in our history," it wrote. "Are the Rangoon Jews paving the way for creating caste distinctions— a feature which we know only too well to be a curse to India?"[40] Another commentator pointed out that adaptation to local customs and conditions, which in other countries was considered grounds for superiority (in England and the United States the earliest Jewish arrivals had looked down on later ones), in India was treated with contempt. Because the Bene Israel had not been in affluent circumstances or until recently occupied positions in the commercial world or in government, the newcomers (Baghdadis) had more status. I. A. Isaac, the Bene Israel journalist resident in Calcutta, criticized those who condemned the Bene Israel because their forefathers had married alien women, when "the forefathers of the whole Jewish nation had committed the same crime," citing Moses, Jacob, Joseph, Esau, and King Solomon.[41]

Only a year after the Rangoon decision another case concerning the right of the Bene Israel to be classified as Jews arose, this time in Bombay. In 1922 the wealthy Baghdadi Sir Sassoon J. David had established a trust that, unlike the Jacob Sassoon trusts, neither discriminated between Jews nor excluded any community.[42] In the late 1920s, the government of Bombay Presidency and the trustees of the Sassoon J. David Fund had negotiated the construction of a special pavilion of the Jamsetji Jijibhoy Group of Hospitals, popularly referred to as the J. J. Hospital. The trust fund would give money for the new wing, on the condition that fourteen beds be reserved for Jews. By the time the construction was completed, the fourteen beds had been reduced to ten, but when the advisory committee for the J. J. Hospital met on 18 June 1936 to discuss the inauguration of these special beds for Jewish patients, Sir Alwyn Ezra, a nephew of Sassoon J. David and the chief trustee of the fund, stated that the Bene Israel should not come under the category of Jews. By this time a number of central European Jewish refugees had established themselves in Bombay; presumably they (but not the local Bene Israel) were included along with the Baghdadis in the term *Jews*.[43]

The advisory committee resolved to consult the government about whether Bene Israel could be classified as Jews and whether they were entitled to the special accommodation. Lieutenant Colonel S. S. Vazdifar, superintendent of the J. J. Hospital, consulted Dr. A. S. Erulkar, the well-known Bene Israel gastroenterologist, who naturally answered that the Bene Israel should be included as Indian Jews, explaining their origin and history and discussing their orthodoxy in religious observances. Erulkar even pointed out that the maternal grandfather of the late Sassoon J. David had been buried in a Bene Israel cemetery in Bombay. Erulkar, himself a member of a Jewish synagogue in London, mentioned that in India, for census and municipal voter registration purposes, Bene Israel were classified as Jews. Finally, he cited the Rangoon decision as precedent.[44] Vazdifar forwarded Erulkar's letter to the Bombay government, which concluded that for all official purposes the Bene Israel community should be considered a part of the Jewish community, as all statistics had been compiled on that assumption and no separate figures for the Bene Israel population were available. That they had remained a distinct group socially was mainly because of their long isolation from Jewish communities in other parts of the world. One official wrote: "There is therefore no ground for Government to introduce an invidious distinction between sections of the general Jewish community or to treat the Bene Israel community as not coming under the generic term 'Jews.' "[45] They were therefore entitled to the benefits of the special accommodation to be offered for Jews in the hospital.

The government in India, in both cases, echoed the decision made by the government in England: no distinctions were to be made between Jews for political or any other purposes. Identity stemmed from religion.

Individual Attitudes

Although no systematic survey has been conducted on the attitudes the Bene Israel and Baghdadis held toward each other in the second quarter of the twentieth century, and although it has not always been possible to conduct in-depth interviews about that period, the comments of various members of both communities are instructive.

The experiences of Baghdadi professionals are particularly revealing. Albert A. Shellim, a magistrate, referred to the Bene Israel as Jews but implied that there were different kinds of Jews, each with its own burial grounds and synagogues. His father, a prominent physician, had associated from the 1920s to the 1940s with Bene Israel doctors such as Jerusha Jhirad, A. S. Erulkar, and Jacob Apteker, who, along with a few other Bene Israel professionals, were very highly regarded in that generation. Albert Shellim himself, as a well-placed professional, mixed in many circles, particularly non-Jewish ones, and joined many non-Jewish clubs.[46] He did not participate extensively in regular Baghdadi Jewish activities nor in the politics of various Baghdadi organizations, although he served as a trustee of one. Similarly, highly educated Bene Israel were often accused after the 1930s of being less involved in communal activities.

The only other Iraqi Jew to become a magistrate (and the first one to do so) was Reginald Mathalone, who was a High Court liquidator in Bombay. He confirmed that most Baghdadis went into business because not enough money could be made in law or the other professions. He himself had never met his contemporary, David Reuben, a Bene Israel Indian Civil Service judge, although he had heard of him. Mathalone recognized the long-standing strained relations between the Bene Israel and the Baghdadis. He knew very little about Bene Israel history but thought that they might have intermarried with non-Jews. Acknowledging that the Iraqis always considered themselves foreigners, he suspected that they also thought they were socially superior to the Bene Israel and also that perhaps color affected their attitudes. Like Albert

Shellim, Mathalone had few Jewish friends and met them only in passing; his friends were mainly Indian and English.[47]

Shanta Chenoy, like her mother, Hannah Sen (a prominent Baghdadi Jew who had founded Lady Irwin College), had married a non-Jew but still considered herself Jewish and identified with the community. She felt that Baghdadis could be arrogant but that the Bene Israel had made a "mistake" in considering themselves Indian because the Baghdadis viewed such assimilation negatively. She confirmed that since color was very important in India, the color of the Bene Israel did not help them vis-à-vis the Baghdadis. However, she thought that most Baghdadi girls were more serious students than the boys, so that marriage was a problem within that community. The boys, after high school or three years of college, always went into business, whereas the Bene Israel entered the professions, government service, or education; for this reason, some Baghdadi girls preferred the Bene Israel boys. Shanta Chenoy also commented on the lack of real orthodoxy among the Bene Israel—such as the infrequency of widow remarriage, which seemed to assimilate to Hindu practices.[48]

Sophie Kelly, the principal of the Hill Grange School in Bombay, admitted that as a child she had looked down on the Bene Israel. As an adult, however, she realized that many of them were more refined than many Baghdadis, that they were intellectuals, professionals, and high government servants, and that many Bene Israel were very orthodox, pious Jews. She attributed the Iraqi discrimination to racial and color prejudice resulting from the British presence, although she acknowledged the influence of Indian society as a whole. Sophie Kelly felt that the Bene Israel were less careful than Iraqis about maintaining Jewish marriage and divorce laws but that some Iraqi families could be just as "mixed up" as Bene Israel families. She also suggested that when most of the Baghdadis left Bombay, those remaining felt that they had to accept the Bene Israel, and some realized that their attitudes had been wrong.[49]

While the Baghdadis tended to look down on the Bene Israel, there were cleavages within the Baghdadi community itself. Those who lived in Byculla were considered unrefined and were looked down on by the wealthier Baghdadis who lived in the Fort and Colaba districts. Byculla Jews sent their children to the Sir Jacob Sassoon Free School, whereas the Fort Jews went to private Christian schools, which had higher standards. Even in *Habonim* (Zionist) camps, the two groups remained apart. Byculla Jews were considered very clannish: they joined Byculla groups, went to synagogue and school with Byculla friends, and had no contact with the outside world until they grew up and got jobs. Fort Jews preferred not to intermarry with them. But Byculla Jews could move up the social ladder by moving to the Fort district. In an article in the *Jewish Tribune* in 1933, Benjamin Moses chided the Fort

Jews for casting aspersions on the Byculla Jews and stigmatizing them as illiterate and unworthy of companionship with their more "enlightened" Fort brethren. He thought that the Byculla Jews were proud of being Jews and revealed their Jewishness more than the Fort Jews, who sometimes even tried to hide their identity. Moses warned that the Fort Jews needed more humility and that, in any case, all Jews should unite at this time, because of the danger of Hitlerism to German Jewry.[50] This intracommunal conflict has a familiar ring to anyone aware of the issues of ghettos, socioeconomic mobility, and assimilation among Jews (and other minorities?) the world over.

Another component of Bombay Jewish society was the small community of white Cochin Jews. In the 1920s, there were about thirty to forty families. They considered themselves Jews of European origin, closer to Anglo-Indians or Parsis, of a higher class than the Baghdadis, whom they felt were interested only in making money and not in education. The Cochin Jews may have been friendly with the Baghdadis, but they preferred that their children marry Europeans. Some Cochinis questioned the Jewishness of the Bene Israel because they had "intermarried with native women and, after all, had learned much of their religion from Cochin Jews."[51]

Interestingly enough, many Bene Israel professionals and other educated people lived in Nagpada, a section of Byculla, often in the same buildings with Baghdadis. The children of the two groups overcame the language barrier through English, mixed at the Nagpada Neighborhood Center or in the convent schools, and became lifelong friends. Bene Israel, of course, were aware of Baghdadi attitudes and could be scornful of Baghdadis. Some Bene Israel felt that, except for a few wealthy Baghdadi families in Fort, most were third rate. They were poor and some were beggars. In the first half of the twentieth century, conservative Bene Israel mothers preferred to have their children (daughters especially) play with Hindu children rather than with Baghdadi children, because the Baghdadis were already living according to a freer, modern, Western lifestyle, too different from the Bene Israel.[52]

In 1913 some educated Bene Israel women had started the Stree Mandal (Women's Association) for poorer, less-educated girls and women. They offered sewing and embroidery classes and published reports in Marathi so that these people could read them. Yet the Stree Mandal never had any contact with the Baghdadi Jewish Women's League. Perhaps they visited each other once or twice, but each was concerned with its own group. Some Bene Israel felt that the Baghdadi women acted more superior than did the men.[53]

Anne Solomon Samson had a Baghdadi mother and a Bene Israel father, as did many of her relatives. At times the parents of a Bene Israel man objected to this arrangement, she said, not because he was marrying a Baghdadi woman, but because they wanted him to marry someone they had already selected for him. Although marriage between Baghdadi men and Bene Israel women was rarer, the parents of the man sometimes objected. Anne Samson's parents attended Magen David (the Baghdadi synagogue in Byculla), where her father was counted in the *minyan* but was never called to the Torah. He apparently did not mind, as he went only to pray, but others did object. Anne Samson was married to a Bene Israel; she and her parents socialized with both Bene Israel and Baghdadis, and many of her Bene Israel-Baghdadi cousins went to the Sir Jacob Sassoon Free School, although she herself had gone to a convent school in the 1950s. To her, the crux of the problem was assimilation, rather than just religion, which she felt could have been worked out. Bene Israel assimilation to Hindu customs and Baghdadi desire to assimilate to the British made the two groups irreconcilable.[54]

Zionism

After World War I, with the emergence of the British mandate for Palestine, the issue of Zionism came to the fore. This development further complicated the question of Indian Jewish identity and affected Jewish attitudes toward Britain.

Bene Israel Conflicts

Although the Balfour Declaration had been issued two years earlier, the turning point for the Jews of Bombay occurred in 1919. Paul Tolkowsky wrote on behalf of the "Universal Zionist Organization" of London to various Bene Israel institutions, informing them that the head office in London was sympathetic to Bene Israel farmers and other workmen in India and thought they would do much better by going to Palestine than they had done in India. Tolkowsky asked for information to place before the board of the Zionist organization: What was the attitude of the Bene Israel toward the Zionist movement? Would they form a branch of the Universal Zionist Organization in India? What was their feeling toward the eventual return en mass to Palestine? What was the number of Bene Israel in Bombay and other places, and with whom should the Universal Zionist Organization of London further correspond?

The Sha'ar ha-Rahamim Synagogue convened a public meeting of the Bene Israel community on 2 April 1919 to consider the question of Zionism, a European ideology that was demanding their attention. Some of the leaders were sympathetic: Jacob I. Apteker, the editor of the *Friend of Israel*, explained that the objects of Zionism were to provide protection for persecuted Jews and to cultivate and beautify Palestine. He assured the 350 people present that Zionism did not want all Jews to go and settle in Palestine; it sought only those who were oppressed. Dr. E. Moses added that another aim was to take possession of Palestine. The Erulkar brothers, however, had obviously given some thought to the matter and were wary. Dr. A. S. Erulkar saw that Zionism had two aspects, intellectual and political. He supported intellectual Zionism, which aimed at the preservation and development of Jewish learning and culture, but he disagreed with the national and political aspirations. In his view, Zionism was not the solution to Jewish oppression because there were more persecuted Jews in Poland alone than Palestine could ever possibly absorb, even if Arabs and other non-Jews were made to leave. Nor would he discuss the pros and cons of national Judaism with supporters of Zionism unless they guaranteed equality, without distinctions of class or color, for all followers of Judaism. Otherwise, Erulkar argued, a Zionist state, assuming that one was set up, would provide an excellent breeding place for racial hatred based on color prejudices, and the bond of religion would be a mockery. Because the Zionists had so far given no assurance to the Bene Israel and because the community in general knew nothing of Zionism, the meeting was not competent, he contended, to arrive at a proper conclusion. He and others suggested that efforts should be made to educate the Bene Israel about Zionism.[55]

Dr. Erulkar's brother David suggested that the Bene Israel not commit themselves in a hurry because other influences had superseded religion to bring various peoples together to form a nation. Indeed, Jews had fought Jews and Christians had killed Christians in World War I in the service of their own nations. For Zionists to form a Jewish nation from peoples who were widely divergent in their civilizations, ways of thought, and economic conditions, he argued, would be to set back the world's progress by several centuries. He too cautioned that the Bene Israel had to think carefully, for Western Jews as a rule were not free from color prejudice, even toward their coreligionists; in his view, the Bene Israel were flatly denied their rights as Jews in the Baghdadi synagogues because of their color. Recalling instances where Western Jews had without any grounds condemned the Bene Israel as converts to Judaism, even as the descendants of slaves, David Erulkar concluded (prophetically perhaps): "If we have to contend against such calumnies in the Diaspora, what chance would there be for a handful of people to stand against overwhelming majorities of men with whom, the past has shown, color can entirely eclipse the obligations which religion entailed?"[56]

Solomon Moses, who presided over the meeting, countered that people would not be expected to sail for Palestine if they voted for Zionism, and he ridiculed the population question as insignificant. Notwithstanding the Erulkars' objections, a majority of those present approved a resolution offered by J. I. Apteker that the meeting was in full sympathy with the Zionist movement in England and appointed a committee, consisting mainly of Bene Israel

Conference people, to consider how they could cooperate with it. The leaders of the Samson faction, or All-India Israelite League, were noticeably absent from this committee.

The *jamat* (assembly) of Tiffereth Israel Synagogue, which was then controlled by the league people, met and passed a more cautious and guarded resolution, stating that the meeting at the school did not represent its views:

> the meeting [of the jamat] was in sympathy with the intellectual aspects of Zionism, but deferred consideration of political or national aspects of Zionism until a) details of the political future of Palestine were finally decided upon and announced, and b) the Zionists have publicly and authoritatively declared that any Bene Israel who choose to emigrate to Palestine shall be entitled in all respects to the full enjoyment of all the rights and privileges, and that no distinction, preference, or disability based on colour prejudice shall be tolerated in the state intended to be set up by the Zionists and that the claims of every coloring people shall be accepted without impugning their purity of race.[57]

One can clearly see the influence of the Erulkars in formulating this resolution. Thus the factionalism that had expressed itself earlier in the management of communal institutions and in attitudes toward the discussion of politics in the conferences now appeared on the issue of Zionism.

Apteker reiterated his pro-Zionist views in a lengthy, well-informed editorial in the Marathi section of the *Friend of Israel*. He summarized the history of the Zionist movement and the current state of affairs in Palestine and discussed the tendency toward and dangers of assimilation by Jews in Western countries. Since Jews the world over were divided on Zionism, Apteker suggested, it was not surprising that the Bene Israel would be too. Yet, he argued, the fears of prejudice were unfounded, because Jews of all colors, from all over, the Middle East as well as Europe, would be going. Thus it was ridiculous to ask the Zionist organization for a guarantee against discrimination. "We [the Bene Israel] should not show our inferiority complex by suggesting that we might be questioned as being true Jews," he wrote. Only those who needed and/or wanted to would go to Palestine and make it a center of Jewish culture and religion. Apteker then outlined the efforts to make Palestine open to Jews by international law, quoting the Balfour Declaration, and urged the Bene Israel to confirm their identity with Jews in other parts of the world by supporting the Zionist movement.[58]

Possibly the context of the developing Indian politics that would allow Jews to participate, but not as a significant community, made the idea of strengthening ties with coreligionists in other countries particularly attractive to many Bene Israel. Would they come to see themselves as Jews first, Indians second?

If the *Friend of Israel,* the conference paper, supported Zionism, the *Israelite,* the league organ, opposed it. In its English columns, the *Israelite* reprinted a resolution on national Zionism passed at the Twenty-Sixth Biennial Council of American Hebrew Congregations; the resolution stressed Judaism as a religion and opposed reviving a Jewish nationality or founding a Jewish state. The *Israelite* also reprinted a notice from the Paris correspondence of the *Westminster Gazette* mentioning that some of the strongest promoters of Zionism at the Paris Peace Conference were violent anti-Semites, especially eastern Europeans, who hoped to rid their own countries of Jews. A later issue of the *Israelite* discussed Arab opposition to Zionism and the views of Faisal, head of the provisional government in Syria and later King of Iraq. Subsequently, pointing out in Marathi that the King-Crane Commission, sent by the United States to Syria to determine the wishes of the population, had reported that the Syrians were opposed to Zionism, the editors argued that the Bene Israel should withdraw from the movement.[59]

Meanwhile, in May 1919, the members of the Jewish community at Karachi elected their leader, Abraham Reuben, to represent the Jews in Sind in connection with the Zionist movement. He wrote to Tolkowsky, then acting Belgian consul in Bombay, informing him that the Bene Israel population of about 650 in Sind was in entire sympathy with the movement *"provided there is nothing against the British Government in its aspiration"* (emphasis his). The community would decide on forming a branch association of the Universal Zionist Organization when it had more information, and he therefore requested details about the movement, suggesting that he might also meet Zionist representatives when he was in England the following May. Reuben at that time was president of the All-India Israelite League; indeed, he wrote on its letterhead. He evidently was more open on the Zionist question than some of his Bombay colleagues. The Zionist head office in London sent him Zionist literature, which he circulated to members of the Jewish community in Karachi and Sind. By the end of the year, the Karachi community had deputed Reuben to proceed to the Holy Land to report on the practical possibilities of Zionism.[60]

In its third annual meeting, in December 1919, the Bene Israel Conference, the organization to which most of the Zionist supporters belonged, passed two resolutions relating to Zionism. In Resolution 12, they expressed their "gratitude to the British Government and to the British people who are the first nation after two thousand years to acknowledge publicly the Jews' rights and privileges as a free community, and to the Allied and Associated Powers who have adopted as an essential element of the Peace Conference the British Government's declaration in favour of a Jewish National Home in Palestine." In Resolution 15, they noted with satisfaction "the resolution passed by the public meeting of the Bene Israel Community of Bombay on April 2, 1919, expressing its sympathy with the Zionist movement and recommending that a Zionist society be formed in Bombay."[61]

The *Israelite* continued to oppose Zionism, mentioning the riots in Jerusalem as further proof that Bene Israel should not emigrate and should not be involved in the political affairs of others.[62]

Looking back in 1977, B. J. Israel felt that Zionism was a major point of difference not between the All-India Israelite League and the Bene Israel Conference, but rather between their respective journals, the *Israelite* and the *Friend of Israel*. Although the league did not take any position regarding Zionism, it did pass resolutions about atrocities in Russia after the war, thereby expressing its awareness of and concern about Jewish problems in other parts of the world. B. J. Israel claimed that his father, Jacob B. Israel, a league leader, was not essentially anti-Zionist: he thought the mandate was a mistake because of Arab opposition but agreed with the basic idea that Jews—with divine guidance—had a right to return to Palestine. He was a great admirer of the Arabs and wanted Jewish colonization of Palestine only with Arab consent and approval. B. J. Israel felt, however, that the Erulkars were very anti-Zionist because they went along with the general nationalist movement in India, particularly in 1917–18, when Gandhi backed the Khilafat movement of the Muslims, partly to get them on his side. The Indian National Congress consistently opposed the idea of the national home for the Jews. Thus, the anti-Zionism of the Erulkars and of Jacob B. Israel stemmed from different sources, although all of them felt a strong Indian identity, one that surpassed, perhaps, their Jewish identity. Many people did not take seriously the potential racial problems in the Jewish state because they never felt they would be required to leave India and go to Palestine.[63]

The Bene Israel continued to watch the Zionist movement carefully. News of the League of Nations award of the mandate for Palestine to Britain and the consequent prospects for the development of the Jewish national home greatly pleased the Jews of Sind and the Zionist supporters of Bombay. In August 1920 David I. Rogow of New York gave a lecture on Zionism to about one hundred Bene Israel in Bombay, exhorting his audience to form themselves into a Zionist organization as a practical way to help the movement, which American Jews, he stated, were supporting. This call seemed to be the push they needed: less than a month later, Zionist sympathizers held another meeting, resolved unanimously to form a Bene Israel Zionist association, and appointed a committee to draft a constitution, with Dr. E. Moses as president and Jacob Apteker as treasurer. D. M. Samuel, the secretary, immediately wrote to the Zionist organization in London requesting a copy of its constitution, a statement of its aims and objectives, and advice on how the Bene Israel branch could affiliate to it. Pleased that the "present great moment in Jewish history was appreciated in Bombay," the head office expressed the hope that the Indian Jews would "do their utmost in collecting a large fund towards the rebuilding of Palestine and thus assist in the redemption of our people." They sent a list of free Zionist pamphlets that they were willing to forward if the Bene Israel wanted to distribute them and help the movement.[64]

That December, Judah Hyam, in his presidential address at the Fourth Bene Israel Conference, raised the question of what active part the Bene Israel, situated where they were, could take in the Zionist movement. If they were only to help in the colonization of Palestine, they might, later on, when funds were organized for that purpose, send persons from the community to receive liberal education at Hebrew University or to settle in the Holy Land. Jacob Apteker, chairman of the reception committee, also expressed his excitement in his address:

> This year is memorable for one of the greatest events that has occurred in Jewish history for the last two thousand years, the recognition of the national status of the Jewish people by the British Government and her allies, by their decision to incorporate the Balfour Declaration in the Treaty of Peace with Turkey and by the acceptance by Great Britain of the Mandate for Palestine as a Jewish National Home and by the appointment as High Commissioner of Sir Herbert Samuel—a man who combines within himself all the higher attributes of a successful British statesman with the heart of a conscientious Jew. . . . The Jews all over the world are thankful and grateful to Great Britain, who was the first to give complete emancipation to her Jewish subjects and who has now emancipated the Jewish land.[65]

Zionist Emissaries in the 1920s

The Baghdadi community had already captured the honor of establishing the first Zionist association in Bombay. In May 1920, a few months before the formation of the Bene Israel branch, three ardent young Baghdadis—E. S. Somekh, J. S. Ezra, and M. Moses—founded the Bombay Zionist Association (BZA). Despite the general indifference of the Baghdadi community, the young men received moral and financial support from a few individuals, including Meyer Nissim. By December they had forty members. David E. Shellim became president, and the association began to issue a monthly bulletin.[66] Eventually, it was the Baghdadi branch, rather than the Bene Israel group, that was to survive, despite its vicissitudes, and carry the flag of Zionism in Bombay.

The World Zionist Organization was eager to encourage the fledgling movement in all countries and, of course, to raise funds for colonization and development. In what might be considered a twentieth-century adaptation of the *shlichim* movement, the organization sent out emissaries to Jewish communities all over the world. In 1921 Israel Cohen, the secretary of the organization, was sent as the first Zionist emissary to the Far East, with an itinerary that included Egypt, Australia, New Zealand, China, and Japan, as well as India. Cohen was canvasing particularly for Keren Hayesod (known at first as the Palestine Restoration Fund and later as the Palestine Foundation Fund). Whereas Keren Keyemet L'Israel (the Jewish National Fund) engaged primarily in purchasing land in Palestine for Jewish settlement, Keren Hayesod had been established to provide funds for workers to settle on the land and to promote industry. Cohen was able to raise substantial sums, despite reservations and doubts on the part of the donors, from the Ashkenazi Jewish communities of Australia, especially in Perth and Melbourne, and from the Baghdadi community in Shanghai.[67]

Arriving in February in Calcutta, which did not yet have a Zionist association, Cohen addressed a meeting in the Magen David Synagogue and commented later on the rather unfriendly attitude and stinginess of David Ezra, the head of the community, who objected to the financial object of the representative's visit. After lecturing on the work of the World Zionist Organization and its institutions, Cohen was able to help the Calcutta Jews establish a Zionist association of which David Ezra, by way of conciliation, was elected president. He then increased his donation. Calcutta's two leading papers, the *Statesman* and the *Englishman,* published a letter from the Zionist emissary on the Palestine Restoration Fund, the *Statesman* also including a sympathetic editorial note. By dint of a week's canvasing, Israel Cohen was able to raise only fifty thousand rupees, the equivalent of three thousand pounds ($11,640); he felt that this comparatively poor financial result was due to, apart from the initial negativism of Ezra, the absence of several wealthy members of the community, the acute financial depression, and the depreciation of the rupee.

In Bombay, Cohen was welcomed by a very large gathering headed by the presidents of both the BZA and the Bene Israel Zionist Society, as well as by Tolkowsky, whom he described as the unofficial head of the Zionists in Bombay. The emissary addressed four public meetings. The first was attended by representatives of both sections of the community. The second was held at the Sir Jacob Sassoon Free School and attended only by Baghdadis: after his address, donations totaling over five thousand rupees were subscribed. The third meeting, held at Cowasji Jehangir Hall and presided over by Professor Patrick Geddes, the architect and planner of Hebrew University, was attended by Jews and non-Jews. In a lecture entitled "Great Britain, Palestine and the Jews," Cohen explained how Jews the world over had been bound together by ties to the Holy Land. Stressing the tragic history of the Jews since the end of the war, especially in eastern Europe, he discussed how the Zionists were now trying to create in Palestine a place of refuge and a center of Jewish civilization and culture. After appealing for liberal contributions, he received pledges for four thousand rupees.[68]

More than five hundred Bene Israel attended Cohen's fourth public meeting, held at their school. Dr. E. Moses referred in an opening speech to the "colour bar" that, he said, had been raised against the Bene Israel by the other Jews in India and inquired whether there would be similar discrimination in Palestine. Cohen assured them that they would be just as welcome as the Yemenites or any other Eastern Jews who had recently arrived in Palestine, and that their services could be utilized with advantage as engineers or skilled artisans or in other ways. He compared the paradise of Bene Israel life in India with the hell of Jews in eastern Europe. Cohen felt that this meeting was the finest he had addressed in India: over eight thousand rupees were subscribed, the largest donations coming from E. Moses, Jacob Apteker, David Abraham Tarankhopkar, and Dr. Benjamin Reuben, all conference people.[69]

Cohen reported that he found the Bene Israel animated by a keen Jewish consciousness, a love for Jewish learning, and a strong desire to do their share in the national task of restoring the Land of Israel. The young men were the most vocal, asking many questions about the developments in Palestine and especially about the relations between Jewish nationality and the citizenship of the countries in which Jews lived. Perhaps their concern over group identity in the light of Indian nationalism was beginning to emerge.

Cohen also made several personal calls, but the results were unsatisfactory, except in the case of E. D. Sassoon and Company, then headed by Sir Victor Sassoon, from whom he obtained a generous check for one thousand pounds. The rest of the donations in Bombay amounted altogether to fifteen hundred pounds. Cohen had hoped to get a substantial donation from Sir Sassoon David, the wealthiest Jew in Bombay, who had been generous to non-Jewish causes; but, Cohen commented, "he seemed to shelter himself behind the bad example of certain notable Jews in London and refused to give anything for the present."[70]

During this visit, Cohen wrote to the president of the Jewish community at Cochin, asking him to collect donations and forward them. On his return journey aboard the S.S. *China* Cohen, upon request, gave a lecture entitled "The Restoration of Palestine under the British Mandate" to the first-class passengers, who included the maharaja of Patiala and many other Indian government officials and military officers.[71]

Tolkowsky was authorized to collect and transmit all funds raised in Bombay. (Later Zionist emissaries also seemed to have greater faith in European or Palestinian Zionists resident in India than in the local representatives.) But as in all fund-raising, Cohen found that noting down subscribed pledges and collecting the actual funds were two different things, and after his return to London, he devoted much of the next two months to correspondence trying to collect the amounts pledged.[72]

Perhaps Cohen's vision of immigration from the Eastern communities had been a bit premature. The unsuccessful absorption of immigrants from Muslim countries in the early 1920s influenced the World Zionist Organization to reduce organized *aliyah* (immigration to Palestine) from these countries to a minimum. In general, organized Zionist activity in Muslim countries became limited to financial support of the World Zionist Association and the national home. In Iraq, the aim of the Zionist institutions "was not to bring the Jews closer to Zionism and *Eretz-Yisrael* (the Land of Israel), nor Zionist education, nor *aliyah* to *Eretz-Yisrael*, but to get money from Iraq."[73] Zionist leaders in Morocco prior to 1923 integrated Zionism with traditional religious thinking. They believed the Zionist organization was created to "gather the dispersed to go up to Zion" and were ready to participate in financing the national enterprise in Palestine and maintaining the World Zionist Organization, expecting that the organization would arrange their immediate *aliyah* and suitable absorption. When it became clear that this expectation could not be accomplished, the Zionist activists in Morocco discontinued their activities within the framework of the World Zionist Organization.[74]

In November 1921, the BZA launched *Zion's Messenger*, "a family newspaper devoted to Judaism, Zionism, Literature and Science in general and to the mental culture and progress of the Jews in the Orient." This journal was clearly a Baghdadi enterprise. Its editor, Florence Haskell, evidently did not feel the *Israelite* and *Friend of Israel*, which she did read, met the Baghdadis' needs. She hoped that *Zion's Messenger* would consolidate the Jews of Bombay and, in time, of India. The new paper often commented on Bene Israel activities. The first issue, in fact, engaged in an argument with the *Israelite* over which community had contributed more during Cohen's visit. Later, *Zion's Messenger* noted that some of the wealthiest Baghdadis, such as A. Raymond, Sassoon J. David, and the Judahs, had not contributed and urged them to give and to take a personal interest in Zionism so that "the Jews of Bombay and India should not be left behind the rest of the world."[75]

While congratulating the editor on the appearance of this paper, Israel Cohen also commented on several matters in the first issue. The paper had incorrectly reported Russian as having been added as an official language in Palestine. Cohen also corrected its report on the amounts remitted to Keren Hayesod, saying that neither group had settled its account, and that he hoped that the paper, by acknowledging the donations hitherto received, would act as a reminder and impetus to those who had not yet redeemed their pledges.[76]

Late in December 1921, Keren Hayesod sent another emissary, Ariel Bension, who came from a distinguished Sephardic Jewish family of Baghdad and was related to the Sassoons. Cohen urged his successor to try to collect the outstanding pledges from his own visit, to see as many members as possible of the Bene Israel Zionist Society, and to advise the Bombay community to hold regular meetings of these organizations. He added in his letter, however: "I think you should know that the relations between the two societies are not particularly friendly and you will therefore have to be discreet in your conversations with their respective representatives."[77]

After Bension addressed a meeting of the most prominent and influential members of the Baghdadi Jewish community in Arabic, the BZA established a Keren Hayesod committee. Bension was successful in persuading A. J. Raymond, the managing director of E. D. Sassoon and Company, and other respected Baghdadis to become officers; he hoped that others would come forward. Until then the poorer Jews in Byculla seemed to have made more of an effort to contribute to Keren Hayesod than had the richer Fort Jews. Bension also persuaded the Bene Israel Society to agree to collect one hundred thousand rupees over the next five years.[78]

The BZA had other tasks as well. During 1921 it had devoted much of its time to ameliorating the conditions of wartime refugees pouring into Bombay from Bukhara and Anatolia until they could be sent to Palestine. However, when it looked as though they might not be able to go, the Zionist Organization of Persia asked the Bombay Jews to absorb, settle, and assist these refugees rather than send them back to Persia.[79] By the following summer, the Indian press began to devote leading columns to the Palestine mandate, the Rutenburg scheme for the Palestine Electric Corporation, and the Zionists in general. Papers such as the *Morning Post* and the *Advocate of India*, which were sometimes anti-Jewish, might be expected to be anti-Zionist, but even the *Bombay Chronicle* and the *Times of India* were expressing anti-Zionist views. S. J. Haskell, as secretary of the BZA, wrote letters to the *Advocate of India* contradicting some of its statements.[80]

Zionist emissaries might request funds, but the Indian Jews saw the visitors as their personal links to world Jewry and sometimes requested assistance in return. At the end of 1922, the BZA, trying to solve the problem of the lack of trained religious leadership, sent Meyer Moses, a former member of its executive, to London to study for the rabbinate, and asked Israel Cohen to help him as he "was rather poor." When Moses arrived in London, he was quite penniless, had no friends or relatives there, had been given minimal funds by Bombay, and was relying totally on Cohen to make arrangements for his study and keep. Cohen urged Bombay and Calcutta to send money but at the same time tried to arrange for local organizations to give Moses a scholarship for his studies at Jews' College. A few years later, Cohen, who had also helped E. Reuben (a son of Abraham Reuben of Karachi) when he went to England to study engineering, wrote to Victor Sassoon on the young man's behalf when he was seeking employment.[81] Even Cochin recognized a certain authority in the Zionists: in November 1922 the elders of two synagogues in Ernakulam wrote to the president of the English Zionist Federation explaining that they had no spiritual and administrative leadership at the moment and requesting that the federation delegate somebody to reorganize their affairs.[82]

In December 1922, when Belle Pevsner arrived in Bombay as a representative of the Jewish National Fund, she was introduced at a public lecture by Sir Jamsetji Jijibhoy, the Parsi leader, who presided. Although she appealed to the Bene Israel community at the fifth session of the All-India Israelite League to help build the Jewish national home, the league still refused to pass any resolutions on the matter. However, the sixth session of the Bene Israel Conference, meeting at the same time, responded by passing a resolution to help the fund. Meanwhile, some prominent Baghdadis, such as Albert J. Raymond, Jack Raymond, and C. D. Silas, seem to have taken over the leadership of the BZA. It was at this point, in early 1923, that Sassoon J. David made his first donation—five thousand rupees—to the Jewish national institutions.[83]

Though the BZA was active in the early 1920s, it is hard to know what was happening with the Bene Israel Zionist Society. In 1924 Israel Cohen complained that he had had no response from Captain Ezekiel, its secretary, to whom he had written several letters, and wondered if the society was still in existence. *Zion's Messenger* in that year commented that the Jewish community of Poona, including the Bene Israel, showed considerable sympathy to Zionism and that several were members of the BZA.[84]

Zion's Messenger seems to have ceased publication in 1927. In that year, Ben Sargon, an advocate of the High Court and an early Zionist, had become the secretary of the BZA and renewed the correspondence that had also lapsed between the association and Israel Cohen.[85] Now, after a five-year hiatus, Keren Hayesod sent another representative, Dr. Alexander Goldstein, to India. He reminded a meeting of the Bene Israel community of the Balfour Declaration, of the threefold increase in the Jewish population of Palestine, of improvements in the country, and of the Hebrew University. When he appealed for contributions of a *shekel* (one rupee a month) per person, some anti-Zionists called this sum exorbitant and said no one would contribute, as the immediate needs of the community were more urgent. More than fifty Bene Israel did contribute this amount, however. Despite the unemployment and poverty in the community, Goldstein's powerful appeal led them to pledge three thousand rupees payable within three years. At the Eleventh Bene Israel Conference that year, Jacob Apteker, the president, took a jab at the Baghdadis:

During the long period of our stay in India, we as well as our ancestors enjoyed the visits of *shelehim* [*sic*] or emissaries from Jerusalem, but through our ignorance, we never could realize until Mr. Zangwill opened our eyes and convinced us, that they were no better than *schnorrers*. But Cohen, Pevsner and Dr. Goldstein brought us into contact with accredited representatives of foreign Jews and the manner in which they sought our co-operation with Jewish causes is a convincing proof of the deeper sympathy with us, of European Jews, than of our Asiatic brethren.[86]

After revisiting Bombay in late 1928 or early 1929, Bension suggested that the head office maintain contact with the BZA, whose "members were young and enthusiastic, but had no influence whatsoever." Bension wanted copies of all communications addressed to Ben Sargon, the secretary, to be sent to Mr. Davidoff, a young Palestinian Jew in Bombay. Again, the Zionist officials tended to rely on European or Palestinian Jews.[87] But he also summed up his impressions of the situation by the end of the 1920s:

I believe we have cause to congratulate ourselves on a fine success in Bombay, not only because the financial results are so much better than our expectations, but because the atmosphere now, for the first time in our Zionist history, is one of warmth and friendliness. Nearly all the mills have been shut down for almost a year, the poorer section is in dire straits . . . the few rich families . . . are . . . frightened by the class struggle going on in India. . . . The Mohammadans have been holding meetings of sympathy with Palestine Arabs and pledging their support for the Arab Holy Places "which are now threatened by the Jews." Because of this agitation we thought it best to avoid all publicity with regard to the mission and I went about my work, quietly convincing Jews, which made the task longer and more arduous, but productive of good results.[88]

This is the first time that a Zionist emissary to India reported on the political situation within India and its relevance to Palestine. From now on, the Zionists' attention was to be drawn to this aspect with increasing frequency.

Palestine and Indian Politics

If Zionist ideology received a mixed welcome among Indian Jews, its impact on non-Jewish thinkers in India ironically threatened to be of greater consequence for the development of the Palestine situation. While the purpose here is not to explore in detail the development of attitudes of Indians, Muslims and Hindus, toward the Palestine issue, this broader political environment not only attracted the attention and response of Indian Jews but also became a primary focus of concern for the Jewish Agency for Palestine, the organization responsible for Jewish immigration and settlement in Palestine.

Mahatma Gandhi's concept of political interdependence with Muslims and his belief that Muslim and Hindu Indians should form a single state determined his attitude toward Zionism. Supporting the *Khilifat* movement, Gandhi made his first public statement on Zionism in his paper *Young India* on 23 March 1921, writing that since Muslim opinion in India "will not tolerate any non-Muslim influence direct or indirect over the holy places of Islam, the most thorny part of the question" was Palestine. Palestine could not be given to the Jews as a result of the war. They should be permitted to worship freely, but Muslims, who had fought in the last war, should not lose control of Palestine. His statements on the Jewish claims to Palestine went unchallenged at the time. The All-India Muslim League concluded that England had to give up its mandate over Mesopotamia and Palestine. Gideon Shimoni has argued that Gandhi's pro-Khilifat position reflected not any serious concern for the welfare of the Turks or Muslims in general, but merely his concern for Muslim-Hindu relations within India:

> His [Gandhi's] role in the *Khilafat* movement elevated him . . . into a position of great all-Indian political influence with the Muslim League . . . and with the predominantly Hindu Indian Congress leadership because he became the crucial link between the communities. At that time, his guidance of the mass-supported *Khilafat* movement into lines of non-cooperation with the British *raj* enabled him to break out of the conventional framework of Indian politics into wider social, religious and geographical bases of support.[89]

When Kemal Ataturk abolished the caliphate in 1924, the Khilafat movement in India disintegrated. King Husayn of the Hijaz now declared himself caliph, but in the same year, the Wahhabis, lead by Ibn Saud, took Mecca and Medina. The Khilafat now split into pro-Hashimite and pro-Wahhabi factions, the Ali brothers favoring the latter. But despite the dissension, the movement left a legacy of hostility to Zionism in India.[90]

The Jewish Agency became concerned, in the late 1920s and 1930s, about the attitude of Indian Muslims and the possible repercussions on British policy in Palestine. The 1929 disturbances in Palestine that resulted from Arab opposition to Zionism, had attracted much attention among Indian Muslims, and the Zionist executive now asked Bombay Jews to report on Muslim reactions and occasionally sent out its own emissaries both to investigate the situation and to propagate the cause. In April 1930 Gershon Agronsky, a Jewish Agency representative, arrived in Bombay two days before the All-India Muslim Conference on Palestine Affairs opened there. He seized the opportunity to rebut some of the anti-Zionist arguments of the speeches and resolutions as reported in the press. The *Times of India* and the *Daily Mail* published editorials calling the Balfour Declaration a "mistake," although arguing that Britain had to stand behind it. Signing himself "Onlooker," Agronsky managed to have a letter published in these two papers and in the *Bombay Chronicle.*[91]

Meyer Nissim, who had just retired as mayor of Bombay, was very helpful in putting Agronsky in touch with Muslim leaders. Although the Zionist representative realized that there were various shades of Muslim opinion in India, he concluded that the relation of Indian Muslims to the Palestinian Arabs must not be omitted from any consideration of the Islamic problem confronting the Zionist movement. Agronsky believed that most of the Muslims were ignorant of events in Palestine, that a large section of the leadership was indifferent, and that "trafficking with Palestine" was the monopoly of the Khilafat leaders, Shaukat and Muhammad Ali. Nevertheless, he warned, in the hands of a minority wishing to exploit the Palestine question, the issue could be made formidable. The All-India Muslim Conference on Palestine Affairs had paid more attention, as it turned out, to the more immediate problem of Muslim relations to the civil disobedience movement in India, but the Palestine question could be and was used as a rallying point. Agronsky also thought that British opinion in the Bombay Presidency tended to minimalize the agitation in regard to Palestine, even though on 19 April ten thousand people had marched through the streets shouting "Down with the Balfour Declaration." "Palestine Day," 16 May, saw an even larger demonstration. These Palestine days were to become annual events in certain Indian cities. Agronsky saw that Hindu nationalists, when their cause seemed to be served, made overtures to the Muslims on this issue.[92]

Agronsky's analysis of the Zionist situation in Bombay in 1930 was also interesting: he thought that the handful of Jews in Bombay had underrated their own importance. The house of Sassoon was indeed very powerful, and its manager, Albert Raymond, commanded great respect. Raymond and Meyer Nissim were nominally Zionists, he felt—at least they had been contributing to Palestine funds since Bension's visit—but they remained aloof from the workaday Zionists, whose number for a small Jewish population like Bombay was not negligible. Agronsky observed that the upper-class leaders of the Jewish community had ignored earlier attacks on Zionism but now had agreed that this policy of quiescence had been a mistake. That all the English newspapers in Bombay had printed Agronsky's long letter on Zionism was encouraging. He therefore recommended that the trustees of the Jewish community (the Baghdadi trustees of the Sassoon Funds, including Nissim and Raymond) assume responsibility for circulating authentic information about Palestine and Zionist work and for responding to every challenge against Zionism. The political secretary of the Bombay Presidency even agreed that it would be useful for the Palestine government to circulate periodically official information about religious questions that might attract attention or cause agitation in India, since most of the information was coming from the Supreme Muslim Council, Indians who visited Palestine, and the Arabic press. Finally, Agronsky recommended that the Zionist organization should "consider without delay what measures could be taken so that Zionism could turn its face . . . to the East to spread proper information about Palestine."[93]

Possibly responding to Agronsky's urging, Joseph Sargon launched the *Jewish Bulletin* (later known as the *Jewish Advocate*, and then as the *Jewish Tribune*) in 1930. Dr. Chaim Weizmann, head of the Jewish Agency and Zionist executive, responded to Sargon's request for a special message to the Jews of India:

> We need the help of the Jews in India particularly in one respect: as they live in the East among diversified races and religions, they can appreciate more deeply than is often done in the West, the special problems connected with the upbuilding of a Jewish community in an Eastern land. They must explain the meaning and true aspirations of Zionism to fellow citizens in the vast realm of India.[94]

Weizmann asked for help in clearing up misunderstandings, especially among Indian Muslims, whom he thought would become friends if they knew the facts. Leo Herrmann, secretary of the board of Keren Hayesod, also welcomed the *Jewish Bulletin* as an organ to dispel ignorance about Zionism and about the building of the Jewish national home among Indian Jewry. Sargon, meanwhile, felt that Indian Jews had done nothing worthy of mention for the development of Palestine, but they could not excuse themselves on the grounds of financial limitation, backwardness, and small population. He urged them to explain the beneficial effect of the work in Palestine on all the inhabitants, so that the sixty million Muslims in India should not exploit the position of their coreligionists in Palestine to wring concessions from the government for themselves.[95]

The paper also campaigned vigorously for greater contributions to the Jewish National Fund (Keren Keyemet L'Israel), especially on the part of the rich, deploring the attitude that Jews elsewhere would look after the Jewish National Fund and that therefore Bombay Jewish charity should look after local needs. The contributions collected from the blue Jewish National Fund boxes were reported periodically, and the paper urged that instead of giving Sepher Torahs to synagogues in memory of the departed, Bombay Jews give donations to the fund, or buy trees or land or inscriptions in the Golden Book of the Jewish National Fund. People were also encouraged to leave money to the fund in their wills.[96]

Although led by pro-British Baghdadis, the BZA and the *Jewish Bulletin* (*Advocate*) took a lively interest in political developments in Palestine and recorded their indignation at a policy that diverged from that originally intended by Balfour and the British government. Reacting strongly to the pro-Arab tilt of the Passfield White Paper of 1930, the BZA cabled a protest to Prime Minister Ramsey MacDonald. When the *Times of India* alleged that

Zionist policy was aggravating economic conditions in Palestine, David I. Sargon, brother of Joseph and Benjamin, and general secretary of the BZA, defended the Balfour Declaration, arguing that the Arabs had not found their economic status slowly but definitely undermined. His letter was printed, as was S. S. Koder's similar letter to the *Madras Mail* criticizing that journal's approval of the Passfield White Paper. The *Jewish Bulletin* (*Advocate*), meanwhile, strongly opposed the white paper, Joseph Sargon noting that Stanley Baldwin, David Lloyd George, Austen Chamberlain, and other leading British statesmen had also disapproved of the document. The paper reprinted a number of important documents in this period: Weizmann's letter to Lord Passfield of 20 October 1930, resigning as head of the Jewish Agency and Zionist executive; a letter to the editor of the *London Times* from Sir John Simon stating that the British policy represented in the Passfield White Paper was a departure from the obligations of the mandate; Ramsey MacDonald's famous letter to Weizmann interpreting the white paper, and Weizmann's acceptance of it; and finally, the revisionists' analysis. Sargon himself did not accept MacDonald's interpretation and still felt that British policy had been reversed.[97]

Later in 1931, when the Labour government fell and Lord Passfield had to retire from active politics, the *Jewish Advocate* expressed satisfaction, saying that Passfield's obstruction of the Zionist movement since his appointment to office had resulted in the loss of Jewish confidence in the Labour government and in Weizmann's resignation. Although the Sargons appreciated Weizmann's contribution to the Zionist movement and knew that he would play an important part in the future, they felt that his moderation had hurt the movement and that he had been an instrument of betrayal. Later, they softened their views toward him.[98]

As Agronsky had realized, the leading Muslim anti-Zionists in India were the Ali brothers, who had led the Khilafat movement. After Muhammad Ali died in March 1931 (he was buried in Jerusalem), his brother Shaukat continued to back the Arabs against the Zionists. He visited Palestine and spoke with many Muslim and Jewish officials, including the mufti, Haj al-Amin, who had particularly impressed him. Shaukat Ali praised the mufti to Sir John Chancellor, the high commissioner of Palestine, saying that Indian Muslims regarded the mufti as the leader of all Muslims. Shaukat Ali was convinced that the Jews wanted to take over not only Palestine, but much of the Middle East. He dreamed of raising funds in Muslim countries to build a Muslim university in Jerusalem and even possibly of establishing a Muslim caliphate in that city. He also regarded the agitation against Indians in South Africa as the work of Jewish traders who, finding themselves displaced by Indians, wished the latter to be expelled from the country.[99]

Some of the Zionists tried to respond to Shaukat Ali's statements and accusations. In reply to a *Times of India* article, David Sargon argued that the Muslim leader was ignorant of the situation in Palestine, was distorting facts, and was working against the efforts of the authorities to promote good-will among Jews and Arabs. J. J. Gubbay, another leading Bombay Baghdadi Zionist, disputed claims Ali had made, advising him not to worry about foreign politics but to devote himself to India and the Indian cause.[100]

In March 1932, upon his return from the Muslim Congress convened by the mufti in Palestine, Ali granted an exclusive interview to the *Jewish Advocate* in which, once again, he denounced Zionism as upsetting the thirteen hundred years of friendship between Muslims and Jews. He also accused the Zionists of abusing the Arabs in the European press. The Jews got the Balfour Declaration, he claimed, because they had helped the British in World War I and had taken advantage of the weakness of the Arabs. Ali predicted that war would break out between Arabs and Jews, and that Muslims would fight against Jewish statehood. Sargon responded by repeating the usual arguments about Jewish colonization having improved the welfare of the Arabs, but the editor also mistakenly claimed that aside from the Palestine disturbances of 1929 instigated by the mufti, there had been no signs of hatred between Jews and Arabs, who lived in the friendliest manner, and that any signs of dis-content were due to the anti-Zionist propaganda carried on by the mufti.[101]

Indian Zionism in the Early 1930s

In the early thirties, the BZA had an uphill fight. Through its organ, the *Jewish Advocate*, it continually urged Bombay Jews to give more, reminding them that as a result of the Depression, the World Zionist Organization was now receiving less from Jews in affluent countries. The association held dances to benefit the Jewish National Fund and ran meetings, which were not always as well attended as the members had hoped. A few young, en-thusiastic members, such as the three Sargon brothers, J. J. Gubbay, and E. S. Somekh, carried the biggest share of the work.[102]

In 1931 a Zionist from Rangoon suggested that an Indian Zionist federation be formed by the branch associations in Cochin, Bombay, Calcutta, and his own city. Such a federation could consolidate the movement in India, he suggested, at a time when anti-Zionist feeling was growing among the Indian Muslims. Several leading Zionists, including some of the officers of the BZA and S. S. Koder, the leader of the Cochin Jewish community, supported the idea. A united Indian Zionist federation could address the public through speeches and statements to the press, help increase Indian Jewry's contri-bution to the various Zionist organizations, and perhaps encourage *halutzim* (pioneers) from India and Burma to settle in Palestine. They could even send a representative to the World Zionist Organization. Shanghai's news-paper, *Israel's Messenger*, approved of the idea, and also suggested that the

World Zionist Organization send an emissary to establish an office in India and act as the leader of Indian Zionism. Other Zionists, including David Sargon, secretary of the BZA, argued that the concept was impractical because the individual organizations were too small to warrant such a federation. Officials of the central office in London, responding to a query from Sargon, said that they were not well enough aquainted with conditions in India to give a definite opinion, but that a centralized federation was useful in a country, such as Australia, where Zionist societies were scattered. They also remarked, disapprovingly, that for the last few years there had been "scarcely any contact worth mentioning" between the various Zionist groups in India and the London organization, and that the sale of the *shekel* seemed to have ended. Help was needed, they concluded, but whether or not it should be in the form of a federation, the local Zionists would have to decide.[103]

In an editorial entitled "Zionism, Why Is It So Lean in India?" the *Jewish Advocate* argued that the "greatest minds of World Jewries spent their lives fighting for Zionism, while Indian Jewry goes aimlessly through life with no worthy object before it." It acknowledged that Indian Jewry was living in the "far-flung East, where we do not even hear the beat of the Jewish heart" and was far away from the world Jewish problems that brought others closer to Zionism. Perhaps those who lived in India, the editorial continued, did not realize fully the benefits of Zionism, not having witnessed pogroms, discrimination, and anti-Semitism. The editorial criticized those who, while saying that they had no time to propagate the Zionist ideal in India, took an active interest in civic affairs that did not concern the local Jewish community.[104]

Certain non-European Jews opposed or ignored Zionism because they believed it would help only Ashkenazi Jews. In Syria, for example, between the wars there were small Zionist organizations and small *Hechalutz* groups (young Jewish pioneers), with more activity in Damascus than in Aleppo, but in general the Syrians saw Zionism as an Ashkenazi movement and were thus ambivalent.[105] In Morocco, a major Zionist debate persisted over whether Moroccan Jews should strive for *aliyah* to Palestine or for assimilation in Morocco (then a French protectorate), helping the Zionist movement through fund-raising.[106] The *Jewish Advocate* ridiculed the Sephardis' excuses and reported with great pride that Sir Percival David, the son of Sassoon J. David, and a patron of Middle Eastern and East Asian art and archaeology, had endowed a chair in this field at Hebrew University in memory of his late father. Although Sargon realized that Jews in India could not claim any credit for this generosity, he hoped that since Sassoon J. David had been born and spent most of his life in India, the act would be a model for other Indian Jews. Also in this period, a Bene Israel of Calcutta, a Mr. Meyer, left twenty thousand rupees (about two thousand pounds) for the purchase of property in Jerusalem, the income from which was to benefit poor Jews.[107]

One hears very little of Bene Israel Zionism in the early 1930s. Perhaps this silence is because they had no journal of their own; yet since the Sargons were so interested in the Bene Israel and reported on many of their other functions, they would probably have mentioned Zionist activities as well, had they occurred. Perhaps their Zionist organization had died out at this time. The central office of the World Zionist Organization in London obviously suspected the same thing. Clearly the central office wondered how to prime the Indian pump in general. No delegate had been sent to India since Bension's last visit because of the expense and trouble involved. Personal letters were addressed to Isaac David and Albert Raymond, explaining the dire financial straits of the movement—the work of immigration, colonization, and education was being jeopardized, teachers not having received their salaries for months—and urging them to contribute generously. Israel Cohen continued to correspond with Indian Jews, encouraging them to buy *shekels* and to contribute to Keren Hayesod. The central office soon realized that if it wished to rekindle the enthusiasm of Indian Jews, it would have to send another emissary. The choice fell upon Adolph Myers of Keren Hayesod.[108]

Myers's arrival in Bombay, in November 1932, was to have a pronounced impact on the Zionist movement of that city, not all of it positive. Myers turned out to be an energetic, charismatic young man whose eloquent writing and speeches greatly impressed people. His purpose was not only to raise money, but also to arouse the Indian Jews' Jewish consciousness. Soon after Myers's arrival, Joseph Sargon extolled his virtues:

> We have known English Jews, cultured Jews, idealistic Jews, Jews with charm, modesty, power of self-expression, but we have never known a Jew that possessed all these qualities and characteristics at one and the same time.[109]

In an effort to win over the reticent, Myers, in a speech to a large and representative gathering at the Fort synagogue, exclaimed:

> Zionism is not a charity. Did you think for one moment that I had come to *beg*, either for myself or for the people, the Jews of Palestine? I certainly do not need your money; nor do they. Though poor, they are rich, far richer than you; rich in the joy and contentment that comes from a sense of common achievement and the common pursuit of a selfless ideal. It is not in *their* name that I come to ask your help and support, but in the name of the whole Jewish people and in the name of generations of Jews yet unborn. It is not others that I ask you to have a care for, but fundamentally, it is for yourselves and your children and your own future as Jews.[110]

This speech created a profound impression upon its hearers and was probably prophetic; most likely the children of many of Myers's listeners did find themselves in Palestine some twenty or thirty years later.

Sensitive to the growing Indian nationalist movement, Myers also gave a public lecture on India and Palestine at Sir Cowasji Jehangir Hall, with V. N. Chandavarkar, then mayor of Bombay, in the chair. At the outset, Myers claimed that he spoke not as an Englishman, but as a Jew coming from the Jewish homeland, and that he spoke on India as an outsider. He proceeded to draw a parallel between Hindus and Jews: more ancient, with a longer history than any other people, both were now coming to a new realization of their historic destiny. But whereas the people of India were at least living on their own soil, the sixteen million Jews were scattered. Both were ruled by Great Britain and both had to work out their relationship to this power. Myers suggested that although dominion status with the greatest possible internal autonomy would ultimately be the most suitable form of government for both, neither country would be ready until it could prevent the small landowning class and self-seeking politicians from establishing an autocracy. He saw the same problems of poverty and indebtedness among the Hindu masses and Arab *fellaheen* (peasants).

Chandavarkar, meanwhile, took the opportunity to point out that the Jews of Bombay had no cause to complain of any differentiation or anti-Semitism and that they were well known to be among the most loyal and most generous of Bombay's citizens. He extolled the Jews for their contributions toward civic welfare, their occupation of eminent positions, and their magnanimity toward cosmopolitan charities. Reflecting current views on communalism, the mayor pointed out with pride that, unlike other minority communities in India, the Jews relied on their own ability and did not seek special representation with safeguards in the new constitution that was being formed.[111] Many Jews who heard these speeches must have experienced a dilemma: with whom should they identify, Indians or Zionists?

Myers went to Bene Israel meetings and rallies and delivered a well-attended lecture on Zionism and Judaism at the Bene Israelite Young Zionist Association meeting. Jacob Ezekiel, the chairman, described the precarious financial position position of the Bene Israel community and regretted the inability of its members to contribute as much as they had in the past, when they had been more prosperous. A Bene Israel Keren Hayesod committee was formed to clear the Jewish National Fund boxes more regularly.[112]

Although Myers formed close friendships with the few stalwart workers of the BZA, he was disappointed to find that most of the leaders of Bombay Jewry held aloof. Once again, a Zionist emissary urged the wealthy Baghdadis, who until now had taken minimal interest, to participate and contribute. The middle-class Baghdadis were still giving proportionately more. Yet Myers purposely did not apply to the Sassoon trust funds for contributions so as not to appear to be competing with local charity needs.

Meanwhile, in order to dispel the notion that Sephardic Jews were not welcome in Palestine,[113] and to invalidate an excuse for not giving, the Jewish Agency reserved ten immigration certificates for Bombay Jews who wanted to come as *halutzim,* even though their need was recognized as far less than that of Jews from eastern Europe. If the Sephardic Jews of Bombay felt themselves neglected, Myers maintained, it was only because of their failure to organize their resources for Zionism and their general lack of initiative.[114]

Nevertheless, Myers's visit was considered an unparalleled success, with better results in Bombay than elsewhere. By December 1932 he had raised 14,000 rupees (6,500 in cash and the rest in pledges), whereas the previous delegate, Ariel Bension, had obtained a total of 9,500 rupees over a three-year period, nearly half of the sum from the Lady Rachel Sassoon Trust Fund. Although some prominent, wealthy Baghdadis declined to contribute, Keren Hayesod was very pleased with the tremendous help Joseph Sargon and the *Advocate* gave to Myers and his mission. Myers, in turn, concluded that the small lights to counter the gloomy economic and spiritual life of the Jews in Bombay were the BZA, the Zionist sports club, and the *Jewish Advocate.* The life of the community was so unorganized and so uncared for, he felt, that the newspaper was essential if all contact among its members themselves and between its members and the outside world was not to be broken off.[115]

Early in 1933, however, the honeymoon between Myers and the Sargons ended. Returning from his campaign in Rangoon and Calcutta to Bombay, Myers suddenly resigned as the official delegate of Keren Hayesod, having realized, he claimed, that the organization's method of fund-raising (trying hard to get money from the wealthy Jewish leaders of the Diaspora) was out of date. He wanted to do something more radical along the lines of cultural Zionism, feeling that it was more important to remain in the Diaspora and try to bring Zionism to the youth, the masses, and the middle classes. Myers had stressed the importance of pioneers in the Diaspora and now wanted to form a nucleus of young people in Bombay who would give their own lives to building up those of their people. He named his movement the Herzlian Brotherhood. Its members would live in a kibbutzlike style, with only the barest necessities, as Jewish missionaries to the *Galut* (Exile) and would donate 10 percent of their income to Keren Hayesod. They were to educate themselves in Zionism and to make a trip to Palestine, then return to devote their lives to the uplift of the local community. Eventually, two "pioneers" from Bombay, David J. Gubbay and Norman H. Hillel, joined his movement. Joseph Sargon suggests that the real reason for Myers's resignation, however, was that he was offered a job with the *Times of India* and preferred to remain in India. The *Times* paid Europeans handsome salaries, and Myers had been recognized in Bombay as a brilliant writer and orator. The Sargons were disillusioned, feeling that it was wrong for Myers not to go back to Palestine, and that he was staying in India purely for his own personal interest and for the money.[116]

Myers's resignation now caused a serious breach in the BZA, which had only twenty-two members toward the end of 1932. There had been a disagreement over forming a federation of Indian Zionists: the Sargons felt it was premature, while others, including Myers, thought it could be done. The Sargons, along with E. S. Somekh, another early founder, resigned from the BZA, which was totally reorganized. A dispute then arose over the ownership of the *Jewish Advocate*, which Joseph Sargon had founded and edited for three years, receiving a subsidy from Keren Hayesod and the Jewish National Fund for its work as the Jewish voice in India. The Zionist executive asked Sargon to continue as a member of the BZA and retain the editorship of the *Jewish Advocate*, subject to the journal reflecting the policy of the association and being under its control. When Sargon rejected those terms, the BZA established a new organ, still named the *Jewish Advocate*, forcing Sargon to change the name of his own paper to the *Jewish Tribune*. Keren Hayesod and the Jewish National Fund now switched their subsidy to the new *Jewish Advocate*, edited by J. F. Haskell. This new *Jewish Advocate*, in a different format, remained the organ of the BZA, became a fortnightly instead of a monthly, and was now sent free to all association members. Those staying with the BZA included J. F. Haskell, Norman Hillel, and David and J. J. Gubbay. The new leaders of the BZA were interrelated.[117]

According to Joseph Sargon, Myers urged the *Jewish Tribune* to promote the immediate establishment of a federation and to endorse his own candidacy as delegate to the next Zionist congress on behalf of Indian Jewry, an idea firmly opposed by the Bombay Baghdadi leaders.[118] For a while, Myers remained an influential figure among the Zionists, persuading new people to enroll in the BZA so that, by May 1933, it had ninety-three members. His wife joined him from England and established a branch of the Women's International Zionist Organization (WIZO) in Bombay. Together, the Myerses formed a children's class in Hebrew and opened a reading room that stocked many periodicals. They also arranged a study trip to Palestine for the Herzlian Brotherhood, but only Adolph Myers, David J. Gubbay, and Norman H. Hillel went. Eventually, Myers disassociated himself from Zionist activities in Bombay, and was no longer even mentioned in the *Jewish Advocate*, which must also have become disillusioned with him.[119]

Just before giving up the *Jewish Advocate* to start the *Jewish Tribune*, Sargon had criticized British policy in Palestine in an editorial objecting to the Shaw, French, and Hope Simpson commissions that had been sent to investigate there. They had been expensive, he argued, and produced only inaccurate, pernicious findings. Efforts should go instead into the work of building up Palestine. But Sargon was not alone in criticizing the British. With Hitler's

rise to power in Germany in 1933, the *Jewish Advocate,* under its new editorship, voiced dismay that the Palestine government, at this moment of
urgent need, had reduced the number of immigration certificates deemed
necessary by the *Va'ad Leumi* (National Council) by 50 percent. With the
economic position of Palestine better than it had ever been, the *Advocate* saw
no need for such restrictions. It also counseled against noncooperation on
the part of either Arabs or Jews, criticizing the Arabs who hoped thereby to
stop Jewish immigration and land purchase, and Jewish extremists who
thought they could obtain increased Jewish immigration and land acquisition.
Instead, the *Advocate* urged, Jews and Arabs should cooperate with the government and with each other.[120]

This theme of cooperation was reiterated by Jacob B. Israel, the now
elderly Bene Israel leader who in 1919 had opposed Zionism because of Arab
opposition, but who by the 1930s seemed to have modified his view. When
Shaukat Ali presented a plan for improving the conditions of Arabs in Palestine and Transjordan, he coupled it with a scheme to oust the Jews from
Palestine. Israel thought Shaukat Ali would do better to advise the Arabs to
work in amity with the Jews, who could develop the deserts. Arab advancement would be possible only by learning from and copying the great work
the Jews were doing in Palestine. "As a matter of fact," Israel wrote, "the lot
of the Arabs in Palestine had never been as happy as it now is by the advent
of the Jews under Zionism."[121] While the observations and protests of these
writers were similar to those being expressed by Zionist sympathizers the
world over, they do indicate that a few Jewish voices in India followed developments in Palestine carefully and had the courage to speak up, even if it
meant criticizing the British.

Indian Politics and Palestine: The Mid Thirties

The Jewish Agency was not alone in its concern about Indian Muslims.
The government of India also watched their attitude carefully. The 1929
disturbances in Palestine had indeed given rise to Muslim agitation in India,
but the government had felt that it was moderate and that, except for holding
meetings where the position of the British government was condemned, Indian Muslims had had no serious reaction. In 1933–34, as immigration to
Palestine from Germany increased, the general view of moderate Muslims
was definitely against making Palestine into a home for the Jews because such
a policy was bound to come into conflict with the economic as well as political
interests of the Arabs. In 1933, an unidentified Muslim who held an important
office in the government of India summarized Muslim feelings:

> Losing lands by sale, unemployment on the increase, no local self-govern-
> ment to speak of . . . [the] Arab condition has continued to deteriorate;
> and now that these matters have come to the notice of the Muslims in India,

feeling has grown that Christian Europe is under financial obligations to the Jewish financial magnates and at their dictation is pursuing a policy of discharging [these obligations] by depriving Arabs of homes and creating a situation which for years to come will be a source of trouble to the civilised world and create bitterness between Muslims and the West.[122]

Certainly Muslims were becoming more vocal. At the twenty-third session of the All-India Muslim League held in Delhi in November 1933, both Haji Rashid Ahmad, chairman of the reception committee, and Hafiz Hidayat Husain, president of the league, identified Indian Muslim interests with those of the Arabs, stating that British imperial interests themselves required that the Balfour Declaration immediately be scrapped. "I hope," said Husain, "that the Government of India will not fail to impress on His Majesty's Government the intensity of feeling created by the present happenings in Palestine among the Muslims the world over, and practically among all Asiatic races."[123] The session adopted a resolution emphatically protesting the policy of trying to make Palestine the Jewish national home and asking the viceroy to convey to the British government the demand of Indian Muslims that the Balfour Declaration be withdrawn.[124]

That same month, a deputation alerted the viceroy to the growing feeling among Muslims in India that British policy was to keep Muslim nations subordinate in order to further imperial interests. Muslim opinion was equally disturbed at the prospect of Jews ousting Arabs from a country whose holy places, in particular Jerusalem, were second in Muslim estimation only to Mecca. The deputation warned that the Hindu Congress party press was using these points to undercut the proven loyalty of the Muslims of India to the British crown. The Jews would soon dispossess the Arabs and place them in a position of permanent inferiority. In sum, the deputation insisted, His Majesty's government should review the whole matter.[125]

In January 1934 the Muslim Religious Congress in Jerusalem drafted a memorandum to arouse the support of Muslims in other countries against Jewish domination. Concerned about this development, the India Office asked the government of India to report on the reactions in India, if any. Although the memorandum was also designed to arouse feelings against the British government for assisting the Jews to oust the Arabs from Palestine, there seemed to be little agitation in India. The government thought that the propaganda either was not being conducted in India or, if it was, was eliciting no response from Muslims there. A bit of propaganda was apparently reaching Afghanistan, however, and trickling into India.[126] Nevertheless, the All-India Muslim League Council, meeting in April 1934, passed a resolution recommending that "a strong and influential deputation wait on the Viceroy" to explain how the Balfour Declaration had "ruined the peace of the Sacred Land."[127] There is no indication of whether a deputation actually did so.

Conclusion

The growth of Zionism offered the possibility of yet another identity to the Jews of India, but the problems between the communities extended into the Zionist arena. Two separate Zionist associations emerged, although the Bene Israel organization often floundered. Zionist fund-raisers were frustrated on both ends of the spectrum: the Bene Israel had very little to give, and the wealthy Baghdadis balked. The Baghdadis might identify with Jews elsewhere in the British Empire and demand equal treatment, but they did not identify sufficiently with (Ashkenazi) Jewish concerns to support Zionism. Only a few middle-class Baghdadis remained consistently interested in Zionism, expressing a strong identification with Jews elsewhere. Soon, however, the Zionist executive had a more pressing problem in India than fund-raising: that of the broader political situation, which would surely have important ramifications. In some ways, the Zionists were more concerned with the attitude of the Indian Muslims than that of Indian Jews.

The question of Jewish identity, complicated within the context of the growing Indian nationalist and Zionist movements, really came to a head in the next years, fostered by the advent of Hitler and increasing anti-Semitism, and the consequent arrival of central European refugees in India. At the same time, events in Palestine were also reaching a critical point in 1936–39, with the government of India becoming increasingly responsive. With war around the corner, the Indian nationalists saw remarkable opportunities to press their case. How would the Jews respond to these converging events?

CHAPTER 6

A HEIGHTENED
JEWISH CONSCIOUSNESS

Jews everywhere were frightened by the course of events in Nazi Germany, the rise of Fascist parties throughout Europe, and the deteriorating situation in Palestine. Such events were bound to affect the political consciousness of Indian Jews and their sense of identity as members of a worldwide religio-ethnic minority. An increasing stream of central European Jewish refugees seeking shelter in India required the local communities to mobilize support to sustain them and to keep the doors open. Suddenly the goals of the Zionist movement and the need for a Jewish homeland seemed more relevant and urgent; those who had held aloof now had to reassess their position. Gandhi's pronouncements on nonviolence as related to the Jews of Germany and on Palestine compounded the matter. At the same time, however, developments within India, such as the implementation of the Government of India Act of 1935, the coming to power of Congress in 1937, and the high unemployment generated by the Depression, competed for the attention of the Jewish community.

As formulated in the Government of India Act of 1935, Britain's policy on communalism, in both political rights and patronage, required the governor to safeguard the "legitimate interests" of racial and religious communities for which "special representation is accorded in the Legislature" and of small or disadvantaged classes, and to secure for them "a due proportion of appointments in our Services."[1] Not only did Jews have no special representation *qua* Jews in any of the legislatures (they had not demanded it), but the government's policy of giving preference in the services to Muslims, other recognized minority communities, and the intermediate and scheduled (backward) classes worked to their disadvantage. As noted above, the Bene Israel were not included as an official "minority community" and, after 1937, were classified as advanced.[2]

Safeguarding
Jewish Interests in India

In 1937 Dr. Elijah Moses, a Bene Israel physician, was elected mayor of Bombay. In 1913, supported by Pherozeshah Mehta, the Parsi leader, Moses had been nominated by the government as a member of the Bombay Municipal Corporation. But, having at one point criticized the policy of the governor in primary education, he lost his seat in 1918. Moses became, in 1925, the first Bene Israel actually to be elected to this body.[3] In successive terms, Moses focused his concern on issues relating to public health, the City Improvement Trust, and the Opium Enquiry Committee. He first ran for mayor unsuccessfully in 1933.

Moses was never officially associated with the Congress party or the nationalists. In the municipal corporation he was an independent member of what was called the "Progressive Group," which was connected with the liberal party or with neutrals. According to B. J. Israel, in his drive to be elected mayor, Moses began supporting Congress but never joined the party. Thus, when the turn came again, in 1937, to elect someone other than a Hindu, Parsi, or Muslim, he won, defeating two Christians, because of political manipulation and the support he got from the nationalists. But his convictions were never as strong as those of the Erulkars. He favored a neutral stance because he felt many Bene Israel depended heavily on government service. After all, he had been the leader of the group that in 1917 had said there should be no politics of any kind in the communal conference.[4] Perhaps the experience of losing his government-nominated seat in 1918 because he was too outspoken reinforced this belief. In any case, Moses did don a Gandhi cap when he was elected mayor in 1937.

The Jews were very proud of Moses' success.[5] He was actually the first Jew to be styled officially as mayor, because only recently had the president of the Bombay Municipality been thus designated. On 20 June 1937, the Bene Israel presented Moses with a congratulatory address:

> That you, a member of a microscopically small Community, should have been elevated to the dignity of the first citizen of Bombay, is evidence of the unique position the Bene Israel community holds in the estimation of the general public and is due recognition of the meritorious services rendered by you to the city in the past.[6]

Moses replied:

> I have not been a noisy or a vocal member of the Corporation for reasons more in the interests of the community than of myself. However, I openly profess my leanings towards the nationalist views. India is the land of our adoption and I submit that we cannot go counter to . . . [her] aspirations. . . . At the same time, we cannot non-cooperate with Government. We must

be both patriotic and loyal. . . . Unless we assert ourselves and take active part in elections and offer ourselves as candidates, our community will never rise in the esteem of other communities in this country.[7]

In presenting the address, I. J. Samson had also referred to the problem of unemployment in the community, hoping that Moses would use his influence to help. To this point Moses replied that he could not do as much for the large number of people who had approached him for job recommendations as he had hoped. He recommended that young people seek higher academic qualifications or take up technical, commercial, or vocational training. The new mayor also felt that the non-Jewish corporators should ensure that the corporation gave members of his minority community a chance.[8]

The Bene Israel were not the only ones concerned about employment opportunities in this period. In an era when communal patronage was still important and the Indian nationalists were demanding more and more opportunities, those minority communities that had benefited from British preference were frightened. The Anglo-Indians represent a very good case in point. By the latter half of the nineteenth century, Anglo-Indians had surpassed most Indians in income and could count on steady, dependable earnings in occupations controlled by the British. They were ill prepared for the greater economic competition resulting from the Indianization of the services in the 1920s, and their prosperity declined. During these years, the community had an outstanding spokesman in the person of Sir Henry Gidney, who, as a prominent member of the Central Legislative Assembly at Delhi, defended the interests and rights of the Anglo-Indians. He led deputations before the secretary of state for India and the Simon Commission and represented the Anglo-Indians at the round table conferences in London. As a result of the efforts of Sir Henry, the government of India in 1934 affirmed the right of Anglo-Indians to certain percentages of reserved jobs in the railways, telegraphs, and customs services.[9]

The Calcutta Baghdadis also felt threatened. Having failed in their efforts to be recognized as Europeans for electoral purposes, their emphasis shifted to the question of communal rights as Jews. In 1937 Isaac David launched a controversy when he wrote a series of articles for the *Jewish Tribune,* which were reproduced by the *Calcutta Statesman.* David lamented

> the absence of any agitation on the part of the Jewish people in India to present their case before the Simon Commission when everybody else, Hindus, Muslims, Indian Christians, Parsees and others, belonging both to the majority and minority communities, were fighting tooth and nail to gain seats for themselves in the Lower Houses of the various Indian Legislatures.[10]

As a result, he argued, the Jews were not represented at all in any of the lower houses, either directly or indirectly with any of the other communities in India, and the interests of all classes would be undermined. David disagreed with those Jews who thought they were already very powerful and influential without that representation. The Jews needed to safeguard their rights as an important and influential minority community, just as Anglo-Indians had done. Like Anglo-Indians, they had joined hands with the British and fought for them, in the Indian defense and other expeditionary forces. Thus the Jews had a very strong claim on the British government for adequate protection of their liberties and rights and their significance in the country.[11]

Finally, David argued that if the Jews did not agitate for themselves now, their claims would probably be lost forever when Indian independence came. "Now we can count on the British Government for support," he maintained, "but what would happen if a greater bulk of the powers are given to the Indians?" David urged that now that the Jews of Bengal had failed to gain European recognition for themselves, all the Jews in India should present their case jointly to Parliament, requesting communal rights:

> Just as English Jews struggled to get their rights and recognition from Government in England, and have really contributed greatly to England, Jews of India must do the same here. Nothing must be spared to get our rights and privileges to live in India with safety and peace with our non-Jewish brethren recognized. We need a permanent settlement of the Jewish question in India. We must contribute our manpower and resources in time of trouble to the Government, just as the Bene Israel did in the past.[12]

This is one of the strongest statements of the unity and distinctiveness of the Jewish community in India that one finds from Baghdadis.

The issue of whether Jews could trust the Indian National Congress to protect their rights was obviously controversial. In 1931 a joint meeting of Baghdadis and Bene Israel in Bombay had voted not to request separate communal representation. Dr. E. Moses now realized that with the growth of political consciousness among all sections of the Indian public, the Jews must consider how to secure for their community a proper share in the administration of the provinces and the country as a whole. He felt, however, that the best route would be to implement the reformed constitution in cooperation with the major communities in the country. "This spirit of harmony and good feeling, I have no doubt," he wrote, "will secure for us a proper position in the economy and polity of the country to which we are entitled."[13] This statement may sound like a plea from a mayor anxious to avoid turmoil, but this position was apparently supported by the Bene Israel journalist I. A. Isaac, who felt that the Jews were "on top" in India and could afford to trust and cooperate with other Indians because India had already tolerated them. If they now asked for special seats, they would look like ingrates. Some Bene Israel, Isaac pointed out, took a prominent part in Congress to show their gratitude.[14]

Isaac David countered that the Jewish poor and middle classes were not "on top" and challenged I. A. Isaac to point to an instance where Jewish boys were taken into government service without some prejudice. When Jews applied for police service, they were told that such posts as sergeants were reserved only for Europeans and Anglo-Indians. This was racial discrimination, David argued.[15] Dr. Moses also recognized that the Bene Israel's chances of admission into government service were "few and far between," and that the struggle for existence had become very difficult.[16]

Aware of the concerns of the minorities, the Congress Working Committee, meeting in Calcutta at the end of October 1937, passed a long resolution formulating its policy on minority rights.[17] In a letter to the *Jewish Tribune*, Isaac David quoted Mohammad Ali Jinnah, in the negotiations between the Muslim League and Congress, as saying that the most vital issue concerning the Muslims and other minorities in India at that time was preserving their rights and interests, especially in view of the introduction of a democratic form of government. David commented:

> It appears . . . that there is already a suspicion of the minority communities in the ultimate good faith of the majority community, and since such a community as the Muslims entertain fear for their future, what are we going to do to ensure our own existence if we are to leave everything in the hands of the major community without getting our own individual rights recognized or formally joining hands with them as Indians?[18]

I. A. Isaac wrote a strong response to David's critique:

> Our community is a microscopic minority and our economic and political interests are in common with the majority community. We have not been recognized in the Indian Act as a minority and are free to seek representation through several constituencies. . . . Our first duty under the circumstances is to create national consciousness by joining the Congress as moderates and fighting for our rights on constitutional lines. . . . Within the Congress we will have immense opportunities and abundance of goodwill for redressing our grievances.[19]

I. A. Isaac asked Isaac David what sacrifices the Jews had made in the present political struggle for freedom to assert their rights so glibly. He suggested that David learn a lesson from the Parsis, who were as much founders of the Congress as the Hindus, had contributed great leaders such as Dadabhai Naoroji, Pherozeshah Mehta, and K. F. Nariman, and yet had asked nothing for themselves as a community.[20] Although David said that he was not against the existing principles of the Congress, which were "in essence purely a non-violence theory," he strongly disapproved of the idea of the Jews breaking away from their loyalty and attachment to the British throne. He reiterated that the Jews throughout the British dominions so far had been working in the interests of the crown and had refrained from taking part in any movement or joining with any other nationals against the government.[21]

These opposing political views may well have reflected communal membership. I. A. Isaac, a Bene Israel—though long resident among Baghdadis in Calcutta—quite possibly identified more with other Indians and therefore trusted them more than did David, a Baghdadi, who perhaps considered himself an "outsider" and felt less confident about his future under Indian rule than under British rule.

Another Bene Israel, Hyam David Hyams, of Ahmedabad, also supported Isaac, arguing that the Congress did not represent any Hindu or Muslim cause but stood for the birthright of every Indian, especially since it had repeatedly declared its policy of "protecting the religious, linguistic, cultural and other rights of the minorities."[22]

"Ben Nee" (a pseudonym for Ben Sargon) insisted that the Parsi community, though a much larger community than the Jewish one, had overcome the disadvantages of minority status and that the Jews could too. He was confident, from the statements of their leaders, that the Indians "who have obtained the power they now wield after much sacrifice and suffering will uphold the legitimate rights and aspirations of the Jews of India who have also worked for the advancement of the country."[23]

It seems, then, that although in 1935 the editors of the *Jewish Tribune* were still hoping for the inclusion of the Sephardic Jews on the European rolls, three years later they had reverted to their original position that the "Jews were Indian" and could trust Indians.

Clearly, most Baghdadis hoped that the British would remain in India. They had struggled, albeit unsuccessfully, to have themselves considered Europeans and they preferred a European government. Though few had any sympathies for Indian nationalism, one notable exception was Maurice Japheth, the well-known Baghdadi journalist (whose family came from Aden), who would later shock members of his community by marrying a Bene Israel woman. Profoundly influenced by Gandhi after meeting him in Nagpur in 1935, Japheth adopted the simple life Gandhi advocated, wrote a number of books about the Mahatma, and openly preached Indian nationalism, though he did not try overly hard to persuade members of his community to join him. He saw himself as an Indian first and a Jew second, and never had any doubts about the importance of Indian independence.[24] In the spring of 1941, Japheth became editor of the *Jewish Advocate*. He was inspired to interview Dr. B. R. Ambedkar, the leader of the scheduled classes, on the question of Jews and Jewishness after reading an article by Ambedkar on the story of Moses, in which he explained how the account of the Exodus and of the leadership of Moses had been a source of personal inspiration, and how he saw in the present condition of the depressed classes of India a parallel to that of the Jews in their captivity in Egypt.[25] "The Jews of India are placid," Ambedkar stated, "they have yet to make their mark in the public life of the country. We expect them to identify themselves with the various phases of the country's aspirations." He had absolutely no fear that anti-Semitic sentiments would be roused if the Jews in India were to come to the fore and expressed his admiration for the new social order being created in Palestine.[26]

No other leaders of the Baghdadi community were really involved with Japheth in these nationalist interests. Some people believed that, like Michael David, Meyer Nissim, head of the Bombay Municipal Corporation in 1929, favored Indian nationalism, but quietly so. Yet others felt that not even Meyer Nissim really identified with India, and that the espousal of nationalist causes by Nissim and others was mainly rhetoric.[27] One Baghdadi reminisced:

> The Baghdadi community was apolitical; they really weren't concerned with politics. Some could barely tell you who the Governor of the state was. They were loyal to the British because they were traders and their interests lay there: they assimilated to the British from that point of view, but they really considered themselves as members of the aristocracy. So there was no real interest in nationalism.[28]

At the same time that these debates on Jewish communal rights and the trustworthiness of Indian nationalists were taking place, the communities had to deal in a very practical way with the influx of central European Jews, particularly into Bombay and Calcutta. This new element also stimulated the Indian Jews' consciousness of themselves as Jews in a wider world, and enriched their Zionist environment, but there were repercussions on a broader, political plane.

The Refugees Arrive

Although a sprinkling of independent European Jews had come to Bombay in the late 1920s, it was not until after 1933, when the refugees began to arrive, that the problems of their absorption demanded the attention of the Jews of India. In 1934 eleven Bombay Jews (mainly established Europeans), headed by A. W. Rosenfeld and A. Leser, formed the Jewish Relief Association (JRA). Originating as a "purely charitable association to assist European Jews who found their way to hospitable India but had no means of livelihood, as in most cases they were victims of racial persecution," the organization at first had little to do, but as anti-Semitism in central Europe and elsewhere intensified, the refugees increased. The JRA established contact with the Central Council for Refugees in London and guaranteed maintenance to the government of India for every refugee admitted into India. Soon the government began granting visas in every instance recommended by the association, and it recognized the JRA, with branches in Calcutta and Madras as well, as the official body representing Jewish refugees in India. Although Sir David Ezra of Calcutta was the president of the JRA and Sir Alwyn Ezra the vice-president (in order to give the organization more prestige in India), and other Baghdadis contributed funds, most of the working members, including the chair and vice-chair, were central Europeans. Until the outbreak of war, about one thousand refugees were admitted with the assistance of the JRA and were distributed all over India.[29]

By the late 1930s boats were arriving in Bombay carrying penniless Jewish refugees en route to China, Colombo, Manila, Hong Kong, and Japan. The JRA tried to help the transit passengers financially, but the resources became more and more strained. Those refugees who could offer guarantees of maintenance while in India, through either relatives or the association, were permitted to land in Bombay; others were not. By 1939 Sir Victor Sassoon had contributed twenty-five thousand pounds (332,500 rupees) to the Council for German Jewry and Sir Alwyn Ezra donated ten thousand rupees to the JRA of Bombay, the highest contribution it had yet received.[30]

Although those European Jews who had arrived penniless were looked down upon by the money-conscious, aristocratic Baghdadis, the more affluent refugees often considered themselves superior to both the Bene Israel and the Baghdadis. Popular with affluent Indians, the European Jews felt they had something in common with Parsis. If they mixed at all socially with their coreligionists, it was only with the upper-class Baghdadis, in whose proximity they lived in the Fort. Most of the Bene Israel lived too far away or had no facilities to entertain or receive the newcomers. The Bene Israel's main contact with the European Jews was through the German doctors, often eminent specialists, who treated them very well, and sometimes without charge. The refugees had their own organizations and involvements and, according to G. L. Gabriel, a German metal-factory owner who arrived in the late 1920s, a different attitude toward Jewish communal institutions and Jewish welfare. The central European Jews ordinarily attended the Baghdadi synagogue in the Fort, but because of overcrowding, rented a separate hall for their own services during the High Holidays.[31] In 1938, the Jewish Club, partially financed by Sir Alwyn Ezra, opened in the Fort area, attracting leading Baghdadis and Europeans as members. Hardly any Bene Israel joined, probably because they did not live in the area, but the club's Literary Circle sponsored a series entitled "Careers for Our Youth" to which they invited some Bene Israel speakers, including Dr. Abraham Erulkar and Rebecca Reuben, the principal of the Elly Kadourie High School.[32]

The "Doctors Problem"

The arrival of the doctors (and other refugees) had repercussions beyond the Jewish community that must be seen within the general context of the dwindling of employment opportunities and the Indianization of the services. Although there were fewer than one hundred Jewish refugee doctors in all of India by 1941, protests began early in 1934, when a Captain Thornton wrote a letter to the All-India Medical Council claiming that German doctors were flooding Bombay "to the great detriment of an already grossly over-crowded profession," and calling for legislation to control the influx. By 10 March 1934 the issue had already reached the Central Legislative Assembly as Nabakumar Sing Dudhoria (representing Calcutta) asked how many doctors from Germany had set up practice in Bombay and why they were coming. If German physicians could work unrestrictedly in India, what would the government do to check the competition with local doctors? Sir Girja Shankar Bajpai, secretary for the Department of Education, Health and Lands, responded that he did not yet have any information. Another legislator, S. C. Mitra, argued that a large segment of public opinion favored inviting or welcoming distinguished scientists or medical men to India from other countries.[33]

Similar ambivalence surfaced a week later, on 18 March 1934, at a large meeting held in Bombay, when Indian dentists and physicians voiced concern over the issue of reciprocity: since Indian doctors were not allowed to practice in Germany, why should India permit German doctors to practice here? They passed a resolution urging the government to enact laws to limit the practice of medicine to the nationals of India. At the same time, however, they recognized the plight of the German Jewish doctors, refugees from Hitler's terror, and decided to afford the victims a haven of refuge and the opportunity to practice in the country.[34]

Shortly thereafter, when the questions of competition and reciprocity were again raised in the central legislature, Bajpai was more forthcoming, saying that the government knew that six or seven German doctors had arrived in Bombay since the beginning of 1934. The All-India Medical Council could take up the question of the disabilities of the Indian doctors in Germany. A few legislators continued to express sympathy for the German Jewish doctors.[35]

The Indian press at this stage was sympathetic to the Jews. The *Bombay Chronicle* argued that a few Jewish physicians, if given refuge in Bombay from Nazi persecution, would not make much difference to the medical profession there. It objected to an appeal to government and the legislature to discriminate against them, as such action would amount to cruel inhospitality toward men who had come to India not to practice medicine, but to escape miseries in Germany. The principle of reciprocity was irrelevant in this case. The *Free Press Journal* and the *Bombay Sentinel* adopted similar positions, the latter noting "that the medical fraternity in Bombay refused to countenance a ban on the Jewish doctors who sought refuge in Bombay, . . .

and will follow ancient Indian traditions of affording shelter from persecution."[36]

But the issue would not die. When, almost a year later, the Bombay Medical Council again considered the question of confining the practice of medicine and dentistry to Indians, the government of Bombay advised that representation should be made to the central government and the All-India Medical Council. Though no more than ten German Jewish refugee doctors had yet established practices in Bombay, in less than a year they had made reputations for themselves. They had many Indian patients, and native states were requisitioning their services. Commenting on their success, a Parsi correspondent to the *Bombay Chronicle* ascribed the reasons for their popularity to "their method of examination, taking medical history, personal interest and time taken for each, scrupulous concern for fact and detail, cooperation of the various doctors who confer together to get a correct diagnosis, and the prominent position occupied by Germany in the medical world."[37]

In December 1938, the All-India Medical Conference suggested prohibiting the immigration of medical practitioners from countries that did not recognize Indian medical qualifications. Although the Bombay government had told its local medical council to take up the refugee issue with the central government and the All-India Medical Council, the central government felt that permission to practice medicine in India was primarily a concern of the provincial governments. In the central legislature, Manu Subedar, representing the Indian Merchants' Chamber, asked on 22 February 1939 whether the government had considered the desirability of transporting some of the German doctors back to their own country. Sir R. M. Maxwell, the Home Department member, replied that they would not be permitted to return; they were, in effect, stateless. Sir Ziauddin Ahmad from the United Provinces asked whether India was to be treated as an asylum for all those people turned out by Germany and Italy. Maxwell's answer was no.[38]

The government seems to have become impatient with some of these attacks. Officials could not see how the forty-two Jewish doctors who had entered by April 1939 could have a detrimental effect on Indian medical interests. Dr. Abraham Erulkar, however, acknowledged that the big towns were overcrowded, yet he believed there was scope in small towns and villages for the refugee doctors.[39]

Soon, however, the problem expanded, for not only the doctors but other European Jewish refugees as well might create economic problems.

Problems of Absorption

By May 1938 the question of admission of Austrian refugees became complicated. Since Austria's annexation by Germany, Austrian passports were no longer valid, but the refugees did not want to take out German travel documents. Should they be required to have documents valid for travel to countries other than India in case they became destitute and had to be deported? The Home Department, recognizing that other countries would be equally wary, decided to risk admitting refugees who, for the time being, had a visible means of support. But India was still afraid of being flooded with refugees who would either shortly become financially dependent or, alternatively, would earn good livings as doctors or other specialists "much to the natural and justifiable resentment of Indians." A minute in a Home Department file dated 21 May 1938 stated:

> These Austrian refugees are likely to become something of a problem. Our aim should be to restrict immigration to such individuals as seem to be of decent standing (preferably vouched for by non-aliens in India) and unlikely by reason of destitution or otherwise to become a nuisance in India. If this is done, the possibility of their becoming "stateless" need not alarm us, as they will in due course become eligible for naturalization.[40]

During this period, the India Office as well as British consular authorities in foreign countries referred a large number of applications for Indian visas from Jewish refugees to the Home Department, which insisted that the applicant must not be politically undesirable and must obtain a guarantee of employment. An exception could be made if the immigrant had substantial funds, but Jews, who would probably be unable to extricate funds from Austria and Germany, would be unlikely to qualify.[41]

By late 1938, however, some Indian members of the Central Legislative Assembly began to question the government's policy on the Jewish refugees in general. One proposed question asked about the number of Austrian-born Jews who had come to India as refugees from Nazi persecution and their civil and political status vis-à-vis Indian nationals with regard to employment and the exercise of the franchise. Though this question did not actually reach the floor, the answer prepared by the Home Department was revealing. Although certain elements in the government had stated that it was not their policy to encourage the entry into India of European or other refugees, the Home Department felt that because of an increasing number of applications, it had had to establish a general policy of admitting only those persons from Austria and Germany who fully satisfied its conditions. It was not possible to say how many were Austrian-born Jews or refugees. They would remain aliens until they became naturalized subjects and until then would not be eligible for any office or for any municipal, parliamentary, or other franchise.[42]

In an editorial in the *Jewish Advocate* entitled "How India Can Help the Refugees," A. E. Shohet observed that the press devoted considerable space to the Jewish problem in Europe and particularly to Nazi Germany and its treatment of the Jews. He felt that the leaders of Congress—Gandhi, Subhas Chandra Bose (the Congress president), and Nehru—were sympathetic. Refugees could not bring funds to India, but, Shohet maintained, more than capital, India needed technicians and experience for its newly expanding industries. Suggesting that the National Planning Committee under the direction of Nehru could play a role, the editor also noted that Jews could contribute to the advance of Indian agriculture. Jewish farmers had shown what they could do for Palestine, Shohet argued. With a little investment, they could establish model farms, which, through partnership and cooperation, might attract educated unemployed Indian youth to agriculture. In this way, perhaps twenty-five thousand Jewish refugees could be absorbed throughout India.[43]

Another advocate of Jewish refugee absorption was Shabdai S. Koder, the leader of the Cochin Jews and their representative in the legislative council of that state. Koder requested that the dewan, Sir R. K. Sanmukham Chetty, allow persecuted Jews to settle in Cochin, but Chetty, who had been discussing this matter with Jewish representatives in Geneva and London, wanted to ascertain whether there were opportunities in the state for Jews to eke out a livelihood. The dewan also realized that immigrants could not receive appointments in the public services of Cochin and he did not want to incur any financial obligations on the part of the government. In May 1939 Edmond de Rothschild, on a three-month tour of India and Burma, reported that the dewan of Cochin had offered to admit 250 Jewish refugee families in a particular area. Unfortunately, nothing seems to have come of this scheme. Around this same time, Paul Singer, an agricultural expert from Palestine who was visiting Mysore to discuss the importation of Dutch cows from Palestine, spoke with the dewan, Sir Mirza Ismail, about the possibility of granting 300 acres of land where thirty Jewish refugee families could settle. Here too, there seems to have been no follow-up.[44]

Jews were not the only ones thinking up absorption schemes. J. R. Glorney Bolton appealed in the *Spectator* to Indian princes, particularly in Hyderabad and Mysore, to organize medical centers in their capital cities and staff them with Jewish refugee doctors.[45] An Indian, M. B. Sant, pointed out that India needed many foreign specialists and that German Jews had been among the leading experts in many lines of industry and commerce. Also in late 1938, J. B. Hearsey, a taluqdar (large landowner) of Oudh (and a friend of Edwin Montagu), proposed to lease a considerable amount of acreage of excellent soil to a limited number of Jews to help with their rehabilitation. But some Home Department officials thought that this area was likely to be almost uncultivatable and they wanted more details. Was Hearsey willing to help the Jews settle in and to guarantee their maintenance? The India Office was prepared to cooperate with the German Jewish Aid Committee in London to investigate such schemes. When this committee inquired about N. G. Chinavis of Nagpur, who had offered to hire one or two German-Jewish agricultural and horticultural specialists, the India Office ascertained that Chinavis was a gentleman of high social standing and one of the leading and enlightened landholders in the province. There is no indication that any of these schemes ever materialized.[46]

Jawarharlal Nehru himself was involved with some proposals to help the Jewish refugees in the fall of 1938. He forwarded to provincial governments a large number of applications he had received, while visiting Vienna, from Jewish experts seeking employment in India. Dr. Syed Mahmud, the minister of education and development in Bihar, had agreed to employ four such Jews in industrial and other development schemes in the provinces, but consulted with Maurice G. Hallett, the British governor of Bihar. When Hallett voiced his fear to Lord Linlithgow that Nehru might attempt to introduce Jewish communists in his scheme to find employment for experts in Bihar, the viceroy agreed that they should keep an eye on developments. Meanwhile, the Intelligence Bureau of the Home Department also had some secret information that Nehru had put two Jews seeking jobs in touch with the managing editor of the *National Herald*. Nehru accused the government of India of obstructing the employment of Jews in India (for example, by requiring guarantees of permanent employment, which no one could give). It was clear that the British government wanted to control the influx of Jews and especially to see whether Nehru's "Austrian friends attempted to get to India."[47]

Not all Indians, however, were so eager to help. The fears of economic competition continued, and in February and March 1939 Indian legislators persisted with their questions about the conditions for admitting refugees. Maxwell stated that no proposal was under consideration to facilitate the immigration of Jews into India on a large scale. In reply to another question, the government stated that it had no precise information about the number of Jews who had entered India during 1938 and 1939 and their countries of origin, as immigrants with valid passports were admitted into India and were not asked whether or not they were Jews. It was even difficult to know how many were immigrants and how many were casual visitors. The government claimed that it had given no relief in any form. It acknowledged that arrangements had recently been made with the secretary of state for India to admit Jewish refugees from dictatorship countries if the Council of German Jewry guaranteed to maintain them for five years and, if the refugees were unemployed at the end of that period, to repatriate them to the United Kingdom. Persons employed at the end of that period were to be regarded as independent. The India Office had been thinking of a "small batch" of Jewish refugees. The government was hedging here in drafting its response, for if it claimed to have no means whatever of identifying Jewish refugees, there would be no way to arrange for their admission with the India Office or the Council of German Jewry.[48]

At this point, the Home Department did not reveal to the legislature that it had authorized visas to 269 Jewish refugees up to the beginning of 1939. In response to another question, Maxwell replied that the government did not intend to stop the migration of foreigners to India, that only Jews who were British subjects were eligible for employment in the services of the crown, and that it was not very easy for these people to get naturalization certificates. When Abdul Qaiym, of the Northwest Frontier Provinces, said he knew of several instances where Russian Jews had been appointed in the Criminal Intelligence Department when local people were without jobs and that it was easy for them to get naturalization certificates, the president of the legislature, Sir Abdul Rahim, retorted: "If you know all this, you need not ask for information."[49]

Notes in the Home Department files indicate that once the Jews were admitted into India, the only means the central government had of obtaining any information about them was through the provincial governments, whom it did consult before granting visas to Jewish refugees to insure that their presence would not adversely affect the interests of Indian nationals. By mid February 1939, however, there was some talk in the Home Department that perhaps the Jewish refugees should be limited to about five hundred, including those who were specialists or relatives of employed foreigners in India.[50]

The Indian press provided another forum for the discussion of policies toward Jewish immigration. In a letter to the *Bombay Sentinel* K. F. Nariman, an eminent lawyer, a former mayor of Bombay, and a former president of the Bombay Provincial Congress Committee, deplored that Jewish refugees in transit were denied the right of entry into India, even for a few hours of sightseeing, unless they could secure a "guarantee" from local inhabitants. Nariman felt this treatment was humiliating, insulting, inhuman, immoral, and perhaps also illegal. What was the sanction for asking a whole community or a section of a foreign population to give a "guarantee" in advance before landing, he wondered. Nariman contended that the required immigration guarantee was too strict, for the government insisted that someone promise to be responsible for the permanent maintenance of the refugee while in India and for the expenses of repatriation if deported, even when the refugee had an employment contract.[51]

On 21 March 1939 the *Hindustan Standard* of Calcutta published an article—originally written in German and published in a German paper, *Valkischer Beohachter*—by Habib ur-Rahman, entitled "The Jewish Question in India: Menace of Influx in Various Spheres." Rahman, an experienced journalist who had Nazi sympathies (he was rumored to be in the confidence of

Goebbels) and whose writing was later banned by the Indian government, stated that until recently there had been no Jewish problem in India because the number of Jews was insignificant, but that this situation was changing because "Mahatma Gandhi, by his unauthorized interference in Germany's policy in regard to the Jews, has set the ball rolling." Gandhi's pronouncements on the Jewish question had rendered dissensions between the Congress and the Muslim League more acute. Rahman was annoyed at Nehru and the United Provinces government, which advocated importing Jewish experts. How can one advocate the removal of all Englishmen on the ground that there are enough Indian specialists and then call Jews into the country, he asked. He quoted the *Indian Nation* in Patna, which had said, "You starve your own countrymen and grant concessions to foreigners," and noted that a medical delegation had protested to Congress's President Subhas Chandra Bose about the immigration of Jewish doctors. In considering petitions from Jews in Europe to settle and practice in India, the Congress party, "which has so strongly agitated over the 'dumping' of foreign specialists in India should follow the same policy with regard to the Jews," Rahman advocated.

A Madras newspaper, the *Indian Express*, emphasized that India was not open for a mass immigration of Jews. Sparsely populated countries, such as Australia, Siberia, and Canada, were more suitable, it pointed out, adding: "It is interesting to note that the Jews as spongers avoid such countries where pioneering work must first be done, but prefer to speculate upon Indian sentimentality." The paper asserted that the Ceylon government had refused the Jews permission to settle, and that the pro-Jewish policy of several Indian states, among them Cochin, had been condemned by the Indian press.[52]

The Indians' concern even extended to the British government's consideration of schemes to accommodate Jewish refugees elsewhere in the empire. When the British discussed settling perhaps 150 refugees in the Kenyan Highlands, both the Foreign Department of the All-India Congress Committee and Indians in the central legislature opposed the proposal, fearing that it would bring about a further deterioration in the economic and political conditions of the Indians and Africans of Kenya. European settlers in Kenya formed an association to oppose such a scheme. A. E. Shohet, the editor of the *Jewish Advocate*, did not see how such a small influx of Jews in Kenya would seriously aggravate the situation, even if the Jews had preference over Indians and Africans in matters of land settlement and employment. Nor could the Indians complain about imperialism, Shohet claimed, as they were as much imperialists in Kenya as the British. Similarly, when the British government proposed to open up British Guiana to the refugees, Indians there demanded the reopening of Indian emigration to British Guiana so that they would not be overrun by an influx of Jews from central Europe and so that Indian settlers could maintain their premier position. This opposition to Jewish settlement elsewhere, Shohet felt, was another reason why Jews should consider only Palestine as a place of resettlement.[53]

Political Challenges and Responses:
Gandhi and the Jews

The attention focused on the refugees was only one of the ramifications of the momentous changes taking place in Europe by the late 1930s. The effect of Nazi propaganda in India and the response of the nationalist leaders preoccupied the more aware members of the Jewish community.

The Jewish press kept a watchful eye not only on events in Germany, but on Indian and world reaction to them. In 1933, for instance, the *Jewish Advocate* noted that the Indian press, including the *Times of India* and the *Evening News*, had strongly condemned the Nazi outrages and sympathized with the Jews; the *Advocate* also approved the League of Nations' admonition of Germany.[54] The *Jewish Tribune* published an editorial in June 1937 against Nazi misrepresentations of the Jews and Jewish ethics. That same month, the anti-British *Bombay Chronicle* attacked the chief rabbi of London, who, in a Thanksgiving service for the coronation of the king and queen, had declared that Britain was the world's strongest hope against "the normal barbarism of political doctrines which deny that common humanity is the bond between man and man and wage war on democratic institutions and organized religion." Criticizing the *Chronicle*'s headline writer, who had characterized the rabbi's speech as "bursting into flattery," the *Jewish Tribune* argued that in the light of Nazi actions, England's declaration that it would not tolerate any injustice to its nationals who did not profess the dominant faith merited the chief rabbi's asserting his faith in that country.[55]

The press may not have hesitated to state its position on the Jewish question, but Mahatma Gandhi, for several years, did. In 1935 Rabbi Louis Wolsey, a Philadelphia Reform rabbi who styled himself a "Jewish Gandhist," sought the Mahatma's advice on how to fight Hitlerism. Gandhi replied:

> I have not a shadow of a doubt that vituperation and returning evil with evil does add to the stock of evil in the world, and therefore does not serve anybody. Non-resistance, however, does not mean passive submission to the will of the persecutor. On the contrary, it means a refusal to submit to his will and preparedness to suffer the consequences of nonsubmission.[56]

A *Jewish Tribune* editorial found this reply vague and unenlightening.

By the end of 1938, however, Gandhi had received many letters asking him to declare his views about both the Arab-Jewish question in Palestine and the persecution of the Jews in Germany. Some of this pressure came from Hermann Kallenbach. He, along with H. S. L. Polak, also a Jew, had been a close associate of Gandhi's during his struggle for Indian rights in South Africa, and had maintained an intimate friendship with him. Neither Polak nor Kallenbach was a particularly observant Jew, but for both their Jewish consciousness was reawakened during the Nazi period.[57]

At the urging of Kallenbach and others, Gandhi finally published a full declaration of his views in the *Harijan* on 26 November 1938. His position on Zionism and the Arab-Jewish question in Palestine will be taken up later. Gandhi expressed his sympathy toward the Jews, seeing them as the untouchables of Christianity. The German persecution of the Jews seemed to him to have no parallel in history. "If there ever could be a justifiable war in the name of and for humanity," he wrote, "a war against Germany to prevent the wanton persecution of a whole race would be completely justified. But I do not believe in any war. A discussion of the pros and cons of such a war is therefore outside my horizon or province." He was against any alliance with Germany, but he also felt that the Jews could resist their organized and shameless persecution, preserve their self-respect, and not feel helpless and neglected:

> If I were a Jew and were born in Germany and earned my livelihood there, I would claim Germany as my home even as the tallest gentile German may, and challenge him to shoot me or cast me in a dungeon. I would refuse to be expelled or to submit to discriminating treatment. . . . And suffering voluntarily undergone will bring them [the Jews] an inner strength and joy which no number of resolutions of sympathy passed in the world outside Germany can. . . . The calculated violence of Hitler may even result in a general massacre of the Jews by way of his first answer to the declaration of . . . hostilities [by the allies]. But . . . even the massacre . . . could be turned into a day of thanksgiving and joy that Jehovah had wrought the deliverance of the race even at the hands of the tyrant.[58]

Gandhi believed that the Jews in Germany had a parallel in the Indian *satyagraha* campaign in South Africa and simply needed a leader to guide them in organized nonviolent action:

> It will then be a truly religious resistance offered against the godless fury of dehumanized man. The German Jews will score a lasting victory over the German gentiles in the sense that they will have converted the latter to an appreciation of human dignity.[59]

The *Jewish Advocate* reacted sharply to this statement. Noting that Gandhi had broken his strange silence on the issue, Shohet argued that the Mahatma was either misinformed or ignorant about the Jewish question in Germany and Palestine and that his remarks were naive, if not tragically inconsistent. In comparing the Jews in Europe with the Harijans in India, Shohet observed, Gandhi forgot one fundamental difference: Jewish homelessness. The Mahatma's advice that the Jews should adopt the policy of *satyagraha* and "insist on a just treatment wherever they are born" was pointless because they had adopted this policy two thousand years ago, and the results were well known. Nor was the parallel with South Africa useful because the South African government did not terrorize and murder Indians as the Nazis did the Jews. A letter from E. J. Samuel of Calcutta reiterated that if Gandhi had not been dealing with the Afrikaners and the British in South Africa and India, but rather with the Nazis, *satyagraha* would not have worked for him. Samuel advised the Jews to practice nonviolent *satyagraha* not necessarily to those who oppress them but to God, who in good time would have mercy on them and relieve their distress.[60]

Nor did Gandhi's statements about Germany's anti-Semitic measures leave him immune from German critics, who said that his writing had not rendered himself, his movement, or German-Indian relations any service. In an exclusive statement published by the Calcutta *Statesman*, Gandhi replied that he was not unprepared for German anger, but that underlying his writing was a friendliness toward Germany. He wanted Germans to realize the value of outside criticism.[61]

To friends who sent him newspaper clippings criticizing his appeal to the Jews to adopt *satyagraha*, Gandhi responded that the Jews had never practiced nonviolence as an article of faith. He quoted the biblical "eye for an eye" phrase and claimed that the Jews wanted the so-called democratic powers to punish Germany for her persecution and deliver them from oppression. Their nonviolence was therefore that of the helpless and the weak.[62] An article appearing in the *Harijan* in late December 1938 reported Gandhi as saying:

> [If Jews were] actively non-violent, . . . in spite of the misdeeds of the dictators, they would say, "We shall suffer at their hand; they know no better. But we shall suffer not in the manner in which they want us to suffer."[63]

Gandhi's views continued to draw protests in the press, both in India and abroad. Shohet reiterated that the Jews had held to the doctrine of non-violence throughout the Diaspora through necessity, as had Gandhi: Jewish nonviolence was no more that of the "helpless and the weak" than Gandhi's was. If India had had the power and resources of Britain or America, Gandhi would probably not have appeared on the scene in his present role. As for the "eye for an eye" philosophy, Shohet said that one had to turn to post-biblical philosophy, literature, and folklore to appreciate the spirit and nature of Jewish nonviolence. A letter from E. J. Samuel interpreted the "eye for an eye" statement to mean that God would punish accordingly, and not that the persecuted would exact the penalties.[64]

Perhaps the most disappointed of all with Gandhi's statements were two prominent Jews then residing in Palestine: the great philosopher, Martin

Buber, and the president of the Hebrew University of Jerusalem, Judah
Magnes. Early in 1939, both addressed to Gandhi letters that, although
concentrating on the Palestine problem, also dealt with his views on the
German question. They too found *satyagraha*—a concept they did not reject—unworkable as a method of resistance against Nazism (Buber himself
had lived under the Nazi regime for five years). Magnes held that the tradition
of Jewish martyrdom provided the same inner strength and dignity as *satyagraha*. There was no reply to these letters, and Shimoni thinks they may have
gone astray, never reaching Gandhi.[65]

The neutral attitude of the Indian National Congress toward the Nazi
persecution also disturbed the Jews of India. The Working Committee of the
Congress showed its sympathy with the Czechs and passed resolutions in
favor of the oppressed people in Spain and China, but passed not a single
resolution in sympathy with the Jews of Germany and Austria. Shohet referred
to this omission in the *Bombay Sentinel,* as did a *Sunday Standard* editorial
writer who admitted the validity of the Jews' reproach against the Working
Committee:

> We (the people of India) have not yet condemned in unequivocal terms
> the brutalities perpetrated on the Jews. Indians are always sympathetic
> towards the suffering of others, and we look to the Congress to take the
> initiative. The present anguish of the Jews should appeal to all those who
> believe in the fundamental rights of human beings.[66]

Shohet felt that a resolution in sympathy with the persecuted Jews would not
only reflect the high moral principles of Congress but would practically nullify
the vicious influence of the Nazi propaganda in India, on which "millions
of rupees are spent annually to pervert the minds of the Indian public."[67]

Gandhi's statements that the Jews had "called down upon the Germans
the curses of mankind," and that to the Jews "revenge is sweet," shocked his
old friend Polak, who wrote letters asking Gandhi to reassure him that he
had been misrepresented. Gandhi confirmed his original statements.[68] Shimoni reports that Gandhi eventually did retract the statement publicly in the
Harijan.[69] Persisting in his efforts to influence Gandhi, Shohet visited the
Mahatma at his ashram in Wardha for four days early in 1939. It is hard to
say whether anything came of this visit except for a Jewish New Year's message
the following September in which Gandhi wished an era of peace for Shohet's
"afflicted people." Meanwhile, as war seemed to be approaching, Gandhi
wrote to Hitler begging him to prevent its outbreak. He also told the viceroy
that he was on the side of England and France from the purely humanitarian
standpoint.[70]

Noting the circulation of Nazi pamphlets and the frequent appearance of
articles extolling the Nazi regime in certain sections of the Indian press, the
Jewish papers worried that the Nazis had free scope in India. Indeed, as early

as 1937 the government had detained postal packets containing circular letters in Urdu from Habib ur-Rahman from Germany, addressed to Muslim newspapers. The government saw an article headed "Assassin Jew Frankforter" as "extremely objectionable and obviously written with the object of creating disaffection towards Britons and Jews and therefore embarrassing to the Government of India." The Jews were accused of being tyrants and assassins of Palestine Arabs.[71] Shohet believed that "the Nazis had wormed their way into Mr. Jinnah's heart and some other leaders of the Muslim League . . . [who] find a strong appeal in the Fascist philosophy of the Nazis and also in the anti-British doctrine."[72]

The *Bombay Sentinel,* a nationalist paper edited by B. H. Horniman (who, although a Congressite, was a severe critic of Gandhi and the Congress Working Committee), had reported that German money was flowing into India to subsidize Nazi propaganda, particularly among the Muslims.[73] On 8 November 1939 the question of Nazi propaganda in Bombay was raised in the Bombay Legislative Council. The government said that it was aware of the presence of a certain Dr. Urchs, who was a Nazi leader, but not of "any extensive propaganda being conducted among the people of the Province." Shohet felt that the answer was both illuminating and face-saving, that the government knew full well that practically all German firms and the consulate were centers of Nazi propaganda in India. The *Jewish Advocate* urged the government to take a firmer stand against the surreptitious methods by which Nazi propaganda found its way into the press.[74]

Zionism in India: 1936–39

The rise of Nazism in Germany had an immediate impact on developments in Palestine. As the Nazi program became clearer, many German Jews flocked to the Jewish national home. Arab fears that they would be outnumbered by the Jews, which had been building for almost two decades, now seemed more justified than ever. From 1936 to 1939, Palestine was rocked by an Arab rebellion directed against both the Jews and the British, riots that elicited grave concern in India as elsewhere in the Muslim world.

Although Gandhi remained silent, other prominent Hindu leaders, including Jawaharlal Nehru, spoke out in favor of the Arabs. The government of India realized that although to most of the Muslim population, Palestine was far too distant to excite much attention, the views expressed by the Muslim deputation in 1933 were now no doubt widely held. Indeed, practically the entire Muslim vernacular press—and some of the English-language journals—criticized the British government. Muslim politicians and leaders took a growing interest in the Palestine situation: on 9 June 1936 the council of the All-India Muslim League passed a resolution expressing sympathy with the Palestine Arabs in their troubles and warning the government that its pro-Jewish policy was causing great excitement among the Muslims of India, who felt that the British statesmen wanted to put insurmountable difficulties in the path of Arab progress. The resolution asked all Muslims in India to observe 19 June as Palestine Day by suspending all business and holding meetings expressing their sympathy with the Arabs. While a few Hindu papers now began to take the same line as the Muslim press, and Palestine Day was observed in many places, the viceroy, Lord Linlithgow, still felt that there was very little real interest in or genuine enthusiasm for the Arab cause. Yet there were signs that Muslims in Egypt and Palestine were trying to stir up Muslim sympathy in India.[75]

A Palestine conference held at Allahabad in July attracted nationalist Muslims, Hindu Congressmen, and communists. Both Hindus and Muslims emphasized the close connection between the Arab struggle in Palestine and the nationalist movement in India. Some speakers suggested that the surest way of helping the Arabs was for Indians themselves to shake off the shackles of British imperialism. Resolutions urging Muslims to boycott British goods and to abstain from enlisting in the army in the event of war were passed. Yet little attempt was made to translate the resolutions into action. Meetings held in other parts of India were poorly attended and focused on subjects other than Palestine and on local problems. An unnamed government analyst wrote of this period:

> The feeling behind this agitation does not appear to be genuine or deep, for it has been engineered by professional mischief mongers and left wing agitators, partly as an electioneering movement. Congress agitators who have expressed their sympathy with the Arabs are actuated by the desire to obtain the Muslims as their allies in their attack on British Imperialism and to repeat the history of the years 1920–21, when the Muslims were moved by their feelings over the Khilafat to join hands with the Hindus in the policy of non-cooperation.[76]

The Jewish Agency Initiative

If the government was not yet overly anxious about pro-Palestinian events in India, the Jewish Agency now became very much concerned. A letter from Moshe Shertok (later Sharett),[77] the head of its political department, to Hermann Kallenbach, Gandhi's friend from South Africa, on 15 July 1936, gives a good insight into the Jewish Agency's efforts to establish contacts with India and to gain its leaders' sympathy and understanding for Zionist work and aspirations:

> It is clear that our political future as a nation returning to its home in Asia must ultimately depend in a large measure on the amount of goodwill and solidarity which we shall succeed in evoking on the part of the great Asiatic civilizations. Even from the purely materialistic standpoint a

> country like India with its vast potentialities holds out to us prospects of
> markets and other economic advantages . . . and we must see to it that . . .
> these prospects . . . [are] not . . . hampered by political or racial prejudice.[78]

Without mentioning names or dates, Shertok indicated that visitors from
India who were impressed with the Jews' work in Palestine had advised the
Zionists to send people to India to acquaint the intelligentsia of the Indian
national movement with Zionist aims and achievement, feeling that such
efforts would find a favorable response in Hindu circles. He informed Kallenbach that Nehru had openly taken a stand against the Zionists and that
Hindu politicians appeared to regard the Jews in Palestine as Western in-
truders and to see the conflict between them and the Arabs as one between
Asiatics and Westerners or Westernizers.

By July 1936, Shertok had decided to send Dr. Immanuel Olsvanger, a
Sanskritist, as a special emissary to India.[79] This mission was not to be a
"political campaign conducted by means of public meetings or interviews in
the press, but a very cautious and discreet method of procedure." If Olsvanger
could establish good personal contacts with a couple of dozen Indian intellectual leaders and get a hearing for the Zionist position in the most important
political and intellectual centers, Shertok would consider the mission a success. He believed that Olsvanger could not only present the Zionist case on
a high cultural level, but could gain the respect, affection, and confidence of
people and "even endear himself to persons with an oriental mentality."[80]

While a delegate for Keren Hayesod in South Africa from 1920 to 1928,
Olsvanger had met Kallenbach, whom he now suggested to Shertok to ac-
company him to India and introduce him to "the right people to talk to."
Shertok, excited to learn that Gandhi had such a close Jewish friend, told
Kallenbach that he desperately needed him:

> the fact remains that by virtue of your signal service to the Indian cause in
> South Africa and your close personal connection with the greatest of living
> Hindus . . . you are in a unique position to help Zionism in a field where
> the resources of the Jewish people are so meagre as to be practically non-
> existent. What you have no doubt regarded as a part of your purely private
> past which has nothing to do with Zionist or Jewish affairs can now be of
> invaluable service to our national movement.[81]

Kallenbach accepted the challenge. He was willing to go on the mission, but
because he had to go to London for business matters, he planned to join
Olsvanger in India.[82]

When Olsvanger arrived in Bombay in September 1936, Meyer Nissim
and A. E. Shohet, who was then heading the Zionist and Keren Hayesod
office in Bombay as well as editing the *Jewish Advocate*, helped him to meet
some Indian political and cultural leaders. His most important entrée, however, turned out to be Sarojini Naidu, a poet, nationalist, and Indian women's

leader, whom he had once met in South Africa through Kallenbach. A politician, and a friend and disciple of Gandhi, Naidu was also sympathetic to Zionism and took Olsvanger under her wing, introducing him to many important people and accompanying him on his visits. She also suggested that Olsvanger meet with H. S. L. Polak, Gandhi's other old friend from South Africa, who happened to be in India just then and was willing to help. Olsvanger, however, felt that Polak's influence had diminished and did not follow up on the offer.[83]

After corresponding with and meeting twice with Nehru, Olsvanger decided that the president of the Indian National Congress knew little about Zionism and was prejudiced against it. Nehru stated that Zionism was a movement of Jewish high finance and that he was against all imperialism, whether German or British. To Olsvanger's remark that the Arabs were supported by Hitler, Nehru replied,

> We have sympathy for the national movement of Arabs in Palestine because it is directed against British Imperialism. Our sympathies cannot be weakened by the fact that the national movement coincides with Hitler's interests.[84]

Shimoni claims that in Palestine as well as in India, Nehru was not willing to recognize more than one legitimate nationalism in the struggle against imperialism.[85]

In an interview with the *Jewish Tribune* Nehru admitted that "he viewed the Palestine question from a very broad angle," and that he had not made a close study of the situation in Palestine, of Zionism, or of the Jewish question. Joseph Sargon, the editor, was not surprised: many Indians had never even met a single Jew and, as a result of their limited reading, did not entertain a very high opinion of them. The principles of Zionism were not widely understood, he felt, partly because the press in India, although it discussed Palestine's political problems, told little about how Eretz Israel (the Zionists' term for Palestine) was being developed. Since the London *Times* and the *Manchester Guardian* published special supplements at certain times of the year on Eretz Israel, Sargon suggested that perhaps leading newspapers in India could do the same, focusing on the economic growth of the country and the wide field it offered for Indian trade.[86]

Nehru's attitude must have greatly disappointed Olsvanger, for the emissary felt he was a much more important leader than Gandhi, whom Olsvanger tended to undervalue. Olsvanger could not accomplish much in his twenty-minute interview with Gandhi at the ashram, as the Mahatma was recovering from illness. In response to Olsvanger's statement that Kallenbach was a Zionist, Gandhi said: "I know, but then he has so many poor relatives."

Olsvanger decided not to broach the subject further but to leave it to Kallenbach (who had been unable to join him in India after all) to take up later.

Olsvanger met with a number of Muslim leaders, such as Abdulghafar Khan and Maulana Irfan of the Khilafat movement, but not with Muhammad Ali Jinnah, who had to go on a trip, but who supposedly said, "I am not interested in the Palestine question. I would love to meet Dr. O. nevertheless: I heard so much about him from Sarojini."[87] Olsvanger found Muslim opinion to be quite diverse and concluded that although most Indian Muslims cared very little about Palestine, the press and resolutions passed at conferences made it look as though all Indian Muslims were anti-Zionist. Olsvanger pleaded with members of the Bombay Zionist Association who had friends in China to try to obtain reliable information about the millions of Muslims there. Perhaps influential Muslims in China could be persuaded to voice their support of the Zionist cause, affirming that the Jews who were resettling Palestine would respect the Muslim holy places and would bring prosperity and cultural and economic uplift to all inhabitants of Palestine and to the whole Middle East.[88]

In the course of his visit, Olsvanger did not restrict his meetings to Hindus and Muslims, but naturally had a certain amount of contact with the local Jewish communities, although he had not come primarily as a fund-raiser. When he visited the Jews of Cochin, he was treated as a state guest. Sargon felt that the State of Cochin could not have shown its sympathy for Zionism in a better manner at a time when anti-Zionist feeling was growing in India.[89]

As a Sanskritist and someone interested in Indian culture, Olsvanger was perhaps in a better position than any of the earlier Zionists to establish a warm relationship with the Bene Israel, whose good relations with Muslims as well as with Hindus could stand the movement in good stead, he felt. Up to now, the Bene Israel had participated minimally in Zionist activities, and previous emissaries, although holding meetings for them, had not made very great efforts to bring the Bene Israel into the Zionist fold. Perhaps, since the earlier delegates were primarily fund-raisers, they had been discouraged by the poverty of the Bene Israel.[90]

Nevertheless, the question of Bene Israel settlement in Palestine was on the minds of many people. At the end of 1934 the first Bene Israel to emigrate to Palestine, M. R. Daniel of the Burma Railways, had gone to Tel Aviv in the "capitalist" category (the label for an immigrant who had sufficient funds to establish a business and who therefore did not have to be provided with a job).[91] In May 1936 Abraham Reuben, vice-president of the Karachi Jewish community, had inquired whether Bene Israel were permitted to settle in Eretz Israel, claiming that some people in Bombay were informed by the last Zionist delegate that they were not. Joseph Sargon reassured him that there were no restrictions on Bene Israel immigration, but noted that although the

Jewish Agency encouraged immigrants from all over, including (dark) Yemenites, Eretz Israel could not absorb the unemployed of any country. Immigration certificates, being so hard to obtain, were given to Jews from
countries in which they were persecuted most; since Indian Jews were not
persecuted, why was it necessary for them to emigrate? Sargon also mentioned
that when the Jewish Agency had, in 1932, granted half a dozen immigration
certificates to Jews from India, those who went "did not prove themselves
worthy" and returned to India, "not being able to live the lives of *halutzim*."
The certificates were wasted and the experiment was not encouraging.[92]

Olsvanger now confirmed that it would certainly be possible to form a
Bene Israel colony in Palestine if the community were truly interested. He
personally believed that a large number of Bene Israel in Palestine would
bring something of the best of the Indian spirit to Palestine and would also
bring a lively contact with India, to the benefit of the Zionists. He also tried
to win over Dr. Abraham Erulkar and to assure him that there would be no
discrimination against the Bene Israel because of their skin color. He urged
Erulkar not to "attach so much importance to one's personal views, that are
influenced by casual personal experiences and interests, when it concerns a
movement that lived and struggled for realization under a hundred different
economic and political structures and constellations."[93]

Olsvanger was able to obtain Marathi books written by the Bene Israel for
the National University Library of Jerusalem and taped a record of Bene
Israel songs. I. A. Ezekiel, the editor of the *Jewish Minister,* a new Bene Israel
journal, commented favorably on Olsvanger's visit and asserted that the Hebrew University should investigate the historical origin of the Bene Israel and
the Cochin Jews.[94] But the action for which Olsvanger is still remembered
today in India (and for which two generations of scholars would now thank
him) was his success in arranging for the publication in Tel Aviv in 1937 of
the *History of the Bene Israel of India,* written by H. S. Kehimkar at the end
of the last century. Olsvanger later was to play an important role in helping
the Bene Israel adjust to Israel when they came in the early years of the
state's existence.

The growing unrest in India, even among Hindus, over the Palestine
question disturbed A. B. Salem, vice-president of the Malabar Jews Association of Cochin, who sent periodic political reports to Leo Herrmann, secretary
to the board of Keren Hayesod. Salem was convinced that it was necessary
to combat the spread of lies and negative opinions vigorously by active propaganda. He wanted Keren Hayesod to contribute some five pounds a month
to supplement the Cochin Jews' cost of a stenographer and publications to
this end. The political department of the Jewish Agency confirmed that it
was important to influence Muslim opinion in the East, particularly so that
public opinion in England would not be misled by reports that the vast

Muslim population there was strongly in favor of the Arabs, but the Agency would not finance Salem, claiming that its funds were limited.[95] Just about this time, however, Olsvanger persuaded the Jewish Agency to fund a local "political agent": A. E. Shohet in Bombay.

From the time of the resignation of Adolph Myers from the Keren Hayesod delegateship and the repercussions thereof, the Bombay Zionist Association had been carrying on a hand-to-mouth existence. By 1936 the *Jewish Advocate,* then in the hands of Shohet, had gradually been enlarged to a sixteen-page monthly. Yet the BZA had very few members and its work was conducted solely by Shohet and J. J. Gubbay, who functioned as Keren Keyemet L'Israel (Jewish National Fund) and Keren Hayesod commissioner. Financially, the BZA was on its last legs. Olsvanger concluded that it was essential to have someone permanently engaged in Zionist work in Bombay. The Jewish Agency, combined with the two national funds, decided to establish and subsidize a properly functioning organization there to serve as a rallying point for Zionists and to create and maintain contacts with Muslims. A subsidy of six hundred Palestinian pounds a year was to provide the salary of one paid official, who would be the secretary of the BZA and the editor of the *Jewish Advocate,* and to assist in the overhead expenses. The man in charge of the work, Olsvanger believed, had to be "one acquainted with the oriental mentality and one who had easy access to all classes of the population and an intelligent and humane grasp of the complexity of the problems." He thought that Shohet, who was just about to finish his university studies, and who had very influential relatives in other Asian countries that he could visit, would be ideal. He suggested to Shertok that Shohet be hired for two to three years and be brought out to Palestine for several months, at the Agency's expense, to be introduced to all branches of the work there.[96]

Olsvanger's attempts to bring about a reconciliation between the Sargon brothers and the BZA had failed. The efforts he made to reorganize the BZA by bringing in the new German Jewish immigrants and the Bene Israel on the committee further antagonized the Sargons, who may have seen in the rebuilding of the association a challenge to their own paper and its claim to represent the Zionists in India. The hostility broke into print. Joseph Sargon, the editor of the *Jewish Tribune,* was furious at the thought of a subsidy going to Shohet, the editor of the *Jewish Advocate* and his rival. Although he had previously stressed the propaganda value of his own newspaper, he now argued that contributing such a sum for Zionist propaganda in India, particularly for a paper aimed at Indians (and especially Muslims), was a waste, because non-Jews would consider a Jewish newspaper sectarian and, if they read it at all, would not take it seriously. Moreover, he maintained, since Indian Muslim sympathy for the Arabs arose from religious affinity and Hindu concern from internal politics, they would not be swayed by a Zionist journal aimed at them. Sargon cited as proof the case of Nehru, who, despite efforts of Zionists to reach him and his own admission of ignorance of Zionist affairs, was still making anti-Zionist remarks. Finally, it seemed wrong to him to use Zionist funds collected elsewhere for Zionist propaganda in India; the money was needed in Eretz Israel, and Indian Jews contributed very little as it was.[97]

In September, Lord Linlithgow telegrammed Sir Samuel Hoare, the secretary of state for India, that Muslim reaction was beginning to harden and was likely to become more embittered as a result of the despatch of troops to Palestine (to deal with the rebellion).[98] He had been disallowing in the Central Legislative Assembly questions and resolutions on Palestine that requested him to convey Muslim feeling to His Majesty's government because they would clearly lead to a discussion of London's policy, which the viceroy felt he did not have adequate material to defend. Linlithgow knew that he would have to receive a Muslim deputation soon; if he could inform it that he had conveyed the intensity of Indian Muslim concern, the hands of the moderates would be strengthened. Yet the secretary of state argued that although a representative deputation of Muslims was preferable to a debate in the assembly, he did not feel justified, on the basis of information supplied by the viceroy, in reporting to the cabinet that Indian Muslim concern could be described as intense. Linlithgow should simply say that His Majesty's government had been kept fully and promptly informed of the strength of Muslim feeling in India and should make clear that the present conflict was political and racial rather than religious in character.[99] Was the previous tendency of the Home Department and the viceroy to minimize Muslim agitation (or simply to misperceive it?) now backfiring? Two months later, an all-Muslim conference devoted to Palestine passed strong resolutions threatening a boycott of British goods and noncooperation with the government in India if Britain did not satisfy Arab demands in Palestine.[100]

Kallenbach, meanwhile, had finally arrived in India in May 1937 and was warmly received by Gandhi, whom he had not seen for twenty-three years. During a two-month visit, he had many discussions on Zionist work in Palestine (which he had just visited) with the Mahatma and other Indian leaders, trying to win their sympathy for the movement. Although Gandhi did not become pro-Zionist, he did become, as a result of Kallenbach's efforts, more sensitive to the Jewish position than he had been previously. He now accepted, in principle, the validity of the Zionists' aspirations, but the goals had to be achieved with Arab approval, not through British power. On Kallenbach's advice, the Jewish Agency prepared for Gandhi a special twenty-five page monograph that explained the rationale of Zionism. After reading it, Gandhi believed that India might be able to play a role in working out settlement talks—he had previously expressed privately to Kallenbach his willingness to assist in bringing about "direct conversations between Arabs and Jews"—but the monograph did not change his basic views. Another close associate of Gandhi's, an Anglican priest, the Reverend Charles F. Andrews, who had become a friend of Kallenbach's, also tried to persuade Gandhi to take a more pro-Jewish position and to work on Indian feelings.[101]

Muslims and Hindus reacted strongly to the Royal Commission Report on Palestine (analyzing the problems and suggesting solutions) that appeared in July 1937. At its Haripura meetings, Congress passed a resolution condemning in no uncertain terms Great Britain's decision to bring about the partition of Palestine and the measures taken to implement this decision. One can understand that Congress, antagonistic toward the idea of the partition of India, would find such a solution to the Palestine problem unattractive. In fact, the conclusion of the Royal Commission Report actually stated that only where one of the parties had been British, as in Britain, Canada, and South Africa, had conflicts of nationalities been overcome and unity achieved, whereas the schisms between the northern and southern Irish and the Hindus and Muslims in India had not yet been composed. The implication seemed to be that partition might be the solution for those conflicts as well as for Palestine.[102] The government felt that Congress had passed the resolution to try to exploit Muslim religious sentiment and to cultivate Muslim mass support.[103]

In October 1937 Shaukat Ali sent a statement on the Palestine issue, signed by all the Muslim members of the central legislature present at the time, to the government, requesting that it warn the responsible ministers in England that they should not lose Indian Muslims for the sake of foreign Jews, who, in a crisis, would not be able to give any help. The statement, which was forwarded to the secretary of state, claimed:

> The partition of Palestine is unthinkable and highly revolting to Muslims of the world. We demand the whole Palestine be handed over to the Arabs, sons of the soil, and the mandate ended as in Iraq. Arabs must be allowed to enjoy self-determination and form their own democratic government. The present repressive and pro-Jewish policy must be stopped forthwith.[104]

M. A. Jinnah, in his presidential address to the All-India Muslim League, meeting that same month in Lucknow, also rejected the partition of Palestine:

> The whole policy of the British Government has been a betrayal of the Arabs, from its very inception . . . this question of Palestine, if not fairly and squarely met, boldly and courageously decided, is going to be the turning point in the history of the British Empire. I am sure I am speaking not only for the Musalmans of India, but of the world . . . when I say that Great Britain will be digging its grave if she fails to honour her original proclamation, promises and intentions . . . which were so unequivocally expressed to the Arabs and the world at large.[105]

On October 17 the session adopted a lengthy, six-section resolution on Palestine in which it demanded the recision of the partition plan and the annulment of the mandate. It also appealed to rulers of Muslim countries to use their influence to save the holy places in Palestine from the sacrilege of non-Muslim domination and the Arabs of the Holy Land from the enslavement of British imperialism backed by Jewish finance. It placed on record its complete confidence in the Supreme Muslim Council and the Arab Higher Committee under the leadership of the grand mufti, and warned the British government

> that if it fails to alter its present pro-Jewish policy in Palestine, the Musalmans of India . . . will look upon Britain as the enemy of Islam and shall be forced to adopt all necessary measures according to the dictates of their faith.[106]

Nonetheless, the government felt that these resolutions were formal protests, and that Muslims had shown only "perfunctory interest" in Palestine.[107]

Indian Jews in the limelight were reluctant to express their views on Palestine. After the Royal Commission Report came out, Sir Victor Sassoon, for one, would not state his opinion on the Jewish state in Palestine or on partition. Dr. E. Moses, the Bene Israel mayor of Bombay, strongly advised the Jewish community not to embarrass the government by "importation of this extraneous bitterness nor allow the dissensions in the Holy Land to interfere with their cordial relations with the Muslims in India." He felt that amicability in India might secure a more suitable settlement of the dispute in Palestine. He proposed direct talks between Arabs and Jews, especially since the Royal Commission Report had recommended partition.[108]

As part of his responsibilities, A. E. Shohet regularly addressed to Eliahu Epstein, the chief of the Jewish Agency's Middle East section, letters from India, which contained excellent political analyses and included newspaper clippings. He explained how the pro-Arab campaign was being more intensively pursued, mainly because of local political conditions. Since Congress had participated in elections and accepted office and was managing to conduct the government in the major provinces without the help of non-Congress Muslims, a keen rivalry had grown up between organized Muslim bodies, each vying with the others to prove the universality of its outlook on Muslim questions. Congress, Shohet felt—here echoing the government's analysis—anxious to show that Muslim interests, even international ones, were amply safeguarded by the national movement, had espoused the Arab cause. Shohet believed that Indian socialists were generally misinformed about Zionist ideology, and thus the imperialist issue loomed very large in the socialist program. Except for the Anglo-Indian press, which supported British policy, the Indian press was anti-Zionist. Many vernacular papers did great mischief among the Muslim masses, he contended, and it would be very difficult to counteract the propaganda of such papers as they catered to party groups with a definite communalist bias. In subsequent letters he discussed issues such as an appeal by Nehru, during a speech on the minorities and the Congress, exhorting Indian Jews to join the Congress party and assuring them of equal treatment, and a resolution on Palestine, framed by Vallabhai Patel, which also called upon the Jews to join hands with the Arabs to fight British imperialism.[109]

Indian Zionism in the Late 1930s

To prepare for his work, A. E. Shohet visited Palestine from November 1937 to April 1938. While there, he wrote a lengthy report to the Zionist offices on the conditions and scope of the work in India, which gives an excellent summary of the situation (or at least his perception of it) at the time. Shohet felt that the chief difficulty facing Zionist work in India was the general disinterest due to a lack of continuous Zionist education and outlook between visits from emissaries. Thanks to Olsvanger's mediation, the BZA, for the first time in its history, numbered a few Bene Israel among its members, with two of them on the executive committee. Now the Bene Israel masses had to be won over. Although poor, the community was by far the largest section of Indian Jewry and politically, Shohet thought, the most important factor in Jewish life in India. He wanted to try to open up this whole new territory in Zionist fund-raising activities, even though it might not pay brilliantly at first, and asked the head offices to prepare special propaganda material, messages of good will and appeals addressed especially to the Bene Israel. Finally, the Bene Israel needed contact with youth movements, especially those interested in spreading the Hebrew language. Shohet wanted to arrange for two Hebrew teachers to be sent to India from Palestine. He also suggested that Zionist societies be started in Ahmedabad and Karachi (where the Jewish communities were almost exclusively Bene Israel) and in Cochin.

Shohet reiterated that until now the middle-class Baghdadi Jews had been the main contributors to Zionist funds in Bombay. Their Zionism had derived partly from their familiarity with things Jewish, particularly the Hebrew language, and partly from their realization of the Jewish problem, which their "none too happy experiences in Iraq" brought home to them. The wealthy, long-established Jews, with few exceptions, had grown indifferent to Zionist ideals. It was important to make Zionism in India significant and attractive to these rich Jews, especially the youth. It was also necessary to seek the assistance of the increasing European Jewish community to give a Zionist tone to Jewish social life. There was no other type of organized Jewish life in India, and Zionism was the only platform on which all sections of the community could meet. He also wanted the Jewish Agency to supply him with first-rate articles written by well-known persons and designed to appeal to non-Jewish readers. Films with commentary that could be shown in conjunction with lecture meetings would be helpful too.

Shohet claimed that the rivalry between the *Jewish Tribune* (the Sargons) and the BZA was unresolvable because it was one-sided and personal. He and Olsvanger believed that the Palestine institutions must cease their contact with Joseph Sargon, as such contact gave the impression that Sargon still had official connections with the Zionist head offices. Shohet felt that he should return to Bombay as the head offices' representative, and not as an official of the BZA.[110]

Sargon, meanwhile, continued to insist that although he published articles criticizing Zionist institutions in Bombay and the attitude of the head offices of the Jewish national institutions in Jerusalem because they were using outside funds to subsidize Zionist work in India (which in other countries was done by volunteers), he was still an ardent Zionist. Sargon, who had always championed the Bene Israel, also criticized the appointment of Shohet as the head offices' representative in India without consulting the Bene Israel.[111]

In May 1938 another Zionist emissary, Dr. Benzion Shein, visited Bombay and discovered that the Bene Israel indeed were very much influenced by Sargon's *Tribune* and rejected Shohet, despite his genuine efforts to bring them into the fold. Shein was most impressed with Shohet and felt it was a pity he had to waste so much time and energy in the fight against the Sargons. Shein recommended that the head offices write strong letters to expose the Sargons to the public and to point out that they were not an institution but three individuals who happened to issue a monthly magazine. Otherwise, they would destroy every good effort being undertaken by the community.[112]

The attitude of the Muslims became increasingly worrisome to the Indian government. Propaganda on behalf of the Palestine Arabs frequently found its way to India from abroad (mostly from Cairo) despite government efforts to prevent its circulation. There were also locally composed appeals and much "objectionable speaking on Palestine," especially in New Delhi and the United Provinces, and a genuine pro-Arab feeling was very widespread. The Central Intelligence Department, however, believed that as long as the Muslim League under Jinnah was not so strongly pro-Arab and concentrated on local matters, the British government had little to fear. But what might happen if Jinnah had to adopt a more pro-Palestinian stance in order to win mass support? Apparently the CID did not take Jinnah's remarks at the 1937 Lucknow session of the Muslim League, or the resolution passed, very seriously. It also felt that Congress Muslims and other groups were all exploiting an opportunity to unite Muslim feelings against the British government and to divert attention from political and religious questions nearer home.[113]

The British government soon abandoned the idea of partitioning Palestine and called for a round table conference in London to which all parties, but not the grand mufti, were to be invited. The Indian press unanimously welcomed the rejection of partition but criticized the exclusion of the grand mufti. Although the Muslim press generally asked for the exclusion of Jews from the conference and freedom for the Arabs to choose their own delegates, Jinnah advised the Arabs to participate in the conference and did not demand the exclusion of the Jews. Most of the Anglo-Indian press, such as the *Times of India*, the *Statesman* (Calcutta), and the *Pioneer of Lucknow*, pointed out that both Jews and Arabs had rights in Palestine and that Britain needed to seek a just settlement between the conflicting interests. The Hindu vernacular press suggested that Jewish immigration be stopped, the rights of Arabs be recognized, and the dream of a Jewish national home in Palestine be abandoned.[114]

The security of the Muslim holy places in Palestine was of paramount concern in a special issue of the *Deccan Times*, a South Indian Muslim English weekly, published on Palestine Day in 1938. The content, most of it anti-Jewish, was translated and appeared in Muslim vernacular papers. Shohet thought that this was the first organized, unveiled attack on the Jews in the Muslim press in India and wondered who had subsidized this publication. Dr. Leo Kohn of the World Zionist Organization believed that the *Deccan Times* had gotten its money from the London Arab Centre; Shohet suspected the Nazis. Maulana Kifayat-ullah, the president of the Jamiat-ul-Ulema-Hind group (the Indian party especially concerned with Muslim religious issues), had returned from a conference in Cairo in a German cargo-boat, which was most unusual for an Indian.[115]

At its Patna session in December 1938, the Muslim League made its views on Palestine very clear in Resolution 5:

> the British Government in Palestine [make] . . . their sympathy for the Jews a pretext for incorporating that country into the British Empire with a view to strengthening British Imperialism and to frustrating the idea of a federation of Arab States and its possible union with other Muslim states. They also want to use sacred places in Palestine as aerial and naval bases for their future military activities. The atrocities that have been perpetrated on the Arabs for the attainment of this object have no parallel in history.[116]

On the third day's meeting, at a particularly vituperous discussion on Palestine, speakers not only reiterated their opposition to British policy and warned that the ninety million Indian Muslims would back the Arabs, but also commented that Britain's atrocities against the Arabs were greater than those of Germany against the Jews. Professor Abdul Sattar Khairi said that both the British and the Hindus were Jews to Muslims, that is, their enemies. When Abdul Khaliq said that "the real Jews of the West were the British, and those of the East were the Hindus, and both were the sons of Shylock," the chair forced him to withdraw his remark. Jinnah said that such statements were not in keeping with the dignity and prestige of the Muslim League and requested the speakers not to be "carried away by passions, but to exercise restraint, not wounding the susceptibilities of other communities."[117] The secretary of state for India refused the request for Indian Muslim representation at the Palestine conference, on the grounds that to widen the basis of the representation for one party would entail doing it for the other as well. Jinnah was greatly disappointed and, at the urging of the Arab Higher Committee, appealed the decision.[118]

Gandhi Speaks Out on Palestine

Kallenbach had urged Gandhi to declare publicly his views on the Arab-Jewish question in Palestine and the persecution of the Jews in Germany. The statement in the *Harijan* of 26 November 1938, which was so unsatisfactory concerning the situation in Germany, was also unfavorable to Zionism. Gandhi here reverted to his 1921 position:

> Palestine belongs to the Arabs in the same sense that England belongs to the English or France to the French. . . . What is going on in Palestine today cannot be justified by any moral code of conduct. The mandates have no sanction but that of the last war. Surely it would be a crime against humanity to reduce the proud Arabs so that Palestine can be restored to the Jews partly or wholly as their national home.[119]

If the Jews insisted on settling in Palestine, they had to secure the good will of the Arabs. Gandhi offered the same solution here that he had proposed for the Jews of Germany:

> [The Jews] can offer *Satyagraha* in front of the Arabs and offer themselves to be shot or thrown into the Dead Sea without raising a little finger against them. They will find the world opinion in their favour in their religious aspiration. There are hundreds of ways of reasoning with the Arabs, if they will only discard the help of the British bayonet.
>
> I am not defending the Arab excesses. I wish they had chosen the way of non-violence in resisting what they rightly regarded as an unwarrantable encroachment upon their country. But according to the accepted canons of right and wrong, nothing can be said against the Arab resistance in the face of overwhelming odds.[120]

A. E. Shohet wrote the first Jewish response in the *Jewish Advocate* of 2 December 1938; he asked, among other things, why Gandhi judged the Jews by the highest spiritual standards, but the Arabs by the "accepted canons."

Eliahu Epstein congratulated Shohet on the comprehensive and dignified reply to the Mahatma but wondered whether Shohet's article would reach those Indians who read the *Harijan*. Although Epstein and Leo Kohn believed that polemics with Gandhi would only help to spread his anti-Zionist views and enable pro-Arab circles in London to make an issue of them, Kohn offered to write an article explaining Gandhi's mistakes in regard to the Palestine question if Shohet could have it published in some prominent Indian papers.[121]

Shimoni suggests that Gandhi would have preferred not to have been pressured into saying anything. He realized that both Arabs and Jews had a strong case and he wished to hurt neither: "But he could less afford to hurt the Arabs than the Jews. For . . . Gandhi was still functioning in a real political field of forces in which Hindu-Muslim fidelity remained the sorely-tried fulcrum in his policy."[122] Although the Muslim League did not accept partition in Palestine, it had been talking about partition in India. Gandhi and the Indian National Congress, therefore, so concerned with Indian unity, could not afford to consider partition as a valid concept at all.

The small group of Zionist intellectuals who favored Jewish-Arab rapprochement and peaceful coexistence, such as Martin Buber, Hugo Schlomo Bergmann, and Judah Magnes, were disappointed with Gandhi's statement. In the letters that Buber and Magnes wrote to Gandhi (which probably never reached him), Buber explained that Zionism was the heart of the Jews as a collective group and that the Bible commanded the Jews to fulfill themselves as a community in the real land of Zion, while Magnes argued the need for a spiritual and intellectual center in Palestine. Both challenged Gandhi's position that Palestine belonged to the Arabs and appealed to him to try to influence the Arabs to practice *satyagraha*.[123]

In March 1939 Kallenbach arranged for Shohet to have an interview with Gandhi. There the young editor voiced his disagreement with the Mahatma's views on Zionism. Shohet eventually learned from a letter from Gandhi's secretary that Gandhi had decided not to say anything publicly about the subject of the interview. Although Shohet felt that the Zionists could not expect anything from Gandhi, since he viewed the Palestinian question as a purely Muslim one, Shohet intended to treat very seriously the Mahatma's suggestion that he keep him informed and send him Zionist literature. The editor also urged Kallenbach to arrange for someone of the political department to correspond regularly with Gandhi.[124]

Indian Zionism on the Eve of the War

Zionist activity seemed to perk up a bit in 1939. Shohet had returned from his visit to Palestine with a Polish-born Palestinian wife, who was able to inject some new life into the movement in Bombay. She established the precedent (common in Europe and America) of collecting for the national funds at weddings as a way to link every new Jewish family with the up-building of Eretz Israel. The effort to link Zionism with Jewish social life was realized by the establishment of the Jewish Club in Bombay. An important by-product of this venture was that Shohet got Sir Alwyn Ezra, the wealthy Baghdadi, to pay a considerable amount of the monthly rent of the club and thus brought him, albeit through the back door, to Zionist work. The published list of Jewish National Fund Blue Box clearances for 1939 revealed seventy-four donors—mostly Baghdadi and European Jews. Although Bombay had not yet received a Hebrew teacher, by the beginning of 1939, Tehilla and Peter Krieger, two Hebrew teachers and experienced youth leaders from Palestine, arrived in Calcutta to work through the Jewish Girls School there. In Cochin, a Malabar Zionist movement was created by a group of young men from Ernakulum.[125]

Keren Hayesod sent another Zionist emissary, Yehuda Nedivi, the town clerk of Tel Aviv, to India in March 1939. Indian Jews were excited to meet a representative of the only all-Jewish city in the world. Shohet, in a *Jewish Advocate* editorial, reminded his readers that the contributions of Jews from central European countries had ceased because of Hitler, and that India and Burma would now have to follow in the footsteps of Britain, South Africa, Australia, and New Zealand in picking up the slack. The arrival of German Jewish refugees in India had given the local Jews an insight into the problems now facing the Jewish people, particularly in Palestine. "When we realize how difficult it is to give shelter and work to only a handful of refugees," the editorial maintained, "we can appreciate what Palestine is trying to do at a time of economic standstill and diplomatic and terroristic high pressure."[126]

Nedivi's activities were not limited to fund-raising, however, for as soon as he arrived, he went on a political mission proposed by the Jewish Agency: Kallenbach had been able to arrange for more interviews. Shohet and Nedivi had formal talks with Nehru and Gandhi in Delhi and met other important leaders such as Sardar Vallabhai Patel, the chairman of the Parliamentary Subcommittee of the Congress and a confidant of Gandhi; Mahadev Desai, Gandhi's secretary and the editor of the *Harijan*; G. D. Birla, a major industrialist and financial supporter of Congress; and Bhulabhai Desai, the head of the Bombay Provincial Congress Committee and the leader of the opposition in the Central Legislative Assembly.

Shohet and Nedivi had what they described as a cordial interview with Nehru on 20 March 1939, but they found him still most decided in his views. When Nedivi talked about how the Jews had helped the Arabs, Nehru replied that he had no doubt of it, because he had discussed the Palestine question with many friends who had been there and knew a great deal about what the Jews were doing. But, Nehru said, they were helping the Arabs just as the

British brought many improvements to India. Shohet countered that the British aided India only to enrich Britain, whereas the Jews were investing their efforts and money into Palestine for that country's own benefit: nothing would be taken out. Nehru recognized the difference but was concerned about the spread of anti-Jewish feelings among the Muslims in Africa and Asia over the question of Palestine. He felt that Palestine could play only a small part in solving the refugee question, and as a gesture to the Arabs, the Jews should agree to a temporary suspension of immigration. Shohet retorted that given the Jews' position in eastern and central Europe and the fact that Palestine had taken nearly half the refugees so far, that solution was impossible. If Jews were allowed to immigrate according to the absorptive capacity of the country, even more could be done. Nehru objected to all types of imperialism. Nor was he convinced that the Jews were building a socialist society in Palestine. He favored a delegation to Palestine to survey the conditions on behalf of the Congress, but India was preoccupied with her own problems and could not send investigators now.[127]

During the interview with Gandhi on the following day, in the presence of Kallenbach, the Reverend Charles Andrews, Mahadev Desai, Pyarelal (Gandhi's secretary), Patel, and others, Gandhi asked why, if the conditions were as described by Nedivi, the troubles were so widespread and the British placed such a large army in Palestine without apparently being able to quell the rebellion. Nedivi replied that the British must be massing soldiers in Palestine for reasons other than safeguarding the Jewish population, which, not wanting the military, was largely defending itself, a right it had clamored for. Gandhi said his own sympathy was entirely with the Jews and asked what more they expected him to do and in what way he could help them. As the Jews were an Eastern people who wanted to return to their ancient home in the East, Shohet and Nedivi argued, Gandhi could help them win the much-needed sympathy and favorable opinion of India, an Eastern nation. The Mahatma reiterated that it would not help the Jews if he were to condemn the way in which propaganda was carried on among the Muslims in India. Muslim opinion was artificially worked up and the Jews had nothing to fear from it, as it was not based on just grievances. Gandhi considered the Muslim League propaganda on the Palestine question as being directed against the Congress. Shohet thought the Mahatma meant that any remarks from him would only lead to greater controversy and publicity. When they raised the question of sending an Indian delegation to Palestine, Gandhi replied that a non-Muslim delegation would be of no use to the Jews.[128]

The report of this meeting comes from Shohet, who was again very disappointed when he received the minutes of the interview from Gandhi's secretary, because he felt that he and Nedivi had been misquoted and that there were many omissions and errors in what Gandhi had said. Although

Gandhi had appeared sympathetic and cordial in the interview, it seemed to Shohet that the minutes had been shaped to conform with the Mahatma's ideology: again, Gandhi would not say anything about the part the Muslims played in the Palestine question, even in the minutes of a private interview. Shohet had a more realistic view of Gandhi than Olsvanger had had, realizing that "today Gandhi is India," and that the Mahatma was indeed in a position to shape Indian public opinion. Shohet and Nedivi still wanted the Jewish Agency to send a "real politician" to meet Gandhi and Nehru, the only person in Congress, they felt, who was interested in international questions. Nehru might not play an important part in the inner cabinet of the Congress, but he did command great publicity in the Indian press, and socialists and youth looked up to him. Sardar Patel, the real power behind Gandhi, was not interested in Palestine and other non-Indian questions at all. Unfortunately, there is no way to judge whether Shohet's report or the notes on the interview are more reliable, but I am inclined to believe Shohet as his political reporting was generally accurate.[129]

In a final assessment, the Zionists' efforts to reach Gandhi would have to be termed unsuccessful. The Mahatma's need to maintain Hindu-Muslim friendship in India prevented him from voicing publicly any support for Zionism.[130]

But Nedivi, after all, had not come to India mainly to speak with Gandhi. When he returned to Bombay, he began his fund-raising campaign in earnest, making a direct public appeal before one of the largest Jewish gatherings in Bombay for many years. The public press was not invited to this lecture, presided over by Meyer Nissim, because Nedivi showed a film about the training of the Jewish Defence Corps and did not want non-Jews, especially Muslims, to see or read about it. But Nedivi's later lecture at the Jewish Club on Tel Aviv was reported prominently in the *Times of India*, which in addition published a long interview with him. He also spoke with youth groups, both Bene Israel and Baghdadi, whom Shohet was having trouble involving in Zionist activities.[131]

After a stay of thirteen days, Nedivi concluded that in Bombay one could rely on the work only of J. J. Gubbay and Erna Petzal, the wife of a German Jewish doctor, who was particularly good at attracting donations from Continental Jews. The other BZA committee members, A. Leser and Fred Klein, two Continental Jews, although both devoted Zionists, were too deeply engrossed in refugee work to be of much help to the Zionists. Nevertheless, in Bombay, the committee members had donated as much as or more than they could really afford, which was more than he could say for the Calcutta committee members.[132]

In fact, by 1939 the Zionists felt that the greatest obstacle to their fund-raising was the local refugee committee, which was collecting monthly subscriptions and lump sums from everyone. A good source of regular income that had been tapped by the Zionists in 1932 had been the Sassoon group of mills, where a large number of poor Jews had contributed fifteen hundred rupees to Keren Hayesod. Now, however, they were being canvased by the local refugee committee and had nothing left to give the Zionists. Other obstacles were the Sargons, who renewed their agitation during Nedivi's visit. The head offices in Jerusalem had told Nedivi to ignore the Sargon issue, but the local committees would not permit him to do so because of the local press war. Nedivi was willing to try to bring about a reconciliation, but J. J. Gubbay insisted that he continue to ignore the Sargons, threatening to withdraw entirely from the BZA's work if Nedivi intervened in what Gubbay termed a personal matter. This the Zionists could not afford. Nedivi also felt that Keren Hayesod and Keren Keyemet L'Israel should agree on their policy toward the Sargons.

Like his predecessors, Nedivi was most impressed with Shohet, whom he found overworked, putting out the *Jewish Advocate* almost single-handedly, and doing a lot of lecturing and organizing. Nedivi suggested a rearrangement of the financial support so that Shohet's salary would be considered not a part of the subsidy to the BZA, but rather a direct salary by Jerusalem, as it was to all its other salaried officials.

In Calcutta, Nedivi found his work hampered both by simultaneous canvasing for other funds and by the presence of the young Edmund de Rothschild of London, then visiting India on a world tour and lecturing everywhere on the desirability of settling refugees in various parts of the British Empire, immigration to Palestine now being very limited.[132] Nedivi got David Ezra to contribute one thousand rupees (Nedivi erroneously claimed it to be the first contribution Ezra had ever made to Zionism). Lady Ezra helped the emissary in soliciting contributions and managed to get two hundred rupees from G. D. Birla, one of the leading industrialists in India. Rothschild even said he wanted to visit Palestine and gave Nedivi a check for five hundred rupees. Nedivi suggested that Jerusalem try to bring Lady Ezra into active participation in any field she chose. He also warned that local Jewish politics in Calcutta involving the Ezras, Ezra Arakie, and the Kriegers (the Hebrew teachers from Palestine) needed to be handled carefully.[134]

Shohet felt that Nedivi's campaign was financially a success. By the time Nedivi left, he had collected 4,951 rupees (including first-time gifts from Sir Alwyn Ezra and Mozelle Nathan) from Bombay, and 4,416 rupees from Calcutta.[135] Nedivi concluded that although the Jewish community in India was numerically small, it was nevertheless potentially important, but needed constant information about Jewish realities the world over, especially, perhaps through films, about what was being achieved in Palestine. Everyone complained that between delegates the territory was left unworked and the enthusiasm aroused was allowed to subside. The emissary also set up machinery to collect and send to the Bene Israel school, in accordance with its wishes, as complete a set as possible of the Hebrew textbooks used in the municipal elementary schools of Tel Aviv. Although he reiterated the findings of earlier delegates that the Bene Israel were very poor and could not supply large funds, Nedivi favored support for the work of Rebecca Reuben, the principal of the school, believing it would have an excellent effect everywhere in India. He also suggested bringing Reuben to Palestine for a visit so that she could examine the educational system and adopt what she could.[136] This proposal was the first suggestion of financing a trip for a Bene Israel to Palestine.

There is no indication that Nedivi visited Cochin, although Mandelbaum observed in this period that Zionism had recently become a common field of interest on which the various castes in Cochin could meet. He mentioned that Zionist representatives had visited the city and "readily implanted their idea and ideal there, and that several young men, from all three castes, were enthusiastic Zionists and worked in cooperation to raise funds for Palestine."[137]

Conclusion

In the period 1936–39 the various themes and events that would affect the sense of identity of the Jews of India came together. The failure to obtain their goal of inclusion on the European electoral rolls forced the Baghdadi Jews of Calcutta to rethink their position. Perhaps they had erred in concentrating on European status, and should now work, in cooperation with the Bene Israel and Cochin Jews, on obtaining communal rights as Jews. The Government of India Act, with its communal preferences in the services, seemed to threaten their economic well-being, and the ever-increasing strength of the Indian nationalists seemed to threaten their political interests. If India were to become independent, who would safeguard Jewish rights? Some politically articulate Bene Israel, however, were convinced that the Jews would not get lost in the shuffle and that the nationalists would protect them.

The European Jewish refugees who were arriving in this period did not get caught up in these issues. They were too preoccupied with their own problems of absorption and acceptance, and in any case, as they considered themselves to be only transients in India during the war years, the position of Jews in an independent India was not uppermost in their minds. If anything, they were more concerned with Zionism, having had firsthand experience of the need for a Jewish homeland. The European Jews' very presence (as well as the reasons for it) thus heightened the local Jewish communities' sense of Jewish consciousness.

It was during this period that the Palestine problem loomed so large: just as European Jews needed a homeland more than ever, Britain, to forestall Arab rebellion in the coming war, prepared to placate the Arabs by moving toward a restriction of Jewish immigration. The importance of Indian opinion, Hindu as well as Muslim, was not lost on Jewish Agency leaders, particularly people like Shertok and Epstein, who feared that Indian antagonism toward Britain's pro-Jewish Palestine policy would encourage Britain to tilt the other way. Thus the Jewish Agency leadership enlisted the help of local Jews, and anyone else, in gaining sympathy for the Zionists, and it sent emissaries to Gandhi and Nehru in an attempt to turn Hindu opinion in favor of Zionism. By the middle of 1939, however, that cause seemed to be lost.

During the war years all these themes—Indian nationalism, Jewish sense of identity, and Zionism, with its implications—began to crystalize. To this period we can now turn.

PART IV
THE WAR AND ITS AFTERMATH

CHAPTER 7

CHALLENGES OF THE WAR

The Indian nationalists understandably felt slighted when, in September 1939, Lord Linlithgow, the viceroy, declared India at war with Germany without consulting with Congress. New confrontations followed. Congress at first offered to support the war effort if Britain would promise India independence after the war and grant immediately more Indian participation and responsibility in the central government. Britain's refusal to transfer such power during the war led to the resignation of congressional provincial ministries. Indian anxiety mounted with the fall of France and the Battle of Britain, but so did suspicions of the British, who continued to postpone all steps toward dominion status until after the war.[1] Britain now counted on her protected minorities in India to rally to her cause, a pressure that divided the Christian community. While the older generation, most white-collar workers, and a vocal group of missionaries openly or quietly supported the British, pacifists and conservatives remained neutral. The influence of a tiny group of younger laymen, pastors, and missionaries who backed the nationalists was limited.[2] For the Jews of India, there could be no ambivalence toward the Allied cause.

Jewish Mobilization for the War Effort

When the war finally broke out, the Jewish communities made their stand clear immediately. Synagogues offered prayers for the speedy termination of the war and the success of Britain and her allies. The Bene Israel of Tiffereth Israel Synagogue stated that, in accordance with their ancient traditions, they were prepared to support Britain in her war against Nazism and oppression. The Calcutta Hebrew Association (Baghdadi) sent a wire to the viceroy, affirming its loyalty to the king and the British government and assuring Linlithgow that "there is not a Jewish soul who will not show his gratitude by sacrificing his all for the success of the British arms."[3] Before the outbreak of the war, Edmond de Rothschild, having visited India for three months, had sent a message to the Jews there through the Jewish Agency, reiterating what many knew: "I have seen that many of the different sections of Jewry are at variance with each other. German Jews, British Jews, Baghdadi Jews, Bene-Israelites [sic] and Cochin Jews must tolerate and co-operate with each other for otherwise a divided Jewry will fall."[4]

Once the war started, the need for Indian Jews to stand together to interpret the Jewish position for the Indian community at large and to mobilize contributions of money and personnel to the war effort seems to have promoted an increased unity. The Bombay Zionist Association arranged for a meeting on 25 October 1939, at which, for the first time, all sections of the Jewish community met on one platform to express loyalty and unanimity of opinion and purpose. Speaking in the name of the Zionists, A. E. Shohet, the Baghdadi editor of the *Jewish Advocate* and the official representative in India of the Jewish Agency for Palestine, supported Weizmann, who had stated that "the Jews stand by Britain and will fight on the side of the Democracies," despite the critical attitude of the Zionists toward the British government on the subject of Palestine.[5] Shohet voiced the Zionists' confidence that if the war would end Hitlerism and reestablish the rule of law and the right to live of small nations, then the Jews' right to national freedom would once again be asserted. Solomon Moses, a Bene Israel solicitor, made clear that the war was not against the German people, but against Hitlerism. John Klein, chairman of the Jewish Relief Association, thanked the government of India, the provincial governments, and the people of the country for the succor and help extended to the Jews who had come there as refugees. The release, so far, of more than half the interned Jews had been ordered, and he hoped that they and the rest would find in India what they had lacked in their own country—security and freedom to work for their advancement and that of the country. The meeting passed a resolution expressing these views, which the viceroy acknowledged through Alwyn Ezra, saying he would forward the communication to the emperor.[6]

The Jewish newspapers and their editors played a leading role in the community in this period. During the first year of the war, the *Jewish Advocate* and the *Jewish Tribune* commented on political events affecting the general effort, particularly within Great Britain, such as the dismissal of Leslie Hore-Belisha (a Jew) as secretary of state for war from the Chamberlain cabinet, the resignation of Chamberlain himself, and the detention of Sir Oswald Mosley and his clique because of his pro-Nazi and anti-Jewish views. Naturally, the papers always commented on Jewish news and problems during the war and began to focus on the position of Jewish refugees in Shanghai. An anti-Nazi broadcast organized by All-India Radio, on which five Jewish immigrants from Germany talked about their experience in Nazi Germany and in concentration camps, also elicited attention.[7] The major concern and thrust of the Jewish press in these early years, however, was to promote the Indian Jewish war effort and to report on its progress.

On 15 July 1940 Bombay Jewry met again to mobilize its forces to help

Britain in the war. Dr. E. Moses presided and the speakers, who included Solomon Moses, M. E. Haskell (a Baghdadi), Joseph Sargon, and A. E. Shohet, once more stressed the need for concerted action by the entire community for the overthrow of Hitlerism. The meeting elected a committee of thirty to translate the resolutions into practice and to plan social and welfare work. The *Jewish Tribune* wrote that "never in the annals of the community was a more representative gathering present." A similar meeting was convened in Poona by Edward Iny, a Baghdadi, and M. R. Reuben, a Bene Israel, who appealed to the community not to lag behind the efforts of Bombay and to join the civic guards and army in large numbers. The gathering, addressed in English, Marathi, and Hindustani, also formed a committee to devise ways of coordinating the community's war effort and collecting donations to the various war funds.[8]

Shohet and Sargon, the editors of the Jewish papers, hoped that the appointment of these committees would accelerate the communities' efforts, for they felt that until now, Bombay Jewry had contributed minimally. The money collected fell short of expectations and some names were conspicuous by their absence from the list of donors and contributions regularly published by the *Jewish Advocate*. By September 1940, forty-six donors had contributed 13,535 rupees. Most of the contributors were Baghdadis, a few were European Jews, and only a handful were Bene Israel. The large donors, those giving over 1,000 rupees, were mainly Baghdadis and Europeans. The Bene Israel clearly constituted the less affluent section of the community: only I. J. Samson and Solomon Moses were able to afford 1,000 or more rupees. Sir Alwyn Ezra and Sir Victor Sassoon, in a category of their own as two of the wealthiest Jews of India, contributed generously from the outset. Sir Alwyn gave 100,000 rupees to the war fund in India in the first days of the war, one of the first and largest contributions from a private individual. He later donated another 30,000 rupees (25,000 from the Sassoon J. David Trust and 5,000 from his personal funds) in support of the Indian Red Cross Appeal of the viceroy. Sir Victor Sassoon, whose contributions to refugee relief were reported to be the highest in the East, donated one million yen to the war fund and also presented valuable jewelry to be sold by auction in America to buy fighter planes for the Royal Air Force, as a gift to help Britain.[9]

Jews also enrolled in the armed forces. Until 1918 no Indian could hold a royal commission: the highest rank an Indian could reach was subedar major, which despite its status corresponded to regimental sergeant major in a British regiment. After 1918 royal commissions were occasionally granted to Indians who came from the proper social status and family. But with the outbreak of war in 1939, the commissions became readily available on a merit basis. Many educated Bene Israel took advantage of the opportunities and became high-ranking officers.[10]

For Baghdadis, however, the issue of Jewish enrollment in the British army became a serious problem. In Calcutta, Colonel C. Warren-Boulton had formed a Jewish platoon, which had attracted many youths. By January 1940, however, the army authorities were questioning the eligibility of Jews for the Indian Auxiliary Force, an adjunct of the Indian Army, and Warren-Boulton had been instructed not to enroll any more. He asked the leaders of the Jewish community to take up the issue with the authorities and support his own representations. In pursuing the matter, the Jewish leaders discovered that unless Jews could establish European descent on the male side, the recruiting officials were strictly justified in excluding them. Representations by Sir David Ezra, D. J. Cohen, and Eric Ellis, of the firm of E. D. Sassoon and Company, were instrumental in persuading the army authorities to allow enrollment in the Indian Auxiliary Force in those cases where the individual was certified by synagogue authorities as being of European descent, even though this lineage could not be proved by documentary evidence. Therefore, Indian-born Jews would not be legally entitled to claim the status of British soldiers, but officials were inclined, in selected cases, to interpret the regulations in a liberal way.[11]

Several members of the Calcutta community also approached Sir Victor Sassoon to use his influence to ascertain the status of the Jews in the Indian Army. The government's clarification was published in the *Jewish Advocate*:

> At present Indian Jews and Anglo-Indian Jews must be enrolled under the Indian Army Act as Indian soldiers. If after enrollment, they are considered by their local military commanders to be habituated to a European or similar style of life and food, they may be granted British scales of rations. Anglo-Indian Jews, but not Indian Jews, get British courtesy ranks in certain units and in all cases accommodation, clothing and medical treatment as for British soldiers. Indian Jews get these services as for Indian soldiers.
>
> Anglo-Indians receive the same pay as Indians unless they are enlisted into British units when they receive British rates of pay.
>
> Any representations regarding the status of Jews of Indian nationality should be sent to the Secretary, Defence Department.[12]

There was some confusion about what was meant by the term *Anglo-Indian Jews* since there were not many Jews who could claim European ancestry in the male line. Both Joseph Sargon and E. M. Musleah assumed that the term referred to Jews from Arabic-speaking countries who had settled in India in the last one to two hundred years; they thought that the more appropriate term would be *Sephardic*.[13] In any case, given the government's reluctance to distinguish between Jews in the 1930s, this declaration was somewhat surprising.

Students of the Anglo-Indian question felt that the British tried to increase their own quota of recruits in India by enrolling Anglo-Indians. Recruiting officers deliberately encouraged, and even compelled, Anglo-Indians, particularly the lighter-skinned members of the community, to register themselves as Europeans, even though officially Anglo-Indians were classified as non-Europeans in the armed services. As Great Britain reserved the air force for the British, Anglo-Indians could not enlist in that branch in India. Nevertheless, some four thousand Anglo-Indians who went to Britain were accepted into the Royal Air Force as British recruits.[14]

Despite these questions, the dual themes of mobilization and unity persisted for the Jews. In March 1941 the Bombay Zionist Association organized a youth conference to bring about closer cooperation among various sections of the Jewish community in Bombay in social, cultural, and educational affairs. Although most of the groups serving on the planning committee were Bene Israel organizations, some twenty institutions from all sections sent official delegates and more than five hundred individuals attended. Many considered the conference to be the most successful Jewish function held in recent years in Bombay. Speeches emphasized the importance of the Jews of India serving as interpreters of Jewish aspirations and ideals to the people of India, millions of whom, A. E. Shohet argued, had never seen a Jew:

> in view of the response to the Nazi anti-Semitic propaganda . . . given by some sections in India up to the outbreak of the war, it was necessary that people . . . should come to know and understand the Jew as he is and not as he is painted by his detractors.[15]

Others hoped that the youth would abandon the prejudices that so far had divided the community and would unite behind a Zionist ideal. A federation of synagogues, the exchange of students and teachers from the two Jewish schools, and closer coordination among the various Bene Israel, Baghdadi, and European women's groups were some of the ideas put forth.[16]

Norman Shohet (A. E. Shohet's brother), a Baghdadi who was now editor of the *Jewish Advocate*, expressed the views of many in his editorial:

> The question of inter-sectional cooperation is the most important issue before the Jewish community in India. For many years past there has been a distinct division between the Bene Israel community—the largest, and historically and intellectually the most important section—and the other locally-established Jews, coming largely from Iraq, who have economically enjoyed a comparatively stronger position so far. This division among the Jewish community has been further emphasized in recent years by the impact of a few hundred refugees from Europe, who more or less have founded a section of their own. . . . What is most unfortunate however, is that few people . . . seem to realize to what extent have these divisions contributed to the disintegration of the community as a whole.
> . . . Suffice it to say that [the reasons for this state of affairs] are fundamentally un-Jewish, and, politically dangerous. . . . The Bene Israel section, for instance, is largely cut off from the main current of Jewish thought and problems; . . . the [Baghdadi] section is intellectually in a backwater, and the Continental section is hard put to it to interest sufficiently the local

people in its relief problems. Close cooperation will automatically solve all these problems. What is then in the way?

First of all the old hostilities are not yet dead. A more formidable obstacle is that the accredited leadership of the various sections—with the exception of the Zionist element—is not interested in, and is unfortunately unable to see the need of communal cooperation.[17]

After the conference, the community organized a standing body, whose meetings were attended by representatives from about twenty-five Baghdadi and Bene Israel groups. They sponsored a Jewish sports meet that created good understanding and cooperation in the community.

The following year the *Jewish Advocate* acknowledged that it had been "singularly lacking in what may be called inside knowledge" of the Bene Israel. A columnist called "Mevaer" asked for a young Bene Israel to edit a page devoted to news and views of particular interest to that community, hoping that Rebecca Reuben would offer her services. Shortly thereafter the paper did publish a lengthy article by an unidentified "Special Correspondent" on the Bene Israel Sir Elly Kadourie High School. In a later issue "Mevaer" criticized a circular, endorsed by the Jewish Relief Association and signed by Baghdadi and European Jews, that called upon the community to observe 20 December 1942 as a day of fasting and mourning in view of the catastrophic situation facing the Jews in Europe. "Mevaer" asked why the largest section of the Jewish community in Bombay, the Bene Israel, had not been asked to sign. He felt that the JRA, if it wanted to, could best heal the "old but apparently still lingering feud" between the two local sections of the community. "Mevaer" argued that services in every synagogue in Bombay, not just in Knesset Eliahu, the Baghdadi synagogue in the Fort, should have been arranged.[18] Such incidents must have caused continuing resentment among the Bene Israel at a time when solidarity was so needed.

The entry of Japan into the war brought the threat to India's doorstep. Calcutta Jews now had to absorb more than twelve hundred Jews (mainly Baghdadis) fleeing from Burma and Singapore. Calcutta became an important base for operations in the Eastern theater of war; as American and British troops arrived in large numbers, the Jewish community provided hospitality for Jewish servicemen and the Judean Club became an active social center.[19] Gandhi, with the war so close, now held out for greater concessions. Rejecting as insufficient the government's offer of a constitutional assembly elected by the provincial legislatures that would draw up a dominion constitution for India immediately after the war, Gandhi, on 9 August 1942, launched the Quit India movement. He argued that the British in India were a provocation to the Japanese and demanded that the British withdraw under threat of a new civil disobedience movement.[20] Congress party leaders were jailed. M. N. Roy, however, believed that the Quit India movement was poorly timed:

India should not upset the British during the war because Hitler was the greatest enemy.

The day after the Quit India movement was launched, a previously scheduled Bene Israel youth convention was held. No notice was taken of the great political event that had happened the night before (although some of the "youths" were in their thirties), and activities went on as planned. Some Bene Israel thought that this action was typical of the apolitical attitude of their community.[21] Some Bene Israel, however, although they did not want to serve actively in political movements, helped the nationalists from behind the scenes. S. R. Bandarkar, later to become the editor of *Maccabi*, took part in Congress functions in 1939 and in the Quit India movement in 1942. He worked underground in the movement, printing bulletins, carrying messages, and passing around pamphlets written by independence leaders in the Parel district. He was caught, detained for several days, and harassed.[22] Two younger sons of Jacob B. Israel were also caught up in the Quit India movement. I. J. Samson's son Arthur was involved with the nationalists, procuring a place where they could make bombs at night. Dr. Erulkar, however, switched his loyalty from Gandhi to Roy in this period, believing it was the wrong time to oppose the British. He would not join the Quit India movement. Another Bene Israel, E. M. Jacob, expressed similar concerns: "What if Hitler were to win the war," he asked, "what would have been the position of Indians? And Indian Jews?" Otherwise, he wanted the British out.[23]

By August 1943 the *Jewish Advocate* could feel proud of the Jewish war effort, considering the community's size and general economic position. Although no statistics were available for the number of Jews who had enlisted in the armed forces, most established families had at least one person serving, and a few had as many as three. A fair number of Jewish young men had secured commissions and some had already attained the post of captain. The navy was the most popular branch among Indian Jewish youths. Refugees who had not yet been accepted in the fighting forces, despite their repeated offers of service, were serving on the home front. The Jewish Division of the Saint John's Ambulance Brigade did its part by offering first aid and other courses.[24] Jews, especially refugees, were also promoting the country's war effort in industrial and technical fields. Jews across India, from national figures like Sir Victor Sassoon and Sir Alwyn Ezra to local business people, were busy with war orders from the government. The creation of the Jewish War Efforts Committee in Bombay had helped somewhat to centralize the work of fund-raising, although the *Jewish Advocate* noted that there was still much to be done. Sir Alwyn Ezra's contributions were singled out for praise: in addition to his initial donations, he had founded Bombay's blood bank, had presented many cash gifts to service canteens, and had provided rent-free resorts, cafes, and reading and rest rooms, as well as a holiday home for

British troops in Kashmir. At the beginning of 1943 he donated twenty-five thousand rupees for amenities and a welfare fund for an Indian Air Force training school near Bombay, and a similar amount for the Royal Indian Navy Benefit Fund. The *Advocate* doubted that any other private individual in India could claim to have done as much.[25]

The Refugee Problem

In addition to mobilizing money and personnel to aid the British war effort, the Jewish communities also had to deal with an increasingly complicated refugee situation. On 1 September 1939, 1,520 German subjects, including women, were registered in British India, not counting those in the Indian states. At the outbreak of war, 850 of these were interned, including all male Jewish refugees, who were technically described as "enemy aliens." Although the solution of the refugees' problems fell most heavily on the shoulders of the Jewish Relief Association, all Jews in India were concerned about them.

A. E. Shohet felt that even if Nazi activities in India were deemed so widespread that the government did not feel justified in taking risks, the decision to intern the Jewish refugees in common with other German nationals was a regrettable step. Other parts of the British Empire had done better. Indeed, the government soon instituted an enquiry commission, the Darling Interrogation Committee, to look into the cases of "friendly enemy aliens." Attached to this committee, A. W. Rosenfeld, the honorary secretary of the Jewish Relief Association, assumed great responsibility, traveling to Delhi to interview officials and visiting internment camps to obtain the release of all bona fide Jewish refugees. Within a couple of months, practically all of them, some 317, were released, along with about 70 other Germans, mainly missionaries.[26] But because the Darling Interrogation Committee did not explicitly state that the refugees were no longer to be regarded as "enemy aliens," their legal position left much to be desired, even though they had all placed their services at the disposal of the government. Shohet advocated that the refugees should be given citizenship as they were willing to fight against their country of origin. Jewish opinion in India was in strong sympathy with "normalizing" the position of the German refugees, and the secretary of the JRA took this matter up with the Home Department.[27]

The internment problem did not end there, however, because new refugees continued to arrive. After the fall of France, public agitation led to the internment of a number of refugees, and a second enquiry commission was established. Once again, A. W. Rosenfeld negotiated to obtain their release. The Indian government decided that even German Jews who had been deprived of their German nationality by the German Ordinance of 25 November

1941 were still liable to internment.[28] Thus, as of May 1943, forty-one Jewish families (sixty-one persons) were still in internment camps, as were sixty-five Jewish refugees sent to India from other countries for internment. The JRA continued its efforts.[29]

At the outset of the war, despite the internment problem, the JRA tried to persuade the government to modify its rules regulating the admission of refugees. It was successful in obtaining the admission of about one hundred fifty persons, mostly aged parents and dependents of those who had already found employment in India. But the JRA was also most anxious that the refugees in India not jeopardize their own position by their conduct, and thus, on 23 September 1939, distributed a circular advising them to behave with circumspection:

> As a result of the War, a certain amount of anti-German feeling is certain to be current in this country and this may easily be turned against the Refugees by ignorant people. Refugees are requested for the sake of themselves, their families and the other refugees to do everything to avoid attracting public attention. They owe this duty also to the Government of India which is showing them great consideration and which might come in for criticism if the fact that a number of German citizens are left free comes specially to the public notice.[30]

The circular urged them not to appear conspicuously in public places, especially in places of entertainment. They were warned not to speak German, even among themselves or over the telephone, and advised to avoid all foreign languages and speak only English, as the "average inhabitant of this country is unacquainted with Continental languages and may mistake any language for German." Of course they were told never to utter a word on political subjects. In short, they were to do nothing that would engender any gossip that could lead to public opinion being directed against all refugees.[31]

The spread of the war had created new problems and added to the responsibilities of the Jewish Relief Association. Refugees from Allied countries and Poland found their way through Russia and Japan to India, where they had to be fed, clothed, and looked after before they could continue to Palestine or North or South America. They often had to be given fares to their ultimate destinations. Later, with the fall of Singapore, Malay, and Burma to Japan, Jewish evacuees to India created yet another challenge. Government-financed hostels were set up, and the JRA was entrusted with running them and coping with the needs of the evacuees.[32]

The *Jewish Advocate*, which published news on the general steps taken to alleviate the refugee problem the world over, appealed for a united effort by all Indian Jews, reminding them that relief was exclusively a Jewish obligation, despite the sympathy shown by the government and other communities. When government maintenance allowances were not sufficient to meet needs, as in the case of the evacuees from Singapore and Burma who were staying in Bombay and Calcutta, the *Advocate* appealed for extra grants for maintenance, medical expenses, food for children, and funds for Passover holidays.[33] Requests for funds were signed by Bene Israel, Baghdadis, and Europeans alike. Calcutta Jewry did not have a working committee, so the burden fell on a few individuals, especially the Ezras. Through the paper, the JRA urged local Jews to make newcomers feel at home, show them around, and entertain them. At times the interests of the refugees and the Bombay committee of the JRA clashed. The committee's philosophy was not to allow the refugees to become dependent on charity, but to assist them by setting them on their feet so that, in time, they could repay the money advanced and give further assistance to themselves. The association pleaded with sympathizers in Bombay and up-country who could advise and find openings for refugees. The refugees, however, wanted the Jewish committees to help them financially all they could.[34]

The JRA was also concerned with the condition of refugees in Shanghai, which, by late 1939, was the only city accepting mass Jewish immigration. The Shanghai Jewish community could not take care of the newcomers alone and the British authorities there, who regarded the Jewish refugees as enemy aliens, added to their difficulties. The *Jewish Advocate*, therefore, urged Bombay Jewry to contribute to their coreligionists in Shanghai as well. A popular way of raising money was to hold a cinema benefit: during this period the money was often divided three ways—one-third each to Shanghai, Bombay, and Calcutta.

Naturalization

The outbreak of the war created the challenges not only of internment and continued absorption, but also of the naturalization of "enemy aliens." By 1939 many Jewish refugees had been in India over five years and were theoretically eligible for naturalization. In the five-year period ending 31 December 1938, the government had granted a total of 338 certificates of naturalization to eligible aliens, but it was hard to say how many were Jews.[35] As we have seen, in November 1914 the prohibition against naturalization of enemy aliens for the duration of World War I had been extended to the subjects of the Ottoman Empire. The central government had refused the request of the Bombay government for the exemption of "selected Baghdadi Jews, non-Muslim Ottoman subjects of 'the Greek race' and natives of Arabia resident in Bombay."

During World War II, the government again had to consider its policy in regard to naturalization of allied, neutral, and enemy foreigners, including bona fide refugees from Germany and Austria. In December 1939 E. Conran-Smith, secretary to the government of India, stated that rather than estab-

lishing a rigid rule absolutely prohibiting the naturalization of German subjects during the war, the government should exercise the greatest caution and
subject every application to close scrutiny. For Germans who were not Jewish
refugees, naturalization would be permitted only in very rare and exceptional
cases. The Home Department realized that the applications from German
Jewish refugees would increase and that some of these individuals might be
able to be naturalized without undue risk.[36] Such was the case, for example,
of a young man, Herbert Jacob Bund, who had arrived in India in 1934 but
could not be included in his father's application for the naturalization of his
family because he was just over twenty-one. He was therefore the only member of the family who was not naturalized, and the government now granted
him the certificate. Dr. Hermann David Laemmle, a skilled ear, nose, and
throat specialist, squeezed in, as did Johanna Rosenfeld, who was living with
her son, A. W. Rosenfeld, already a naturalized British subject "who had
done useful work for the Jewish Relief Association."[37]

On 15 February 1940, however, the question of Jews was addressed more
specifically in a letter from E. Conran-Smith to the chief secretaries of the
provincial governments. He stated that although fairly adequate and reliable
information was available about the activities of Jewish refugees of enemy
nationality in India, no means existed, owing to the outbreak of the war, of
obtaining information about their antecedents and connections in Europe.
There was a distinct risk that pressure could be brought to bear upon naturalized German Jews through their relatives in Germany:

> The Government of India had decided, therefore, that as a general rule,
> Germans, *whether Jewish refugees or not*, will not be naturalized as British
> subjects during the war, unless the case presented exceptional features.
> Such exceptional cases would be considered and decided on their merits.[38]

Once this policy of excluding Jews also was established, the only exception
made was that of Fanny Deckert, a Jewish orphan who was a ward of the
Jewish Relief Association, which was considering sending her to Britain for
education. Her mother had been a naturalized British subject.[39]

India was aware that it was adopting a position different from that of
London, which was more lenient toward Jewish refugees, but the government
felt that conditions in India were different from those in the United Kingdom,
where public opinion was a more important element of support to government and where aliens were subject to much more critical surveillance by
their neighbors.[40]

The strictness of the government's new policy after 15 February 1940
greatly disturbed the Jewish Relief Association. Its president, Sir Alwyn Ezra,
whose contributions to the war cause were well known, informed the Home
Department that although the government had said that in principle the

naturalization of German Jewish refugees would be considered (every case on its merits), a number of requests had been returned with the decision that the applicants could apply again after termination of the war. Ezra wrote, "It is felt that this new decision will cause a great amount of nervousness amongst refugees who . . . have every desire to terminate their former nationality and become useful citizens of their new fatherland and the British Empire." In its response, the government simply reiterated its policy, explaining that exceptional cases would still be considered. Ezra wrote back that the provincial governments always returned the applications: could the government of India arrange for the provincial governments to submit them to the central authorities to be scrutinized uniformly for special features? He also asked about a proposal he had made personally in Delhi for the issue of interim papers for those refugees who were willing to hand over their German passports, simply to clarify their status.[41] But nothing changed. Soon the prohibition of naturalization of Germans, both Jews and Aryans, was extended to cover European aliens in general during the war unless their cases were exceptional.[42]

In the years following, the Home Department applied its policy quite rigidly. Applications from German or Jewish refugees who had been in India over five years, who had served in the Indian Army, often as doctors, and who were strongly recommended by their European superiors, all were turned down.[43] The Jewish Relief Association of Bombay now tried to enlist the aid of Sir Jeremy Raisman, finance member in India (and a Jew). They informed him that all Jewish refugee doctors of military age had volunteered for the Royal Army Medical Corps (which was not open to Indians in India, who had to join the Indian Medical Service) and that those who were not admitted to military hospitals had been employed as civilians by the government in evacuee camps, internment camps, and parole centers. Several older doctors were working as civilians in British military hospitals. The total amounted to fifty doctors. The JRA suggested that Raisman take up with the government the question of the naturalization of these doctors, at least of those who had already been in India five years or more, most of whom had given up very good practices in order to work against the Nazis. Raisman apparently did follow up, because the government files contain a letter from the Home Department to K. C. Roy of the Finance Department in May 1944, explaining the government's position. Government service in the defense forces in any capacity would not in itself justify an exception being made, since several other European subjects of enemy or other alien nationalities were in similar situations, and it would be embarrassing to pick out the Jewish refugee doctors for particularly favorable treatment. They should therefore await the termination of hostilities.[44]

Continued Relief Efforts

Simultaneous with its efforts to resolve the naturalization question, the JRA continued its day-to-day welfare work. It operated a hostel in Bombay for all Jewish refugees who could not afford to maintain their own homes and gave free board and lodging to those who had no work. The association did not believe in doles. In most cases, when the refugees found work, they paid something back to the hostel. By late 1942 the JRA had about three hundred members all over India, and an annual budget of thirty to forty thousand rupees, of which perhaps twelve to fifteen thousand were paid by refugees who had established themselves with the help of the association.[45]

The annual meetings of the JRA were well attended. By 1943 it seemed to be the most representative Jewish organization in India, to which every Jew turned. Its original scope of providing aid to Jews from central Europe who wanted to settle in India or who were on their way to Shanghai had expanded to assisting Jewish refugees from all over. Early in 1943, 1,227 survivors from Poland, including 900 orphaned children, arrived in Karachi in transit to Palestine. The JRA sent a delegate, Dr. H. Cynowicz, a Polish Jew who had settled in Bombay, to report on their condition and to organize help.[46] The *Jewish Advocate* wrote, "Unfortunately, we in India are not yet properly organized to contribute our legitimate share towards a sane and sound solution of the Jewish problem." At its 1943 annual meeting the JRA discussed trying to strengthen its ties and contacts with other Jewish groups and communities in India. They all had to prepare themselves for the postwar period, when the problem of coordinating help to the survivors of the mass slaughter of European Jewry would require strongly organized communities in each country. F. W. Pollack, a German Jew who had been living in Palestine and was now resident in Bombay, expressed the hope that the JRA would understand the needs and play a leading role in uniting all Jews in Bombay, indeed throughout India.[47]

Anti-Semitic Responses

According to the 1941 census of India, the Jews numbered 22,480 in a total population of 389,000,000.[48] While India had no history of anti-Semitism, many Jews feared it because of German propaganda and the views of Subhas Chandra Bose. Bose, who had succeeded Nehru as president of the Indian National Congress, had said in 1938, at the time of the November pogrom (*Kristalnacht*) in Germany: "We in India are keenly sensitive on the question concerning racial equality and we naturally share the indignation of the whole civilized world at the atrocious reprisals on the entire Jewish community in Germany for the criminal act of an unbalanced boy." But Bose resigned from his position in 1939 and formed the pro-Fascist All-India Forward Bloc. The organization was declared illegal and Bose was arrested. When released, he disappeared and later turned up in Berlin. His party was banned on grounds of contact with the enemy. On 21 August 1942 the *Jewish Chronicle* of London reported that Bose was anti-Semitic and had published an article in *Angriff*, the organ of Goebbels, in which he described Indians as the real ancient Aryans and the brethren of the German people. He had said that the swastika was an old Indian sign and that anti-Semitism must become a part of the Indian freedom movement, since the Jews, he alleged, had helped Britain to exploit and oppress the Indians. The *Jewish Advocate* expressed horror at Bose's statement about a Jewish role in India's exploitation but added, "one may expect anything from one who has traveled the road to Berlin in search of his country's salvation." Norman Shohet pointed out how insignificant a part in the economic and political life of the country the Jews of India actually played. He also mentioned that other Indian leaders had so far not shown any anti-Semitic leanings, but that on the contrary, Gandhi, Nehru, Dr. B. R. Ambedkar, and others had been positively friendly to the Jews. He doubted that anti-British demonstrations in Bombay bore an anti-Jewish character or that Germany's anti-Semitic propaganda would fall on receptive ears in India, despite Bose, but he hoped that the government would be on guard.[49]

There were some receptive ears in India, however, because of the economic situation. According to official reports, about 400,000 Asiatic British subjects had arrived in India between 8 September 1940 and the end of 1943; evacuees from territories that were occupied or threatened by Japan, they included 986 Jews. The number of Europeans and foreigners who came to India as evacuees from all parts of the world since the beginning of the war was 11,368.[50] The presence of the Indian evacuees from Asia was creating quite a problem for the Indian government, because the expense of maintaining them stimulated the inflationary trend in the country. The Central Employment Bureau was established to help these statutory Indians find temporary jobs, as most of them wanted to return as quickly as possible to the countries from which they had been evacuated. The government tried to persuade these refugees to join the defense services, which might prove the quickest and cheapest way of getting back to Burma and Malaya once the war was over.[51]

By mid 1943, some two thousand Jewish refugees had settled in India. They had opened new factories, manufacturing goods never before produced in India; they were serving as experts, including doctors, all over the country; they were functioning as merchants with worldwide connections, finding new markets for Indian goods and new sources of supply. Their very success, however, gave rise to continued Indian anxiety about employment and inflation. When questions were raised in the Central Legislative Assembly about the government having recruited twenty-two Czech and Polish refugees to work in munitions, Sir Homy Mody, the member for supply, replied that to ameliorate the scarcity of technically trained men, the government recruited as many suitable people as possible, regardless of nationality, that every possible chance was given to qualified Indians, and that all appointments were only for the duration of the war.[52]

The economic situation gave rise to anti-Semitic comments. At the annual general meeting of the Bombay Chamber of Commerce in the spring of 1943, J. M. B. Gibbon, the outgoing president, claimed:

> Added to the ranks of our home-grown profiteers we seem recently to have acquired an imported article as well. Since India threw open her hospitable shores to the many unfortunates who were driven by the invader from their homes, there has sprung up especially in Bombay, a whole tribe of traders whose activities have been most unwelcome.[53]

The *Sunday Standard*, a Bombay paper with an anti-Semitic bias, responded to these remarks with a new campaign of attacks against the Jews, especially the refugees. Every Sunday, a columnist styling himself "Janus" published derogatory articles referring to the Jews as "alien parasites." Since Gibbon had made no mention of a particular class of refugees, the *Jewish Advocate* argued that only anti-Semites would infer from his statements that he had meant only the Jews. But Munilal Mehra, representing the Amritsar Piece-goods Association at the All-India Yarn and Cloth Merchants Conference, remarked in an interview with the *Bombay Sentinel*:

> To the ranks of those speculators of India are joined the foreign traders' trade, and are the foreign refugees who had to evacuate their homelands on account of the Fascist and Nazi brutes and found a peaceful home in India. Government knew all this time that both these types are biggest hoarders of cotton cloth and have made big fortunes by speculation and hoarding the cloth.[54]

Here too, the *Jewish Advocate* insisted that Mehra did not specify a particular community.

The *Jewish Advocate* believed that the JRA's figures on Jewish refugees in India, especially those of European origin, should receive wide publicity in India to contradict the implications of Mehra's statement. The Jewish evacuees from Burma and the Far East had lost practically everything and were largely dependent on government assistance. Of the 1,120 Jewish refugees from Europe in India, only 68 individuals were carrying on businesses of their own and could be classified as traders. The *Jewish Advocate* wrote:

> It would be a slander on the majority of these merchants to suggest that all of them are profiteers and speculators. But even if they were, it is obvious

that the part the Jewish refugees can play in the profiteering and speculating ramp that runs through the length and breadth of India, is at the worst of negligible proportions. . . . It's a mistake to attribute the present inflationary mess in which 400,000 people find themselves to the activity of 68 Jewish refugee merchants.[55]

The JRA broke down the figures on Continental Jews as follows:

Women and Children	350
Still in Parole Centers or internment camps	147
Commercial employment, clerks, etc.	225
Doctors and Dentists	127
Technicians and Professional men	110
Merchants and Businessmen	58
Aged (unemployed)	25
Manufacturers	20
Inmates of Hostel (unemployed)	18[56]

Of the technicians and professionals, some were in direct government employ and most were working in industrial establishments engaged in war production. Of the doctors and dentists, twenty-nine were serving in the Royal Army Medical Corps as commissioned officers and eleven as civil medical practitioners at military hospitals. Of the twenty manufacturers, some were engaged in war and government orders.

How to handle the problem of anti-Semitism in the press was clearly a concern of the entire Jewish community. One leading Bombay Baghdadi, Albert J. Gubbay, suggested that offensive news items, letters, and articles appearing in the *Sunday Standard* should receive replies not by any individual—dozens of protests had been sent in but none was ever published—but by the Bombay Jewish Relief Association, in consultation with the executives of the responsible Jewish bodies in the city.[57]

The propaganda became so pronounced that in June 1943 Pollack convened an informal meeting of some prominent Jews, who decided to create the Central Jewish Committee from the existing Jewish institutions in Bombay to represent and defend Jewish interests. In 1944 Victor Sassoon became the first president, although his role, as usual, was that of a figurehead: he gave money but would not accept any operational responsibility. Dr. E. Moses became chairman. Other officers included Pollack, A. W. Rosenfeld, and Eric Ellis.

The legislative questioning about refugees and evacuees continued. In late 1944 Sardar Sant Singh of West Punjab asked the Home Department member of the Central Legislative Assembly whether the government policy in regard to Jewish immigration was initiated by the government of India or by His Majesty's government in Britain. Sir Francis Mudie replied that the policy originally followed by the government of India and several other countries was to give refuge and protection to Jews who were persecuted by anti-Semitic laws. Subsequently, when the number of Jews seeking entry into India began to increase, the government of India was constrained to restrict the number of future immigrants. Although he did not state when the change occurred, Mudie did indicate that the present policy was to admit only those who could undertake work of national importance, those whose cases presented special features (e.g., dependents of Jews who were already in India), and those who might otherwise fall into enemy hands.[58]

Zionism: The War Years

If the immediate problems of mobilization for war and dealing with the refugees were uppermost in the minds of Indian Jews during the war years, the relevance of Zionism was no longer in doubt. The MacDonald White Paper of June 1939, restricting Jewish immigration into Palestine just at the moment when Jews most needed a haven, intensified the Zionists' campaign. Their greatest fears had materialized. Although the Jewish Agency seems to have expended less effort to reach Indian nationalist leaders after the outbreak of the war—with all its attendant problems—the head offices were still concerned with local Zionist work.

Sent out to report on conditions in late 1939, Dr. S. Lowy focused on three questions. Was a continued investment in the creation of a Zionist organization in Bombay worthwhile? Was A. E. Shohet the right man for the work to be carried out there? What might Keren Hayesod and the Jewish National Fund expect in the near future from the activities of their office in Bombay? Lowy found that the Bombay Jews, especially the younger generation, were receptive to education about Zionism and were grateful for assistance in raising their cultural standard, which he found very low. But, echoing previous Zionist delegates, he expected very little financial support from these poor people. In his opinion, a real Zionist organization did not exist in Bombay at this point. Only a few people took an active part in Zionist functions. Dr. Petzal, whom Lowy believed had been the driving power of the Zionist movement in Bombay, had been interned. His wife had had to resign her post on the Zionist committee. Like other emissaries, Lowy seemed to have more faith in the Continental Jews; he felt he had even had to convince J. J. Gubbay to continue the work. Shohet, he thought, had undertaken tasks beyond his abilities. There was no way he could edit the *Jewish Advocate*, work for the Jewish Agency, Jewish National Fund, Keren Hayesod, and the *shekel* fund, and also run the Jewish Club and the Young Zionist Club, both of which he had established.

To Lowy, Shohet's strength lay in propaganda, journalism, and politics, not in fund-raising, but without his collaboration Zionist work would collapse altogether. The institutions should continue investing in Shohet, even though the local fund-raising did not cover the cost.[59] Shohet, meanwhile, continued his political analyses for the Jewish Agency. In reporting some correspondence between the viceroy and Muhammad Ali Jinnah in November 1939, Shohet voiced his fear that "His Majesty's Government, which had steadfastly refused to grant a voice to the Muslims of India in the affairs of Palestine during the Palestine Conference, has now altered its policy and is willing to 'appreciate the importance of the points' which the Muslim League is now raising." The Congress could not bring in the question of Palestine in its demand for a declaration of war aims, but the Muslim League could.[60]

The league's position was expressed again at its twenty-seventh session in Lahore on 24 March 1940, when it passed a resolution on the Palestine question:

> [The Muslim League] places on record its considered opinion, in clear and unequivocal language, that no arrangements of a piecemeal character will be made in Palestine which are contrary in spirit and opposed to the pledges given to the Muslim world, and particularly to the Muslims in India, to secure their active assistance in the War of 1914–1918.[61]

If the Muslim communal organization continued to register its views, so did its Jewish counterpart. Although the Bene Israel seemed to have no direct contact at this point with the head offices of the Zionist organizations, the Bene Israel Conference, meeting that same month in Bombay, passed a resolution that "expressed its full sympathy with Zionism and conveys to their brethren in *Erez Israel* its great admiration for their achievements." The conference also highly praised the results of the *halutzim* in Palestine, and when the question of unemployment in India was taken up, members hinted at a "return to the land"—agriculture and Palestine. Hayeem Ezekiel, who held a B.A. in agronomy, said: "Why should not the unemployed class of the Bene Israel take up agriculture again?" Many Bene Israel were apparently also impressed by the fluency with which Hebrew had been revived and was being spoken in Palestine.[62]

Even *Habonim* (a Zionist youth organization with branches in many countries) which in Bombay was composed mainly of Baghdadi youth and had shied away from Zionist activities because of the political implications, gradually became more Zionist. At its fifth anniversary celebration in February 1940, the Bombay branch stressed that although one of the aims of the movement was to make boys and girls realize their responsibilities as citizens of the state in which they lived, it also wanted to instill in them an active interest in the Jewish national revival and particularly in the Hebrew language.[63]

With the onset of the war, demands for contributions to alleviate the plight of the refugees competed even more strongly with requests for funds for Palestine. Various groups in Bombay continued to sponsor events and social functions such as tea dances, sewing parties, raffles, supper parties, and Purim dances as benefits for Palestine. In order to reduce expenses, the *Jewish Advocate* was cut back from a fortnightly to a monthly by July 1940, but soon after it began devoting a whole page each month to WIZO (Women's International Zionist Organization) in order to keep Jewish women in India in touch with the organization's activities throughout the world. WIZO functions in India included fund-raising bazaars, theater performances, bridge parties, dances, and work for the national funds as well as the welfare of Jewish soldiers in India. Baby clothes, handmade in India, were dispatched to Palestine. (WIZO-sponsored home industries' goods from Palestine, however, did not sell well in India because the prices were too high.) The Bombay branch had almost 160 members by 1943, while Calcutta had about 70; they were predominantly Continental Jewish women, with a few Baghdadis. No Bene Israel belonged. Meetings and lectures were well attended and both the Bombay and Calcutta branches eventually formed small youth groups for the younger girls.[64]

In January 1941 Dr. Immanuel Olsvanger returned to India, five years after his earlier visit, this time as an emissary of Keren Hayesod. Norman Shohet, now replacing his brother as editor of the *Jewish Advocate*, commented that Olsvanger had forged a link between Indian Jewry and Palestine as no delegate before him had done. Since his last visit, the editor continued, the Jews had learned that there was no salvation for the Jewish people but a home of their own: the Zionist thesis had proved itself. Olsvanger was now returning to India to "assist us to make our due contribution, as a Jewish community which is still free, to consolidate what already exists in Palestine, in order to enable it to be the most compelling factor at the Peace Conference which will follow the war."[65] A reception committee, which included leading Baghdadis, Continental Jews, and Bene Israel, was organized to invite people to Dr. Olsvanger's public lecture, entitled "The Situation in Palestine Today." A lecture intended for the Bene Israel and a reception held by them for Olsvanger were well attended, perhaps because the community was so pleased at his achievement in getting Kehimkar's *History of the Bene Israel* published. In response to Bene Israel questions about Jews ousting the Arabs in Palestine, Olsvanger countered that the Arabs were ousting the Jews, as could be seen from the increase of the Arab population, many of whom had been attracted into Palestine from the surrounding Arab countries by the Jewish economic enterprises and by general improvements in health and education. Someone suggested that Olsvanger arrange for the publication of the facts, with figures and illustrations showing the benefits derived by the Arabs in Palestine, in some leading newspapers in India to counter the anti-Zionist propaganda there.

"Your ancestors came here at the time of the destruction of the Second

Temple; we want you in Palestine to assist us in the building of the third temple," Olsvanger told the Bene Israel, repeating his invitation many times to send a few youths for settlement. At his suggestion, a small *halutz* committee, consisting of Rebecca Reuben, I. Samuel, E. M. Jacob, and I. A. Isaac, was formed to consider such a scheme. The Shohets had pressed Olsvanger to place the committee under their guidance, but he had not even consulted them—wishing, apparently, to allow the Bene Israel autonomy in this matter. The Shohets did meet with the committee to discuss the Jewish Agency's proposal to send out a man to train *halutzim* in India for Palestine. The *halutz* committee would have to bear only the cost of running the agricultural training farm. But eventually the Bene Israel decided not to go ahead with the plan. The Shohets were very disappointed, for they saw enthusiasm and talent for *halutzim* work among Indian Jewish youth, whom they believed ought to be represented in Eretz Israel. Norman Shohet suggested that having the Jewish Agency send three or four young men to Palestine for special training, in preparation for work among the Jewish youth of India, would be more effective than having an outsider come to India. Calcutta also wanted to send two young people. In addition, the Bombay Zionist Association offered to finance the journey to Palestine of a delegation of young people who were not interested in training for youth work, but who were prepared to settle on the land.[66]

That doubts about Zionism still prevailed were evident at the sixth Bene Israel Youth Day, held on 27 April 1941, where a debate was held on whether or not the Bene Israel should be in favor of Zionism. Although some said yes, arguing that Zionism was merely the political expression of an existing Jewish nationalism, others opposed the movement. Two non–Bene Israel guests, Dr. H. Reissner (an American sociologist) and A. E. Shohet, both of whom had been to Palestine, also spoke, urging the Bene Israel youths to ally themselves with Jewry all over the world in the task of building a Jewish commonwealth.[67]

By the end of Olsvanger's 1941 visit to Bombay, his campaign had yielded the highest total yet collected by any Zionist delegate in that city. Having come at a critical period for the world in general and for Palestine in particular, he had easily convinced people of the importance of his cause, and individual contributions were larger than ever—especially from some of the wealthier members of the Baghdadi community. Ironically, the largest single gift came from a non-Jewish source: 2,000 rupees from the Tata Industries (one of the leading industrial conglomerates in India). An additional 1,000 rupees was given by the trustees of Sir Ratan Tata. These wealthy Parsis thus contributed more than one-fifth of the total collected, 14,757 rupees. The smaller contributors consisted mainly of Continental refugees; again, only a half-dozen Bene Israel names appeared. But the children of the Sir Elly

Kedourie School donated 23 rupees, the cost of five trees in Palestine. The names of Sir Alwyn Ezra and the Sassoons do not appear on the contribution list; perhaps they were giving anonymously.[68]

In the spring of 1941 Maurice Japheth, the Baghdadi journalist, became the editor of the *Jewish Advocate*. A staunch Zionist despite his sympathy for Indian nationalism, Japheth strongly promoted the cause in his editorials and frequently published news about American Zionism, its views and its conventions, claiming that the Americans would now have to take the lead in the coming struggle. When Sir Victor Sassoon visited India, Japheth urged that Sir Victor, who apparently had suggested that the Jews could go elsewhere—to Brazil, for example—learn more about Zionism and Palestine, as he only knew one side.[69]

Early in 1942 the Sargons left India for America and closed their newspaper, the *Jewish Tribune*, leaving the *Jewish Advocate* as the only Jewish paper in India. An editorial board, consisting of Japheth, the Shohet brothers, and F. W. Pollack, was formed. The *Jewish Advocate* was enlarged to twelve pages, in a new style and format, and gave special attention to local news. It also launched a wider advertising and subscription drive, having only three hundred subscribers, compared with the *Jewish Tribune*'s one thousand.[70]

The Jews were not the only Indians watching American Zionist activity. The All-India Muslim League evidently knew about the Biltmore program (urging the removal of present restrictions on Jewish immigration to Palestine and the conversion of Palestine into a Jewish state), adopted by American Zionists in May 1942 in New York, for at its Delhi session in April 1943, the league passed Resolution 12, which expressed concern with Zionist pressure on the United States government to influence the British government. The league perceived that the aim of this new Zionist move was to make the Jewish majority in Palestine a *fait accompli* by opening Palestine's doors to the Jewish war refugees. The league reiterated its support for Arab national demands. These views were confirmed the following year, when at its Karachi session the league passed Resolution 6, which urged the abolition of the mandate system and the creation of the independent countries of Palestine, Syria, and Lebanon. The league also demanded that France liberate Morocco, Tunisia, and Algeria.[71]

The Zionist emissaries continued to visit India. Early in 1942 the well-known Jewish journalist Harry Levin came to India as a delegate of Keren Keyemet and collected a large sum of money, mainly from Continental and Baghdadi Jews. Again, the Tatas gave generously, as did Sir David Ezra of Calcutta this time. Sir Jeremy Raisman, the British Jewish official in the central government's Finance Department—and one of the few civil servants who was open about his Jewish identity—was included in the list of Calcutta contributors. In that year, with the threatened Japanese invasion, many Jews were evacuated from Calcutta and it was difficult to get a campaign or Zionist activities going with any great success.[72]

The following year, Keren Hayesod sent Joshua Leibner, a young member of an American settlement in Palestine, to canvas in Bombay and Calcutta. Partly because the communities had increased in numbers from within and without, and partly because of their increasing awareness of the needs, the results were excellent; almost seven times larger than they had ever been before. After considerable pressure, Alwyn Ezra, who by now had resigned as director of the Sassoon Dawn Mills and had dropped out of social life, gave 2,000 pounds (1 Palestinian pound then equaled a little less than 13 rupees). L. Ovadia, the director of Messrs. E. D. Sassoon and Company, gave 1,500 pounds from the firm, the largest sum he could give without authorization from Sir Victor Sassoon. Ovadia wanted the money to go toward saving as many lives as possible, especially children, from the occupied countries. The Tata trusts were again very generous. In all, over 15,500 Palestinian pounds were subscribed for Keren Hayesod, and other monies came in for Keren Keyemet and the *shekel* drive.[73]

A portrait of the Zionist situation in Bombay in mid 1944 by F. W. Pollack reveals a good deal of activity but gives the impression that only the Continential Jews could handle Zionist affairs properly. A Mr. Starosta had founded the Maccabi movement, the strongest Jewish organization in Bombay, with 750 young memnbers. WIZO had 180 members. Five *halutzim* had left India for youth training in Palestine. Pollack himself and a number of Palestinian soldiers were giving regular lectures to a study group of young people on various Jewish and Zionist topics. But he felt that the Bombay Zionist Association was doing very badly. Although it had 75 to 80 members, he was pessimistic about a successful fund-raising drive because so many well-to-do people had left Bombay and thus "Zionism is again in danger to become an affair of the lower middle class Baghdadians only, which means that neither the Continentals nor the upperclass Baghdadians will contribute to the Funds." Three strong Continental workers had left Bombay and Pollack, left alone with "a few of our Baghdadian friends," found it difficult to cooperate with the Shohet brothers.[74] The BZA, meanwhile, took the management of the *Jewish Advocate* away from Pollack, who started a political and economic bulletin of his own. Dr. Leo Lauterbach of the Jewish Agency's organization department was disturbed that this personal element had developed into a quarrel that had culminated in the resignation of Norman Shohet from the BZA; he blamed the impetuosity and ambition of Pollack.[75]

A few months later, a Dr. Mechner visited India on behalf of Keren Keyemet. He described some of the personalities working for Zionism, singling out Rebecca Reuben, who was using Jewish National Fund materials in the Bene Israel school, and F. W. Pollack. *Habonim* still consisted of Baghdadis only; in talking about WIZO, he particularly mentioned the Continental women who seemed to be running it. The Zionist office by then was being run by a young, non-Jewish Indian who capably looked after the correspondence, collected from the Jewish National Fund boxes, and knew every Jewish family. Mechner's perceptions are revealed by the advice he gave to future delegates: since only a handful of real Zionists (the committee members) expected serious information, speakers should prepare six or seven general lectures (for committees, women, youth, Maccabis, drawing room gatherings, and public meetings), remembering that most audiences had almost no Zionist or Jewish education, held nebulous ideas about Eretz Israel, and confused Zionist aims with charity; some people were also opposed to Jewish political movements in general. "Finally," he wrote, "they are orientals, fond of rhetoric, sentimental, prone to mystic conceptions." The Continental Jews he found indifferent, skeptical, and assimilationist. He felt that *halutz* ideas should be brought home to the youth, stressing that physical work, which was despised among Indians, had a peculiar personal and national value in Palestine. There also seemed to be a new audience in the many Jewish soldiers of the Allied armies who met at the Bombay Jewish Club. Mechner recommended that canvassers should talk not in rupees, but in Palestinian pounds, and that delegates should not draw money from locally collected Zionist funds for their own expenses.[76] During this period, collections were also held through the Zionist Forces Welfare Department in India from British, American, Canadian, Palestinian, and Indian Jewish servicemen, with the local army chaplains conducting the drive. Over thirty-five hundred rupees were collected from servicemen in the spring of 1945.[77]

As the end of World War II approached, and with it, the prospect of an independent India and possibly an independent Jewish state, the Jews became even more concerned about their future. Would there be anti-Semitism in India? Would Jews be free to follow their own religion and enjoy the rights of citizenship? In an interesting article entitled "The Future of the Jews in India," published in the *Jewish Advocate* in 1944, Maurice Rassaby, a Calcutta Baghdadi, noted that not everyone would be able to afford to go to Palestine; most people might have no option but to stay in India. He assumed that the Jews of a free India would have a position similar to those of England and America and that citizenship would involve responsibilities as well as privileges. But Rassaby believed that the prerequisites for citizenship were not very evident among Jews of India:

> For us to become full-fledged Indian citizens will mean first and foremost complete allegiance to India as our mother country. We shall have to realize we are Indians as much as we are Jews. Palestine will have to be our spiritual home just as Mecca is for the Muslims. We must realize once and for all that we will no more be "proteges" of Great Britain or any other country,

but free and equal citizens in our own right, responsible to one power alone—the Government of India.[78]

He also recognized that to achieve a lasting good will between the Indians and the Jews, the latter had to regard the problems that had confronted India and its peoples for centuries as their own. In the long run, tranquility in India would mean peace and security for the Jews, but Indians would not tolerate from any alien minority, he claimed, the attitude of snobbishness and superiority they associated with the Europeans. The Jews of India were not guiltless: "There are some among us that cannot help regarding the Indian as inferior to ourselves. There are some in fact who openly declare themselves against the principle of Indian self-government."[79] Rassaby felt that people could get away with such an attitude while India was not yet independent, but that such a perspective, which was unwarranted and foolish, was more likely to produce anti-Semitism in the future Indian state than any other factor. He suggested that Jewish leaders ensure that the Jews would become an asset to India and not a liability. Educational facilities for Jewish youth, mainly in Calcutta, were antiquated and inadequate, he argued, and the Jews had no hospital of their own where their religious needs could be accommodated. Despite several Jewish capitalists, there were large numbers of Jewish poor. He thought that the Jews had to take on more responsibilities for their communal affairs.

Rassaby's views, unusual for a Baghdadi, elicited an interesting response from L. Firestein, who said that although he understood the author's "good and natural feelings" for a democratic Indian state, working to attain a homeland for Jews should be every Jew's first consideration. Firestein was obviously not an Indian Jew and had no reservations about a strong Zionist position.[80]

Whatever their feelings about Zionism, the ending of the war was the Jews' first priority. When victory finally came, the Central Jewish Board of Bombay, representing all Jewish organizations in the city, arranged a service at Magen David on Thanksgiving Day, 13 May 1945, to offer prayers to God for the victory of the Allied nations in Europe. Over two thousand people, including servicemen, attended. Special prayers, prepared by the chief rabbi of the British Empire, Dr. J. H. Hertz, were offered and the service was conducted by the Jewish chaplain of India Command, the Reverend M. A. Lew. Speeches stressed the significance of the Allied victory for the Jewish people.[81]

Conclusion

The war years continued to reflect Bene Israel ambivalence about Indian nationalism. Even most of those who were attracted to it remained loyal to Britain, unwilling to follow Congress's lead in pressing for greater independence as the condition for its support of the colonial power's war effort. The

Bene Israel position was similar to that of Anglo-Indians and most Indian Christians, but for the Jews the issue had a much broader context than simply the future of India: Jews in India, Palestine, and everywhere else, for that matter, had no choice but to back the Allied powers. If the Bene Israel had ever been hazy about the full ramifications of being Jewish, the daily headlines and the presence of Continental refugees in their midst must have cleared up any misconceptions. There was little they could do financially to promote refugee absorption or Zionism, but they now understood more fully the need for a Jewish homeland.

The Baghdadi Jews, whose loyalty to Britain was never questioned, emerged with a higher profile in these years. The upper classes, particularly the Sassoons, Ezras, and their ilk, were asked to give to everything—the British war effort, refugee absorption, and Zionist work. They responded generously to the first two, and somewhat more than in the past to the third. They attempted to use their influence, when possible, to assist the refugees with problems of admission to India and naturalization. The middle-class Baghdadis, meanwhile, continued with the day-to-day work of the Zionist organization and the newspapers, enlisting Bene Israel when they could, and cooperating, more or less, with the Continental Jews, whose experience made them valuable assets to the Zionist cause.

With the prospect of an independent Jewish state in Palestine now looming larger as the ultimate refuge for survivors of the war, the debate over identity heightened for the Indian Jews. With the war over, Britain would now be totally absorbed with problems in both Palestine and India, perhaps pulling out of both, and Indian Jews would be forced to decide where their future would be.

CHAPTER 8

THE POSTWAR DILEMMA

The Impact of Indian Independence

The end of the war did not solve Britain's problems in India; nor had anyone expected the tide of nationalism to be stemmed. Responding to widespread civil disorders in 1946, during which Muslims and Hindus were fighting each other and both were fighting the British, the Labour government announced that the subcontinent would be partitioned and that on 15 August 1947 two separate states—India and Pakistan—would become independent.

The granting of independence caused waves of concern among all the minority communities, including those Muslims who remained within India. What it meant to be a minority was to change in the postcolonial era. One writer has said:

> As the dominance of a national elite replaces that of a foreign elite, the internal balance between multiple ethnic groups assumes a new alignment. The colonial authority must at least make a show of neutrality toward local groups, a policy that often prompts them to show special favors towards minorities to weight the balance against majorities or especially powerful corporate units. . . . Then independence brings a new set of partialities, namely those favored by the indigenous elite. A new balance is struck, sometimes influenced by power considerations and sometimes by open retaliation against hated colonial favorites now stripped of their former protection.[2]

Most minorities had profited from the privileges of separate electorates and preferred representation in the services that the British had granted to counter the influence of the Hindus in the Congress party. With independence, both would be eliminated. Independent India was to vote as one nation; except for some reservations for the scheduled classes, jobs were now open to competition.[3] Although competent Indians could now enter top-echelon positions that had previously been reserved for the British, the minority groups that had relied on the reservations in the lower-echelon jobs were fearful that they would not do so well in the competitive examinations. Finally, the anticipation of communal nepotism in the private sector intensified the anxiety. In a society where development is slow, wages are low and unemployment is rising,

> parochial loyalties to family, caste, religious community, provincial origin
> and language, take precedence over the needs of competence, complete
> objectivity and fairness in employment. . . . This is obviously perceived by
> the minority members as discrimination against them. The demoralizing
> influence of such perception is that people give up the struggle to improve
> their competence. Consequently, whenever opportunity is available, they
> are left behind. Thus the "self-fulfilling" prophecy comes true.[4]

For some of the smaller communities, such as Jews, Anglo-Indians, and even Parsis, which simply did not have a large enough pool of highly placed people, the job situation began to look grim. To be a Jew, some suspected, might be quite different in postcolonial India from what it had been under the British. We can better understand the attitudes of the Jews after independence if we examine what was happening in other communities in India.

The Muslims, representing perhaps 25 to 30 percent of the population of British India, now found themselves to be a much smaller community, living in an atmosphere of suspicion that they were disloyal to India. They had lost not only the privilege of separate electorates, where they could nominate and elect their representatives, but also their own political party, the Muslim League. In colonial India, Muslims had more than their share of jobs in the Indian Civil Service. After independence, most high-level Muslim officials in New Delhi migrated to Pakistan, so that in the 1960s, the proportion of Muslims in the Indian Administrative Service decreased. They were also underrepresented in the lower rungs of the bureaucracy in the capital. When Urdu was abandoned by all branches of the government, many Muslims with that mother language found the competitive examinations in Hindi for government posts more difficult. Others feared discrimination if they did take them. Employment in the private sector became increasingly difficult, as Muslim industrialists and businessmen who had supported the Muslim League now emigrated to Pakistan, where they filled the posts left by the departure of the Hindu and Sikh commercial classes.[5]

Indian Christians, too, felt the repercussions of the British departure. After independence, they renounced the privilege of the colonial separate electorates. Christians had been well represented in the colonial services before 1947, and because of their high literacy, many retained positions in government offices, especially in New Delhi, but they too were better represented in lower-grade government positions than in the higher echelons. Christians also felt that they encountered prejudice when they applied to Hindus for jobs in the urban private sector, where they lacked the support of joint family or caste. Some Christians used Hindu surnames to hide their identity.[6]

Perhaps more than the other groups, the Anglo-Indians offer an interesting comparison with the Jews, particularly the Baghdadis, another urban minority with a veneer, at least, of European culture and an attachment to the British. Unlike the Baghdadis, however—although similar to the Bene Israel—the Anglo-Indians had no real tradition of entrepreneurship. During much of the colonial era, Anglo-Indians had looked to British authority to protect their interests and, when necessary, relied on their own national leaders like Sir Henry Gidney and Frank Anthony to "wrest concessions from the Government." Fearing, as did all minorities, that their reserved jobs would be lost with independence, the Anglo-Indians headed off this situation through political action. Anthony, a lawyer who was a member of the Constituent Assembly, got through a provision in the new constitution for the nomination of Anglo-Indian representatives to the Lok Sabha ("People's Assembly," or the lower house of the Indian Parliament) and the state assemblies for a period of twenty years (later renewed). Appointments to positions in the railroad, customs, postal, and telegraph services were to be reduced gradually until all reservations ceased, thus preventing a sudden disruption of employment for those still dependent on government service and allowing for occupational adjustment.[7]

A few Anglo-Indians who had served in the British bureaucracy for many years were very loyal to India after independence and were willing to continue serving the new government. But despite the safeguards, most Anglo-Indians feared they would lose both political and economic security in independent India, and the younger generation and middle and upper classes particularly began to migrate to England, Canada, Australia, and New Zealand. Perhaps more than half of the entire Anglo-Indian population moved abroad. Those who remained in India (perhaps fewer than a hundred thousand) have not suffered the persecution that they anticipated, but men still worry about unemployment, finding it hard to compete for top public- and private-sector jobs.[8]

In Schermerhorn's view, the Anglo-Indians, probably more than any other minority in India, have a borderline position in society. Since independence, they have felt that they will not be accepted by the dominant group unless they assimilate to its values and lifestyle, but that would mean abandoning their European standards of dress, diet, family life, education, and language. They are living between two cultural worlds: European and Indian—not really wanted in either, but wanting to be part of both, especially the European.[9]

Emigration from independent India was a solution that appealed not only to Anglo-Indians. Many elements of the Indian population, including Parsis and even the sons of affluent Hindu businessmen, migrated to Britain, Canada, and the United States.[10] The almost simultaneous emergence of both

India and Israel as independent states provided a special emigration opportunity for the Jews.

Once Indian independence was granted, most of the Baghdadis, having always spurned identification with the "natives," now doubted that they would be comfortable in the new India. Their attachment to Britain also hurt them, as it had the Indian Christians and Anglo-Indians. Although most Parsis had not wanted the British to leave, the active participation of their leaders in the early years of the struggle made them more acceptable and enabled them to identify completely with Indians and the new nation. The policy of Indianization worked against the Baghdadis, not so much in connection with jobs in government service, to which they had never been greatly attracted, but in trade. In order to preserve foreign currency for industrialization and to protect indigenous products, the Indian government issued regulations controlling the export of foreign exchange and restricting the import of nonessential commodities. This action seriously hampered the business of many small entrepreneurs as well as of the many wealth Baghdadis who had been engaged in the import and export of luxury items. In the 1950s, the Middle East political situation led to the Arab boycott, whereby Arab countries and firms would not trade with any firms doing business with Israel. It became very difficult for Baghdadi Jews to continue their trade with Arab countries, particularly Egypt and Iraq. Jews had to take in Indian partners and use Indian names. With family, connections, and funds abroad, the Baghdadi upper classes were free to migrate to Western countries such as England, Canada, and the United States, and to Australia. Many Baghdadi Jewish cloth traders who had major dealings with Manchester now settled there. Even less-affluent Baghdadis who had relatives abroad or who could find a source of livelihood in the West also departed, with a relatively small percentage going to Israel.[11]

Of those Baghdadis who stayed, some felt that their businesses suffered once the community disintegrated—not because they were Jews, but because they were not Indians. They lost the business of the departing Jewish community, and other Indians patronized their own communal enterprises. Some Baghdadis also had a minimal command of Indian languages, which, coupled with communal preferences, made it harder for them to get jobs and promotions. There were no longer enough Jews around to "protect" them. Some Baghdadis felt that certain members of their community left because they were too lazy to compete under a merit system—although they proved they could work well when forced to in Israel, for example, when they joined a kibbutz or the army. Thus, the Baghdadis, who had come to India mainly for trade and had not been interested in becoming Indian or taking up Indian customs, unless it was convenient, simply left when the British did, as much for the sake of their children, who had not been brought up in Indian ways and languages, as for themselves.[12]

By the early 1980s, hardly eight hundred Baghdadi Jews remained in India. Some were engaged in domestic commerce. Many were elderly or retired professionals or businessmen who could not take their money out of India and/or who enjoyed a standard of living there that they could not maintain abroad. Others were indigent dependents of the Sassoon trust funds.

After independence, the main concern of the Bene Israel was jobs. No longer would one get preferential treatment in the government bureaucracy by mentioning the service of one's father or grandfather. No longer would a note from a Jewish official to a British official almost guarantee a job. Ironically, with the departure of the British, many more opportunities became available: whereas originally twenty people might have been recruited for a service, now one hundred or one hundred fifty vacancies might be announced. Yet the Bene Israel, like the Muslims, seemed to shrink from competition and did not apply to take the examinations, although many of them probably could have gotten in on merit. They seemed to think that without the British, they had lost their protectors, and they would be discriminated against, even though nepotism and the idea of protecting one's own community had not yet set in strongly.[13]

A few Bene Israel, however, were able to take advantage of new opportunities at the very top of the services that were opened up to competent Indians of all classes, once the British moved out. The leader of the Jewish community in New Delhi, Ezra Kolet, got his job as secretary of shipping and transport because he was number one in a competitive examination taken by three thousand applicants. He doubts that this post would have been available to Indians in British times. Nor, in British days, would there have been Bene Israel running for chief of staff of the army or navy, as occurred after independence. The number of Bene Israel with commissions in the army and air force has been considerable in the last thirty years.[14] Other Bene Israel claim, however, that very few members of their community could actually take advantage of these unusual opportunities as very few were advanced enough to compete for such high positions. Others, meanwhile, lost out when lower positions were given to the scheduled classes. A few Bene Israel who could have had extensions of their government service when the British left chose not to, because they did not want to work under chaotic conditions. Bene Israel encountered the same communal nepotism in the private sector as did the other minority groups. And as more and more members of the Bene Israel community departed for Israel, those who applied for positions in large corporations began to hear, "We're reluctant to hire you because we'll invest in your training and then you'll leave for Israel."[15]

There is no doubt that economic factors contributed to the emigration of both Bene Israel and Baghdadi Jews after India received her independence. One might postulate, however, that had Israel not emerged as an independent state at around the same time, the vast exodus of Bene Israel might not have occurred. Feeling more confident in themselves as Indians, and having fewer connections in the West, the Bene Israel might well have adjusted to the new political situation in India. The Baghdadis, on the other hand, never having felt Indian and having options outside of India, were almost predestined to leave. The extent to which Zionism and the pull of Israel influenced both groups remains to be examined.

Indian Zionism after the War

The events in Palestine in the mid and late forties, culminating in the establishment of the State of Israel in May 1948, gave a new impetus to Zionism in India. Bombay Zionism went through a crisis after November 1948, with the death of J. J. Gubbay, whom Japheth described as "the most powerful and popular exponent of Zionism in India." J. S. Ezra, another of the three founders of the Bombay Zionist Association, then became its president and chairman, offices he held until his death in 1967.

In July 1948 F. W. Pollack began to edit and publish a magazine called *India and Israel*. He now described himself as a private citizen of Israel who had lived in India for many years; he wanted to present a less-biased report on Israel than was available in the Indian press and to give a portrait of the new Jewish state. His first editorial enumerated the Jews who had helped India in her fight for freedom: Kallenbach and Polak, Louis Fisher, Emmanuel Celler, Harold Laski, and others. *India and Israel* was a serious, highly professional magazine, containing much less local news and more international coverage than previous Indian Jewish periodicals. Editorials, articles, and columns, many contributed from world Jewish sources, featured reports about Israeli and Indian Jewish life, Indians (Jewish and non-Jewish) who had visited Israel, the history of Palestine, Arab life in Israel and other Middle Eastern countries, conditions of Jews in oriental countries and South Africa, and Indian press reviews on Israel. The extensive political material focused particularly on Indian-Israeli relations, but also on Japan and South Africa. It also covered the Bahais in detail. *India and Israel* was published until 1953, when Pollack returned to Israel after a thirteen-year stay in India.

Indian-Israeli Relations

India was one of the eleven countries represented on the United Nations Special Committee on Palestine. Along with Iran and Yugoslavia, India disapproved of the majority plan of partition, recommending instead a federal state of Palestine. Given this position, and Congress's previous stance, it was not surprising that India joined most Arab and Asian states in voting against the General Assembly's Partition Resolution of 29 November 1947. Once the Jewish state came into existence, it took India more than two years to recognize Israel, waiting until Turkey and Iran took the step before making her own declaration.[16] A few days before Indian recognition was announced, Israel appointed F. W. Pollack as trade commissioner for Southeast Asia, with headquarters in Bombay. Despite the grant of recognition, diplomatic relations were held up because the Indian government was concerned about its minority of forty million Muslims, although they had not seemed particularly shocked at the recognition.

In early 1952 conversations were held at New Delhi between an Israeli representative and Nehru and other senior Indian officials over the establishment of diplomatic relations. Nehru knew that since India had recognized Israel, it was logical to exchange representatives. Despite the initial optimism, nothing materialized, partly because Moshe Sharett (Shertok), then foreign minister of Israel, insisted on reciprocity, and Nehru, although ready to have Israel establish a legation in Delhi, was not prepared to establish a mission in Israel. Now, added to the problem of the domestic politics was the Pakistan question. Nehru feared that establishing diplomatic relations with Israel would cause the Arab states to support Pakistan on the controversy over Kashmir, a conflict frequently on the agenda of the United Nations, where India needed Arab votes. Nehru also feared that India's trade with the Arabs, especially her imports of oil, would suffer. Further, his efforts to lead the Third World countries in a posture of nonalignment contributed to the government's sympathy with the Arabs. Thus, India refused to send any representative to Israel, and Israel could establish only a consulate general in Bombay. The office of trade commissioner was now changed to consul, so Pollack became Israel's first consular representative in India, to the disappointment, perhaps, of some Baghdadis, who felt that an Indian Jew should have had the honor.[17]

Despite the hostility of the Congress party and the government, other elements in India saw advantages of good relations with Israel. Socialist groups such as the Praja Socialist party of India recognized Israel's strength as a valuable democratic force in an Asia menaced by communism. Rightist Hindu parties such as the Jan Sangh, the Hindu Mahasabha, and Swatantra, and "cultural organizations" such as the Rashtriya Swayamsevak Sangh, viewed Israel as a possible future ally against Muslim aggression. Commenting on India's vote against Israel's admission to the United Nations, the Hindu press, along with members of Parliament, had urged in 1949 that the country recognize Israel.[18]

Meeting in Vijayawada in 1965, the Central Working Committee of the

Jan Sangh party, in discussing the necessity to reorient Indian foreign policy, passed the following resolution:

> Israel is the only really democratic country in West Asia. It is a highly developed country and has been playing an increasingly important role in the economic development of newly emerging African countries. . . . By developing closer relations with Israel, India would not only contribute to stability in West Asia but will also improve her position in a number of African States. It is therefore imperative that India must have full diplomatic relations with Israel.[19]

An editorial in the Jan Sangh journal, the *Organiser*, noted that Israel was as real as the United Arab Republic (Egypt) and was a fact of international life. If African countries could have diplomatic relations with both Israel and Arab countries, why did India refuse? "Are Arabs going to dictate [to] us what our foreign policy shall be?" the *Organiser* asked. It accused the UAR of "Jewbaiting" and criticized the government of India for supporting the UAR against Israel.[20] The party believed that India could partly checkmate Pakistani influence in the Middle East by normalizing its relations with Israel. The *Organiser* also argued that Israel "is the hope of all the Jews the world over; and it is the symbol of stability in a very unstable part of the world."[21]

The party's Central Working Committee reiterated its position at its session in Simla in June 1967, when it criticized the government's pro-Arab stance in the Six-Day War and, once again, called upon it to establish full diplomatic relations with Israel. It also called for the Arabs and Israelis to reconcile their differences and cooperate, demanding that Israel withdraw from areas it had occupied and that the Arab nations acknowledge Israel's existence. Two years later, at its fifteenth all-India session in Bombay, the Jan Sangh party called for India to mediate between Arabs and Israel: "The present policy of touch-me-not towards Israel is neither rational nor national. It is a partisan policy with communal motivations and overtones."[22]

If the anti-Muslim stance of the Hindu rightist parties led them to prefer Israel to the Arab states, the idea that India could serve as a mediator was expressed in 1956–57 by others, such as A. R. Wadia, a member of Parliament from Bombay, and the *Eastern Economist*, which published an editorial that criticized Israeli aggression in the Suez-Sinai War of 1956 yet nevertheless argued that in the light of Israel's political importance, it was absurd for India not to have a diplomatic representative there.[23] The Indian government's position was also criticized by members of India's Parliament and certain newspapers on the ground that India was cutting itself off from a useful source of technical assistance and cooperation. Meanwhile, by 1967, several hundred Indians, including nonofficial delegations, had visited Israel or gone there for training.[24]

The government also appeared to be out of step with popular opinion. Egypt was highly respected by Indians between 1957 and 1965 because of the Nehru-Nasser alliance, but lost a great deal of popular esteem after its defeat in the 1967 war, when Israel acquired a more favorable image. People wanted the government to adopt a policy of greater neutrality and "less active" association with the Arabs. The Indian image of the entire Arab world deteriorated further in 1971, when Arab leaders remained silent during the Bangladesh crisis, although Egypt's performance in the Yom Kippur War in 1973 restored her status in Indian eyes, and Israel lost some ground.[25] Informal discussion with Indians certainly gives the impression that the people of India as a whole, with the exception of Muslims, are not anti-Zionist but actually quite sympathetic to Israel, regardless of their government's position. Hindus, however, sometimes reveal that their anti-Arab views stem not so much from their pro-Israeli sentiments as from their domestic anti-Muslim ones.

In August 1950 the All-Indian Zionist Federation was formed at the instance of the Bombay Zionist Association. Although it turned out to be short-lived, it did allow all Zionists to celebrate on a massive scale, with rallies, meetings, and several articles in the local and national press, India's recognition of Israel. The BZA then formed the Indo-Israel Cultural Society to function "as an arena in which Indian friendship with and goodwill for Israel would be promoted," an unofficial, nongovernmental institution to foster understanding between the peoples of the two countries. The initial meeting was attended by a large number of Jews and an even larger number of non-Jews. But the BZA received strict and insistent instructions from Israeli authorities to suspend immediately all activities connected with the society. The Indians never understood the reasons and were very disappointed. Some members of the BZA, especially Maurice Japheth, were demoralized by the Israeli official attitudes toward the association's first attempt to sponsor the friendship society. It is probable that in working diplomatically to achieve better relations with India, the Israelis did not want to embarrass the Indian government by a visible pro-Israeli organization that might antagonize Indian Muslims. Only after the 1967 war could the Indo-Israel Friendship League be formed, this time at the request of more than thirty Indian members of Parliament.[26]

The *Jewish Advocate* ceased publication in the early 1950s but reappeared in July 1958, thanks to J. S. Ezra, as the *Indo-Israel Review*. Shellim Samuel, a Bene Israel lawyer, became the editor, and the publication remained the organ of the Bombay Zionist Association, with the purpose of interpreting India and Israel to each other and promoting friendship and cooperation between their peoples. The sixteen-page *Review* focused mainly on Israel and its leaders, with many articles contributed, especially by Israelis. As *India and Israel* had ceased publication in 1953, the *Indo-Israel Review* for a while was the only Jewish newspaper in English published in India.

In 1968 three members of the BZA, including Maurice Japheth, resigned from the association and formed the separate Indian Zionist Organization (IZO), which eighteen other people immediately joined. The secessionists felt that overemphasis on personalities and irreconcilable ideological differences within the BZA were causing too much conflict to enable it to work constructively. Perhaps they also wished to free themselves from the influence of Hersh Cynowicz, the Polish Jew who was beginning to dominate Jewish affairs in Bombay at this time (undermining local leadership), and who had become one of the leaders of the BZA after J. S. Ezra died. The Indian Zionist Organization wanted to extend Zionist activity to important fields that were not covered by the BZA but was prepared to work with the BZA if it was willing.[27] The Indian Zionist Organization began publishing its own journal, *Shalom*, in 1969. In 1972 the two Zionist groups managed to combine to elect a delegate to the Twenty-eighth Zionist Congress, selecting Albert Talegaokar, a Bene Israel from the BZA. For the first time, they claimed, in over half a century of the Zionist movement in India, an Indian-born, Indian Jew left India to be a fully accredited, elected delegate.[28]

Indian Jewish Emigration to Israel

Immigration from India to the new State of Israel was initially organized by J. S. Ezra and H. Cynowicz, who concentrated on sending Jews in refugee camps, particularly from Afghanistan, to Israel.[29] A Jewish Agency immigration office was set up in Bombay in September 1950, with Aryeh Ganz as the first director. At first, Pollack, the new trade commissioner, said that only European and Arab Jews who really needed homes should go to Israel. Then, when there was more room, American and Indian Jews, who were not suffering from anti-Semitism, persecution, or homelessness, could go. This attitude did not please the Indian Jews, many of whom are reported to have said to Pollack, in effect, "It's our homeland too, so don't say we can't go."[30]

Among the first immigrants were youngsters who, attracted by the Jewish Agency's activities and propaganda, pressured their parents to let them go. Under the auspices of Youth Aliyah and through the efforts of Rabbi Solomon D. Sassoon of Letchworth, England, a training center for Indian Jewish children was established in Lavee, eight miles from Tiberias. The parents intended to follow soon, and in the first wave some comfortable, educated families with long ties to Zionism, such as the Aptekars, did go and settle in Israel. While some Bene Israel observers have claimed that it was the attachment to Judaism and the attraction of Israel, if not to Zionism *per se*, more than the economic conditions in India that motivated the Bene Israel in particular, others believe that the difficulty of finding jobs in India and the prospects of a higher standard of living in Israel were the main determinants.[31] Although it has been suggested that had Israel not emerged as an independent state, the Bene Israel might not have left India, the reverse may also be true: had the British not left India, fewer Bene Israel might have gone to Israel. The closing of the Sassoon mills in 1945 threw many Jews out of work. The Sassoons had transferred much of their business to China in the 1930s but maintained ownership of the Bombay mills. When the war came, they had to close the business in China and they shifted their interests back to Bombay again. The later liquidation of the Bombay operations impelled many to migrate. A man who lost his job was often advised to "go to Israel." He would see the consul, make preparations, and within two months he and his family might leave. Sustained planning was not always involved.[32]

Immigration from India peaked in 1950–52. Conditions in Israel turned out to be very difficult: many went there expecting it to be the Holy Land and found that it was a country like any other. Certain professionals who had good degrees, high qualifications, and experience in India as physicians, teachers, and government officials, for example, found that in Israel, where Western-educated professionals seemed to be preferred, they were given subordinate posts. Some Bene Israel came to feel that Israel was really looking more for laborers from India. Indeed, some of the Bene Israel manual workers, such as craftsmen and carpenters who could barely make ends meet in India and who emigrated with the aid of the Jewish Agency, could earn a good living in the new country and soon have luxuries they did not enjoy in India. Some even settled in *kibbutzim* and *moshavim* (other types of agricultural cooperatives).[33]

By the end of 1952, there were approximately three thousand Indian Jews in Israel, and the grievances of a small group were beginning to make news. Despite the success of some, a number of Bene Israel who had been clerks, carpenters, or mechanics in India found themselves in Beersheba doing hard manual work that they disliked, and being discriminated against, they felt, in housing. In protests in Israel, in letters home and even to the Indian press, they soon began to accuse the Israelis of color prejudice, an issue that had always troubled the Bene Israel when considering the merits of Zionism. Their grievances were examined by a special enquiry commission of the Jewish Agency headed by Dr. Immanuel Olsvanger, an old friend of the Bene Israel, who had been helpful in the adjustment of Indian Jews to Israel. Olsvanger found that fewer than thirty-five families, mainly in Beersheba, were unhappy, and that they had been stirred up by agitators—a few Bene Israel men. In his view, many of the complaints were not justified. Nevertheless, the Israeli government finally paid for the repatriation to India of some twenty families—150 persons in all—who wanted to return. These families created quite a stir when they claimed to the Indian Parliament that there was color discrimination in Israel. Back in India, however, they found themselves stranded without jobs and housing and soon pleaded to be allowed to return to Israel. They admitted that it was their own failure to come up to the high standards of the pioneering country, repented their action, and petitioned to Prime Minister David Ben-Gurion, as "misguided children" to be sent back. The Jewish Agency was understandably reluctant to pay for yet another trip but eventually relented. By December 1954 most had been flown back to Israel.[34]

A Bene Israel Marathi paper, *Maccabi*, criticized Israel, its immigration policy, and immigrants to the country. Many Bene Israel resented *Maccabi* and some suggested that Pollack might add a few pro-Zionist Marathi pages to *India and Israel* to order to counter *Maccabi*'s criticisms. Gradually, many professional people and other Bene Israel with very good jobs, especially those who were not able to go to the West or to Australia, emigrated to Israel, often to enable their children to participate in a richer Jewish life and education and to have greater marriage prospects.[35]

Not all Bene Israel, of course, wanted to leave India. Some felt that the country had been very good to the Jews and that it would be wrong and ungrateful for them to run away simply because India had become independent and the State of Israel existed. Some Jews should stay in India and prove their loyalty, they said.[36]

An excellent portrayal of some of the contradictory pulls on the Bene Israel can be found in the novel *Shulamith* by Meera Mahadevan.[37] The author, born Miriam Jacob in Karachi, was a Bene Israel married to a Hindu. She was well known not only as an author, but as the founder, in 1969, of Mobile Crèches, a voluntary women's organization for the care of the children of poor construction workers. The lead characters in *Shulamith* discuss the conflict between the devotion to India, which has always succored them and is their home and identity, and the pull toward Israel, the Jewish national home. The difficulties of Bene Israel adjustment in Israel are treated movingly.[38]

Whatever the difficulties were, the marriage issue created the most resentment. Although the question of the Bene Israel's status as full Jews in regard to marriage with other Jews was raised in Israel in the 1950s by some Orthodox Jews, who feared that the Bene Israel's past ignorance of Jewish law relating to divorce and levirate marriage made them unacceptable, it was not until May 1961 that the controversy came to the fore. At that time—when the Ashkenazi Chief Rabbinate happened to be vacant—the Sephardic chief rabbi of Israel, Rabbi Itzhak Nissim (from Iraq) refused to declare that the Bene Israel were acceptable as proper Jews for purposes of marriage. Individual rabbis could now refuse to perform marriages between Bene Israel and other Jews unless the Bene Israel party underwent ritual conversion. As one Bene Israel observer put it,

> the slur of presumptive bastardy was cast on the whole community, rendering its members barred in perpetuity from marrying outside their own tainted group. This slur naturally reflected itself in all social dealings.[39]

As the world press carried reports of protests against racial and color discrimination, angry letters and comments appeared in the Indian press, and Bene Israel institutions in India slowly began to respond. The Chief Rabbinate Council, persuaded by the government of Israel to examine the question, ruled in October 1961 that there was no basis for forbidding marriages with members of the Bene Israel community and therefore such marriages were permitted. But certain Orthodox circles in Israel and the United States would not accept the ruling and pressured the Chief Rabbinate to issue a directive, which it did in February 1962, requiring rabbis functioning as marriage registrars to investigate the female lineage and also all divorces that might have taken place among the ancestors of the Bene Israel party to a mixed marriage "as far back as is possible." No marriage was to take place in any case of doubt without reference to the Chief Rabbinate. This directive made the situation even worse than it had been before the ruling of 1961, for in requiring an investigation, it "gave fresh life and official recognition to the doubts about the legitimacy of every individual member of the Bene Israel community—doubts . . . which the ruling of 1961 solemnly purported to have removed once [and] for all.[40]

The directive engendered new protests in and out of India. Bene Israel intellectuals wrote letters to Orthodox authorities in Israel and the United States. A group of young activists formed the Bene Israel Purity Justification Committee of Bombay and waged a militant campaign in support of the Bene Israel Action Committee, which had been created in Israel to fight against the slur on that community's purity and orthodoxy. Suggesting that Nissim's Baghdadi origin was not irrelevant to their plight, the Bene Israel felt that their future existence in Israel would be problematic if they were not allowed to marry Jews other than Bene Israel unless they underwent conversion. The Chief Rabbinate would not relent. The appellate marriage registrars appointed by the government to review refusals to perform mixed marriages permitted all such marriages to take place, but the Bene Israel Action Committee's request that the directive and the humiliating investigations it called for be withdrawn was refused.[41]

The Jewish Agency and Israel's Ministry of Religious Affairs tried to find a solution toward the end of 1962 by proposing that machinery be established in India to regulate marriages and divorces according to Israeli rabbinical standards. The Bene Israel objected, some even writing to the government of India, not wanting Indian Jewry to fall within the jurisdiction of religious authorities in Israel. An Israeli rabbi who visited Bombay in June 1963 encountered vigorous protests and admitted that the directive of the Chief Rabbinate was discriminatory in effect and inconsistent with the ruling of October 1961. But he was not able to come up with any satisfactory solution.[42]

Despite hunger and sit-in strikes staged by the Bene Israel Action Committee, the Israeli government declared that it had no jurisdiction in the matter and that, in practice, there was no discrimination. By spring 1964, the Bene Israel committees had worked out plans for concerted action in Israel and India. Now President Itzhak Ben Zvi intervened. At a meeting on 31 July 1964, with spokesmen of the Bene Israel Action Committee, at which the minister for religious affairs and the Sephardic chief rabbi were present, the president proposed that the directive of 1962 apply to "immigrants from every distant land," not just the Bene Israel. This compromise was rejected by the Bene Israel, who organized a mass demonstration in Jerusalem on 5 August 1964. Two to three thousand Bene Israel converged on Jerusalem. Their procession to the headquarters of the Chief Rabbinate was accompanied by some fifty sympathizers, including Mapam (left-wing labor) party supporters and Professor Yigal Yadin. Other parties now came out in favor of the Bene Israel, but the National Religious party continued to support the Chief Rabbinate.[43]

An emergency meeting of the Knesset was convened on 17 August 1964. Prime Minister Levi Eshkol moved a resolution that affirmed that the Knesset viewed the Bene Israel as Jews in all respects and with the same rights as all other Jews, including matters of personal status; called on the Chief Rabbinate to remove the causes of any feeling of discrimination among the Bene Israel; and called on the Bene Israel to end their sit-in strike outside the Jewish Agency office. Although four opposition parties proposed separate resolutions asking specifically for the cancellation of the directive, the government-sponsored resolution was passed, with members of the National Religious party, as supporters of the government coalition, voting for it. "It is tragic," wrote B. J. Israel, "that the authorities in Israel should by their intransigence have reduced religion to a matter of political expediency and compromise." On 31 August 1964 the Chief Rabbinate finally issued a statement deleting all reference to the Bene Israel in the directive, which was made applicable to anyone whose family status was in doubt.[44]

For the Baghdadi Jews in India, Indian independence, more than Israeli statehood, motivated them to leave, and most went to London and Australia, rather than to Israel. Nevertheless, there was a substantial emigration of Baghdadis to Israel. Some had gone to Palestine in 1946 and had come back disappointed. J. J. Gubbay thought it was because they were unprepared, and so he started a camp for them near Alibagh, where they could learn farming, Hebrew, and cooperative living. The first *aliyah* from Calcutta arrived at Kfar Blum in 1945. By 1950 hundreds of Calcutta Baghdadis, including a number of businessmen and professionals, were waiting to go to Israel. Between 1945 and 1952 that city's Jewish population, which had been mainly Baghdadi, dropped from approximately 3,400 to fewer than 2,000, a large proportion of those who left having settled in Israel. By 1961 there were 1,165 Jews in Calcutta.[45]

When the State of Israel was proclaimed, the Malabari Jews of Cochin were particularly eager to go, out of a strong Zionist urge. For them, the ideological factor may have been more compelling than the economic one. Their immigration was delayed, however, because Israeli authorities were concerned with the prevalence of elephantiasis, a mosquito-borne disease that causes the legs to swell to enormous size and that affected many Jews as well as other inhabitants of Cochin. When the Jewish Agency specialist sent to investigate the problem determined that the condition was not contagious, approximately two thousand Cochin Jews migrated to Israel between 1953 and 1955. They settled in the Negev (Nevatim), the Galil (Kfar Ofer), the Jerusalem corridor (Mesillat Sion), and elsewhere, mostly in agricultural settlements. Having transmitted their communal assets to Israel, they were well provided for, but they too initially had considerable trouble adjusting to Israel.[46]

In 1951 there were 26,781 Jews in all of India. By 1961 this figure had dropped to 18,533, and by 1971 to 5,825. Many of the Jews who remain in India now do so because they cannot take their money—in the form of savings and pensions—out of India. Wealthy Jews who are leading a comfortable life in India would have to struggle in Israel. Also, some Jews cannot go because, by the late 1970s, Israel would admit only those who could support themselves or had a means of support in Israel, but not the aged and infirm, unless they came from countries where the Jews were becoming extinct or were in trouble, such as Pakistan. In such cases, the Jewish Agency would make appropriate advance arrangements, such as an old-age home or a nursing home. But the Jewish Agency was reluctant to bring people to Israel from an active community, such as exists in India, where the Jews can take care of their own people. Israel had limited funds and needed to spend them on young couples. Nevertheless, in the late 1970s, some four hundred or so a year were emigrating from India, but perhaps 40 percent were "problem" cases: for example, Jews who had once converted to another religion but wanted to revert to Judaism in order, the Jewish Agency representative thought, to go to Israel for economic reasons, bringing with them their gentile spouses and children.[47]

In the 1980s the trickle continued, particularly among the younger Bene

Israel. The attachment to Israel remained great, and even parents who wished to remain in India themselves were proud that their children were going to Israel.

Jewish Communal Relations
in Independent India: An Overview

By the early 1950s the population of the Jewish communities in Bombay had declined considerably. In 1951 there were 20,213 Jews in the city; in 1961, 12,366.[48] Not only had many Baghdadis and Bene Israel left, but most of the European Jewish immigrants, who had considered themselves transients in India, had also departed, often joining relatives in Western countries or settling in Israel. Many of the remaining refugees eventually died of old age in India. In 1980 only a handful of European Jews remained in Bombay. Despite the dwindling of the communities, little was done at first to try to bring the remnants of the Baghdadis and Bene Israel together, with the exception of cooperation on periodicals and in certain organizations. Efforts were made in the late 1950s and early 1960s to revive the Jewish Club as a community organization with a Jewish atmosphere. For a short while, the club enjoyed an active life, holding lectures and meetings, but it soon disintegrated into mainly a card-playing center, frequented by non-Jews as well.[49] In 1957 Bernard Heller, a visiting American rabbi, founded a Young Men/Women's Hebrew Association to bring Baghdadi and Bene Israel youth together. Having club membership and activities shared by males and females from both groups was quite an innovation. The group, which met in the Jewish Club, attracted only the most sophisticated Bene Israel and fewer Baghdadis, most of whom came from poorer families. It foundered quickly. Meanwhile, membership in the Bombay Zionist Association and the B'nai Brith was open to all: Baghdadis, Bene Israel, Cochinis, and foreign Jews did participate.

The Central Jewish Committee that had been founded in Bombay during the war to counter anti-Semitic propaganda in India continued in the postwar period as the Central Jewish Board, with a general coordinating function. Dr. E. Moses, a Bene Israel, replaced Sir Victor Sassoon as president, and Meyer Nissim, a Baghdadi, became chairman. Membership was by organization, and at first very few Baghdadi organizations joined the Central Jewish Board; only the Maccabees and the Bombay Zionist Association, which drew their members from both communities, were early participants. Although additional Baghdadi organizations followed suit, gradually, by the early 1960s, the Central Jewish Board became once again a Bene Israel institution. Baghdadi withdrawal was partly due to increased emigration among that community, leading to the disintegration of the communal organizations. Eventually, Dr. E. Moses resigned and his position was taken by Hersch Cynowicz, whom many Bene Israel disliked, believing he was too susceptible to Baghdadi influence. When the problem of Bene Israel marriages arose in Israel in the early 1960s, the Central Jewish Board of India remained silent. Although Cynowicz was controversial in the Indian Jewish community, he had a certain power and contacts with the government, and so was able to accomplish a fair amount in areas of Jewish concern such as travel documents, preservation of cemeteries, and leave on religious holidays. The Board also addressed itself to matters such as Hebrew education, shortages of *mohels* and *shohets,* and emigration to Israel. Gradually, Bene Israel organizations also disintegrated, some continuing to have a president and a letterhead but little membership. By the mid 1970s the Central Jewish Board was practically defunct.[50]

In the late 1950s and 1960s, a number of Bene Israel synagogues, including many in the villages, affiliated with the American Union of Orthodox Synagogues and tried to persuade the Baghdadi synagogues to join them. Albert Manasseh, head trustee of the Sassoon trusts, accepted the position of president of the Federation of Orthodox Synagogues but was merely a figurehead. He acted as an individual, not as a representative of the Baghdadi synagogues, which refused to participate. According to the trust conditions, the Baghdadi synagogues could not affiliate with the Union, but they may have sympathized with its activities. Thus, the activities of the federation were purely Bene Israel, as was its journal, *Mebasser,* to which Baghdadis never contributed. When Orthodox rabbis came to India, there were never joint Bene Israel-Baghdadi events. Other Bene Israel synagogues formed another federation, the United Synagogue of India, which affiliated with the World Council of Synagogues, supported by the American Conservative Jewish movement. In India, however, the beliefs and practices of the Bene Israel synagogues were identical, no matter to which federation they belonged.[51] Meanwhile, at about this same period, a very charismatic European rabbi, Hugo Gruyn, presided over the liberal synagogue, the Jewish Religious Union. Attendance increased tremendously under his leadership, and although the membership was still predominantly Bene Israel, approximately twenty Baghdadis were members at this time.

The community's educational institutions changed considerably. In the 1940s and 1950s, the Sir Jacob Sassoon Free School (Baghdadi) declined. Discipline became lax. Many wealthy children returned to the private Christian-run schools, and only poorer Baghdadis remained, partly because they depended on the free meals and medical checkups.[52] As the Baghdadis emigrated, the school began admitting more Bene Israel children, especially in the late 1950s. By this time, the Elly Kedourie School (Bene Israel), which had been Anglo-Vernacular—Marathi up to the fourth standard, introducing English as a medium of instruction in the fifth, and teaching only in English from the seventh on—dropped English and became a completely Marathi medium school. Consequently, many Bene Israel sought admission to the Sassoon school, and those with influence with Shalom Abraham, its Bene Israel headmaster, succeeded. By 1954–55, this school was the only one offering both English and Hebrew.

Eventually, as the number of Jewish children declined, the Sir Jacob Sassoon Free High School applied to the charity commissioner to have the trust deed changed so that it could admit non-Jewish children and charge fees. Eager to discourage communal institutions, the government readily agreed, and in 1971, when the total Jewish population of Greater Bombay was only 3,607, the school was opened to non-Jewish children as well. It continued to admit many neighborhood children, now primarily Muslim, but it was still attractive to Bene Israel families. In the late 1970s, about half of the 250 children in the school were Muslim. The feeding trusts established at the school provided that only Jewish children should be fed, but the school tried to feed all who needed it for a nominal fee. The non-Jewish children said Hebrew prayers in the morning but, according to informants, there was no real communal feeling.[53]

Intermarriage between Baghdadis and Bene Israel during this period was still very rare, and when it did occur, it was generally a Baghdadi woman marrying a Bene Israel man. An outstanding exception occurred when Maurice Japheth, the well-known journalist from the Baghdadi community, married an educated woman from a prominent Bene Israel family. Japheth, although of Iraqi origin, actually came from Aden, and Jews of Aden had always been friendlier with the Bene Israel than the Baghdadis in India were. Perhaps also, because of his position, Japheth could defy convention and marry a Bene Israel, although many Baghdadis were disturbed.[54] After Japheth's marriage, more Baghdadi men married Bene Israel women, but when Baghdadi–Bene Israel marriages occurred in Bombay, the Baghdadis checked in Bene Israel synogogues to be certain that the parents of the Bene Israel partner were Jews. If a *Kala* Bene Israel wanted to marry a Baghdadi, Tiffereth Israel, a Bene Israel synagogue, performed a conversion for a fee. The Baghdadi synagogues performed conversions up until the mid 1960s, but the Beth Din of London asked them to stop, as they did not have the competent authorities—a religious court with three rabbis.[55]

When the controversy over intermarriage arose in Israel in the early 1960s, prominent Baghdadis in Bombay differed in their reaction. Some felt that the Israeli rabbis were right to question the Bene Israel according to the *halachic* rules and were amazed that they were eventually forced to recognize them because of political pressure.[56] Others, such as Reginald Mathalone, the trustee of the Sassoon J. David Trust, who cannot be considered typical, approved of the recognition:

> [The Bene Israel] are Jews, and very religious ones. More religious than we. . . . The Baghdadis have always considered themselves superior to them. I don't know why. Jews are Jews. They're even having a tough time in Israel because there's color prejudice, which is a shame.[57]

Nor could national emergencies fully pull the two communities together. In 1962, when India was attacked by China, two friends, Judge Arthur Samson, a Bene Israel, and Magistrate Albert Shellim, a Baghdadi, formed the Jewish Defence Committee. Eventually the High Court told them that they should not participate in such an activity because they were judicial officers. Baghdadis and Bene Israel held a joint meeting, but each group voted for its own candidate for chairman and vice-chairman. The Bene Israel were outnumbered; they gradually withdrew, nothing was done, and the committee never functioned.[58]

The town that always seemed to escape Bene Israel-Baghdadi friction was New Delhi. Here the Jewish population remained small, consisting mainly of Bene Israel in government service, a few Baghdadi Jews, occasional Cochini Jews, and a few foreign Jews connected with the diplomatic corps, business, the media, or academia. The number of Bene Israel families living in New Delhi and its surroundings never exceeded twenty, reaching its peak in the 1950s and 1960s. In the 1950s, all Jews met for services at the residence of a member of the Delhi Jewish Welfare Association, inserting notices in newspapers to announce High Holiday services so that tourists, students, and temporary residents could attend. Eventually they built a prayer hall, the Judah Hyam Hall. Jews in Delhi worshiped and socialized together and were buried in the cemetery without a dividing wall, but the community was an artificial one.[59]

In Bombay, however, the friction between the two groups—and also between factions within each group—continued into the late 1970s, when fewer than four thousand Bene Israel and two hundred fifty Baghdadis remained in Bombay. At this time, the Baghdadi synagogue Knesset Eliahu paid eight Bene Israel to come each morning to form a *minyan*, but the Bene Israel still had difficulties with burials: they were running out of space in their own cemetery but were not permitted to use the Baghdadi cemetery in Byculla— which did have extra space—because according to the Sassoon trust deed, it was meant for Baghdadis.[60]

In 1979 representatives of the Baghdadi and Bene Israel communities in Bombay and Delhi were able to overcome their differences sufficiently to form the National Council of Indian Jewry (to replace the defunct Central

Jewish Board), which has survived into the mid 1980s. Its aims include representing the Jews at national functions, conferences, and meetings of minorities; expressing their views on important social, economic, and political questions; recommending to the government legislation on the personal laws of the Indian Jewish community; preserving Jewish culture and tradition; spreading knowledge of Judaism; and promoting the study of Jewish history and literature.[61] Various youth groups in Bombay, eager to promote the unity of the Jewish community, formed the Federation of Indian Jewish Youth in 1985.

Small Jewish communities still exist in Cochin, Calcutta, Poona, and Ahmedabad, and each has a few energetic, committed leaders. Whether they will be able to prevent the total disappearance of the Jews in these towns is difficult to predict. It is likely, however, that the center of Jewish interest in India in the future will remain in Bombay, and the preservation of the vitality and institutions of that community remains uppermost in the minds of Indian Jews today.[62]

CONCLUSION

For anyone reflecting on the history of the Jewish communities in India, the main question is why, after so many centuries of peaceful coexistence, Indian Jews left almost en masse after World War II? If they, unlike their counterparts in so many countries, were not threatened by persecution or anti-Semitism, why should the simultaneous emergence of an independent India and an independent Israel impel them to emigrate? The remnants of Jews in India to this day, after all, have not fared badly.

This study suggests that the changing nature of group identity in India, in particular the evolving sense of what it meant to be a Jew in India, was the underlying cause. If one accepts the view that in modern India "institutional changes, initially introduced during the colonial period, established new arenas of competition and defined the groups that were in a position to compete,"[1] and the implication that for all groups the movement was away from a caste-defined hierarchy into a more competitive society, one can understand why, for the minorities, ethnicity was likely to become a more pervasive mode of identification. With traditional patterns of relationships undermined, ethnicity in a culturally pluralistic society would be the solution for Parsis, Anglo-Indians, Indian Christians, and, during the British era, Muslims and Jews as well. For the last two groups, however, an international context—a world of coreligionists beyond India—also affected their destinies.

The cultural and religious autonomy that the Jews enjoyed under the caste system in the premodern period, which was acceptable to Hindus, worked well for Jews in the colonial period. With British encouragement, they made the transition from a castelike designation to an ethnic identification. Simply the presence of the culturally distinct British in India, even before their different conception of Indian society began to make itself felt, had far-reaching effects for the Jews. In the early nineteenth century, the exposure to Western Christian missionaries, whose translation of the Old Testament into Marathi and teaching of Hebrew greatly increased the Bene Israel's familiarity with and understanding of Judaism, enabled the Jews of India to forge closer links with the wider Jewish world. These ties were strengthened once the Bene Israel learned English, had access to the religious writings of English-speaking Jews, and eventually formed a branch of the Anglo-Jewish Association. They had been Jewish in a particularly Indian way; now they adopted the beliefs, practices, and concerns of Jewish communities elsewhere.

For the Baghdadis, however, the same British presence that had encouraged them to come to India in the first place also posed a potential threat. The racial separation between Indians and British that the colonial pattern fostered led the Baghdadis to fear that they would lose their status if they were associated with their darker-skinned, native coreligionists, the Bene Israel. In their desire to assimilate to the British and to be considered European, both socially and politically, the Baghdadis drew even further away from the Bene Israel, about whose Jewish authenticity they had some question anyway. Issues of purity, caste, and color, which would have affected relations between the two groups in the ordinary Indian environment, were intensified in the British colonial context.

If the British tendency after 1870 to define and count castes and other ethnic groups forced all Jews to deal with the issue of ethnicity, the emergence of Indian nationalism in the same era profoundly affected several ethnic communities, especially those who in any way might be associated with the colonial power. For the Bene Israel, the ambivalence surfaced in various forms. When they, along with other castes, formed voluntary communal organizations during and immediately after World War I, the tension was articulated in their attitudes toward politics. Most Bene Israel, concerned with the dependency of the community on the British for employment in the public services, were reluctant to jeopardize their position at a time when competition seemed to loom larger. They thus shied away from political discussion. Those individuals most closely identified with India felt that a communal organization had to deal, on occasion, with political matters. Moreover, they believed that they could entrust their future to Indian nationalists and saw no need for separate communal representation in the coming Montagu-Chelmsford reforms. Other Bene Israel leaders were reluctant to take such a stance publicly.

As the question of communal representation came increasingly to the fore in the 1920s and 1930s, the Bene Israel did debate whether Jews should seek separate electoral representation to safeguard their interests. Yet they ultimately decided against it. Although most Bene Israel were not actively nationalist or even very sympathetic to nationalist interests, they did not wish to suggest that they were different from most Indians and needed special treatment. The Baghdadis of Calcutta, however, demanded an alternative arrangement. Reluctant to be lumped together with "native" Jews or Indians, they sought to be included in the European electorates: if they were given full privileges in other parts of the British Empire, why should they not enjoy the same status in India? The Baghdadis' identification with Indians was practically nonexistent. As the nationalist movement grew, so did the fears of the Baghdadis, except for a few individuals.

In those years, as the Baghdadis and Bene Israel struggled to work out their relationships to each other and to Indian nationalism, the growth of Zionism opened yet another channel of identity. Far removed from the centers of Jewish life, the Jews of India were nevertheless aware of events affecting their coreligionists elsewhere—such as the persecution of Jews of eastern Europe after the war, and the British occupation of Palestine and its implications for the future of world Jewry. The central Zionist offices, eager to reach out to Jewish communities all over the world, initiated the contact with India. Now the Jews of India were faced with the same dilemma as Jews everywhere: would they see themselves as simply a religious minority in the country they had inhabited for so long, or would they shift gears and define themselves as part of an ethnic "nation" that needed a home of its own? Many Bene Israel showed some interest in Zionism, although they were uncertain how it would directly affect them. Others, however, disturbed by the way in which the Bene Israel had been viewed by other Jews in the past, had reservations. Would they be considered full Jews in a Jewish state? Behind this question was the implication that Indian Jews would do better to see themselves first as Indians, rather than as Jews. Although the Bene Israel did form on-again, off-again Zionist organizations, it was a handful of middle-class Baghdadis who kept the Bombay Zionist Association alive. Wealthy Baghdadis, like their counterparts elsewhere, tended to be assimilationist (or at least deeply enmeshed in affairs where they lived) and were not very supportive of the Zionist movement, either politically or financially.

It is ironic that the European leaders of the Jewish Agency, more than the Jews in India themselves, realized the significance of India in the Zionist effort. They recognized the potential connection between Muslim pressure on the British in India and British policy in Palestine and, encouraged by the shrewd political observations of some young Baghdadis, they saw the desirability of contacting Hindu leaders such as Gandhi and Nehru, in order to convince them of the Zionist position.

Events in Europe in the 1930s confirmed the reality of the Indian Jews' links with the wider Jewish community. The rise of Hitler and Nazi anti-Semitism, chronicled in the newspapers and radios for all to read and hear, forged a heightened sense of solidarity with their suffering brethren, a number of whom were now arriving on Indian shores. Their awareness of the sympathy of many gentiles—in and beyond India—for their coreligionists impelled Indian Jews to seek a more positive statement from Gandhi.

In the years just preceding World War II, certain British attitudes had disappointed the Jews of India. For the Bene Israel, the failure to be recognized as a special minority for recruitment to the services seemed threatening. For the Baghdadis, the failure to get themselves included on the European electoral rolls made them more fearful about safeguarding their interests. The policy in Palestine was becoming desperate for the Jews. The actual outbreak of the war, however, separated the sheep from the goats. While Hindu and Muslim nationalists, now in a position to make the fulfillment of their demands the condition for full cooperation with the British, were reserved toward the war effort, certain minority groups, such as the Anglo-Indians and the Jews, were more supportive. Despite their dissatisfaction with the white paper on Palestine of 1939, the Jews of India displayed the same loyalty to the Allies as Jews elsewhere. There was simply no choice. For most Bene Israel, their identification with their persecuted coreligionists and their overriding loyalty to the British outweighed any identification with Indian nationalism they might have had. Their sense of an ethnic identity within India had now developed into an ethnic consciousness that encompassed Jews around the world.

In the first half of the twentieth century, many Bene Israel had an ambiguous and ambivalent relationship with the British. They constantly expressed their gratitude and loyalty to Great Britain yet remained aware that, throughout their history, India was the one country that had not persecuted Jews. Many felt it would be unwise to tie themselves too closely to England, as the split would eventually come. Most were political fence-sitters and so were protected on all sides. Pro-British in their heart of hearts, they turned to nationalism gradually. By 1947, most of the Bene Israel in India had become staunchly pro-Gandhi, but the development had been slow and natural. Now it is very fashionable for them to look back and say that they were always in favor of Gandhi. Most Indians today want to work up nationalist pasts for themselves even if they did not have them in the 1930s and 1940s. Few are ready to admit that they ever admired the British or wanted them to rule. But active Bene Israel nationalists were quite out of step with the rest of the community and very much in a minority, although their views were perhaps more important than their numbers might indicate.[2]

Thus, the challenges confronting the Jews of India in the nineteenth and twentieth centuries—British rule and the opportunities it made available, the nationalist movement, and "Judaism reawakening in its various forms, secularist, religious, and Zionist"—were closely interrelated. These challenges seemed to point to three options for the Jews as an ethnic group in the postwar period: a communal cultural autonomy within a pluralistic, egalitarian, independent India; a greater affirmation of their ethnicity through the espousal of Zionism and emigration to Israel; and emigration to other countries.[3]

The emergence of an independent Israel was an enormous lure. The economic uncertainties expected for all Indians after independence, coupled with the special opportunity for emigration provided by the birth of the State of Israel, enticed many Jews to leave. But it was the strong sense of an ethnic

Jewish consciousness that had developed during the British raj, particularly among the Bene Israel, that enabled them to embrace this option.

One also cannot help speculating whether the partition of the subcontinent into two religiously determined states did not in some way affect the thinking of Indian Jews about the relationship between religion and territory as an element of communal identity.[4] It is certainly possible that had Zionism and the State of Israel not afforded an alternative, the Jews of India, at least the Bene Israel and the Cochin Jews, would have remained as an ethnic group in a pluralistic, independent India. The Baghdadis, on the other hand, seemed destined to leave once the British did. Their economic interests and their lack of identification with Indians almost compelled them to emigrate, but only some, whose identification with Jewish ethnicity sufficiently outweighed opportunities available elsewhere, went to Israel.

In a thoughtful piece written in the early 1970s, B. J. Israel articulated some of the concerns of his community members who had remained in India, concerns that were echoed throughout the Jewish world:

> The question of identity for the Indian Jew is not just an academic one, what with the Zionist demand for some sort of link between Jews throughout the Diaspora and the State of Israel, and the Zionist belief that the Jews are in exile on the one hand and the Jan Sangh cry in India for Indianization on the other hand. . . . In so far as being an Indian consists exclusively in being a member of a political entity of a secular character, one can be both a complete Jew and a complete Indian. India respects a diversity of religious and cultural outlooks and does not fear extra-territorial ties on the part of its citizens—like affiliation with world Jewish unions. . . . Those of us who value our Indian citizenship are under no obligation to extend our religious loyalties as Jews to the political state of Israel. . . . If there is a danger on the Jewish side in Political Zionism, there is a danger on the Indian side in the shrill cry of Indianization that has been raised recently. . . . If to be an Indian requires one to renounce the ties of Jewish brotherhood with our coreligionists abroad, there is no place in India for the Jews. If, as some claim, we are required as Indians to adopt the ideological basis of Hindu culture on the ground that it alone is indigenous to the Indian soil, then again there is no place for the Jews in India except as strangers enjoying India's hospitality as do so many foreigners temporarily resident here.[5]

The central issue for the Jews of India today is the very survival of their community. With perhaps only five thousand Jews remaining in India and twenty-five to thirty thousand now in Israel, their institutions in India are struggling to keep alive. Synagogues and prayer halls are gradually closing or finding their membership shrinking. Decisions must be made about the future of those synagogues that are no longer functioning, especially in the Konkan villages from which the Jewish populations have emigrated. Some Bene Israel feel strongly that the Jews owe a great debt to India, where they have always been treated well, and that they should not abandon her. They believe they have an obligation to remain as an active, meaningful, united community with proper leadership. To forfeit its representation in a given country is also a loss to Judaism. Others, like Ezra Kolet, the leader of the Delhi community, fear assimilation as a potential problem. It is the disintegration of the community through assimilation, rather than through emigration, that would disturb him. He feels that the younger generation of Indian Jews has little Jewish identity or concern, and he fears that those who leave India will go not to Israel, but to Western countries.[6]

What might have happened to the Jews in India had India not become part of the British Empire? Would the Bene Israel have remained a castelike group in villages within a hierarchically organized society, having little contact with the Jewish world beyond India?[7] Would Bene Israel-Baghdadi relationships have deteriorated as they did? Would the Baghdadis even have come in such numbers had it not been for the British presence? Although these questions cannot be answered definitively, it can certainly be said that the evolution of Bene Israel identity would have been played out in another context and that the relationship of the Jews to both Indian political development and Zionism would probably have been very different.

Looking from the perspective of comparative Jewish history, one is struck by the uniqueness of the Bene Israel story. They had become increasingly religiously observant and had identified themselves with Jewish ethnicity and world Jewry, without experiencing the anti-Semitism felt elsewhere in the world. Even the emergence of Israel and India's pro-Arab tilt had hardly affected their position. Their emigration to Israel was conditioned not, as in so many Eastern countries, by a persecution resulting from the creation of the State of Israel, but by an attraction to the Holy Land and an uncertainty about postcolonial India.

It is ironic that the Bene Israel have actually experienced more prejudice at the hands of Jews—first the Baghdadis in India, and then the Israelis—than they have from non-Jews. Whether predicated on ethnic, religious, economic, or color discrimination, the tendency of some Israelis to set them apart has been a disappointment to many Bene Israel. It is thus small wonder that observers of the Bene Israel experience are currently watching the absorption and integration of the Ethiopian Jews with interest and concern, and that they are dismayed by the refusal of some rabbis to recognize Ethiopians as full Jews or to perform "mixed" marriages unless the Ethiopian partner undergoes a ritual conversion.[8]

One cannot be certain whether the tiny remnants of Jews in India will be able to preserve the special character and heritage of their communities, nor whether a distinctive identity can be maintained by the Indian Jews already in Israel. How will the effort of this latter group to maintain their culture and traditions affect their integration into Israeli society? Indeed, what does it mean to be an Indian Jew in Israel? This book cannot really answer those questions, yet it may help to clarify some of the issues that were in ferment while the Jews still constituted vibrant, active communities in India and to shed some light on the changing nature of what it meant to be a Jew in India.

GLOSSARY

Hebrew Terms

Aliyah. Lit. "going up"; honor given a Jew to ascend the reading desk platform in a synagogue to recite the blessings over the Torah. Also used to mean immigration into the Land of Israel.

Ashkenazi. Originally applied to Jews living in northern France, Germany, and later, Scandinavian and Slavic countries. Now applied to Jews who follow the ritual developed in these regions.

Beth Din. Jewish religious or civil court of law.

Cohan (Cohen). Jewish male of priestly descent.

Eretz-Yisrael (Eretz-Israel, Erez Israel). Lit. "Land of Israel"; used in the Bible, Talmud, and other Jewish literature to refer to Palestine.

Galut. Lit. "exile"; land of Jewish dispersion, particularly those lands where Jews were subject to persecution. Related to Greek term "diaspora" (lit. "scattering") which generally refers to the dispersion of the Jewish people outside of Israel.

Get. Writ of divorce with text strictly prescribed by Jewish law. According to Orthodox tradition, a divorced wife may not remarry unless she has received a *get* from her former husband.

Gubbai. Synagogue treasurer.

Habonim. Youth organization of the Labor Zionist Movement, promoting Jewish values, Zionism, and pioneer work in Israel.

Haham (hacham, hakham). Lit. "wise" or "sage"; title used by Sephardic or Oriental Jews for a rabbi.

Halacha. Corpus of written and oral Jewish law.

Halitza. Ceremony whereby a childless widow becomes free to marry someone other than a brother of her deceased husband. The surviving brother formally refuses to marry the widow.

Halutzim. Lit. "pioneers"; groups of young Jews who emigrated to Palestine to rebuild the Jewish national homeland.

Hechalutz. Zionist pioneer movement started in 1917 to prepare young Jews physically and spiritually to settle in Palestine in cooperative communities.

Hazan (chazan, hazzan). Reader or cantor; official in synagogue who leads worshippers in prayer.

Kashruth. Lit. "fitness" or "legitimacy"; foods, sacred objects and persons meeting the religious requirements of traditional Jews.

Kedusha. Lit. "holiness"; name of certain prayers in the synagogue liturgy uttered as a proclamation of the majesty and holiness of God.

Keren Keyemet L'Israel. Jewish National Fund; instrument of world Jewry founded in 1901 to purchase and develop land in Palestine (Israel) on behalf of the Jewish people.

Keren Hayesod. Palestine Restoration Fund (later Palestine Foundation Fund); organized in 1920 to develop the Jewish national home by funding agricultural settlement, industry and other immigrant projects and institutions.

Ketuba. Marriage certificate outlining the woman's rights in the event of divorce or of her husband's death.

Kol Israel. Lit. "everyone of Israel"; i.e., the Jewish people.

Kolel. Visitor from Palestine; often Ashkenazi Jews seeking charity.

Kosher. Lit. "fit" or "in proper condition"; designation for ritually pure things, especially food permitted to be used in accordance with Jewish dietary laws.

Matza. Unleavened bread made of flour and water eaten by Jews during the festival of Passover.

Meshuchrarim. A division of Cochin Jewry referring to descendants of converted, manumitted slaves: the so-called brown Jews.

Mikveh. Public ritual bath maintained by a Jewish community. Its use for purposes of purification and cleanliness is a requirement of traditional law.

Minyan. Minimum number of Jewish males above the age of thirteen required by Orthodox Judaism for certain congregational prayers.

Mitzvah (pl. *mitzvot*). A religious and moral obligation.

Mohel. Ritual circumcisor who performs the ceremony on the eighth day after birth of the male child.

Pogrom. (Russian: "riot" or "devastation"); term applied since 1881 to violent anti-Jewish attacks.

Responsa. (Latin: "answers"); branch of rabbinic literature comprised of written opinions and rulings on matters of Jewish law in response to queries.

Schnorrer. Beggar who considered the receiving of alms as his vested right.

Sephardic (Sephardi). Originally applied to Jews of Spanish and Portuguese origin; later applied to all Jews (including Oriental) who follow the ritual developed in Spain and Portugal.

Sepher Torah. Lit. "Book of the Torah"; roll of parchment upon which the five books of Moses are written and from which the designated portion of the Torah is read in the synagogue.

Shaliach (pl. *shlichim*). Emissary from the Jewish community in Palestine to Jewish communities in the diaspora.

Shekel. Name of Hebrew coin from 66 A.D. on. Refers to a membership fee in a Zionist organization. Also the unit of currency in Israel today.

Shema. Lit. "hear!"; one of the most important Hebrew prayers affirming the Jewish faith. It begins: "Hear, of Israel, the Lord our God, the Lord is One."

Shofar. Horn of a ram sounded in the synagogue service, particularly during the services for the New Year and the Day of Atonement.

Shohet. Person who slaughters animals for food according to Jewish laws and regulations.

Simhat Torah. Holiday marking the completion of the annual cycle of the reading of the Torah; a series of processions with the Torah scrolls takes place during the synagogue service.

Tallith (Tallis). Rectangular prayer shawl with fringes at the corners used for worship.

Tebilah. Bath for ritual cleansing.

Torah. First five books of the Bible, known as the Pentateuch or the Five Books of Moses; in a broader sense, term applied to the entire body of Jewish traditions.

Va'ad Leumi. National Council of the Jews in Palestine during the British Mandate.

Yahudis (Yehudis). Lit. "Jews"; term used by Baghdadis and Bene Israel to refer to Baghdadi Jews.

Yibboom. Biblical injunction whereby a man is required to marry the widow of his deceased brother if the brother has died childless.

Yichus. Jewish ancestry or descent.

Yom Kippur. Lit. "Day of Atonement"; holiest day in the Jewish religion.

Indian Terms

Arya Samaj. Major nineteenth-century Hindu reform movement started in the Punjab by Swami Dayananda.

Ashram. Residence or hermitage of a saint or guru engaged in some form of religious instruction.

Collector. Chief administrator and magistrate in a revenue district.

Devnagara. Script in which the Sanskrit and Hindi languages are written.

Dewan (Diwan). Chief officer of an Indian state.

Gita. Short for *Bhagavad Gita* ("Song of the Blessed One"), the sacred book consisting of a long dialogue between Krishna, an incarnation of Vishnu, and Arjuna, a noble warrior; part of the Hindu epic, the *Mahabharata.*

Gora. Lit. "white"; used by Bene Israel to designate members of their community who descended from mothers who were originally (i.e., not converted) Jewish.

Harijan. Lit. "child of God"; Mahatma Gandhi's name for an untouchable.

Hartal. Strike; the soul is too shocked by some abuse to be able to attend to practical affairs for a time.

Jamat. Arabic term used by Bene Israel for the general body of synagogue members or a local community.

Juma prayers. Muslim prayers recited at noon on Friday.

Ka'aba. Shrine of the sacred black stone in Mecca.

Kaiser-i-Hind. Lit. "Emperor of India"; title of the British monarch as ruler of India. Also the name of a medal awarded since 1900 for important and useful services to India.

Kaji (Kazi). From the Arabic *kadi* (judge); originally a hereditary community leader or religious teacher of the Bene Israel who traveled throughout the Konkan to officiate at ceremonies and to settle disputes.

Kala. Lit. "black"; used by the Bene Israel to designate Bene Israel who were believed to have descended from non-Jewish mothers or from those who had converted to Judaism.

-kar. "Inhabitant of"; suffix affixed to names of villages to form surnames of Bene Israel, e.g., Kehimkar means "inhabitant of Kehim."

Khan Bahadur. Title of respect or honor given to distinguished Muslims, Parsis, and Jews. *Bahadur* means "hero" or "champion."

Khan Sahib. Title of respect or honor given to distinguished Muslims, Parsis, and Jews. *Sahib* means "master."

Khilafat. Caliphate, the line of succession to the prophet Muhammad. A movement to protest the division of the Ottoman Empire and to strengthen the authority of the Ottoman Caliphate.

Lakh. One hundred thousand (100,000).

Lok Sabha. Lit. "house of the people"; lower house of the Parliament of the Republic of India.

Lokamanya. Title meaning "world respected."

Mahabharata. One of two major Indian epic poems, it describes the battle between two branches of a royal family. It includes the *Bhagavad Gita.*

Maharaja. Lit. "great king"; ruler of an Indian State.

Malida. A ceremonial food offering and recitation of prayers for special occasions.

Maulana. Title used by a Muslim cleric.

Mem Sahib. Lady, mistress, term of respect used for European women.

Mofussil. Rural hinterland.

Mohallah (Mohall). Quarter for particular caste or group in Indian cities.

Parsis. Descendants of Zoroastrians who moved to India in the early eighth century after the Arabs conquered Persia (Iran).

Raj. Rule, empire, kingdom, administration.

Ramayana. Indian epic centered around the King Rama, an incarnation of Vishnu.

Rao Bahadur. Title of respect or honor given to distinguished Hindus. *Bahadur* means "hero" or "champion."

Rao Sahib. Title of respect or honor given to distinguished Hindus. *Sahib* means "master."

Sabha. Lit. "council" or "house"; a voluntary caste association to promote the mobility and well-being of the caste and caste-consciousness.

Sahib. Master; term of respect used by Indians when addressing or speaking of a European.

Sardar. Title of respect often, but not only, used for Sikhs.

Satyagraha. Lit. "soul force" or "truth force"; non-violent resistance or non-cooperation—Mahatma Gandhi's form of political agitation.

Sepoy. Indian policeman; later any Indian soldier in a European army.

Shanwar Teli. Lit. "Saturday oil-presser"; caste-like designation for the Bene Israel in the eighteenth and nineteenth centuries in the Konkan because they were oil-pressers who abstained from work on the Sabbath.

Shetia. Wealthy merchant class of Bombay in the late nineteenth century.

Shudra. Fourth rank in the traditional caste system; includes groups such as peasants and artisans.

Stree Mandal. Women's Association.

Subedar Major. Highest commissioned rank in the Indian army open to Indians until 1918.

Swadeshi. Lit. "of our own country"; the movement to promote goods made in India.

Swaraj. Self-government, self-rule, freedom, independence.

Taluqdar. Large landholder, responsible for revenue collection.

NOTES

Introduction
(Pages 1–7)

1. Itzhak Nissim, *Benei Yisrael: Piskei Halakkah* [Bene Israel: Halachic Decision and the Sources for the Investigation of Their Laws and the Question of Their Origins] (Jerusalem, 1962) is a collection of important rabbinical correspondence and other pertinent documents relating to the Bene Israel compiled by the Chief Rabbinate of Israel during the controversy over their eligibility to marry other Jews. See also B. J. Israel, "The Bene Israel Struggle for Religious Equality in Israel," in his *Bene Israel of India* (New York, 1984), 88–97. The adjustment of the Bene Israel in Israel is the subject of a D.Phil. dissertation entitled "Bene Israel Indian Jews in Lod, Israel: A Study in the Persistence of Ethnicity and Ethnic Identity," by Shalwa Weil, University of Sussex, England, 1977. See also Schifra Strizower, "The 'Bene Israel' in Israel," *Middle Eastern Studies* 2 (1966): 123–43. See below, chap. 8.

2. An excellent brief introduction to the Jewish communities of India is by the Bene Israel author Benjamin J. Israel, *The Jews of India* (New Delhi, 1982). More accessible perhaps is Walter J. Fischel, Paul Gottlieb, and Avigdor Herzog, "India," *Encyclopedia Judaica* (hereafter called *EJ*), 1971 ed., 8:349–60. Walter J. Fischel, *Ha-Yehudim be Hoddu* [The Jews in India: Their Contribution to the Economic and Political Life] (Jerusalem, 1960), focuses on the medieval and early modern periods. T. V. Parasuram, *India's Jewish Heritage* (New Delhi, 1982) is popular and derivative, but a useful summary. On the Jews of Cochin, see Walter J. Fischel, "Cochin in Jewish History," *Proceedings of the American Academy for Jewish Research* (hereafter called *PAAJR*), 30 (1962): 37–59; and Fischel's "The Contribution of the Cochin Jews to South Indian and Jewish Civilization," *Commemoration Volume, Cochin Synagogue Quatercentenary Celebrations* (Cochin, 1971), 15–64. A readable introduction to this community and a summary of Fischel's work are found in his article entitled "Cochin," *EJ*, 1971 ed., 5:621–28. David G. Mandelbaum, "The Jewish Way of Life in Cochin," *Journal of Jewish Social Studies* (hereafter called *JSS*) 1 (1939): 423–60, a pioneering historical and ethnographic study with useful bibliographical notes, has now been supplemented by his "Social Stratification among the Jews of Cochin in India and in Israel," *Jewish Journal of Sociology* 17 (1975): 165–210, which has been reprinted in Thomas A. Timberg, *Jews in India* (New York, 1986), 61–120. Schifra Strizower, "The Jews of Cochin," *Exotic Jewish Communities* (London, 1962), 88–124, relies heavily upon Mandelbaum's earlier study, and upon Louis Rabinowitz, *Far East Mission* (Johannesburg, 1952), but adds more recent sociological observations. A pamphlet, S. S. Koder, *History of the Jews of Kerala* (Cochin, 1974), presents the views of this leading member of the Cochin community, who has facilitated the research of many foreign scholars. Barbara C. Johnson (Barbara Johnson Hudson),

"Shingli or Jewish Cranganore in the Traditions of the Cochin Jews of India, with an Appendix on the Cochin Jewish Chronicles," M.A. thesis, Smith College, Northampton, Massachusetts, 1975, incorporates recent Indian scholarship. On the adjustment of Cochin Jews in Israel, see Gilbert Kushner, *Immigrants from India in Israel* (Tucson, 1973).

The classic work on the Bene Israel, written by a member of the community at the turn of the century but published forty years later, is Hayeem S. Kehimkar, *The History of the Bene Israel of India*, ed. Immanuel Olsvanger (Tel Aviv, 1937). Other studies by Bene Israel authors include Shellim Samuel, *Treatise on the Origin and Early History of the Beni-Israel of Maharashtra State* (Bombay, 1963) and Moses Ezekiel, *History and Culture of the Bene Israel in India* (Bombay, 1948). Benjamin J. Israel's generous cooperation and works have influenced many researchers. His studies have been collected in Benjamin J. Israel, *The Bene Israel of India* (New York, 1984). Walter J. Fischel, "The Literary Activities of the Bene Israel in India," *Jewish Book Annual* 29 (1971–72): 5–11, and his "Bombay in Jewish History in the Light of New Documents from the Indian Archives," *PAAJR* 38–39 (1972): 119–44, focus on specific aspects of Bene Israel history. A more recent ethnographic study is found in Schifra Strizower, *The Bene Israel of Bombay* (New York, 1971). See also Shirley B. Isenberg, *India's Bene Israel: A Comprehensive Inquiry* (forthcoming).

Walter J. Fischel, "The Immigration of 'Arabian Jews' to India in the Eighteenth Century," *PAAJR* 33 (1965): 1–20, discusses the origin of the Baghdadi community in India. Stanley Jackson, *The Sassoons* (New York, 1968), and Cecil Roth, *The Sassoon Dynasty* (London, 1941), both devote considerable attention to the Bombay period in the history of this famous family. David S. Sassoon, *History of the Jews of Baghdad* (Letchworth, 1949), chap. 33, covers the Bombay period as well. Baghdadi Jews from Calcutta have published several works about their community. The most scholarly treatment is Ezekiel M. Musleah, *On the Banks of the Ganga: The Sojourn of Jews in Calcutta* (North Quincy, Mass., 1975). Isaac S. Abraham, *Origin and History of the Calcutta Jews* (Calcutta, c. 1970), is a more popular treatment of customs and practices. Esmond David Ezra, *Turning Back the Pages: A Chronicle of Calcutta Jewry* (London, 1986), has some useful information, particularly on population and genealogy.

Thomas A. Timberg, *Jews in India* (New York, 1986) contains some useful studies on all three communities. For a study of the Jewish communities in India in the late 1970s, see Joan G. Roland, "The Jews of India: Communal Survival or the End of a Sojourn?" *JSS* 42 (1980): 75–90.

3. M. N. Srinivas, *Social Change in Modern India* (Berkeley, 1966), 120. On concepts of pollution and purity, see M. N. Srinivas, *Religion and Society among the Coorgs of South India* (Oxford 1952), chap. 4. See also Bernard S. Cohen, *India: The Social Anthropology of a Civilization* (Englewood Cliffs, N.J., 1971), 115, 124.

4. Srinivas, *Social Change*, 6, 7, 14, 148, 149; Timberg, "On Indian Jews," in *Jews in India*, 7, sees a kind of "Hebraization"—greater attention to education in Hebrew—as a kind of Jewish parallel to Sanskritization. He suggests that, in merging with Zionism recently, "Hebraization" has a broader significance for the average Indian Jew than Sanskritization has for most Hindus.

5. E. R. Leach, review of Srinivas, *Caste in Modern India*, in *British Journal of Sociology* 14 (Dec. 1963): 377–78; Mckim Marriott, "Interactional and Attributional Theories of Caste ranking," *Man in India* 39(2) (1959), cited in Strizower, *Bene Israel of Bombay*, 26.

6. Cohn, *India*, 3; Srinivas, *Social Change*, 14, 75.

7. Srinivas, *Social Change*, 75. See also Louis Dumont, *Homo Hierarchicus* (Chicago, 1980), 210.

8. On ethnic diversity and cultural pluralism, see R. A. Schermerhorn, *Ethnic Plurality in India* (Tucson, 1978). See also Dumont, *Homo Hierarchicus*, 203.

9. B. J. Israel (personal communication, 6 Feb. 1979). See Schifra Strizower, "Jews as an Indian Caste," *Jewish Journal of Sociology* 1 (1959): 44, 47, 48, and *Bene Israel of Bombay*, 21–27. Strizower cites an informant who said that even in the late 1930s, the Hindus in the Konkan still thought their food utensils would become polluted if the Bene Israel touched them. Strizower felt that although the Jews had been influenced by the Hindu caste system, they were not in fact a caste. The position of the Bene Israel within Indian society was not mystic and preordained, bound up with the religious conception of Hinduism. R. K. Jain, Review of *The Children of Israel:* [British edition of *The Bene Israel of Bombay*], by Schifra Strizower, *Jewish Journal of Sociology* 15–16 (1973–74): 127, has pointed out that the attribution of Saturday oil-presser (*Shanwar Teli*) status to the former Bene Israel villagers was not a genuinely birth-caste attribution but an occupational-caste one. He feels that mechanical and individual pollution may have characterized the Bene Israel's ritual relations with caste Hindus without an element of reciprocity entering into them. Srinivas, *Social Change*, 18, shows how the lifestyle of the dominant group in a local region could prevail in a reverse situation in the nineteenth-century Punjab, where Hindus adapted to Sikh and Muslim practices. Hindu women did not appear in public in overwhelmingly Muslim areas. Hindus did not recite Sanskrit mantras and sent their children to schools run by Muslim clerics. Brahmins donned the sacred thread only at the time of marriage.

10. Strizower, *Bene Israel of Bombay*, 30, talks of a "subcaste-like relationship" between *Gora* and *Kala*—pointing out that although they coexisted, they were not interdependent, and that *visa-à-vis* Indian society, they formed an undifferentiated group. See below, chap. 3, 66–67.

11. Cohn, *India*, 78. Nathan Katz (personal communication, 30 Sept. 1987) has pointed out that British racism and Indian caste attitudes had an affinity that made British domination all the easier. On how the British dealt with the caste system, see below, chap. 1, 24–26, and chap. 2, 32.

12. The existence of Jews in Cochin has been documented as far back as c. A.D. 1000 and a segment of them, the Malabari (the so-called black Jews) probably arrived in India much earlier. Their knowledge and strict observance of Judaism were reinforced by continuous communication with Jews from many lands throughout the medieval period. These international contacts also enabled them to play an important role in trade, which was partly responsible for the high status they enjoyed with the Hindu rulers in Cochin. The Indian environment seems to have contributed to the division of the Cochin Jews into three endogamous subgroups that observed castelike distinctions.

13. Schermerhorn, *Ethnic Plurality*, 12–13, 183–86; Government of India, Ministry of Information and Broadcasting, *India, 1986* (New Delhi, 1987), 14; Dumont, *Homo Hierarchicus*, 203; Mandelbaum, "Social Stratification," in Timberg, *Jews in India*, 100. See Shalva Weil, "Symmetry between Christians and Jews in India: The Cnanite Christians and the Cochin Jews of Kerala," in Timberg, *Jews in India*, 176–204. For an interesting discussion on upward mobility of a caste through conversion to Catholicism see S. B. Kaufmann (now Susan Bayly), "A Christian Caste in Hindu Society: Religious Leadership and Social Conflict among the Paravas of Southern Tamilnadu," *Modern Asian Studies* 15 (2) (1983): 203–34.

14. Article 366(2), quoted in Schermerhorn, *Ethnic Plurality*, 211.

15. Schermerhorn, *Ethnic Plurality*, 13, 210–13, 234, and chap. 9. See also Frank Anthony, *Britain's Betrayal in India: The Story of the Anglo-Indian Community* (Bombay, 1969), and V. R. Gaikwad, *The Anglo-Indians: A Study in the Problems and Processes Involved in Emotional and Cultural Integration* (Bombay, 1967).

16. Schermerhorn, *Ethnic Plurality*, 262–71, 286–87. See Eckehard Kulke, *The Parsees in India* (New Delhi, 1978).

Chapter 1. Jews and Society in Premodern India
(pages 11–28)

1. The upper classes were deported and lost their separate identity, although reports of their continued existence in various parts of the world as the Ten Lost Tribes prevailed throughout history (2 Kings 18:11) (Strizower, *Bene Israel of Bombay*, 10–15). Strizower suggests that the Ten Tribes theory of origin may have originated with Christian missionaries or Jewish travelers and then passed into Bene Israel tradition.

2. Hayeem S. Kehimkar, the classic Bene Israel historian of his community, believed that the Jews arrived around 175 B.C. (Kehimkar, *History of the Bene Israel*, 6–12). The shipwreck legend is similar to that of the Chitpavan Brahmins of Maharashtra. See Kehimkar, 15, and B. J. Israel, *Religious Evolution among the Bene Israel of India since 1750* (Bombay, 1963), 4.

3. B. J. Israel, *Jews of India*, 19. Shellim Samuel, *Beni-Israel*, believes that they arrived in the mid eighth century B.C. before the fall of Samaria, the capital of the Kingdom of Israel.

4. John Wilson, *Appeal for the Christian Education of the Bene Israel* (Bombay, 1866), cited by Strizower, *Bene Israel of Bombay*, 19 n. 11. Wilson, a prominent missionary who worked with the Bene Israel in the mid nineteenth century, had revised his original theory that the Bene Israel were descendants of the Ten Tribes who had settled in India at an earlier date. See John Wilson, *Lands of the Bible* (Edinburgh, 1847), 2:667–79.

5. See B. J. Israel, *Jews of India*, 20; Allen H. Godbey, *The Lost Tribes: A Myth* (Durham, N.C., 1930), 317, 345; Strizower, *Bene Israel of Bombay*, 15.

6. Cited in B. J. Israel, *Jews of India*, 15.

7. See B. J. Israel, *Jews of India*, 14–20, for a full discussion of these theories. See also Kehimkar, *Bene Israel*, 41; Ezekiel, *History and Culture*, 13; and Fischel, "Bombay in Jewish History," 141. There is no indication of whether or not David Rahabi was the first Cochin Jew to encounter the Bene Israel. See Strizower, *Bene Israel of Bombay*,

35–36. Although other early travelers and even Arab historians refer to Jews in India, there is no proof that these Jews are Bene Israel. See Timberg, *Jews in India*, 4, 10 n. 3. Current work by B. G. Gokhale and Brenda Joseph in the Maharastran and Peshwa Archives might turn up scattered early references.

8. See Kehimkar, *Bene Israel*, 74–75; B. J. Israel, *Religious Evolution*, 4. Fischel, "Bombay in Jewish History," 127–31, discusses the use of this term as well as the term "Native Jew Caste," which appears in British Bombay records.

9. B. J. Israel, *Religious Evolution*, 3, 7.

10. See Shalva Weil, "Names and Identity among the Bene Israel," *Ethnic Groups* 1 (1977): 201–19, and Benjamin J. Israel, "Bene Israel Surnames and their Village Links," in Israel, *Bene Israel of India*, 120–66.

11. B. J. Israel, *Religious Evolution*, 6. On the custom of *malida*, a ceremonial food offering and recitation of prayers for special occasions, see W. J. Fischel, S. B. Isenberg, and B. J. Israel, "Bene Israel," *Encyclopedia Judaica Yearbook* (1976), 244. Stephen Sharot, "Minority Situation and Religious Acculturation: A Comparative Analysis of Jewish Communities," *Comparative Studies in Society and History*, 16 (1974): 352, has pointed out that Jewish acculturation was much greater in those societies where the dominant religion was syncretic than in those societies where the dominant religion was insular.

12. Srinivas, *Social Change*, 10, includes in the category of poor, near-untouchable Hindu groups living just above the pollution line the many artisan and servicing castes such as goldsmiths, blacksmiths, carpenters, potters, oil pressers, toddy tappers, shepherds, and basket makers. For a discussion on how the Bene Israel aspired to assimilate to the Agris, a local Maharastrian caste that was higher in status than the Telis, and thus adopted many of their customs, see Ezekiel, *History and Culture*, 27, 30–32. By the mid eighteenth century, oil pressing was no longer the prominent occupation of the Bene Israel, but they still retained the name (see B. J. Israel, *Religious Evolution*, 4). For a discussion of how the Bene Israel fit into the caste system and their own assimilation of some of the values, see Strizower, *Bene Israel of Bombay*, 21–31. In 1920 Abraham Samuel Tarankhopkar published an article entitled "Bene Israel," in Marathi, in the Bene Israel periodical *Friend of Israel*, July–Sept. 1920: 82–85, on the low status of Bene Israel in the villages in earlier periods; the article so angered the community that it passed resolutions deploring its publication. See also, *The Israelite*, Jan.–Feb. 1921: 15–16.

13. Kehimkar, *Bene Israel*, 45–47, chap. 11; Strizower, *Bene Israel of Bombay*, 37–38; B. J. Israel, *Religious Evolution*, 7–8.

14. Throughout the eighteenth century, the three European-founded ports of Calcutta, Bombay, and Madras tended to be settled on a caste basis, and as in other Indian cities, much of the local government was actually in the hands of caste-based groups living in their own quarters, *mohalls*. In Bombay, which developed early as a shipbuilding center, great efforts were made to attract Parsi builders from Gujurat. See Cohn, *India*, 93–94.

15. An oft-told legend explains the founding of this synagogue. During the Second Anglo-Mysore War (1780–84), a Bene Israel commandant in the British Native Infantry Regiment, Samuel Ezekiel Divekar, and several other Bene Israel soldiers were

captured by Tippu Sultan's forces. Divekar vowed that if he were released, he would build a synagogue. The story goes that when he and his brother were brought before Tippu, the sultan's mother, watching the trial from behind a curtain and hearing that the prisoners were Bene Israel, asked that the brothers not be executed, as their community was frequently mentioned in the Koran. Divekar was eventually released and did build the synagogue in the Jewish section of Bombay. A variation on the story is that he was released through the intervention of David Rahabi, who then brought Divekar to Cochin, where he was so impressed by the Jewish synagogues that he vowed to build one in Bombay (B. J. Israel, *Religious Evolution*, 7; Kehimkar, *Bene Israel*, 190–92, 255–56). See also *Indian Jewish Yearbook, 1969* (Bombay), 72–73. These traditions are analyzed most recently by Brenda Joseph, "Samaji's Synagogue: Tales and Traditions," in Timberg, *Jews in India*, 361–66. Katz (personal communication, 30 Sept. 1987) has pointed out that according to the Cochinis, Divekar died while attempting to purchase a Sefer Torah in Cochin and is buried in the cemetery at Ernakulam. He thinks they have confused him with someone else.

16. Roth, *Sassoon Dynasty*, 58.

17. After 1848, other synagogues were established in Konkan towns and villages. See Kehimkar, *Bene Israel*, 181–84; B. J. Israel, *Religious Evolution*, 7; Strizower, *Bene Israel of Bombay*, 39.

18. The group arriving in 1826 also included a Michael Sargon, a Cochin Jew who had converted to Christianity and was employed by the Madras Missionary Society. Sargon worked among the Bene Israel, opening six Marathi schools, which lasted until 1832. Although he became quite involved in communal affairs, he did not seek to convert the Bene Israel. See Fischel, "Bombay in Jewish History," 140–43.

19. Kehimkar, *Bene Israel*, 66–68; B. J. Israel, *Religious Evolution*, 9–11; Strizower, *Bene Israel of Bombay*, 40–41. Wilson also introduced Hebrew into the syllabus for the matriculation and the higher examinations of Bombay University. On the contact between the Bene Israel and the missionaries, see Shirley B. Isenberg, "Paradoxical Outcome of Meeting of Bene Israel and Christian Missionaries in Nineteenth-Century India," in Timberg, *Jews in India*, 348–60.

20. B. J. Israel, *Religious Evolution*, 1, 10–11; Isenberg, "Paradoxical Outcome," 351–52.

21. B. J. Israel, *Religious Evolution*, 13. The missionary Rev. J. Henry Lord reported in 1894 that although most Bene Israel were traditional Jews, a small number were interested in the reform Judaism practiced by some Europeans (J. Henry Lord, *The Jewish Mission Field in the Bombay Diocese* [Bombay, 1894], 15).

22. Schermerhorn, *Ethnic Plurality*, 269. See also Cohn, *India*, 106.

23. See Fischel, "Immigration of 'Arabian Jews,'" 1–20, and "Bombay in Jewish History," 131–38.

24. Fischel, "Bombay in Jewish History," 132–35 n. 36. Reissner says that in 1837 there were 350 Baghdadis in Bombay and 307 in Calcutta, and a total of 6,951 Jews in all of India. He cites as sources Wilson, *Lands of the Bible*, 2:667, 681, and W. H. Sykes, "On the Population and Mortality of Calcutta," *Quarterly Journal of the Statistical Society of London*, Mar. 1845: 2. See H. G. Reissner, "Indian Jewish Statistics (1837-1941)," *Jewish Social Studies* 12 (1950): 350. In the 1830s, Jews from the Ot-

toman Empire monopolized almost the entire retail trade of Bombay, according to the *Gazetteer of Bombay City and Island* (Bombay, 1909) 1:452, as cited by Christine Dobbin, *Urban Leadership in Western India: Politics and Communities in Bombay City, 1840–1885* (London, 1972), 154. See also Roth, *Sassoon Dynasty*, 57–58 and Thomas A. Timberg, "Baghdadi Jews in Indian Port Cities," in Timberg, *Jews in India*, 275.

25. Dobbin, *Urban Leadership*, 16. See also Roth, *Sassoon Dynasty*, 44–48, 50. As advances in education under British auspices in the late nineteenth century enabled Hindu merchants and dealers to trade directly with the Europeans, they no longer needed Parsi middlemen. The Parsi position in commerce declined as the Khojas became business rivals, and eventually the Jews displaced the Parsis in the China trade. See Schermerhorn, *Ethnic Plurality*, 276.

26. Roth, *Sassoon Dynasty*, 54–57; Chaim Bermant, *The Cousinhood* (New York, 1971), 224.

27. Roth, *Sassoon Dynasty*, 60–61; Jackson, *Sassoons*, 33.

28. Quoted in Dobbin, *Urban Leadership*, 23. Dobbin, 20–21, points out the close relationships between members of this *shetia* (wealthy merchant) class that spanned divisions of caste and was based on a community of interests and a common way of life. Most had town houses in the Fort area. See also Roth, *Sassoon Dynasty*, 64–65; Schermerhorn, *Ethnic Plurality*, 274. On the Parsis in this period, see Kulke, *Parsees*, 120–32.

29. On the development of the Bombay cotton industry, see Morris David Morris, *The Emergence of an Industrial Labor Force in India: A Study of the Bombay Cotton Mills, 1854–1947* (Berkeley, 1965), chap. 3.

30. Roth, *Sassoon Dynasty*, 76, 80–81, 86–87; Jackson, *Sassoons*, 47, 52–53.

31. Roth, *Sassoon Dynasty*, 102. See also Jackson, *Sassoons*, 48, 62–66. E. D. Sassoon was registered as an Indian firm, David Sassoon and Company as a British firm. In 1886, however, the Sassoon Mills were exclusively under Parsi management: managers, heads of departments, and engineers. See S. M. Rutnagur, ed., *Bombay Industries: The Cotton Mills* (Bombay, 1927), 314.

32. The school is often referred to as either the Sir Jacob Sassoon Free School or the Sir Jacob Sassoon High School, or simply the Sassoon School. On these trusts, see below, chap. 3.

33. David Sassoon, *History of the Jews of Baghdad*, 203, 208–9. See also Isaac Abraham, *Origin and History*, 14; Thomas A. Timberg, "The Jews of Calcutta," in Timberg, *Jews in India*, 28–39; Musleah, *Ganga*, chaps. 13–14. By the 1880s, it was reported that Baghdadi Jews had taken over practically all of the remaining trade between India and China (Dobbin, *Urban Leadership*, 154). Ezra, *Turning Back*, 1:16, suggests that earlier generations of Arabic-speaking Jews in Calcutta learned Hindustani first, and then English. Very few could read or write any Indian languages.

34. See Howard M. Sachar, *The Course of Modern Jewish History* (New York, 1977), 306–9, 327–28, 494–96. See Srinivas, *Social Change*, 3. A similar hierarchy worked for Indian Muslims: "It was better to be Arab than Persian than Afghan than indigenous Indian convert, say, from Bengal. Over time and space, one had journeyed from relative purity to relative impurity, whether one was Hindu or Muslim, and it was of the highest importance to maintain as much of the purity as possible" (David

Lelyveld, "Fissiparous Tendencies and All That: Parts and Wholes in Modern India," preliminary draft, presented at China-Harvard Seminar, J. K. Fairbanks East Asian Research Center, Harvard University, 11 Apr. 1986, 27).

35. Kehimkar, *Bene Israel*, 94–96; Shirley B. Isenberg, unpublished manuscript on the Bene Israel (c. 1977), 84. Nathan Katz (personal communication, 30 Sept. 1987) notes that most observant Baghdadis in Bombay and Calcutta still will not eat meat from a Bene Israel *shohet* (slaughterer).

36. Fischel, "Bombay in Jewish History," 138–39; Ida Cowan, *Jews in Remote Corners of the World* (New York, 1971), 221. Dumont has observed that adherence to a monotheistic and egalitarian religion is not enough, even after several generations, to lead to the disappearance of the fundamental attitudes on which the caste system is based. In discussing the survival of caste attitudes among Christian converts in a Hindu environment, he cites a seventeenth-century example of Christians who were originally of the *Shudra* caste who insisted that Christians who were formerly un-touchables worship in a different building at the same service. Rome managed to have them worship in one church, but in different parts, separated by a wall or a barrier. Remnants of this attitude persisted into the late nineteenth and early twentieth centuries. See Dumont, *Homo Hierarchicus*, 204–205; 408 n. 102 j and l. Mandel-baum, who also observed castelike distinctions among non-Hindus in India, felt that the social structure of Kerala Hinduism formed the matrix for the social organization of Christians, Muslims, and Jews: "Though their respective scriptures decreed that all who kept the faith were ritual equals, that idea was challenged by the hierarchical perspective of the Hindus around them, who took rigid stratification and the radiation of pollution to be axiomatic. So if the devotees of these imported egalitarian religions were to be taken as worthy, respectable people by the majority in the religion, they too had to demonstrate their relative purity, at least by keeping the more polluted of their own faith at a suitable social distance" (Mandelbaum, "Social Stratification," in Timberg, *Jews in India*, 100). See Mattison Mines, "Muslim Social Stratification in India: The Basis for Variation," *Southwestern Journal of Anthropology* 38 (1972): 334–49.

37. The first record of such correspondence dates to 1843, when the head of the Calcutta congregation (which seems to have had less of a problem with the Bene Israel than the Bombay Baghdadis had), in writing to the *haham* in Baghdad, reflected the warm relationship that existed between the Baghdadis and the few "B'nai Yisroel" in that city: "They all conduct themselves as we do in accord with Rabbinical Law, observing all the *Mitzvot* [commandments], keeping apart from Rabbinical prohibi-tions and not omitting a word from the instructions of the sages. . . . They give birth to sons and circumcise them as we do and when they grow up they teach them Talmud Torah with our children. They are today exactly as we, without any differ-ence, and we always call them to the *Sepher Torah* [to read from the Bible] in accord with the custom of the Jewish people. May we give them our daughters, and may we take their daughters?" (Itzhak Nissim, *Benei Yisrael*, 1–2, as translated by the Bene Israel Purity Justification Committee in *And Ye Shall Teach Them* 10 [June–July 1962]: 11). A copy of the enquiry with a note saying "the reply will help you too" was sent to Baghdadi Jews in Bombay for comment (Weil, "Bene Israel Indian Jews in Lod,"

54). Unfortunately, the *responsa* (answers) of the Baghdad *hahams* to this query have not been preserved.

38. Israel Joseph Benjamin, *Un An de Séjour aux Indes Orientales (1849–50)*, trans. from Hebrew by D. L. Alger (France, 1854), 15–18.

39. Benjamin J. Israel, interview, 19 Oct. 1977.

40. Nissim, *Benei Yisrael*, 13, 15. The letter, published in the newspaper *Doresh Tov Le'amo*, is the first known rabbinic statement on the status of the Bene Israel. See Weil, "Contacts between the Bene Israel and the Holy Land from the Eighth Century B.C.E. until 1948: An Ethno-Historical Perspective," in *The Sephardic and Oriental Jewish Heritage*, ed. I. Ben-Ami (Jerusalem, 1982), 172.

41. B. J. Israel, *Jews of India*, 21–22. Kehimkar, *Bene Israel*, 218, writing at the end of the nineteenth century, made this claim.

42. Schermerhorn, *Ethnic Plurality*, 214–17; Gaikwad, *Anglo-Indians*, 22–23; Anthony, *Britain's Betrayal*, 18–19, 20–22.

43. S. S. Mazgaonkar, "Bene Israelites in the Indian Army," *Israelite* 8 (Nov.– Dec. 1924): 153–54; Sassoon, *Jews of Baghdad*, 35–36; Kehimkar, *Bene Israel*, 200, 219, chap. 9; Musleah, *Ganga*, 334–35; B. J. Israel, *Jews of India*, 22. B. J. Israel (interview, 26 Aug. 1980) has suggested that the communities that fought on the side of the British do not now, after independence, try to deny this. There was no feeling that to have sided with the British was an act of treason or defiance of nationalism. Bene Israel cooperation with the British amounted mainly to taking jobs with them as new openings were provided.

44. B. J. Israel, *Jews of India*, 22. Other groups showing preference for careers in the army were Sikhs, Pathans, Gurkhas, Rajputs, Marathi Brahmins, Jats, Ahirs, Dogras and Coorgs (Srinivas, *Social Change*, 71).

45. *Bene Israelite* 2 (4 Nov. 1895): 2.

46. *Bene Israelite* 4 (11 Feb. 1897): 4.

47. National Archives of India (hereafter cited as NAI), New Delhi, Home Department, Public, 1907, part B. no. 111, p. 131.

48. B. J. Israel, *Jews of India*, 22.

49. Dumont, *Homo Hierarchicus*, xlviii, 4. Many anthropologists have rejected this idea of hierarchy separated from power. For a discussion of this criticism, see Dumont, xxxi–xxxvii.

50. Dumont, *Homo Hierarchicus*, 227–30, 258–60. David Lelyveld, "Fissiparous Tendencies," 5. I am grateful to David Lelyveld for clarifying Dumont's work in relation to my specific concerns.

51. Srinivas, *Social Change*, 30, 75.

52. Ibid., 32, 41. Kerala had a complex matrilinear system in which the ruler and Brahmins "shared" highest status (Nathan Katz, personal communication, 30 Sept. 1987). See M. G. S. Narayanan, *Cultural Symbiosis in Kerala* (Trivandrum, 1972), chap. 1.

53. Bernard S. Cohn, "Notes on the History of the Study of Indian Society and Culture," in *Structure and Change in Indian Society*, ed. Milton Singer and Bernard S. Cohn (Chicago, 1963), 13–15.

54. Ibid., 15.

55. Ibid., 15–18. See also Srinivas, *Social Change,* 95–96.

56. David Lelyveld, "Fissiparous Tendencies," 18–19.

57. According to Srinivas, *Social Change,* 95–96, the new rulers now replaced "the historical role which Indian rulers had played as the final arbiters of the ranking of castes within their jurisdiction, including the ability to promote as well as demote castes, . . . the ranks accorded to castes in census reports became the equivalent of traditional copper-plate grants declaring the status, rank and privileges of a particular caste or castes." Castes claimed to be recorded in the census as a high caste, and thus had a new, government-sponsored channel of caste mobility. It was not until the 1941 census that the column about caste was eliminated.

58. David Lelyveld, "Fissiparous Tendencies," 19–20.

59. Ibid., 4–5. For a discussion of how the Saint Thomas or Syrian Christians of Kerala established firmer communal boundaries and "began to behave according to notions of fixed communal interests," moving away from their former hierarchical integration within a Hindu society, see Susan Bayly, "Hindu Kingship and the Origin of Community: Religion, State and Society in Kerala, 1750–1850," *Modern Asian Studies* 18(2) (1984): 177–213.

60. David Lelyveld, "Fissiparous Tendencies," 21. See also David Lelyveld, *Aligarh's First Generation: Muslim Solidarity in British India* (Princeton, 1978), 8–9.

61. Srinivas, *Social Change,* 92, 98; Cohn, *India,* 130. For a discussion of the extent to which the British may have indirectly consolidated caste by the attention they gave to it and, through the ranking of castes, may have promoted the establishment of the caste associations, see Dumont's discussion of G. S. Ghurye, *Caste and Race in India* (New York, 1932) and G. S. Ghurye, *Caste and Class in India* (Bombay, 1950) in *Homo Hierarchicus,* 220–22, 412–13 n. 112 a–d.

62. B. J. Israel, *Religious Evolution,* 12–13; Strizower, *Bene Israel of Bombay,* 152; Ezekiel, *History and Culture,* 45–47.

63. On communal activities in Calcutta, see Musleah, *Ganga,* chaps. 9, 10, 11, 15, 16.

64. David Lelyveld, "Fissiparous Tendencies," 21; Cohn, *India,* 104–5.

65. Cohn, "Notes," 3; Srinivas, *Social Change,* 82, 58, 90.

66. Srinivas, *Social Change,* 77, 79, 82–83.

67. Srinivas, *Social Change,* 28, 90–91; Schermerhorn, *Ethnic Plurality,* 319. David Lelyveld, "Fissiparous Tendencies," 8–9, has suggested that initially the Muslims took less advantage. See also David Lelyveld, *Aligarh,* 68–101.

68. Kulke, *Parsees,* 147. In the first elections, held in July 1873, 29 of the 2,669 Jews living in Bombay were enfranchised, but only 3.6 percent of them voted, the lowest percentage of those eligible who actually exercised their franchise of any community. The Parsis, who accounted for 6.8 percent of the population, comprised 26 percent of the electoral roll, with 1,040 eligible. Of them, 22.3 percent actually voted. Some 21.9 percent of eligible Goan Christians and 31.5 percent of the 167 eligible Europeans voted. Dobbin, *Urban Leadership,* 173–75, suggests that the percentages of those who voted reflected the educational state of the various communities. See also India, *Census, 1872,* Bombay Presidency, 2:98.

69. David Lelyveld, "Fissiparous Tendencies," 4. See also Stanley Wolpert, *A New History of India* (New York, 1977), 256.

70. Srinivas, *Social Change*, 55; Cohn, *India*, 77.

Chapter 2. *The Emergence of Indian Nationalism*
(pages 31–64)

1. Srinivas, *Social Change*, 85, 133; Cohn, *India*, 101.

2. Ainslie T. Embree, *India's Search for National Identity* (New York, 1972), 25; see also 23–24.

3. Srinivas, *Social Change*, 85; see also Embree, *India's Search*, 27–29.

4. Cohn, *India*, 105–6.

5. Hannah Arendt, *The Origins of Totalitarianism* (New York, 1966), 183; see also 158, 180. Arendt distinguishes between racism and race-thinking: "Race-thinking was a source of convenient arguments for varying political conflicts, but it never possessed any kind of monopoly over the political life of the respective nations. . . . Racism sprang from experiences and political constellations which were still unknown and would have been utterly strange even to such devoted defenders of 'race' as Gobineau or Disraeli. . . . It is highly probable that the thinking in terms of race would have disappeared in due time . . . if the 'scramble for Africa' and the new era of imperialism had not exposed humanity to new and shocking experiences. Imperialism would have necessitated the invention of racism as the only possible 'explanation' and excuse for its deeds, even if no race-thinking had ever existed in the civilized world" (ibid., 183–84). See also B. N. Pandey *The Break-up of British India* (New York, 1969), 21–23, on how the findings of British scholars that Sanskrit linked Indians with Europeans in a common racial origin challenged the racist attitudes of British imperialists. See also Hugh A. MacDougall, *Racial Myth in English History* (Hanover, N.H., 1982), chaps. 6 and 7.

6. Percival Spear, *India: A Modern History* (Ann Arbor, 1961), 306–7. Srinivas, *Social Change*, 80, 82.

7. Cohn, *India*, 61. Sir Percival Griffiths, *The British Impact on India* (Hamden, Conn., 1965), 275–76.

8. Schermerhorn, *Ethnic Plurality*, 220. See also Kenneth Ballhatchet, *Race, Sex and Class under the Raj: Imperial Attitudes and Policies and Their Critics, 1793–1905* (London, 1980).

9. Cohn, *India*, 102.

10. Srinivas, *Social Change*, 85; Embree, *India's Search*, 29–36. On early Indian nationalism and the formation of the Congress in this period, see John R. McLane, *Indian Nationalism and the Indian Congress* (Princeton, 1977), and Anil Seal, *The Emergence of Indian Nationalism: Competition and Collaboration in the Late Nineteenth Century* (London, 1968).

11. Pandey, *British India*, 49–53. "Swaraj is our birthright" was Tilak's phrase. He wanted independence first and social reform afterward. See Srinivas, *Social Change*, 84, 86, quoting Spear, *India*, 314. See also Louis Dumont, "Nationalism and Communalism," *Contributions to Indian Sociology* 7 (1964): 62–64. On Tilak and Gokhale,

see Stanley Wolpert, *Tilak and Gokhale: Revolution and Reform in the Making of Modern India* (Berkeley, 1962), and B. R. Nanda, *Gokhale: The Indian Moderates and the British Raj* (Princeton, 1977).

12. Dumont, *Homo Hierarchicus*, 327; Cohn, *India*, 106–7. Tilak argued that it was the Hindu's religious duty to further nationalism. He interpreted the Gita as sanctioning violence in a righteous cause and saw nationalism as a religiously given righteous cause. Gandhi also used the Gita as his basic religious text and derived from it a counterdoctrine of nonviolence. See Cohn, *India*, 55, and Wolpert, *Tilak and Gokhale*, 67–82.

13. Spear, *India*, 409. See also Embree, *India's Search*, 36–40. In 1882–83, the National Muhammadan Association (founded in 1855) demanded special compensatory privileges and separate representation of the minority (whether Hindu or Muslim) in local self-government. Some Hindus condemned special privileges and separate representation as weakening the country in the 1850s. Dumont, *Homo Hierarchicus*, 324, writes: "Thus, such privileges were in the air long before the time when the British are sometimes said to have invented them." On early communalism, especially Hindu-Muslim and Hindu-Sikh, see C. A. Bayly, "The Pre-history of 'Communalism'? Religious Conflict in India, 1700–1860," *Modern Asian Studies* 19(2) (1985): 177–203. See also Hafeez Malik, *Sir Sayyid Ahmad Khan and Muslim Modernization in India and Pakistan* (New York, 1980).

14. Embree, *India's Search*, 50–52; Srinivas, *Social Change*, 74; Pandey, *British India*, 63–68. The Parsis also became politically active in the middle of the nineteenth century, forming associations that tried to influence the British Parliament toward more favorable provisions for India. Parsi leaders Pherozeshah Mehta, D. E. Wacha, and Dadabhai Naoroji were moderates, loyal to the crown. Naoroji was elected the first president of the Indian National Congress in 1885. See Schermerhorn, *Ethnic Plurality*, 275, and Kulke, *Parsees*, chap. 3. See also R. P. Masani, *Dadabhai Naoroji* (Delhi, 1960).

15. Srinivas, *Social Change*, 86; McLane, *Indian Nationalism*, 362–369. See also Richard Cashman, *The Myth of the Lokamanya: Tilak and Mass Politics in Maharastra* (Berkeley, 1975). In 1905, Indians manifested a burst of political activity over the partition of the province of Bengal—which the British insisted was too large—into two new states, one predominantly Muslim, the other Hindu. Bengali leaders, particularly Hindus, saw this division as furthering the British policy of "divide and rule," and widespread disturbances ensued. Bengal was reunited in 1911, the same year in which the imperial capital was shifted from Calcutta to New Delhi. The agitation over Bengal confirmed in some leaders their belief that they would achieve self-rule only through direct action (Cohn, *India*, 106–8). Unfortunately, neither Musleah, *Ganga*, nor Ezra, *Turning Back*, mentions the Calcutta Jews' reaction to the partition.

16. Cohn, *India*, 107.

17. Embree, *India's Search*, 52–54.

18. *Bene Israelite* English 2 (2 June 1958): 1; 2 (4 Nov. 1895): 1–2. Also *Israel Dharmadeep* 2 (11 May 1883): 129–30; 7 (21 June 1895): 93. See India, *Census, 1881*, Bombay Presidency, 1:162.

19. *Satya Prakash* 2 (9 Apr. 1879): 74, (9 May 1879): 82, (5 Aug. 1879): 108; *Israel Dharmadeep* 1 (25 Nov. 1881): 39.

20. *Curiosities of Judaism* (Marathi) (Bombay, c. 1887), 58.

21. Ibid., 75. The Baghdadi Jews of Calcutta appointed a committee to plan the jubilee celebration and sent a delegation of five to the viceroy to present a message of loyalty and good wishes, signed by twenty-two leading Calcutta Jews and addressed to the queen on behalf of the community. The synagogues were illuminated for the occasion. Musleah, *Ganga*, 336–38.

22. *Curiosities of Judaism*, 62–65.

23. *Dyanoda*, 24 Mar. 1887, as quoted in *Curiosities of Judaism*, 65. B. J. Israel (interview, 28 Dec. 1977) has commented that Bene Israel history really starts with the British: the community really does not know how it lived before that, except that it was left alone. The community was very backward, he feels, in terms of its religious knowledge and position in society. The conditions created by British rule enabled its members to come forward and encounter the missionaries.

24. Griffiths, *British Impact*, 232–33, 280–81. For an expression of similar points of view by Parsis, see Kulke, *Parsees*, 134–35.

25. *Bene Israelite* 4 (July, 1897): 5; see also *Bene Israelite* 4 (30 June 1897): 1–2.

26. Ibid., 5 (Sept.–Oct. 1898): 1; see also 4 (Aug.–Sept. 1897): 2.

27. *Israel Dharmadeep* 4 (20 Mar. 1885): 123; B. J. Israel, interview, 12 Oct. 1977. See also Duncan M. Derrett, "The Administration of Hindu Law by the British," *Comparative Studies in Society and History* 4 (1961–62): 10–52.

28. *Israel Dharmadeep* 7 (4 Jan. 1895): 1.

29. Ibid. 7 (15 Mar. 1895): 40.

30. Ibid. 7 (15 Nov. 1895).

31. *Friend of Israel* 1 (Mar. 1898): 17. *Friend of Israel* (Marathi) 8–9 (Aug.–Sept. 1898), 66, also congratulated the government for its generosity in having liberated Lokamanya Tilak in 1898, six months earlier than it had intended to. On Ranade, see Richard P. Tucker, *Ranade and the Roots of Indian Nationalism* (Chicago, 1972) and Ramabai Ranade, *Ranade: His Wife's Reminiscences* (Delhi, 1963). For similar Parsi concerns over identity, see Kulke, *Parsees*, 167–69. For an interesting discussion of Muslim identity, see David Lelyveld, *Aligarh*, chap. 2.

32. Letter from accountant general, Bombay, no. A. 1/1757, 3 May 1877; Government Resolution no. 2156, Military Department, 16 May 1877; letter from C.M.A., no. 578, 7 May 1877; Government Resolution no. 12948, Military Department, 5 June 1882; letter from the commissariat general no. 441-k-65 1882, 22 May 1882; Government Resolution no. 5698, Military Department, Bombay Castle, 17 Nov. 1886. I am indebted to I. I. Shapurkar for having furnished me with copies of these materials.

33. *Curiosities of Judaism*, 90. See also *Israel Dharmadeep* 4 (1 May 1885): 143–44. On the Volunteer Corps, see McLane, *Indian Nationalism*, 46–48.

34. Quoted in the *Bene Israelite* 4 (30 July 1897): 2. They suffered not in their capacity as Jews, but because of their loyalty to Great Britain.

35. Ibid.

36. B. J. Israel, interview, 28 Dec. 1977. On the rift between the Bene Israel and the Baghdadis in this period, see chap. 3.

37. Schermerhorn, *Ethnic Plurality*, 218–19, citing Noel P. Gist and Roy D. Wright, *Marginality and Identity, Anglo-Indians as a Racially-Mixed Minority in India* (Leiden, 1973), 17, 59.

38. *Israelite* 5 (1921): 204. Some Bene Israel have said that a Bene Israel serving in Bombay got Indian rates of pay, but one serving outside got European rates (George Solomon, interview, 16 Aug. 1980). Others have claimed that Bene Israel even in Bombay got European rates, especially police sergeants. B. J. Israel (interview, 28 Aug. 1980) recalls that his maternal grandfather, who served in the telegraphs department until around 1900 or 1905, got European rates, but that much of his service was in Sind, away from Bene Israel main centers. Israel's father and uncle received Indian rates. In a later period, when government civil employees could have either European or orthodox Indian-style housing, Bene Israel were given the former (Ezra Kolet, interview, 7 Aug. 1977). Many Bene Israel worked in the railroads and the telegraphs departments, living among Anglo-Indians and Indians who were westernized and went to English schools (B. J. Israel, interviews, 12 Oct., 21 Dec. 1977).

39. See I. A. Ezekiel, "David Abraham Tarankhopkar," *Maccabi*, Apr. 1960: 5. On the Israels, Samsons, and Erulkars, see chap. 4.

40. *Friend of Israel* (new series) 1 (Oct.–Nov. 1916): 6; 3 (Apr. 1918): 39–40; 4 (Sept.–Oct. 1919): 105, 107; 5 (Oct., Nov., Dec. 1920): 95. (The original series of the *Friend of Israel* had ended in 1898.)

41. B. J. Israel, interview, 13 Jan. 1978.

42. The attempt to use Hindi as a national language and the language of administration had led to serious disturbances, particularly in the south. The use of a regional language as the medium of instruction in colleges deters non-native speakers from becoming teachers and students. See Cohn, *India*, 40, and David Lelyveld, "Fissiparous Tendencies," 25–31.

43. *Friend of Israel* (Marathi) 3 (Sept.–Oct. 1918): 109–12; Jacob B. Israel, "The Marathi of the Bene Israel," *Israelite* (Marathi) 5 (Mar.–Apr. 1921): 64–69.

44. The Christian schools placed a great deal of emphasis on the education of women. Meanwhile, Sir Jamsetji Jijibhoy contributed generous funds to establish schools for poor Parsis in Bombay and outlying areas, as the Sassoons had done for the Jews (Schermerhorn, *Ethnic Plurality*, 191, 273). See Kulke, *Parsees*, 81–91.

45. Sir Sayyid Ahmad Khan helped establish Aligarh University to introduce modern and scientific higher education for Muslim students of the middle and upper classes, but it had little effect on the community as a whole. Sir Syed's concern for westernization and his Anglophilia were not shared by most Muslim religious leaders, although most of the Muslim League leaders who founded Pakistan were followers of his. See Schermerhorn, *Ethnic Plurality*, 163. See also David Lelyveld, *Aligarh*, 68–92.

46. As good English boarding schools were not available for girls, females from the most educated Bene Israel families were sent to the High School for Indian Girls at Huzurpaga, Poona, a Marathi boarding school (B. J. Israel, interviews, 12 Oct., 9 Nov. 1977).

47. *Friend of Israel* 2 (Apr. 1917): 41.

48. Ibid.

49. Edmund Leach, the anthropologist, in discussing political and cultural units in highland Burma, observed: "For a man to speak one language rather than another is a ritual act, it is a statement about one's personal status: to speak the same language as one's neighbours expresses solidarity with those neighbours, to speak a different language from one's neighbours expresses social distance or even hostility" (E. R. Leach, *Political Systems of Highland Burma* [London, 1954], 49, as cited in Cohn, *India*, 40).

50. *Friend of Israel* 2 (Apr. 1917): 41. Some Bene Israel wanted to establish their assimilation to Europeans and Eurasians: men adopted Western clothes, girls wore dresses. Occasionally, certain individuals might be embarrassed if a woman wearing a sari visited them while Europeans or Eurasians were present (*Israelite* [Marathi] 5 [Mar.–Apr. 1921]: 67–68).

51. *Friend of Israel* 2 (May 1917): 52; 2 (June 1917): 64–65.

52. Ibid. 2 (July 1917): 75–76. The prophecy partly came true: by the 1970s, most highly educated Bene Israel could not express themselves in an educated Marathi, although they could speak well enough to servants. The ignorance of Marathi among the professionals was in part responsible for the clerk class's loss of confidence in them. The lack of communication as well as the difference in lifestyle contributed to the cleavage between the two classes of Bene Israel (B. J. Israel, interview, 28 Dec. 1977).

53. In an address to an Anglo-Indian audience in the 1930s, Sir Henry Gideon warned: "If we are to be acceptable to the future India, we must at once completely reorientate our ideas, our outlook and our objects in life, especially our educational system; so that we may become more sons of India than aliens, as we are now regarded by all Indians, thanks to our educational system which is entirely alien to Indian nationalism and aspirations" (quoted in C. N. Weston, *Anglo-Indian Revolutionaries of the Methodist Episcopal Church* [Bangalore, 1938], 130, as cited in Schermerhorn, *Ethnic Plurality*, 223.

54. *Friend of Israel* (Marathi) 3 (Sept.–Oct. 1918): 109–12; 5 (July, Aug., Sept. 1920): 82–85; and *Israelite* (Marathi) 5 (Jan.–Feb. 1921): 4. Editorials such as this one and a series of articles by A. S. Tarankhopkar, which appear in the *Friend of Israel* in 1920 and which claimed that the Marathi of the Bene Israel was poor because the community as a whole was lower class, angered many Bene Israel, who canceled their subscriptions to the periodical. This dispute eventually contributed to the demise of the *Friend of Israel*, which ceased publication in 1922. (B. J. Israel, interviews, 9 Nov. 1977, 13 Jan. 1978.) Marathi was required up to standard four in all schools until 1932–33, when it became compulsory up to matriculation; by 1937, students had to take an examination in the mother tongue.

55. Cohn, *India*, 107–8.

56. *Friend of Israel* 2 (Mar. 1917): 26.

57. Ibid., 34.

58. Embree, *India's Search*, 56–58. Theosophy, following primarily Buddhist and Brahminic ideas, taught a pantheistic evolution and the doctrine of reincarnation. Its followers believed in a universal brotherhood of humanity without distinction of race, creed, or color.

59. Ibid., 58–59; Pandey, *British India*, 83–86, 97–99.

60. Pandey, *British India*, 101. On Parsi communal organizations, especially the Parsi Central Association, see Kulke, *Parsees*, 211–16.

61. *Israelite* 1 (June 1917): 108. For a detailed examination of Bene Israel communal activities in this period, see Joan G. Roland, "A Decade of Vitality: Bene Israel Communal Development (1917–1927)" in Timberg, *Jews in India*, 285–347.

62. *The Bene Israel Conference Imbroglio*, a letter to the Bene Israel community by Jacob B. Israel, Abraham S. Erulkar, D. J. Samson, I. J. Samson, and Aaron Benjamin, 1 Dec. 1917 (Bombay, 1917): 3; M. A. Moses, interview, 7 Dec. 1977. In an unpublished manuscript, Shirley Isenberg has pointed out that David Erulkar's anti-British affiliations ruined his career as an advocate, but that in his later positions with the Scindia Steam Navigation Company, as a technical advisor to the Empire Chartering Committee, and as a member of the governing board of the International Labour Organization of the League of Nations, he continued to fight for the cause of Indianization (237ff.). Sol Erulkar (interview, 31 Mar. 1978) said that his father, David, felt that only someone as strong as Tilak could free India.

63. *Bene Israel Conference Imbroglio*, 4–7.

64. J. B. Israel later said that he was against those who sought to achieve their objectives by unconstitutional means. He was disturbed that the Erulkars had taken such a prominent part in Tilak's movement. He did not see the value of people marching so prominently in processions (B. J. Israel, interview, 30 Nov. 1977). On these Bene Israel nationalist sympathizers, see chap. 4.

65. *Friend of Israel* 2 (Nov. 1917): 131–33; 2 (Dec. 1917): 142.

66. *Bene Israel Conference Imbroglio*, 7–8.

67. J. B. Israel, *Letter No. 1 to the Bene Israel Community of British India*, 21 Nov. 1917: 1–3.

68. *Friend of Israel* 4 (Mar.–Apr. 1919): 24.

69. *Israelite* 1 (July 1917): 3.

70. Quoted in Percival Spear, *A History of India* (Middlesex, 1970), 2:185.

71. Embree, *India's Search*, 59–60; Pandey, *British India*, 100–101.

72. Some lower castes prayed for the perpetuation of British rule. "It needed the inspiring leadership of Gandhi and the Civil Disobedience Movement of the 20s and 30s to cut across caste and regional differences and bring the Indian masses into the nationalist stream" (Srinivas, *Social Change*, 107).

73. Pandey, *British India*, 101–2.

74. W. C. Smith, *Modern Islam in India* (Lahore, 1943), 185. See also Srinivas, *Social Change*, 142.

75. Srinivas, *Social Change*, 87–88.

76. Dumont, *Homo Hierarchicus*, 317.

77. I am grateful to B. J. Israel for a copy of this address. The other signers were (M. M.?) Ezekiel, Rahamim J. Ezekiel, Samuel S. Mazgaonker, and Jacob E. Solomon. Jacob B. Israel could not have signed this petition while he was still in government service. By 1917, however, he had retired (B. J. Israel, interview, 30 Nov. 1977). In 1911, the Jewish population was 19,956; in 1921, 20,643 (Kingsley Davis, *Population of India and Pakistan* [Princeton, 1951], 179).

78. A copy of this text was furnished to me by B. J. Israel, but the name of the paper is illegible. Although most leading Parsis wanted a separate electorate, H. P. Mody felt that it would not be necessary if the government guaranteed that the city of Bombay would be strongly represented in the provincial legislative council. See Kulke, *Parsees*, 193–94.

79. B. J. Israel has furnished me with a copy of this cartoon from the weekly *Sandesha* (The Message) supplement, 2 Dec. 1917.

80. B. J. Israel, interview, 21 Dec. 1977; Jacob B. Israel, *Letters to the Bene Israel Community*, no. 7, 6 June 1918.

81. *Friend of Israel* 2 (Dec. 1917): 143–44.

82. *Letters to the Bene Israel*, no. 7, 6 June 1918.

83. Embree, *India's Search*, 60–61; Pandey, *British India*, 109.

84. S. S. Mazgaonker, *Occasional Thoughts*, no. 8, 1918: 5–16. Mazgaonker had been an editor of *Israel Dharmadeep* (1893–96) and a signer of the address to Montagu. Montagu, actually, was not particularly sympathetic to Zionism.

85. *Report of the First Bene Israel Conference*, 36; *Israelite* 2 (Jan. 1918): 25–26.

86. J. B. Israel pointed out that Dr. Joseph Bamnolkar Benjamin was an old Congressman who had actually seconded a similar resolution about commissions for Indians at the eighteenth session of the Indian National Congress in 1902, so he must have known of the political implications of the resolution now passed by the Bene Israel Conference (Jacob B. Israel, *Letters*, no. 6 [n.d.], 4–5; no. 7 [6 June 1918], 5). B. J. Israel recalled that Dr. Benjamin was warned that his brother's career in the government's political department might be affected if he took too prominent a part in Congress, so he withdrew around 1918. He did not become involved in politics except during this period. He was always a moderate, never a follower of Gandhi (B. J. Israel, interview, 30 Nov. 1977). See *Israelite* 2 (Jan. 1918): 26.

87. *Friend of Israel* (Marathi) 3 (March 1918): 32.

88. *Israelite* 2 (Aug.–Sept. 1918); 2 (Oct. 1918): 141–42.

89. B. J. Israel, interview, 3 Jan. 1978. Some individuals, such as Dr. Jerusha Jhirad, an outstanding Bene Israel physician, straddled both groups and tried to reconcile them.

90. *Friend of Israel* 4 (Mar.–Apr. 1919): 22–24.

91. B. J. Israel (interview, 3 Jan. 1978) suggests that the league's refusal to join indicates that the cleavage was deeper.

92. *Israelite* 3 (Nov.–Dec. 1919): 146–49; *Third and Fourth Bene Israel Conference Reports*, 1919–1920 (Bombay, 1922): 13, 16, 73, 81–82.

93. On the adoption of Western dress, see Ezra, *Turning Back*, 18–19.

94. See Jackson, *Sassoons*, 46–47, 53, 91. When Albert did celebrate his knighthood four years later, Indians were included among the thousand guests. Albert eventually became an English baronet, a title later inherited by Philip Sassoon.

95. Ezra, *Turning Back*, 234, 269 n. 14, 305–7, 372.

96. Quoted in Roth, *Sassoon Dynasty*, 68. When Bombay's first political association, the Bombay Association, was founded in 1852, David Sassoon was elected to the managing committee (Kulke, *Parsees*, 154). I am not certain, however, how long he served.

97. *Bene Israelite* 3 (3 July 1896): 2. Neither *Thacker's Indian Directory* (Calcutta, 1899) nor any of the Bombay Governor's Council *Proceedings* 30–40 (1892–1902) lists Mrs. Solomon David Sassoon as a member. Sassoon J. David, Bart. (1849–1926) was a member of the large interrelated family of the Sassoons and Ezras. He made his money in the cotton industry and in 1905 was chairman of the Bombay Millowners' Association and president of the Central Bank of India (Rutnagur, *Bombay Industries*, 705).

98. On the Jewish Girls' School, see Ezra, *Turning Back*, 363–69.

99. Musleah, *Ganga*, 333–34, 344–45; Kulke, *Parsees*, 138–40.

100. See Musleah, *Ganga*, 344.

101. National Archives of India (hereafter, NAI), New Delhi, Home Department, 1886, Judicial A. Proceedings, Nov., nos. 150–53, 204–6. See also Musleah, *Ganga*, 344. Aden actually had two groups of Jews, one connected with Yemen and another connected with Basra and, therefore, with the Baghdadis. By 1854, some three hundred Bene Israel were also in Aden, having arrived with the British to serve in the forces and the police. See Shalva Weil, "Bene Israel Indian Jews," 49.

102. Musleah, *Ganga*, 344. *Paerah* was a four-page weekly Hebrew newspaper published from 1878 to 1889. See Ezra, *Turning Back*, 362–63. In 1938, a Bombay High Court decision, in a case involving the will of a Jew from Aden, recognized the applicability of Jewish law on one issue but on another aspect rejected the Jewish law of *kimli* (whereby a party in possession of property can cite two reliable texts of Jewish law in his favor, and his title thereupon becomes indefeasible) because the doctrine was inconsistent with the Indian Evidence Act of 1872 (Messa vs. Messa, Indian Law Reports: B 1938, 529–649).

103. Musleah, *Ganga*, 345. E. M. D. Cohen, the secretary of the school, tried to build up its status by inviting distinguished personalities, such as the viceroy's wife and the governor and the chief justice of Bengal, to preside over the annual distribution of prizes (Ezra, *Turning Back*, 365).

104. Home Department File no. 1908, Edu. Pt. B. Pro. no. 74. Unfortunately, there is nothing further in the files to indicate what eventually happened.

105. At first reluctant to apply for a government grant, lest it compromise the school's independence, E. M. D. Cohen finally relented toward the end of the century because of the school's financial problems (Ezra, *Turning Back*, 366).

106. A. Isaac, *Letters and Speeches* (Calcutta, 1917), 96–99. Isaac, a Bene Israel, took the side of the Baghdadis, who, in seeking European classification for the Sephardic Jews, would probably have excluded him. Isaac was associated with Ezra Arakie, a wealthy Baghdadi barrister and Cambridge graduate. At the end of 1915, the Jewish Girls' School was raised to the Senior Cambridge Standard (Ezra, *Turning Back*, 366). The Free Boys School that was founded in 1882, also to counter missionary influence, was recognized as a European school in 1930, receiving a large government subsidy. It graduated its first Senior Cambridge student in 1935. The Christian Hebrew Mission School was finally closed in 1922 (Timberg, "Jews of Calcutta," 30–31).

107. I. A. Isaac, letters to the *Statesman*, 31 Jan. 1914, 24 Jan. 1917: in *Letters and Speeches*, 103–6; *Zion's Messenger* 2 (May 1922): 19.

108. Musleah, *Ganga*, 346.

109. B. J. Israel, interviews, 12 and 19 Oct. 1977. For anti-Jewish attitudes toward Sir Philip Sassoon in England, see Jackson, *Sassoons*, 130, 145–47, 172, 183–85, and Chaim Bermant, *The Cousinhood* (New York, 1971), 233–34. For an interesting comparison between the Baghdadis and the Armenians, see Timberg, "Jews of Calcutta," 34–40. A comparison might be made with the position of the Jews in late nineteenth-century South Africa who were eager to gain admission to exclusive British clubs as a way of achieving some social status and preserving their economic security and permanent settlement in South Africa. See S. Gertrude Millin, *Rhodes* (London, 1933), 14, 85.

110. The Calcutta community's contribution to the war effort was a modest one. Not many joined the armed forces; of those who did, one, Captain David Ezra of the Royal Garrison Artillery, was killed in action in France. Contributions in cash and kind for the benefit of the armed forces were donated from time to time and the community attended to the religious needs of Jewish troops in India, largely through the efforts of the Reverend E. M. D. Cohen (Ezra, *Turning Back*, 263, 371–72).

111. NAI, Simla Records 1, 1915, Government of India, Home Department, Political A. Proceedings, Feb., nos. 1–67. According to census reports, there were 1,920 Jews in Calcutta in 1911. They would have been predominantly Baghdadis, but no nationality statistics are given (*Census of India*, 1911, vol. 5: City of Calcutta, part 1: *Report by* W. H. Thompson [Calcutta, 1913], 43).

112. Reginald Mathalone, a prominent Bombay Jew whose father came to India from Baghdad in 1892, said that when his father played poker with his friend, the commissioner of police, the friend would jokingly threaten him by saying, "I'll intern you" (Reginald Mathalone, interview, 28 Nov. 1977). Joseph Nissim, a Baghdadi Jew in the Indian Civil Service who occupied the posts of legal remembrancer to the government of Bombay and judge in the Satara District of Bombay Presidency, pleaded on behalf of Baghdadi Jews on this issue (*Shalom*, Sept.–Oct. 1972: 12). The British soon had to deal directly with these minority groups in Iraq when they established their rule in that area after World War I.

113. NAI, Delhi Records 1, 1915, Government of India, Home Department, Political A. Proceedings, Nov., nos. 160–61. Home Department, Notes, Political A. Proceedings, Jan. 1916, nos. 239–42. It would seem, therefore, that about 10 percent of the Baghdadi Jews in Calcutta were Ottoman nationals (cf. note 111). In 1911 there were a total of 832 Armenians in Calcutta (*Census of India*, 1911, 5:43). Timberg (personal communication, 2 Sept. 1987) suggests that most would have been Iranian nationals.

114. NAI, Simla Records 5, 1915, Government of India, Home Department, Public A. Proceedings, Jan., nos. 131–36.

115. NAI, letter from H. Tonkinson, additional deputy secretary to government of India, Home Department, Public A. Proceedings, June, 1920, nos. 363–64 (printed) from Delhi records 3, 1920.

116. Two supporters of the conference, Solomon Moses and Ezra Reuben, could also be considered very Indian. Reuben was less loyal to the British, despite his position as subjudge of the Khaburi District, and more identified with the nationalists (B. J. Israel, interview, 3 Jan. 1978).

Chapter 3. A State of Complex Identities
(pages 65–85)

1. This interpretation was suggested to me by B. J. Israel, interview, 19 Oct. 1977. See Jackson, *Sassoons*, 35, Musleah, *Ganga*, chap. 17, and Pandey, *British India*, 213.

2. India, *Census*, 1881, Bombay City and Island, 50. The total Jewish population for India in that year was 12,009 (*Census*, 1881, General Report, 1:23).

3. B. J. Israel, interview, 19 Oct. 1977.

4. Strizower, *Bene Israel of Bombay*, 28–29. The influence of the Indian environment on these attitudes is complex: parallels can be seen in the case of the Cochin Jews. In Cochin, the white Jews believed that the black (Malabar) Jews did not have proper *yichus*—Jewish ancestry or descent—because they were the offspring of converts to Judaism. Not all, but some of these converts had been manumitted slaves (*meshuchrarim*), sometimes called "brown" Jews. There were black *meshuchrarim* and white *meshuchrarim*, depending on whether the family for which their ancestors had worked was itself a white or black family. The black Jews of Cochin claim, however, that they are not the descendants of converts, slaves or otherwise, but rather that they are the original Jews of Cochin and that the white Jews are a later migration, which arrived in the sixteenth century. In accepting the black Jews and *meshuchrarim* as Jews but not as social and ritual equals because of their flawed descent, the white Jews, according to Mandelbaum, acted in accord with the practice of superior castes. But their behavior was contrary to Judaic law and tradition, which held that properly manumitted and converted slaves, as well as others converted according to prescribed ritual, were fully Jews and entitled to ritual equality. Mandelbaum points out that the Malabar and *meshuchrarim* Jews did not accept their personal inferiority and repeatedly protested the attitudes of the white Jews. Similarly, in protesting the assumptions of superiority by the Baghdadis, the Bene Israel were acting in a way that would be expected of a Hindu subcaste regarded as inferior by a group slightly higher in the caste ranking (Mandelbaum, "Social Stratification," 69–70, 72, 82–83, 96–98).

5. See *Satya Prakash* 1 (4 May 1878): 88.

6. *Bene Israelite* 3 (8 Oct. 1896): 2. See also *Jewish Chronicle* (London), 9 Feb., 11 May, 6 July 1883; 15 May 1885. A series of articles in *Israel Dharmadeep* also responded to the *Jewish Chronicle* columns, but the author suggested that the distinctions made between *Kala* and *Gora* were perhaps unfortunate. See *Israel Dharmadeep* 2 (30 Mar. 1883): 110; 2 (13 Apr. 1883): 113–14; 2 (22 June 1883): 161; 2 (10 Aug. 1883): 185–86. See also B. J. Israel, letter to *Jewish Chronicle*, 10 Dec. 1971: 25. The color distinction noticeable among Cochin Jews does not prevail between *Gora* and *Kala* Bene Israel.

7. In 1880 a dispute in print between two noted Bene Israel authors, Solomon Daniel Navgaoker and Benjamin Shimson Astemkar, over whether or not the distinction between *Gora* and *Kala* should be obliterated, led to a lawsuit. See *Satya Prakash* 2 (12 Dec. 1878): 29–36; 4 (6 Oct. 1880): 15; 4 (4 Nov. 1880): 23; 4 (1 Jan. 1881): 44; *Times of India*, 24 Dec. 1880. See also Strizower, *Bene Israel of Bombay*, 29.

8. *Times of India*, 20 July 1895 (anonymous letter to editor, but obviously from a Bene Israel); *Bene Israelite* 2 (3 Dec. 1894): 3; 2 (1 Feb. 1895): 2. See also Kehimkar,

Bene Israel, 162–63. B. J. Israel, interview, 26 Aug. 1980; Marge Gubbay, interview, 30 Aug. 1980.

9. Shirley Isenberg, unpublished manuscript, 92. She quotes this letter from the wardens of Cochin, 14 Nov. 1899, and claims that from the religious point of view, the Cochin black Jews were *halachically* pure Jews and were probably more learned and orthodox at that time than the Cochin white Jews. See also Mandelbaum, "Social Stratification," 85. The Baghdadis also felt that there were religious differences between themselves and the Cochin Jews, especially the black and brown Jews, whose dress and customs were similar to those of their Malayali neighbors. The Baghdadis identified with the white Jews, many of whom were of Baghdadi or Syrian origin (B. J. Israel, interview, 19 Oct. 1977).

10. B. J. Israel, "The Problem of Marriage for the Bene Israel in Israel," *Mebasser* (Bombay), June 1962: 9.

11. At a Jewish Sabbath service, there are seven readings from the Torah, during which prescribed passages are read by members of the congregation who are called to the pulpit for this purpose. The first reading is reserved for Cohens and the second for Levis, but the readers for the third through sixth readings are chosen in turn. The seventh reading can be divided into two parts and often the right to read each is sold to the highest bidder. Extra readings are not regarded as essential to parts of the service. In later periods, Bene Israel were not permitted to participate in the first readings in Baghdadi synagogues.

12. *The Hebrew and the Voice of Sinai* 3 (11 Jan. 1907): 89.

13. Ibid. and 3 (1 Feb. 1907): 104–5.

14. *The Bene Israelite* 2 (1 Feb. 1895): 2. B. J. Israel could not understand why the Baghdadis ever would have made such an offer unless it was made when they had just arrived in India. But he could see why the wealthy Bene Israel would refuse the offer: they did not think well of Baghdadi women in general, partly because the poorer ones seemed to follow the Arab custom of girls earning their dowries through prostitution. The first case of intermarriage that B. J. Israel knew of was that of Moses Samson, a Bene Israel who, already married, married a Baghdadi as his second wife around 1890 (B. J. Israel, interview, 12 Dec. 1977).

15. B. J. Israel, interview, 26 Aug. 1980. In 1893, while reporting a love marriage between a Bene Israel boy and a Baghdadi girl and the fact that many Bene Israel were pleased with this rapprochement, the editor of *Israel Dharmadeep* asked: "If members of our community were to keep an eye on the white skin of the Baghdadi girls, then what will happen to our Bene Israel girls?" (*Israel Dharmadeep* 5 [1 Dec. 1893]: 104). Srinivas, *Social Change*, 29, has pointed out that a caste group is generally endogamous but occasionally endogamy coexists with hypergamy. The caste considered to be lower gives its females to the higher caste in a one-way relationship. This arrangement results in a scarcity of females in the lower group and of males in the higher. If Baghdadi girls were marrying Bene Israel boys, which group was considered higher?

16. B. J. Israel, "The Problem of Marriage," 9; *Jewish Minister* 2 (19 May 1937): 14.

17. *Satya Prakash* 3 (3 Oct. 1879): 8; 3 (16 Nov. 1879): 17; 4 (17 Mar. 1881): 63;

4 (14 May 1881): 88; 4 (10 Sept. 1881): 119; 5 (9 Oct. 1881): 7; *Israel Dharmadeep* 7 (18 Jan. 1895): 9; *Bene Israelite* 2 (4 Nov. 1895): 2.

18. *Israel Dharmadeep* 7 (6 Dec. 1895); *Bene Israelite* 3 (7 Jan. 1896): 1; *Friend of Israel* 2 (June 1899): 1–2.

19. *Satya Prakash* 4 (27 June 1881): 98–99; 10 (16 Jan. 1881): 46–47; 11 (31 Jan. 1881): 50–51.

20. *Jewish Chronicle* (London), 10 Feb. 1883. See R. Anderson and A. Thompson, *Report of the Deputation to the Indian Missions Made by the American Board of Commissions for Foreign Missionaries* (Boston, 1856), 28–29. See also *Satya Prakash* 5 (9 Oct. 1881): 6. See also Anglo-Jewish Association, *12th Annual Report* (1882–83), 11, and *Report of the Israelite School of the Anglo-Jewish Association* (1882–83), 6–7. Some scholars have argued that the Baghdadi contributions to the Bene Israel were quite insignificant, considering the extensive philanthropic work of the Sassoons and Ezras. See Shalwa Weil, "Bene Israel Indian Jews," 55. In the 1890s, out of a total of 7,700 rupees received annually for the Israelite schools, only 800 rupees were donated by the Sassoon family (Kehimkar, *Bene Israel*, 246). Similar instances of communal exclusivity occurred within the American Jewish community, where German Jews, although maintaining their own institutions, helped establish others for East European Jews. See Stephen Birmingham, *Our Crowd: The Great Jewish Families of New York* (New York, 1967), 290–97; Irving Howe, *World of Our Fathers* (New York, 1976), 230–35, 498; Sachar, *Modern Jewish History*, 307–9.

21. *Bene Israelite* 3 (4 June 1896): 2; 3 (8 Oct. 1896): 2.

22. J. M. Ezekiel, witness for plaintiffs, evidence, Rangoon Court Case (22 Feb. 1935), 150–51. (The Rangoon Court Case was a dispute that took place in the mid 1930s, over Bene Israel rights in the Musmeah Yeshua Synagogue in Rangoon. It is covered fully in chap. 5.) B. J. Israel (interview, 19 Oct. 1977) says that his parents were married in about 1892 in the Baghdadi synagogue in Poona, but that soon after, such marriages were stopped. The Poona cemetery today is divided into Bene Israel and Baghdadi sections. The Bene Israel synagogue manages the cemetery but the Sassoon trustees do the major repairs.

23. Musleah, personal communication, 21 Oct. 1981.

24. Testimony of E. E. Moses, evidence, Rangoon Court Case (26 Mar. 1935), 29–32. Moses said that he did not really know what the difference between the Bene Israel and Baghdadis was. Isenberg, unpublished manuscript, 86, has observed that the Baghdadis, who were so un-Indian and such orthodox Jews, in preventing the Bene Israel from being called upon to read the Torah in the Baghdadi synagogues, "acted against all non-Indian Jewish custom and precedent and in this respect manifested a kind of Indian discriminatory caste behaviour." In 1835 New York's Sephardic Congregation Shearith Israel took steps to make the admission of German Jews more difficult. See Charles Silberman, *A Certain People* (New York, 1985), 42–43.

25. B. J. Israel, interview, 22 Dec. 1977.

26. Office of the Sassoon Charity Trusts, Ballard Estate, Bombay, Trust Deed of the Jacob Sassoon Bombay Jewish Charity Fund, 13 Feb. 1899, clause no. 6.

27. Office of the Sassoon Charity Trusts, Ballard Estate, Bombay, Trust Deed of the Bombay Jewish Burial Ground, 28 Dec. 1908, p. 1; Trust Deed of the Lady Rachel

Sassoon Dispensary, 12 Dec. 1912, clause no. 4; Trust Deed of the Sir Jacob Sassoon Passover Food Trust Fund, 18 Dec. 1911, clause no. 3. In the late 1970s, however, Moshe Sultoon, a trustee of the Sassoon trusts in Bombay, said that although the Sir Jacob trusts did exclude the Bene Israel, recently they had come in "through the back door." The doctors at the dispensary had been told that if Bene Israel applied, they were to be treated and given medicine. Word got around that if a poor Bene Israel wrote for help to pay for glasses, dental work, or medical bills, Sultoon, although he could not give any money from the trusts, would give it quietly out of his own pocket. Sometimes Albert Manasseh, a Baghdadi trustee living in London who contributed ten to twenty thousand rupees a year to make up the trust deficits, reimbursed Sultoon for the money that he gave under the table to Bene Israel. Sultoon (interview, 20 Oct. 1977) argued that the Bene Israel had their own funds and institutions that should help them but did not. Neither the 1868 trust deed endowing the Byculla Synagogue (Magen David) and its adjacent schools nor the 1885 one endowing the Fort Synagogue (Knesset Eliyahu) excluded Bene Israel when noting that these institutions were meant for "those of the Jewish religion and faith."

28. *Jewish Chronicle*, 25 June 1909: 20; 3 Sept. 1909: 21. *Times of India*, 23 Sept. 1909: 8. Jacob B. Israel, unpublished letter to the *Jewish Chronicle*, 29 Sept. 1909. I am grateful to B. J. Israel for providing me with copies of this material.

29. Solomon M. Vakrulkar, "Our Synagogues and Their Functions: An Address to the Bene Israel," 8 Dec. 1907 (Bombay, 1909), 12–14, 23.

30. I. J. Samson, "Marriage and Divorce among the Bene Israel," *Israelite* 1 (Aug. 1917): 150–52; "The Religious Beliefs of the Yehudis" (Marathi editorial), *Israelite* 1 (July 1917): 135–38; Isenberg, unpublished manuscript, 84–84a. For an interesting discussion of how Calcutta Baghdadis handled the problem of races on the Sabbath, see Ezra, *Turning Back*, 471. An unusual accommodation to Jewish needs was made by the Bombay Tramway Company, which issued official tram tickets that could be purchased on a weekday to be used on the Sabbath, when Jews could not carry money—although truly Orthodox Jews would not ride, either.

31. Gaster Papers, Moccatta Library, University College, London, letter from I. E. Sargon to Gaster, 25 Aug. 1911.

32. Gaster Papers, letter from Gaster to Sargon, 25 Oct. 1911.

33. Jacob B. Israel, *Israelite* 1 (Jan. 1917). See also Lord, *Jewish Mission Field in the Bombay Diocese*, 82–89.

34. B. J. Israel (interviews, 12 Oct., 28 Dec. 1977), observed that Asians or Asiatics were considered one step above the native Indians, but both Indians and Asians despised the Anglo-Indians even more than the Europeans despised the Indians. Even as the Bene Israel became more westernized, they never claimed to be Europeans or Eurasians. See also B. J. Israel, *Khan Bahadur Jacob Bapuji Israel* (Bombay, 1960), 24–25.

35. Many of these articles were by Jacob B. Israel and D. J. Samson. See the *Israelite* 1 (Jan. 1917): 4–6; 1 (Apr. 1917): 66–70; 1 (May 1917): 86–89; 1 (June 1917): 108–13, 117 (Marathi); 1 (July 1917): 128–30; 1 (Aug. 1917): 149–52; 1 (Oct. 1917): 180–81; 3 (Jan.–Feb. 1919): 1–2; 3 (Mar.–Apr. 1919): 32–34; 3 (May–June 1919): 58–60; 3 (July–Aug. 1919): 95–97; 3 (Sept.–Oct. 1919): 117–20. The people in charge

of the *Israelite* resented Baghdadi attacks on the Bene Israel more than the editors of the *Friend of Israel,* who were more likely to make reference to Baghdadi events and affairs.

36. I. J. Samson, "Marriage and Divorce among the Bene Israel," *Israelite* 1 (Aug. 1917): 150–52.

37. The introduction of reforms and the British legal system involved the changing or abolition of customs claiming to be a part of religion. The British insisted that religious customs satisfy the test of reason and humanity if they were to be allowed to survive (Srinivas, *Social Change,* 49). In the early 1920s, the Bene Israel addressed the problem of polygamy. The Bene Israel Conference favored prohibition of polygamy enforced by synagogues and prayer halls; the league advocated legal prohibition. By 1924 it had become increasingly difficult for a Jew to marry a second wife in the synagogues of Bombay, at least without the consent of the living wife. But if consent could not be obtained and reconciliation failed, problems involving divorce ensued. Bene Israel found it very expensive to resort to the High Court and therefore the community considered the formation of a communal tribunal for trying matrimonial cases, to be appointed either by the community itself or by the legislature, as the Parsis had done (*Israelite* 6 [1922]: 106; 8 [1924]: 6–7). In 1925 a Jewish divorce case involving two Baghdadis appeared before the High Court of Bombay; Bene Israel and Baghdadi "experts" were called to testify. The court, ruling that it had jurisdiction and would apply Jewish law, concluded that the Jews of Bombay were generally monogamous and could not lawfully contract a second marriage except in certain cases. It also acknowledged that among Jews divorce was allowed on the grounds of adultery or cruelty, and that in such cases the courts could dissolve a Jewish marriage. Jews would no longer need a ritual *get* executed by the husband; the wife would be granted a decree *nisi* for divorce. (Whether Jewish authorities would recognize this document and permit the woman to remarry was another question.) Further, the court could order permanent alimony in a matrimonial suit between Jews. The judge also suggested that the Jewish community consider either establishing a *beth din* (religious court), as in Jerusalem, Baghdad, and London, or seeking special legislation similar to the Parsi Marriage Act, to settle matrimonial disputes. (28 Bombay Law Reports, 328; Indian Law Reports, 50 [1926]: 369–94).

38. "Yibboom or Halitza?" (Marathi editorial), *Israelite* 1 (June 1917): 117–18. I. J. Samson, "Marriage and Divorce among the Bene Israel," *Israelite* 1 (July 1917): 129–30, and 1 (Aug. 1917): 150–52.

39. Gaster papers, letter from A. Benjamin to Gaster, 27 Apr. 1936; Gaster to Benjamin, 12 May 1936.

40. Gaster papers, Benjamin to Gaster, 29 May 1936.

41. Gaster papers, Gaster to Benjamin, 10 June 1936.

42. I. A. Isaac, "Queer Beliefs of the Arab Jews," *Israelite* 1 (Oct. 1917): 180–81.

43. *"Hazzans"* (Marathi editorial), *Israelite* 1 (Apr. 1917). See also 1 (July 1917): 135–38 (Marathi); 1 (Oct. 1917): 164; 2 (Aug.–Sept. 1918): 123; 7 (Sept.–Oct. 1923): 148 (Marathi); 7 (Nov.–Dec. 1923): 179 (Marathi).

44. B. J. Israel, *Religious Evolution,* 15.

45. These informants do not recall Bene Israel begging, although in 1917 Jacob

Apteker and Dr. E. Moses, two Bene Israel leaders, had commented on this problem in the communal journals. They believed that professional begging among the Bene Israel had emerged around 1905, as a result of the Indian custom of giving doles to the poor. Both men argued for the establishment of a Bene Israel shelter for the poor and an orphanage to alleviate these problems. See *Friend of Israel* 2 (June 1917): 62–63; *Israelite* 1 (Apr. 1917): 65.

46. B. J. Israel, interviews, 12 Oct., 28 Dec. 1977. See *Jewish Tribune* 2 (Mar. 1934): 25. In the census of 1901, seven Baghdadi women even listed their occupation as prostitutes. Some prostitutes from the Calcutta community attended synagogue on the Day of Atonement (Ezra, *Turning Back,* 61, n. 36, 453). As early as 1894, the Reverend J. Henry Lord, *Jewish Mission Field,* 19–21, claimed that some two hundred European "Jews and Jewesses" were engaged in prostitution in Bombay and that the government had deported some of them because they were "purveyors of vice." In 1916 the Jewish Association for the Protection of Girls and Women (London), having heard about Jewish prostitution in India, wrote to the government of India to find out how extensive the problem was and whether or not they could undertake work in India to eradicate it. The central government wrote to the provincial governments asking for information on Jewish prostitution and discovered that the main centers were Calcutta, Rangoon, and Bombay, with a total of 101 European Jews and 85 Asiatic Jews identified as prostitutes. The European Jews, mainly from central and eastern Europe, were professionals who had already been in the business for some years in Middle Eastern cities before coming to India, especially Bombay and Bengal. They would be unlikely to reform, the government thought. The Asiatic Jewish prostitutes, however, who carried on their trade with more secrecy than the Europeans, were mainly girls from low and depressed classes. They either had been recruited voluntarily in Baghdad, where they were prostitutes before being brought to India, or were the victims of parents and guardians who employed them as commercial speculation. The government felt that the Jewish Association for the Protection of Girls and Women might well do useful work among the Asiatic Jewish prostitutes. See NAI, Home Department, Judicial A. Proceedings, Mar. 1916, nos. 99–101, and A Oct. 1916, 245–57 (1916). Proceedings, Jan. 1917, no. 14 (1917). Sir Jacob Sassoon, with whom the association had communicated about the problem in 1909, felt that the trade could best be fought at the ports of embarkation, as the law in India made it difficult to eradicate the traffic in Bombay (*Jewish Chronicle* [London], 25 June 1909, 20).

47. *Friend of Israel* 1 (Oct.–Nov. 1916): 6.

48. *Israelite* 1 (Sept. 1917): 163.

49. There are some interesting parallels among the Parsis. Kulke points out that when the rise of Indian nationalism led to the formation of a new Indian historical consciousness, Parsis lacked an attachment to Indian history and responded with a rediscovery of their own Iranian past. He traces the Iranian "renaissance" among Parsis to the mid nineteenth century, when they learned about the terrible situation of Zoroastrians in Iran and tried to help them. In 1922 the Iran League was founded to strengthen the connection of Indian Parsis with Iran and their coreligionists there. But, Kulke writes: "From the time that a reorientation toward the Iranian nation and

its cultural heritage can be observed among the Parsees, their search for their own ethnic, social, cultural, historical and national identity only became more complicated. Their cultural and national frame of reference became divided into three socio-cultural and political dimensions: Indian, Iran and England. This psychological identity conflict characterizes the Parsees' search for group identity as well as their political behavior since about 1900. The result was a permanent identity crisis, a permanent loyalty conflict, even if it was not always consciously felt." (*Parsees*, 144) In the early twentieth century, some Parsis even proposed that their entire community should emigrate from India and found a separate Parsi colony somewhere, perhaps in Baluchistan or East Africa. See Kulke, *Parsees*, 142–46.

50. Abraham David, "Sheluhei Erez Israel," *EJ* 14:1358–68. Over the centuries, the *shlichim* played an important role historically not only in sustaining relationships between Palestine and the Jewish communities in the Diaspora, but also in compiling and publishing reports about the various communities they visited.

51. The frequency with which *shlichim* came is attested to by Eleazar Arakie of Calcutta, who mentioned that between 1843 and 1863, twenty *shlichim* arrived in his city (see Musleah, *Ganga*, 406–14). On the details of *shlichim* in Calcutta, see Musleah's excellent summary, ibid., 509–17.

52. Trans. by Weil, "Contacts" 172. See also Walter J. Fischel, *Unknown Jews in Unknown Lands: The Travels of Rabbi David D'Beth Hillel (1824–1832)* (New York, 1973).

53. Weil, "Contacts," 172.

54. *Bene Israelite*, 3 (7 Jan. 1896): 1.

55. I. J. Samson, "The Communal Economy of the Bene-Israel," *Israelite* 2 (Mar. 1918): 44–46. Occasionally, private emissaries who were subject to severe economic hardship were given letters of recommendation signed by the heads of the communities in Eretz Israel and authorizing them to collect on their own behalf (David, "Sheluhei Erez Israel," 1360). Several reports of Sha'are Rason Synagogue up to 1918 contain references to charity given to *hahams* and *kolels* (visitors from Jerusalem). See Strizower, *Bene Israel of Bombay*, 68, and *Sha'are Rason Synagogue, 1840–1968*, 34–35.

56. *Satya Prakash* 3 (29 Jan. 1880): 41; 3 (8 Aug. 1880): 100; *Israel Dharmadeep* 6 (6 Apr. 1894): 39; 6 (1 June 1894): 52; 6 (6 July 1894): 64; 6 (2 Nov. 1894): 123; 7 (5 Apr. 1895): 56–57; *Bene Israelite* 2 (3 Dec. 1894): 2. Wilson was perhaps returning a favor. When he visited Palestine in 1843, he carried a letter of introduction from Arabian Jews in Bombay telling the Jews of the four holy cities that Wilson, a resident of Bombay, was a great man and was sympathetic to Israel. Wilson apparently also gave Pingle some useful preparatory information for his trip. See *India and Israel* 1 (Sept. 1948): 16, and Kehimkar, *Bene Israel*, 77. I cannot trace copies of Ghosalkar's and Pingle's works, nor have I ever seen them quoted.

57. *Bene Israelite* 4 (30 July 1897): 1. On the attitude of English and American Jews toward the congress, see Walter Laqueur, *A History of Zionism* (New York, 1972), 101–6, 402–3.

58. *Bene Israelite* 4 (Oct.–Nov. 1897): 4.

59. Kehimkar, *Bene Israel*, 224–25.

60. N. E. Roby to Theodor Herzl, 15 Oct. 1901, quoted in Fischel, "Early Zionism in India," *Herzl Yearbook* 4 (1961): 310. Roby (Naphtali Eliahu Rahabi) was a scholar interested in Jewish history. Fischel, 312–13, sees this letter as an indication that the Jewish community in Cochin must have followed the contemporary Jewish scene in Europe closely.

61. The names he listed from Cochin were Isaac Elias Hallegua, Samuel S. Koder, and Jacob Hay E. Cohen. The people mentioned in Bombay, Mrs. S. D. Sassoon, Jacob E. Sassoon, and Sassoon J. David, were all Baghdadis. From Calcutta he suggested David Joseph Ezra Co., J. R. J. Liveroy, and B. Meyer (Fischel, "Early Zionism," 311–12, 316–17). There is no way of knowing whether Roby had sought the prior assent of the people he listed.

62. Roby's letter was published in *Die Welt*, no. 45 (8 Nov. 1901): 2. See Fischel, "Early Zionism," 314, 321. Despite their orthodoxy, the Cochin Jews apparently did not have the same qualms as the Bene Israel about a "man-made" restoration.

63. Musleah, *Ganga*, 415; Central Zionist Archives (hereafter cited as C.Z.A.), Jerusalem, Z3/962, Correspondence, Central Zionist Organisation and S. G. Cohen, Zionist Association for India, 5 Nov. 1913, 4 Feb. 1914. See also "Zionism," in I. A. Isaac, *Letters and Speeches*, 76–77. This article was reprinted from the *Jewish Messenger*, 29 Aug. 1913. In 1914, the Central Zionist Organisation also contacted the Poona Jewish Benevolent Association, trying to interest them in the movement, but there is no record of a response (C.Z.A. Z3/962, letter to Secretary of the Poona Jewish Benevolent Society, 1 July 1914).

64. *Friend of Israel* 2 (June 1917): 62. The May article was reprinted from a source called *Common Sense*, with no further data given (*Friend of Israel* 2 [May 1917]: 52).

65. *Times of India*, 13 Nov. 1917: 6; 15 Nov. 1917: 8.

66. Ibid., 20 Nov. 1917: 4; 30 Nov. 1917: 8.

67. *Friend of Israel* 2 (Dec. 1917): 144; 3 (Sept.–Oct. 1918): 102. Musleah, *Ganga*, 415. See also Ezra, *Turning Back*, 372.

68. Gideon Shimoni, *Gandhi, Satyagraha and the Jews: A Formative Factor in India's Policy towards Israel* (Jerusalem, 1977), 20–25. On the Khilafat movement, see Gail Minault, *The Khilafat Movement* (New York, 1982). See also R. P. Masani, *Britain in India* (Bombay, 1960), 119–21.

69. Syed Sharif uddin Pirzada, ed., *Foundations of Pakistan*, All-India Muslim League Documents, 2 (1924–47), appendix 1, All-India Muslim League, Delhi, 11th session, 30–31 Dec. 1918, p. 583.

70. B. J. Israel, letter to Percy Gourgey, 3 Jan. 1972.

Chapter 4. Indians, Jews, or Europeans?
(pages 89–127)

1. Srinivas, *Social Change*, 87; Cohn, *India*, 108. Spear, *History of India*, 2:190–91.

2. Spear, *History of India*, 2:190.

3. Ibid., 192. Minault, *Khilafat Movement*, 66–72.

4. *Israelite* 4 (July–Aug. 1920): 95. David Erulkar had been particularly moved by Tilak's humility (Sol Erulkar, interview. 31 Mar. 1978).

5. Quoted in ibid. 4 (Nov. 1920): 167.

6. *Israelite* 5 (1921): 3–4.

7. Ibid., 5 (1921): 207–8; 6 (1922): 75. See below, 115–16.

8. *Israelite* 5 (1921): 202–3. One wonders if the president of the All-India Israelite League would have expressed such unswerving loyalty to the British.

9. Reading had been vice-president of the Anglo-Jewish Association but had to resign the post upon his new appointment; Claude Montefiore, the organization's president, hoped the new viceroy would find the occasion to visit the association's school in Bombay (*Israelite* 5 [1921]: 2, 13). Ezra, *Turning Back*, 527, recalls that when he was a young boy in Calcutta, his father held up to him the example of Lord Reading, who later became foreign secretary.

10. *Friend of Israel* 6 (Jan.–March 1921): 6.

11. *Zion's Messenger* 1 (Jan. 1922): 27.

12. *Israelite* 6 (1922): 9–10.

13. *Israelite* 5 (1921): 43, 51–53, 94. I have not been able to locate Fraser's pamphlets. The quotes are taken from the *Israelite*. Fraser's views echoed those of certain people in Britain who were displeased that two Jews were in charge of Indian policy. They associated a "Jewish conspiracy" with the break-up of the British Empire in India. See Gisela Lebzelter, *Political Anti-Semitism in England, 1918–1939* (London, 1978), 20–21, 50–51, and Colin Holmes, *Anti-Semitism in British Society, 1876–1939* (London, 1979), 145–46, 207.

14. *Statesman* (Calcutta), 1921, quoted in *India and Israel* 4 (1951): 28.

15. Ibid., 94.

16. Arthur Berriedale Keith, *The King and the Imperial Crown* (London, 1936), 423. Keith suggests that the prime minister, Lloyd George, had been on close personal terms with Lord Reading and "was not forgetful of friends who had in early days been of decisive help" (424).

17. *Jewish Tribune* 8 (Aug. 1937): 2.

18. *Indian Social Reformer*, 17 July 1937: 723. The editorial is unsigned, although the editors are K. and S. Natarajan. It is possible that Keith himself held Jews in "no high honour." Elsewhere in his book, he attributed King George V's support of the Jewish National Home in Palestine to his father's many Jewish friends and to its advocacy by Sir Herbert Samuel, "a member of a great financial family. . . . The scheme involves grave obligations and anxiety" (Keith, *Imperial Crown*, 418).

19. *Israelite* 6 (1922): 57–58, 121–23 (Marathi). B. J. Israel (interview, 3 Jan. 1978) informed me that the articles were by Mazgaonker. Israel did not know who the "Indian Jews" referred to might be. Perhaps they were sons or grandsons of Indian-commissioned Bene Israel, because a number were still in the army until about 1915—remnants of the old recruitment. In any case, Baghdadi Jews did not serve in the Indian army in this period.

20. *Israelite* 6 (1922): 109–10. In *Cochin Jew Town Synagogue*, a guide to the Paradesi Synagogue for visitors written in 1929, A. B. Salem described the Passover ceremony, stressing the traditional devotion of Jews to personal liberty and independence and drawing a parallel between Moses and Aaron and Gandhi and Nehru (Mandelbaum, "Social Stratification," 94–95).

21. *Israelite* 7 (Jan.–Feb. 1923): 7.

22. M. D. Borgawkar, "The Viceroyalty of Lord Reading, First Year," *Israelite* 6 (May–June 1922): 74–76.

23. M. D. Borgawkar, "The Viceroyalty of Lord Reading, Second Year, April, 1922 to March, 1923," *Israelite* 7 (Mar.–Apr. 1923): 35. To compensate for the loss of revenue when the newly created Tariff Board abolished the cotton excise, Reading doubled the salt tax, which fell most heavily upon the poorest peasants and landless laborers, whose work in the hot sun required substantial salt intake. This increased salt tax was to become the rallying cry for Gandhi's renewed *satyagraha* in 1930. See Wolpert, *New History*, 308.

24. *Israelite* 7 (Mar.–Apr. 1923): 37.

25. M. D. Borgawkar, "The Viceroyalty of Lord Reading, Third Year, April, 1923 to March, 1924," *Israelite* 8 (1924): 63–67.

26. The *swadeshi* movement had developed in 1905, as one of the responses to Lord Curzon's partition of Bengal. *Swadeshi* might be translated as "things belonging to India"; the campaign was launched to use Indian raw materials instead of shipping them to Britain and buying them back as finished goods; its aim was to strengthen the Indian economy while at the same time hurt the British. This idea stemmed from the nationalist conviction that the poverty and economic backwardness of India were due to British rule. See Embree, *India's Search*, 48–49, and, for Gandhi's attitude toward foreign cloth, 77–78.

27. *Israelite* 7 (1923): 41.

28. Dumont, *Homo Hierarchicus*, 444 n. 16.

29. Ibid., 329 (and see 330), 416 n. 114d. On the intricacies of representation and government under British rule, see Beni Prasad, *India's Hindu-Muslim Question* (London, 1945). See also Pandey, *British India*, 118–23.

30. *Friend of Israel* 6 (Apr.–June 1921): 45. On Parsi opposition to home rule, see Kulke, *Parsees*, 190–92.

31. The memorandum was published in the *Israelite* 8 (Sept.–Oct. 1924): 124–27. At its 1924 conference in Delhi, Congress passed a resolution calling upon all Hindus and Muslims "to extend full tolerance to the minor communities of India and to deal with them in all questions of communal intercourse with justice and generosity" (Resolution no. 7, Delhi Unity Conference, 26 Sept.–2 Oct. 1924, in *Congress and the Problem of Minorities* [Allahabad, n.d. (1947?)], 86).

32. *Israelite* 9 (Jan.–Feb. 1925): 3.

33. *Bene Israel Review* 1 (Mar. 1926): 4–5.

34. *Israelite* 10 (1926): 106.

35. *Bene Israel Review* 1 (Oct.–Nov. 1926): 1.

36. "Our Retired Editor, Mr. I. J. Samson," *Israelite* 10 (1926): 25–26.

37. *Bene Israel Review* 1 (Aug. 1926): cover, 2, 10.

38. See Cohn, *India*, 59.

39. Arthur Samson, interview, 29 Aug. 1980. Arthur came to disagree with his father, feeling that Gandhi was too soft and too moral. I. J. Samson would not allow his son to speak against Gandhi in public, arguing that the Indians would lose much more if they fought the British physically rather than pushed them out economically.

40. Pandey, *British India*, 125.

41. *Report of the Eleventh Conference* (1927), 15.

42. The idea of a *hartal*—whereby the soul is, in theory, too shocked by some abuse to be able to attend to practical affairs for a time—had been proposed by Gandhi as a means of protest (Spear, *History of India*, 2:191).

43. Arthur Samson, interview, 29 Aug. 1980. I. A. Ezekiel, "Mr. I. J. Samson," *Maccabi*, July 1960: 5–6.

44. The Simon Commission also denied that communal tension would disappear if communal representation were abolished. It saw as the true cause of Hindu-Muslim rivalry the struggle for political power and the opportunities it would confer (Indian Statutory Commission [Simon Commission] Report, cmd. 3569 [London, 1930] 1:29–30). See Dumont, *Homo Hierarchicus*, 330. Also on minority safeguards, see K. K. Aziz, *Muslims under Congress Rule, 1937–1939: A Documentary Record* (Islama-bad, 1978), 1:61–62.

45. Griffiths, *British Impact*, 327–30; Pandey, *British India*, 130–34.

46. Arthur Samson, interview, 29 Aug. 1980. Although there is no way of corrob-orating this story, Arthur Samson has generally proved to be a reliable source.

47. I. A. Ezekiel, "He Walked Humbly without Knowing It," *Maccabi*, Jan. 1961: 5. Isenberg, unpublished manuscript, chap. 5 n. 28; I. A. Ezekiel, "Obituary," *Maccabi*, May 1960: 5. On M. N. Roy, see Leonard A. Gordon, *Bengal: The Nationalist Movement, 1876–1940* (New York, 1974), 136–56, 254–59.

48. B. J. Israel, interview, 13 Jan. 1978.

49. E. M. Jacob (interview, 5 Dec. 1977) commented that the Bene Israel govern-ment employees did not want to be in the position of Anglo-Indians, but could not speak out. When German Jewish doctors began arriving in India and Indian doctors protested against the competition, Dr. Erulkar, along with other prominent local doctors with high incomes, said the new arrivals should be allowed to practice (I. I. Shapurkar, interview, 22 Oct. 1977). Sol Erulkar (interview, 31 Mar. 1978) says that his father, David, was moved by a strong Indian patriotism. And see below, 178–80.

50. Nissim Ezekiel, interview, 12 Jan. 1978.

51. B. J. Israel (interview, 13 Jan. 1978) reports that his father and the Erulkars never discussed politics at home, but rather talked in David Erulkar's office in Bom-bay. He thinks that perhaps his father might have been much less involved in con-troversial politics if he had not been linked with the Erulkar brothers, who, along with I. J. Samson, were the real activists. Samson had probably gotten his brother D. J. to sign the Montagu representation, just as J. B. Israel had gotten his brother, Shalom, to sign it.

52. B. J. Israel, interview, 19 Oct. 1977; Pandey, *British India*, 141–42. The non-Brahmin movement was started by the wealthy and somewhat westernized leaders belonging to peasant or higher castes. If they sought political power, it was because that power could be translated into economic terms, in obtaining good jobs and entry into careers for one's castefolk. In Madras, Bombay, and Bengal, the leaders of the backward classes movement, which sought to abolish all distance between castes, stayed clear of the nationalist movement and strongly supported the British. The scheduled castes (Harijan) movement originated gradually as part of the backward

classes movement, although it acquired distinctive overtones (Srinivas, *Social Change*, 72, 111). For a discussion of the origins, activities, and claims of the so-called non-Brahmin movement, see G. S. Ghurye, *Caste and Race* and *Caste and Class*.

53. J. B. Israel's father, grandfather, and great-grandfather had served the British. The communities connected with military service, even those with partly mercenary motives, had some kind of bond with the British. Up until 1921–22, the Israels had pictures of the king and queen in their home (B. J. Israel, interviews, 12 Oct., 19 Oct. 1977).

54. Other Indians—business and commercial interests, landlords, and moderate intellectuals—also opposed the civil disobedience campaign, believing that the time had come for negotiations. See Embree, *India's Search*, 105.

55. *Times of India*, 7 July 1930.

56. J. B. Israel, letters to the *Times of India*, 4 Feb., 24 Apr., 16 and 31 May, and 9 July 1930; 22 Jan. 1931; 4 Jan., 1 Apr., and 17 Sept. 1932. Also *Illustrated Weekly of India*, 13 Aug. 1980. I am indebted to B. J. Israel for providing me with copies of these letters.

57. Cohn, *India*, 109.

58. B. J. Israel, interviews, 12 Oct., 13 Jan. 1978. Two Bene Israel recalled that in 1931 a big meeting with Gandhi was held. The Jews asked what should they do and Gandhi advised them to consider their own safety as a small community. He said, in effect, "If we win, you'll be with us, but don't be against us" (Bension and Sam Abraham, interview, 7 Sept. 1977). Dr. A. S. Erulkar once noted in pencil, on the back of a scroll, that when he asked Gandhi what the position of the Indian Jews in the fight for independence should be, the Mahatma's reply was: "They must decide for themselves." I am indebted to Dr. Sol Erulkar, the nephew of A. S. Erulkar, who showed me this note. In 1933, when A. S. Erulkar asked Gandhi why he did not include people from other groups, including the Jews, in his movement, Gandhi reportedly replied: "If you could influence any Jews or put me onto some, I would like it. They must feel absolutely secure from molestation by Hindus and Mussalmans" (Sol Erulkar, interview, 31 Mar. 1978). The report of this exchange surprised B. J. Israel (personal communication, 11 May 1978), who said that Gandhi did not exclude other groups. In April 1938 Nehru, in a speech on the minorities and the Congress, exhorted Indian Jews to join the Congress and assured them that they would be given equality of treatment (CZA, Jerusalem, 899/55, letter from India, A. E. Shohet, 12 Apr. 1938). On the Christians, see Schermerhorn, *Ethnic Plurality*, 192.

59. I have not come across I. J. Solomon's name in any other connection with nationalist views. B. J. Israel (personal communication, 20 June 1978) thinks he was a lawyer who once stood for election to the Bombay Legislative Council.

60. *Bombay Chronicle*, 21 July 1930. Sir Victor Sassoon was antinationalist and probably would have frowned upon such activities. On the complex evolution of the attitudes of business circles toward the Indian National Congress, see Claude Markovits, *Indian Business and Nationalist Politics, 1931–1939: The Indigenous Capitalist Class and the Rise of the Congress Party* (Cambridge, 1985).

61. *Bombay Chronicle*, 21 July 1930. Dr. Erulkar had a reputation as a brilliant orator. Much later, I. A. Ezekiel recalled his speech at that initial meeting: "There

was no high-sounding phrase mongering here; he made no appeal to your emotions, for he appealed only to your reason. It was the simplest possible exposition I have ever heard in the philosophy of freedom of man, freedom of nations, the why and wherefore of it" (Ezekiel, "He Walked Humbly without Knowing It," *Maccabi*, Dec. 1960: 7).

62. *Times of India,* 7 July 1930.

63. *Times of India,* 1 Aug. 1930.

64. Arthur Samson, interview, 29 Aug. 1980. Percy Gourgey, letter to *Jewish Chronicle,* 17 Dec. 1971. The president of Lady Irwin College, Hanna Sen (a Baghdadi married to a Hindu), was a nationalist sympathizer. A leftist group of Baghdadis in Calcutta after World War II was also pronationalist (Thomas Timberg, personal communication, 5 Oct. 1987).

65. Resolution of Working Committee, 21 Jan. 1931. Reprinted in *Congress and the Problem of Minorities,* 116.

66. *Jewish Advocate* 2 (Sept. 1931: 233. India, *Census, 1931,* summary volume, Imperial Table 16.

67. *Jewish Advocate* 2 (Mar. 1931): 121–22, 128.

68. B. J. Israel, interview, 21 Dec. 1977. Interestingly, he felt that the Bene Israel were less westernized than the upper-class Parsis were. Despite B. J. Israel's perception, the Parsis' attitudes in this period were actually quite divided. According to Kulke, a minority, led by middle-class intellectuals, felt the solution to their identity crisis lay in integrating into the emerging Indian nation as fully as possible. These Parsis considered themselves Indians first, and thought other minorities would have to develop this consciousness too if chaos were to be avoided. Active in the national movement, they were opposed by most of their coreligionists as traitors to the British and their own community. The experiences of K. F. Nariman, the leader of the Bombay Congress, are particularly interesting. See Kulke, *Parsees,* 146, 194–211, 228–37.

69. Griffiths, *British Impact,* 275–76.

70. This identification meant that the strategy was not one of "group mobility that affirmed the values of the caste system, but a rejection of the system and a joining in the battle for abolishing it." Eventually, Ambedkar led many of his followers to convert to Buddhism, thus seceding from Hindu society, so that they would no longer be restricted by the hierarchical ideology of the caste system (Cohn, *India,* 140–41); Srinivas, *Social Change,* 73.

71. See Masani, *Britain in India,* 154–55, on Gandhi's fast.

72. B. J. Israel, interview, 28 Dec. 1977. The fast succeeded. Dr. Ambedkar, in a scheme known as the Poona Pact, agreed to withdraw his claims for separate electorates, in exchange for which certain seats would be reserved for the scheduled castes. After primary elections by a scheduled caste electorate to select the candidates, the scheduled caste representatives would be elected by all Hindus. (Griffiths, *British Impact,* 331; Pandey, *British India,* 135).

73. B. J. Israel, interviews, 28 Dec. 1977, 28 Aug. 1980.

74. Interviews: B. B. Benjamin, 22 Dec. 1977; M. A. Moses, 7 Dec. 1977; Sam Israel, 11 Jan. 1978.

75. *Jewish Tribune* 6 (Mar. 1935): 24–25.

76. NAI, Home Department, no. 29/1/31 Ests. (1931): F 14/21/34 Ests. Home 1934.

77. NAI, Home Department, F. 29/5-1, 1928, serial nos. 1–13. Appendix 2, serial no. 12, endorsement from Finance Department, no. F.25 II R. II, 10 July 1929. Also F. no. 10/1/29 Ests.; no. 159/29 Ests. Home Department no. 29/1/31 Ests. 1931. Although eventually disallowed, a question had been raised in the central legislature about Bombay's policy: N. Anklesaria complained that in no other civilized country outside of British India was "backwardness in education an essential qualification for preferment in the matter of Government appointments" and said that this policy was one of discrimination that was keenly resented by the classes adversely affected (Legislative Assembly, notice received 13, 131. Home Department F. no. 29/131, Ests., 1931).

78. Srinivas, a South Indian Brahmin, has devoted much attention to the anti-Brahmin movement of the backward classes, both under the British and after independence. He admits that Brahmins, especially those from Madras and Bengal, usually predominated in the civil service (Srinivas, *Social Change*, 66–68, 102, 105, 114, 153).

79. *Friend of Israel* 2 (Mar. 1971): 29. Srinivas, *Social Change*, 112, says that there was a widespread desire among non-Brahmin castes in the 1950s to be categorized as "backward," as it was their best hope of securing education (especially technological and medical education), prestigious and well-paid employment, and mobility in the class as well as caste system.

80. *Israelite* 5 (1921): 5; 8 (1924): 7. Abigail Moses (Dr. E. Moses' wife) was at the time president of the Government Anglo-Vernacular Girls School at Thana.

81. Government Resolution, Finance Department, 4457-12 Oct. published in *Bombay Gazette*, 4 Nov. 1926, reproduced in *Bene Israel Review* 1 (11 Oct. 1926): cover, 1–2.

82. B. J. Israel, interviews, 12 Oct., 9 and 30 Nov. 1977.

83. They were probably referring to low absolute numbers. In 1931 26 percent of the Jews were literate in English, second in percentage only to Parsis, of whom over half were literate in English. Christians had only 9 percent, Jains, 3 percent (Davis, *Population*, 185).

84. NAI, Home Department, F. 14/28/135 Ests. (S) 1935.

85. Interviews: B. J. Israel, 28 Dec. 1977; E. M. Jacob, 5 Dec. 1977. Nathan Katz (personal communication, 30 Sept. 1987) has pointed out some overlapping of the Jewish and Anglo-Indian communities in Cochin, especially for those Cochinis living in Fort Cochin, traditionally an area of European settlement, rather than in Jew Town. In the mid 1980s, the secretary of the Cochin Anglo-Indian Association was a Cochin Jew. See also N. Q. King, "A Preliminary Note on some Jewish Anglo-Indians," in *Jewish Tradition in the Diaspora*, ed. M. M. Caspi (Berkeley, 1981), 191–96.

86. NAI, Home Department, F. 31/5/39, Ests. 1939. Also 31/46/45, Ests. 1945. See also Musleah, Ganga, 350–51.

87. NAI, Home Department, F. 31/46/45, Ests. 1945.

88. B. J. Israel, interviews, 13 Jan., 30 Aug. 1978, felt that Bombay Christians and Bene Israel were a little behind in the legal profession, partly because most legal litigations were commercial and it was difficult for people to establish themselves in

the profession unless they had ties with commercial communities. He knew of only two Baghdadis who were taken into the Indian Civil Service (I.C.S.): A. M. Gubbay, controller of currency, who retired prematurely from the service around 1895, and Joseph Nissim, Meyer Nissim's brother. Samuel Solomon, a Calcutta Baghdadi, entered the I.C.S. in the late 1920s, serving in both the judicial and executive branches (Ezra, *Turning Back*, 378–80). The only Bene Israel in the I.C.S. was David Reuben, the High Court judge in Bihar. David Lelyveld (personal communication, 26 July 1986) has pointed out that there were no Anglo-Indian judges and that Anglo-Indians did not reach positions of distinction.

89. B. J. Israel, interview, 12 Oct. 1977. During World War I, David Ezra, a Calcutta Baghdadi, was a captain in the Royal Garrison Artillery (Musleah, *Ganga*, 63).

90. Joseph B. Schechtman, *On Wings of Eagles* (New York, 1961), 89–90.

91. NAI Home Department, 1919. Police, Part B, Proceedings, Aug. 1919, nos. 161–63.

92. Ibid.

93. *Zion's Messenger* 1 (Dec. 1921): 1–2; also see 1 (Nov. 1921).

94. *Zion's Messenger* 1 (Jan. 1922): 28. The *Israelite* 5 (1921) (Marathi): 221–22, felt that it was a disgrace for the people of Bombay that such riots had broken out on the arrival of the Prince of Wales, and that they could have been avoided if the government had asked the Volunteer Corps to look after the arrangements.

95. Musleah, *Ganga*, 346.

96. NAI Home Department, F. no. 291/1929, Public, 1929, Political, 13 May 1929.

97. Ibid., W. S. Hopkyns, officiating chief secretary to the government of Bengal, 22 June 1929. Legislative councillor was the highest political office attained by a Calcutta Jew. In 1941 Cohen was awarded the Order of the British Empire, a citation for meritorious service (Musleah, *Ganga*, 343). On Cohen, see Ezra, *Turning Back*, 306–7. The Jewish population of Calcutta had remained relatively static between 1901 and 1931 (Ezra, *Turning Back*, 432).

98. NAI, Home Department, F. 291/1929, Public, 1929, C. W. Gwynne to the chief secretary to the government of Bengal, no. F-291/29, 7 June, 13 July 1929.

99. Ibid., David Ezra to chief secretary to the government of Bengal, 20 Aug. 1929.

100. Ibid., government of Bengal, no. 165116 A, 5 Sept. 1929; no. 19388 A, 9 Nov. 1929; government of Bombay, Reforms, 72/29, 19 Nov. 1929.

101. Ibid., David Ezra to A. H. Kemm, 4 Nov. 1929.

102. Musleah, *Ganga*, 347.

103. Ibid.

104. Ibid., 348–49.

105. Ibid., 349–50.

106. Ibid., 350.

107. Great Britain, Official Report, Fifth Series, Parliamentary Debates, Commons, 1934–35, 29 Apr.–17 May, 30:890–99. Also, *Jewish Chronicle*, 10 May 1935: 16 (Parliamentary Correspondence). The Anglo-Indians were a special case; the British felt guilty about them, responsible for their existence.

108. Smiles mentioned their connection with the Calcutta Turf Club and the fact that they had won nearly all the principal races in India (House of Commons, 7 May 1935, p. 903). On the Calcutta Jews and horseracing, see Ezra, *Turning Back*, chap. 14. Perhaps the Baghdadis were anxious to be recognized as Europeans for both political and social reasons because they sensed some British anti-Semitism as they tried to move into aristocratic circles and became direct competitors in business.

109. Ibid., 903–9.

110. Ibid., 905–6, 911–13. *Jewish Tribune* 6 (1935): 6.

111. *Jewish Chronicle*, 17 May 1935: 33, Parliamentary Notes.

112. *Jewish Chronicle*, 24 May 1935: 10, Notes of the Week. It is not clear who the disapproving "authoritative Jewish quarters" were.

113. *Jewish Chronicle*, 31 May 1935: 18.

114. *Jewish Tribune* 6 (June 1935): 4–5.

115. Letter from S. S. Koder, Jr., to *Jewish Tribune* 6 (July 1935): 14. Samuel Shabdai Koder (1869–1941) was a prosperous merchant and industrialist and a great benefactor to his community, instrumental in raising its educational standards. The first Jewish Councillor of the British Cochin Municipality, he was its chairman for six years. He represented Mattancherry in the first and second Cochin Legislative Council and was managing director of the Ferry and Transport Service and the Cochin Electricity Company. His son, Shabdai Samuel Koder, became the recognized leader of the Jewish community in South India and beyond and served for a time as a member of the Cochin Legislative Council (Fischel, "Early Zionism," 318–19).

116. *Jewish Tribune* 6 (June 1935): 7.

117. Esmond Ezra, himself a Calcutta Baghdadi, writes: "It is difficult to see how the sponsors of the moves to secure the label 'European' for the community could logically have hoped to succeed. The Jews of Calcutta, with few exceptions, are Semites whose ancestors had lived for generations in West Asia. Whatever else they might or might not be, they are certainly not Europeans and the arguments their representatives advanced from time to time over a period of more than fifty years from 1885 onwards were doomed to failure and deserved to fail" (*Turning Back*, 243 n. 25).

118. Embree, *India's Search*, 107–9; See also Pandey, *British India*, 136–40.

119. Nissim was first elected to the Municipal Corporation by the justices of the peace (who could elect sixteen members) in 1915 to fill the vacancy caused by the death of Sir Pherozeshah Mehta. After a temporary absence from India, Nissim was nominated by the Indian government toward the end of 1922. From 1923 until his retirement in 1940, he was elected by the Fort area (Meyer Nissim, "When I was Mayor of Bombay," *India and Israel* 1 [Sept. 1948]: 14–15). Alwyn Ezra at one point represented the British Chamber of Commerce in the Bombay Corporation. See also *Jewish Advocate* 4 (Feb. 1933): 6; (July 1940): 10.

120. Sassoon J. David, for example, was a prominent man, but Meyer Nissim was not. The Jews rarely had more than one municipal councillor at a time, and sometimes none. At present, unless a non-Hindu is very prominent, he has no chance of being elected mayor. There were barely three or four Parsis in the whole corporation in the late 1970s (B. J. Israel, interview, 16 Nov. 1977).

121. *Times of India* 2 (October 1931): *Jewish Advocate* 3 (Mar. 1932): 342; 9 (Jan. 1939): 13; *Jewish Tribune* 10 (Mar. 1939): 4.

122. The interpretation of independence as dominion status at the Imperial Conference in 1926 raised the issue in India (Spear, *History of India,* 2:186).

123. *Jewish Advocate* 2 (Mar. 1931): 114–15; 2 (May 1931): 159–60; 2 (June 1931): 177; 2 (July 1931): 190; 2 (Oct. 1931): 241; 3 (June 1932): 425. Michael David, interview, 29 Aug. 1978; B. J. Israel, interview, 14 Sept. 1977.

124. "Not to make political demands was to support the status quo and, in fact, the Bene Israel remained loyalists till 1947 and they genuinely regretted the departure of the British" (B. J. Israel, quoted in Schermerhorn, *Ethnic Plurality,* 258).

Chapter 5. Intracommunal Struggles and Zionism
(pages 128–170)

1. *Zion's Messenger* 1 (Jan. 1922): 27; 3 (Jan. 1923): 17.

2. Wealthy Bene Israel had apparently been permitted to marry there, as long as they brought their own *hazans* and *ketubas* (marriage certificates), until the Baghdadis discovered that a Bene Israel bride had been a widow at the time of her marriage. As widows are not permitted to marry in synagogues, the Baghdadis were incensed and refused the use of the synagogue for Bene Israel weddings until about 1930. Even today, a Bene Israel wedding held in a Baghdadi synagogue must be recorded on the register of a Bene Israel, not the Baghdadi, synagogue (Shirley Isenberg, interview, 1 Jan. 1978; Lily Samson, interview, 10 Jan. 1978); *Jewish Tribune* 8 [Aug. 1937]: 10. Unfortunately, the minutes of the managing committee of the Baghdadi synagogues are available only for the period after 1938. Aaron Samson, a Bene Israel witness in the Rangoon synagogue case, said that when he was in Calcutta, prior to 1926, he was permitted to read the Torah from the pulpit for original readings (Evidence [21 Mar. 1935], 197).

3. *Jewish Tribune* 2 (Mar. 1934): 18, 19, 21, 25. B. J. Israel, *Religious Evolution,* 12; Strizower, *Bene Israel of Bombay,* 131–32. Kehimkar, *Bene Israel,* chap. 10.

4. See *Jewish Tribune* (4) 1 (Apr. 1933): 16–17; 7 (Apr. 1936): 13; 8 (Mar. 1937): 20. In February 1933 the *Jewish Advocate* was taken over by a new management. The Sargons continued to publish their own paper, but changed its name to the *Jewish Tribune* (see below, 166–67). This situation complicated the numbering of both periodicals. The *Jewish Advocate* reverted back to volume 1:1 with the issue of 24 Feb. 1933. The *Jewish Tribune* for a while used two volume numbers, one to show its continuity with the "old" (Sargon) *Jewish Advocate* and the other to show that it was a new publication. The system is so confusing that readers wishing to follow up references should go by dates, rather than volume numbers, for the years 1930–35.

5. *Jewish Advocate (Tribune)* 3 (Sept. 1932): 485.

6. *Jewish Tribune* (4) 1 (Apr. 1933): 21. These views seem to contradict those expressed in June 1935, when the editorial supported the efforts of the Sephardic Jews to be included in the European electoral rolls (see above, chap. 4, p. 123). E. G. Moses (interview, 5 Nov. 1977), a Bene Israel lawyer, thought that by 1932–33, Baghdadi attitudes toward the Bene Israel had begun to change because the Baghdadis were becoming better educated.

7. *Jewish Tribune* (4) 1 (Apr. 1933): 16.

8. "Communal Problems," *Jewish Tribune* 2 (Aug. 1934): 5, 21. In 1935, the Baghdadis did found the Bombay Jewish Association to take an interest in community matters, particularly in the area of education.

9. *Israel Dharmadeep* 8 (Jan. 1885): 64–65. See also Musleah, *Ganga*, 343.

10. NAI, Home Department, F. no. 47/8/40, Public, 1940.

11. *Eleventh Bene Israel Conference Report, 1927*, 1.

12. NAI, Home Department, F. no. 47/1/34, Public, Home 1934; *Jewish Advocate* 1 (Oct. 1930): 53–55; 1 (Nov. 1930): 67; 1 (Jan. 1931): 85; 1 (Feb. 1931): 103. *Jewish Tribune* 6 (Mar. 1935): 5.

13. *Jewish Advocate* 10 (14 July 1939): 15; 10 (11 Aug. 1939): 14; 12 (Apr. 1943): 11.

14. Albert Elias, interview, 3 Jan. 1978.

15. At his death in 1937, Professor Ezekiel Moses Ezekiel (who was also a lawyer) was described by the *Jewish Tribune*, a Baghdadi newspaper to which he had contributed special articles and book reviews, as the most learned Hebrew scholar in Bombay, in fact, in India. He had served as honorary professor of Hebrew at Saint Xavier's college and as Hebrew examiner to the universities of Bombay and the Punjab (*Jewish Tribune* 8 [Mar. 1937]: 20). He had previously taught in the Israelite School but had resigned after a disagreement with its founder (*Jewish Minister* 2 [Mar. 1937]: 20 [Marathi]).

16. *Israelite* 6 (1922): 11; *Zion's Messenger* 1 (Nov. 1921): 3; 1 (Feb. 1922): 4.

17. *Jewish Advocate* 1 (Jan. 1931): 88–89; *Jewish Tribune* 6 (May 1935): 7; 6 (Sept. 1935): 3.

18. General Register of Pupils attending the Sir Jacob Sassoon High School, Byculla, Bombay. The register starts in 1913, but the first Bene Israel admission is noted in 1922. Some Bene Israel, however, would not have sent their children to the Sassoon school even if they could have, because better English schools were available and the higher academic standards were more important to them than the Jewish atmosphere (B. J. Israel, interview, 12 Oct. 1977). Also, B. R. D. Kelly, interview, 20 Sept. 1977.

19. Sophie Corley, interview, 5 Dec. 1977 (ORT is an abbreviation for three Russian words meaning "Society for Rehabilitation and Training"); Mrs. Malyanker, interview, 12 Dec. 1977.

20. Roth, *Sassoon Dynasty*, 223–29; Rutnagur, *Bombay Industries*, 189–211, 512. See also *Jewish Advocate* 3 (Mar. 1932): 353; 10 (25 Aug. 1939): 14. In 1931 European- and Jewish-controlled mills accounted for 43 percent of paid-up capital and about 30 percent of spindles, looms, and workforce. But in the 1930s, while many Indian groups made large investments, the major British and Jewish groups did not expand (Markovits, *Indian Business*, 30, 61, 198). By the mid 1950s, Gujaratis and Marwaris had replaced Parsi, Muslim, and Jewish dominance in the cotton industry (Kulke, *Parsees*, 123–24). On the Marwaris, see Thomas A. Timberg, *The Marwaris: From Traders to Industrialists* (New York, 1979).

21. B. J. Israel, interview, 19 Oct. 1977. He knew of only one Bene Israel who had a position of real responsibility in the Sassoon organization, a mill manager in the Manchester Mill, one of the smaller enterprises. But he also knew of a Bene Israel manager in the Gujarati mills. Knowledgeable Bene Israel disagreed over whether the mills preferred Bene Israel or Baghdadis in hiring.

22. Morris, *Industrial Labor Force,* 46 n. 22, 50, 61, 205.

23. *Zion's Messenger* 3 (Feb. 1923): 3; 3 (Mar. 1923): 1.

24. Hannah Reuben, interview, 28 Nov. 1977.

25. M. A. Moses and A. B. Moses, interview, 22 Dec. 1977. Sam Hallegua, a Cochin Jew in Bombay who was a spinning master in the Jacob Sassoon Mill, reports that he was often asked by M. A. Moses to employ a Bene Israel (interview, 6 Jan. 1978). On labor officers, see Morris, *Industrial Labor Force,* 137–38.

26. Hannah Reuben, interview, 28 Nov. 1977. Shirley Isenberg (interview, 27 Jan. 1978) thought that the Sassoons gave high jobs in the mills only to their own relatives. In the fourteen Jewish-owned mills in 1925, practically all of the managers were Europeans; the one exception, A. J. Hallegua, a Cochin Jew, was manager of the Meyer Sassoon Mill. There were seven Jewish assistant managers (mostly Baghdadis), one Jewish mechanical engineer, and two Jewish weaving masters, one of whom was European (there was also a Jewish weaving master in a Hindu-owned mill) (Rutnagur, *Bombay Industries,* 121, 293–94, 300, 186–215).

27. Sixteen directorial positions in those same nine factories that year were occupied by Parsis, nine by Hindus, six by Muslims, and six by Englishmen. Twenty directorial positions in fifty-six mills owned by non-Jews were also held by these same Jews, mainly Sir Sassoon David and A. J. Raymond (Kulke, *Parsees,* 126; Rutnagur, *Bombay Industries,* 278).

28. Sam Hallegua, interview, 6 Jan. 1978. He too felt that the mills had provided great opportunities for Jewish employment.

29. Interviews: M. A. Moses, 22 Dec. 1977; Shalom Abraham, 16 Sept. 1977; Hannah Reuben, 28 Nov. 1977; Rachel Daniel, 6 Dec. 1977; Sophie Corley, 5 Dec. 1977; I. I. Shapurkar, 7 Oct. 1977.

30. *Jewish Tribune* 8 (Sept. 1937): 10–11.

31. Ibid. 8 (Oct. 1937): 1–2.

32. Ben Nee, "In the Communal Arm Chair," *Jewish Tribune* 8 (Oct. 1937): 6. Rustam Khusrokhan, manager of the E. D. Sassoon accounts, in voluntary liquidation in 1977, said that Sir Victor Sassoon never identified with Jews very much. Unlike Sir Jacob Sassoon, he was always reluctant to stress his Jewishness (Khusrokhan, interview, 20 Oct. 1977). Timberg (personal communication, 6 Oct. 1987) suggests that Sir Victor may have shown himself differently to Jews and non-Jews.

33. By 1945 most British firms had sold out to older Indian associates (see Timberg, *Marwaris,* 78). After selling the mills, Sir Victor had a great deal of trouble repatriating the money to England, as the Indian government wanted tax payments. Sir Victor paid the taxes under protest and tried for years to recover the funds. Although he finally won in court, as of 1977, the company was still trying to get the money out of India (Rustam Khusrokhan, interview, 20 Oct. 1977). Interviews: Sarah Samson, 22 Dec. 1977; Walter Abraham, 2 Dec. 1977; Sam Hallegua, 6 Jan. 1978; Rachel Daniel, 6 Dec. 1977. In Calcutta, the large industrial group of B. N. Elias, with its jute mill, cigarette factory, and other companies, played a similar role in providing employment for Jews, particularly after World War I. When the Eliases disposed of their companies to a Marwari family in 1973, they were criticized for not safeguarding the jobs of Jews (Ezra, *Turning Back,* 325–46).

34. Judgment in High Court of Judicature at Rangoon, Original Civil Jurisdiction, 9 Apr. 1935. Civil Regular no. 85 of 1934. J. M. Ezekiel and one vs. C. S. Joseph and others. Published in *All India Law Reporter*, Rangoon Section (1935), 6–8.

35. Evidence, 8, 64; Judgment in High Court, 221.

36. J. E. Joshua, witness, 22 Feb. 1935, Evidence, 167–69.

37. *Jewish Tribune* 2 (4) (June 1934): 4. Gaster papers, Gaster to J. M. Ezekiel, 16 Nov. 1934.

38. Judgment in High Court, 221.

39. Gaster papers, J. M. Ezekiel to Gaster, 5 June 1935; Gaster to Ezekiel, 20 June 1935. Gaster later wrote to Ezekiel: "I consider it a disgrace that Jews should fight against Jews . . . to establish . . . various degrees of purity of descent. It is a dangerous procedure and absolutely against the Jewish spirit. Even a proselyte who comes to us is a full-blooded Jew from a national and religious point of view, still more so . . . the Bene Israel who have been Jews for ages and whose original descent could not be impugned" (25 Mar. 1937).

40. *Jewish Tribune* 2 (Mar. 1934): 5. This article was contradicted by an editorial written in June 1935, supporting the inclusion of Sephardic Jews on European electoral rolls. See above, 123.

41. *Jewish Tribune* 2 (Feb. 1935): 5, 12; 6 (Aug. 1935): 17, 18.

42. Clause 13a of the trust deed of the Sassoon J. David Trust Fund, 28 June 1922, states that it is meant "for the relief and benefit of the poor and indigent members of the Jewish or any other community of Bombay or other parts of India or of the world." I am indebted to Reginald Mathalone for making a copy of this deed available to me.

43. Although Sir Alwyn's name does not appear in the government file on the case, most Bene Israel believe that he, a Baghdadi Jew, first raised the issue. See *Jewish Minister* 2 (Mar. 1937): 19 (Marathi); *Mebasser* 1 (15 June 1961): 22. Even Reginald Mathalone, the trustee of the Sassoon J. David Fund in the late 1970s, did not deny Sir Alwyn's role in the affair (Reginald Mathalone, interview, 28 Nov., 13 Dec. 1977). On Sir Alwyn Ezra, see Ezra, *Turning Back*, 248.

44. Government of Maharastra Archives, Elphinstone College (hereafter called GMA), Bombay, General Department, no. 1630/33 B. Letter from A. S. Erulkar to S. S. Vazifdar, 6 Aug. 1936. Also, Vazifdar to surgeon general with government of Bombay, 13 Aug. 1936. E. D. Ezra, *Turning Back*, 559, noted that in London, David Sassoon, whose home Ezra (then a student) visited regularly in 1937 for Sabbath services, had his Bene Israel servants participate in the prayers.

45. GMA, Bombay, General Department, no. 1630/33 B, official's note on file. The official was actually B. J. Israel. Mathalone (interview, 24 Nov. 1977) feels that the government decision on the J. J. Hospital case was correct.

46. Albert A. Shellim, interview, 18 Nov. 1977.

47. Reginald Mathalone, interview, 28 Nov. 1977.

48. Shanta Chenoy, interview, 22 July 1977. Perhaps the difference in occupational orientation of the two groups accounted for the lack of competition between them.

49. Sophie Kelly, interview, 18 Aug. 1978.

50. Na'im Gubbay, interview, 13 Sept. 1977; Benjamin Moses, "Nagpada Jewry," *Jewish Tribune* (4) 1 (1933): 711.

51. Flo and Sam Hallegua, interviews, 7 Dec. 1977, 6 Jan. 1978.

52. Jerusha and Leah Jhirad, interviews, 18 Oct., 17 Nov. 1977; Isenberg, unpublished manuscript on Bene Israel, 189.

53. Rachel Daniel, interview, 6 Dec. 1977.

54. Anne Solomon Samson, interview, 23 Dec. 1977.

55. *Israelite* 3 (1919): 74.

56. Ibid., 75.

57. Ibid., 76–77.

58. *Friend of Israel* 4 (Mar.–Apr. 1919): 28–32 (Marathi).

59. *Israelite* 3 (July–Aug. 1919): 101–2, 115 (Marathi), 3 (Sept.–Oct. 1919): 123.

60. See also C.Z.A. Z 4/2472. Reuben to Tolkowsky, 13 Aug. 1919; Reuben to secretary of Central Office of Zionist Organisation, 27 Nov. 1919.

61. *Third and Fourth Bene Israel Conference Reports, 1919–1920* (Bombay, 1922), 8–12, 75–76.

62. *Israelite* 4 (Mar.–Apr. 1920): 59 (Marathi).

63. B. J. Israel, interviews, 9 Sept., 14 Oct. 1977. On the Indian National Congress's attitudes toward Zionism, see Chap. 6 below.

64. C.Z.A. Z 4/2472. Abraham Reuben to secretary of Zionist Organisation, London, 14 June 1920; D. M. Samuel to Zionist Organisation Central Office, London, 28 Aug. 1920; Zionist Office of London to D. M. Samuel, 23 Sept., 6 Dec. 1920. *Friend of Israel* 4 (July–Sept. 1920): 72–73, 76.

65. *Fourth Annual Bene Israel Conference Report*, 41, 84, 88. *Friend of Israel* 4 (Jan.–March 1921): 5.

66. *Zion's Messenger* 2 (May 1922): 1–2.

67. Israel Cohen, *The Journal of a Jewish Traveler* (London, 1925), 36–39, 54–65, 128–31. In these years the name of the Zionist organization varied. It was sometimes known as the Universal or Central Zionist Organization, depending on the correspondent.

68. *Friend of Israel* 4 (Apr.–June 1921): 39–40. Tolkowsky's identity remains something of a mystery. The first name of the person who wrote to the Bene Israel from London in 1919 was reported as Paul. The person described as the head of the Bombay Zionists in 1921 was the acting Belgian consul and was called William. Is it the same person? A Shemuel Tolkowsky, born in Belgium, had settled in Palestine in 1911 and served under Weizmann in London as a member of the Zionist political committee (1916–18) and as secretary of the Zionist delegation at the Versailles Peace Conference (1918–19). (Benjamin Jaffe, "Shemuel Tolkowsky," *EJ* 15:1211).

69. *Friend of Israel* 4 (Apr.–June 1921): 40–41; Cohen, *Journal*, 255.

70. C.Z.A. Z 4/1902, Israel Cohen to Zionist Executive, 27 Mar. 1921; See also Z 4/2472, Israel Cohen to Victor Sassoon, 29 Jan. 1926.

71. C.Z.A. Z 4/1902, Israel Cohen to Zionist Executive, 27 Mar. 1921.

72. *Friend of Israel* 6 (Apr.–June 1921): 41.

73. Zvi Yehuda, "The Place of Aliyah in Moroccan Jewry's Conception of Zionism," *Studies in Zionism* 6 (1985): 202.

74. Ibid., 199–201.

75. *Zion's Messenger* 1 (Nov. 1921): 1–2, 7–8, 18; 1 (Dec. 1921): 2–3, 21.

76. C.Z.A. Z 4/2472, Israel Cohen to Florence Haskell, 15 Dec. 1921.

77. C.Z.A. Z 4/2181, Israel Cohen to Bension, 6 Dec. 1921. *Zion's Messenger* 1 (Feb. 1922): 3. Apparently some Jews of Calcutta hesitated to fulfill their pledges because they were concerned about riots in Palestine and Churchill's statements and wondered whether the Balfour Declaration would be implemented. Cohen deplored the murder of Jews by Arabs in Jerusalem but said it was necessary to prove that the Zionists' work results in the advancement of everyone in the country (C.Z.A. Z 4/2472, Israel Cohen to E. M. D. Cohen, 29 Dec. 1921).

78. *Zion's Messenger* 1 (Mar. 1922): 1–3; C.Z.A. Z 4/2181 I, Bension to Directorate, Keren Heyesod, 10 Mar. 1922.

79. *Zion's Messenger* 1 (Dec. 1921): 2–3, 21.

80. *Zion's Messenger* 2 (May 1922): 1–3, 20; (July 1922): 1–2, 52–53; (Aug. 1922): 57–58. *Advocate of India*, 21 June 1922.

81. C.Z.A. Z 4/2472, S. H. Haskell to Israel Cohen, 1 Dec. 1922; Israel Cohen to S. H. Haskell, 28 Dec. 1922; Israel Cohen to B. A. Ferst, secretary, Jewish War Memorial, 16 Mar. 1923; Israel Cohen to Sir Victor Sassoon, 29 Jan. 1926.

82. Fischel, "Early Zionism in India," 327–28.

83. *Zion's Messenger* 3 (Jan. 1923): 1–2, 14, 16, 17; 3 (Feb. 1923): 2.

84. C.Z.A. Z 4/2472, Israel Cohen to S. H. Haskell, 11 June 1924; Z 4/15641, Israel Cohen to Ben Sargon, 22 Mar. 1927; *Zion's Messenger* 4 (Feb. 1924): 59; *Report of Eighth Bene Israel Conference* (1924), 21.

85. C.Z.A. Z 4/15641, Israel Cohen to Ben Sargon, 22 Mar. 1927.

86. *Report of Eleventh Bene Israel Conference* (1927), 26–27.

87. After 1924, eastern European Jewish youth who had been educated in France and had been Zionist activists there came to Morocco and took the lead in Zionist activity in that country. They emphasized the philanthropic-emancipation elements, rather than the national-political aspect of Zionism. Addressing itself to the intellectual, mainly non-native element, the local Zionist organization grew apart from the main Jewish community, which had limited means and demanded immediate *aliyah* (Zvi Yehuda, "Place of Aliyah," 201).

88. C.Z.A. Z 4/15641, communication from Dr. Bension, 21 Jan. 1929, reprinted in a letter from Leo Hermann, secretary of the Board of Keren Heyesod, to Zionist executive, 5 Feb. 1929.

89. Shimoni, *Gandhi*, 26; see also 20–27; *Young India*, 23 Mar. 1921: 93–94. Two months later, Gandhi wrote that the British mandate was "an act of treachery toward Indian Mussalmans and of pillage against the world's Mussalmans" (*Young India*, 25 May 1921: 162). Pirzada, *Pakistan* 1:562–63.

90. Minault, *Khilafat Movement*, 206–7; Shimoni, *Gandhi*, 27.

91. C.Z.A. Z 4/4129, Gershon Agronsky, "Notes of a Visit to Bombay on Behalf of the Jewish Agency," 17 Apr.–2 May 1930.

92. Ibid.

93. Ibid.

94. *Jewish Bulletin* 1 (Dec. 1930): 71.

95. Ibid., 78; 1 (Nov. 1930): 57–58; 1 (May 1930): 10–11; 1 (Dec. 1930): 71, 78.

96. *Jewish Advocate* (formerly *Jewish Bulletin*) 1 (Jan. 1931) 86, 91–92; (Feb. 1931) 99–100, 107; 2 (Mar. 1931): 124.

97. *Jewish Bulletin (Advocate)*, 1 (Nov. 1930): 57–59, 61, 64–65, 68, 76–77; 1 (Feb. 1931): 109; 2 (Mar. 1931): 116, 132–37.

98. *Jewish Advocate* 2 (June 1931): 173; 2 (Aug. 1931): 207; 2 (Sept. 1931): 221–23; 3 (May 1932): 390.

99. NAI, Home Department, F. no. 95/1931 pol. 1931; *Jewish Advocate* 2 (Apr. 1931): 152; 2 (July 1931): 129, 198–99; 2 (Oct. 1931): 253; 2 (Nov. 1931): 273–74.

100. *Times of India*, 11 June, 13 July 1931, reprinted in the *Jewish Advocate* 2 (Aug. 1931): 218.

101. *Jewish Advocate* 3 (Mar. 1932): 338–39, 362–63. The *Jewish Advocate* 2 (Jan. 1932): 311, claimed that Gandhi and other delegates to the Round Table Conference had been very much impressed by the Zionist case submitted to them in conversations they had with the Nahum Sokolow and Selig Brodetsky.

102. See, for example, *Jewish Advocate* 2 (Sept. 1931): 221, 223–24; 2 (Oct. 1931): 241, 245; 2 (Nov. 1931): 262–64, 270–71; 2 (Dec. 1931): 279–80, 287, 290; 2 (Jan. 1932): 299; 3 (Apr. 1932): 376; 3 (Sept. 1932): 485–86.

103. *Jewish Advocate* 2 (June 1931): 176–77; 2 (July 1931): 194–95, 202–3; 2 (Nov. 1931): 268–69; 2 (Dec. 1931): 294; 2 (Jan. 1932): 313–15; 3 (Mar. 1932): 342–43.

104. *Jewish Advocate* 3 (June 1932): 417.

105. Walter Zenner, "The Jews of Syria: An Historical Perspective," paper presented at Symposium on Syrian Jews, City University of New York, 17 Nov. 1986.

106. See also Yehuda, "Place of Aliyah," 202–10.

107. *Jewish Advocate* 3 (Apr. 1932): 379; 3 (Oct. 1932): 540; 3 (Nov. 1932): 555–56.

108. C.Z.A. Z 4/15641, chairman of Council [of World Zionist Organization] to Albert Raymond and Isaac David, 13 Feb. 1932; *Jewish Advocate* 3 (June 1932): 413, 415–16; 3 (Oct. 1932): 508–9; 3 (Nov. 1932): 555, 558, 574.

109. *Jewish Advocate* 3 (17 Nov. 1932): 585. This edition was a special number of the *Advocate* brought out on the occasion of Myers's visit.

110. Ibid., 591.

111. Ibid., 593, 594, 599.

112. *Jewish Advocate* 3 (Dec. 1932): 618, 621; 3 (Jan. 1933): 641. It is not clear exactly what the Bene Israelite Young Zionist Association was or when it was formed. E. M. Jacob (interview, 5 Dec. 1977) recalled that he was the secretary of a Bene Israel Zionist association that was formed before Myers's arrival and that lasted only two years. The original organization founded as a result of Israel Cohen's visit apparently had died out.

113. By the late 1920s, the World Zionist Organization had greatly reduced organized *aliyah* from Muslim countries.

114. *Jewish Advocate* 3 (17 Nov. 1932): 581–82, 597–99.

115. *Jewish Advocate* 3 (Dec. 1932): 604, 624–25. In this period there were approximately thirteen rupees to a British pound and four rupees to a dollar.

116. E. M. Jacob, interviews, 5 Dec. 29 Dec. 1977; Joe Sargon, interview, 23 Dec. 1980.

117. *Jewish Advocate* 3 (17 Nov. 1932): 507; 3 (Jan. 1933): 649; 3 (Feb. 1933): 671–72; 1 (4) (24 Feb. 1933): 3–5, 8, 12; (10 Mar. 1933): 4, 5, 10, 13–15. C.Z.A. S 51456, head of Keren Heyesod to E. J. Samuel, 22 June 1922.

118. C.Z.A. Z 4/15641, Joseph Sargon to Israel Cohen, 10 Mar., 24 Mar. 1933. Sargon wrote to Cohen, hoping that since the new paper, the *Jewish Tribune*, would run exclusively on Zionist lines, with the same objective as the *Jewish Advocate*, the Zionist executive would continue to support only the *Tribune*.

119. *Jewish Advocate* 1 (7 Apr. 1933): 13; 1 (28 May 1933): 5, 18. Adolph Myers was apparently still in Bombay in 1941, for his name appears in that year's list of contributors to the Jewish National Fund (*Jewish Advocate* 11 [Mar. 1941]: 11).

120. *Jewish Advocate* 3 (Jan. 1933): 630; 1 (28 May 1933): 4; 1 (7 Apr. 1933): 4.

121. Jacob B. Israel to *Times of India*, 17 May 1933.

122. NAI, Home Department, F. 22/85/36 Pol. 1936.

123. Pirzada, *Pakistan*, 2:209, 223.

124. Ibid., 225–26.

125. NAI, Home Department, F. 22/85/36 Pol. 1936.

126. NAI, Home Department, F. 106/35 Pol. 1935.

127. Pirzada, *Pakistan*, 2:232.

Chapter 6. A Heightened Jewish Consciousness
(pages 171–210)

1. *Instruments of Instructions to the Governor-General and Governors* (London, 1935), Cmd. 4805: 13. See chap. 4 above.

2. *Jewish Minister* 2 (July 1937): 5.

3. When the Bombay Municipal Act was passed in 1888, the government could appoint sixteen of the seventy-two councillors. It tried to include members of minorities, who might not succeed at elections. Of five Jews who were members of the corporation from 1908 to 1948, Dr. Elijah Moses and Meyer Nissim, a Baghdadi, were the only councillors who were regularly elected. Sassoon J. David was also nominated by the government. See *Jewish Minister* 2 (July 1937): 3–4; *Bene Israel Review* 1 (Feb. 1926): 1–2; and *Free Press Journal*, Apr. 1938.

4. B. J. Israel, interview, 12 Oct. 1977. Others have also suggested that Moses probably supported the nationalists for political convenience (I. I. Shapurkar, interview, 7 Oct. 1977). Moses' daughter, however, claims that he was very pro-Congress and friendly with V. C. Patel and others. He thought independence would be good, but also got along well with the British (Dr. Ruby Solomon, interview, 7 Oct. 1977).

5. The *Jewish Tribune* 8 (May 1937): 1–2, 5, gave him a long editorial write-up. The *Jewish Minister*, a Bene Israel journal published in the late 1930s, never mentioned nationalist politics, even though it was edited by I. A. Ezekiel, who was interested in politics. It remained quite parochial, concentrating on local and communal affairs; it did not even have a foreign news column. Its Marathi columns expressed pride at Moses' election, hoping that the entire nation would acclaim the Bene Israel community because of him (*Jewish Minister* 2 [Apr. 1937]: 7–9). See *Mayor's Fund Week Souvenir*, Bombay, Nov. 1960, 59.

6. The text is found in the *Jewish Minister* 2 (July 1937): 1–2.

7. Ibid., 3–4.

8. Ibid., 5–6; *Jewish Tribune* 8 (Sept. 1937): 4.

9. Schermerhorn, *Ethnic Plurality*, 219–22.

10. Isaac David, "Calcutta Jewry and Unity," *Jewish Tribune* 8 (Mar. 1937): 13.

11. Isaac David, "Calcutta Jewry and Unity [part 2]," *Jewish Tribune* 8 (Apr. 1937): 6.

12. Isaac David, "Calcutta Jewry and Unity [part 3]," *Jewish Tribune* 8 (May 1937): 11; June 1937): 6.

13. Dr. E. Moses, "Special Message to the *Jewish Tribune*," *Jewish Tribune* 8 (Sept. 1937): 9.

14. I. A. Isaac, letter to the editor, 29 Oct. 1937, *Jewish Tribune* 8 (Dec. 1937): 16.

15. Isaac David, letter to the editor, 14 Dec. 1937, *Jewish Tribune* 8 (Feb. 1938): 13–14.

16. *Jewish Minister* 2 (July 1937): 5.

17. *Congress and the Problem of Minorities*, 128–29.

18. *Jewish Tribune* 8 (Feb. 1938): 13–14.

19. I. A. Isaac, letter to the editor, 11 Mar. 1938, *Jewish Tribune* 9 (Apr. 1938): 19–20.

20. Ibid. The Parsis, actually, not having been granted separate electorates, felt insecure and sought to safeguard their interests in a future independent India (Kulke, *Parsees*, 196–97).

21. *Jewish Tribune* 9 (June 1938): 17.

22. H. D. Hyams, letter to the editor, 5 Apr. 1938, *Jewish Tribune* 9 (May 1938): 21–22. Hyams is quoting Resolution 16, "Protection to Minorities," of the Congress session of 1937 at Haripur. See *Congress and the Problems of Minorities*, 134–35.

23. *Jewish Tribune* 9 (June 1938): 5. He doubted whether "one Jewish member of any legislative body could have achieved anything for his people."

24. Lily Samson, interview, 10 Jan. 1978; Flo Hyam (Japheth's sister), interview, 14 Oct. 1977. Japheth's books include *Pursuit of Truth* (Bombay, 1948) and *Mahatma Gandhi* (Bombay, 1968). Some Baghdadis felt that Japheth had good intentions and a genuine interest in national politics, but that he was confused and very subjective, that he never got away from the fact that he was Jewish. "He was involved with the Central Jewish Board, the All-Indian Jewish Federation, Gandhian ideals, socialism— everything all at once. He needed to be truly secular," one Baghdadi later commented, "rather than lumping the national movement with Jewish interests" (Albert Elias, interview, 3 Jan. 1978).

25. The article had been published in the *Bombay Sentinel* and was reprinted in the *Jewish Advocate* 11 (Oct. 1941): 9.

26. *Jewish Advocate* 11 (Nov. 1941): 9.

27. Moshe Sultoon, Ezra Mir, interview, 9 Sept. 1977. In Nov. 1930, Meyer Nissim had been a speaker at a meeting, banned by the police, to protest "unchivalrous, brutal and inhuman treatment" by police against Indian women at a flag salutation ceremony on 26 Oct. (*Jewish Advocate* 1 [Nov. 1930]: 63). At a banquet at the Corporation Hall to which he had invited the government of Bombay and leading citizens, Nissim had permitted the Congress flag, along with others, to be hoisted at the entrance. British members of the Indian Civil Service were furious, and the governor reportedly almost walked out of the party (Meyer Nissim, "When I was Mayor of Bombay," *India and Israel* 1 [Sept. 1948]: 14–15).

28. Albert Elias, interview, 3 Jan. 1978.

29. *Jewish Advocate*, Oct. 1942: 7, 11. In 1933–35, another Jewish refugee problem, one unrelated to the war, developed. Hundreds of Jews from Russia, Persia and Afghanistan, in transit in Afghanistan, were seeking admittance into India. Some may have been Russian and Bokharan Jews who had been living in Afghanistan since 1917 under difficult conditions and had been unable to acquire Afghan citizenship. Others may have included Afghan Jews who were expelled from many towns and robbed of their possessions after the assassination of Mohammed Nadir Shah in Nov. 1933. In Kabul and Herat, where these Afghan Jews were allowed to reside, they were subjected to stringent restrictions in work and trade (Schechtman, *Wings of Eagles*, 258–59, 264). Some of these Jews wanted to stay in India, others wanted to proceed to Palestine. In 1934 the government of India allowed a substantial number of these refugees to enter, although many of them were not easily absorbed economically. As they had no national passports, there was nowhere else they could go. The Indian government feared that a number of these Jews, especially the Russians and the Persians (who were often of Russian origin, with fraudulently acquired Persian papers, and engaged in the fur trade as smugglers in Soviet interests) might be Bolshevik agents. The Jews in Afghanistan wanted to leave; the Afghan government wanted them out. Powerful Jewish organizations in England exerted considerable pressure on India to help these refugees. The government decided to grant a limited number of visas to Jews who wished to remain in India after ascertaining that their connections in India were satisfactory. Others could be given transit visas if they had valid papers for elsewhere and India was the only transit route. But in any case, the government insisted on guarantees that these Jews were not Soviet agents and expected the Afghan Foreign Office to help on this matter. (NAI, Government of India: Foreign and Political Department, General Branch, file no. 181, G serial nos. 1–24–1935). In 1936 there was a further evacuation. Between 1932 and 1938, 721 Afghan Jews arrived in Palestine (Schechtman, *Wings of Eagles*, 262, and Erich Brauer, "The Jews of Afghanistan," *Jewish Social Studies* 4[2] [1942]: 121–27). How many came through India is uncertain.

30. *Jewish Advocate* 9 (2 Dec. 1938): 10, 14; 9 (30 Dec. 1938): 2, 4, 11; 9 (13 Jan. 1939): 14; 9 (27 Jan. 1939): back cover; 9 (24 Feb. 1939): 15.

31. Strizower, "Ten Tribes of Bombay," *Jewish Chronicle* 1 July 1961, has pointed out that although the central European Jews were not all Orthodox, they were never asked by the Baghdadis to prove that they were really Jewish. They were accepted. Some Bene Israel remember the German Jews as being uppity and snobbish and not mixing even with the handful of Bene Israel whose religious leanings were similar, the members of the progressive Jewish Religious Union (which met in an area where German Jews did not live). In the 1950s, however, when Hugo Gruyn became the rabbi and a synagogue, Rodeph Sholem, was built, a few of the Europeans who had remained became interested (Leah Jhirad, interview, 18 Oct. 1977; Mr. and Mrs. G. L. Gabriel, interview, 22 Nov. 1977; Reginald Mathalone, interview, 28 Nov. 1977; A. Leiser, interview, 10 Nov. 1977). In 1937, when Knesset Eliahu, the Baghdadi Fort synagogue, decided to charge for seat reservations, a few of the European Jews switched over to Magen David in Byculla or the Bene Israel synagogues (*Jewish Tribune* 8 (8 Oct. 1937): 5.

32. *Jewish Advocate* 9 (4 Nov. 1938): 14; 9 (2 Dec. 1938): 14; 10 (13 Sept. 1939): 27.

33. Central Legislative Assembly, *Debates,* 10 Mar. 1934, starred questions and answers, no. 434: 2:1981–82.

34. *Jewish Tribune* 6 (Mar. 1935): 36. Dr. A. S. Erulkar, along with other prominent Indian doctors (who had large incomes and therefore were not affected), helped to persuade the Indian government to let these refugees enter. E. M. Jacobs (interview, 5 Dec. 1977) recalls that Gandhi supported their entry, arguing that India was a land that welcomed everybody.

35. Central Legislative Assembly, *Debates* 4, 3 Apr. 1934, question no. 602, 3088–90.

36. *Jewish Tribune* 2 (Apr. 1934): 23.

37. Letter from Rustom Dadachanji, 28 Feb. 1935, to *Bombay Chronicle,* cited in *Jewish Tribune* 7 (Apr. 1936): 16 See also *Jewish Tribune* 6 (Mar. 1935): 36.

38. Central Legislative Assembly, *Debates* 1, 4 Feb. 1939, question no. 52: 144–45; 13 Feb. 1939, question no. 324: 1:741–42. NAI, Home Department, F. 22/9/39, Pol. 1939, question no. 622.

39. NAI, Home Department, F. 22/46/39 Pol. 1939; Central Legislative Assembly, *Debates,* 15 Apr. 1939, no. 1738: 4:3774. See also *Jewish Advocate* 10 (14 July 1939): 14, 10 (25 Aug. 1939): 3.

40. NAI, Home Department, F. 17/83/38 Pol. 1938.

41. NAI, Home Department, F. 17/444/38.

42. NAI, Home Department, F. 8/27/38 Pol. 1938.

43. *Jewish Advocate* 9 (27 Jan. 1939): 2–3.

44. *Jewish Advocate* 10 (4 Nov. 1938): 14; 10 (19 May 1939): 14; 10 (11 Aug. 1939): 10. *Jewish Tribune* 10 (Mar. 1939): 35.

45. *Jewish Advocate* 9 (9 Sept. 1938): 18–19. Richard Freund, a visiting Jewish scientist, had a long talk with Sir Akbar Hyderi, the prime minister of Hyderabad, about the possibility of bringing a few first-rate German-Jewish scientists to Osmania University (CZA S 25/3586, Richard Freund to Eliahu Epstein, 7 Oct. 1937).

46. *Jewish Tribune* 10 (Mar. 1939): 26; NAI, Home Department, F. 17/195/38, Pol. 1939, letter, J. A. Thorne, secretary to government of India to Hearsey, 20 Sept. 1938; 17/143/38, Pol. 1938.

47. NAI, Home Department, F. 153/38, Pol. 1938. M. G. Hallett to Linlithgow, 30 Oct. 1938; Linlithgow to Hallett, 3 Nov. 1938.

48. Central Legislative Assembly, *Debates,* 6 Feb. 1939, question no. 139, 1:257–58; 9 Feb. 1939, question no. 240: 581–82. *Jewish Advocate* 9 (24 Feb. 1939): 15. NAI, Home Department, F. 22/2/1939; 22/9/1939, Pol. 1939.

49. NAI, Home Department, F. 22/9/39, Pol. 1939, question no. 622.

50. Ibid.

51. *Bombay Sentinel,* 21 Feb. 1939; *Jewish Advocate* 9 (24 Feb. 1939): 4, 15; *Jewish Tribune* 10 (Mar. 1939): 33.

52. NAI, Home Department, F. 22/46/39 Pol. 1939; Central Legislative Assembly, *Debates,* 15 Apr. 1939, question no. 1738, 4:3774. See also *Jewish Advocate* 10 (25 Aug. 1939): 3.

53. *Jewish Advocate* 10 (28 July 1939): 15; *Times of India*, 4 Aug. 1939; *Statesman*, 24 Aug. 1938: 6. See also Central Legislative Assembly, *Debates*, 4 Feb. 1939, starred question no. 56, 1:148–49; 8 Feb. 1939, starred question no. 188, 1:415–16; 24 Aug. 1938, short notice question and answer, 5:922–24.

54. *Jewish Advocate* 1 (7 Apr. 1933): 5; (23 June 1933): 3.

55. *Jewish Tribune* 8 (June 1937): 2.

56. Ibid. 6 (July 1935): 18.

57. Shimoni, *Gandhi*, 3–14, 37–38.

58. *Harijan*, 26 Nov. 1938: 352–53.

59. Ibid., 353.

60. *Jewish Advocate* 9 (2 Dec. 1938): 2–4, 12–13.

61. The statement was reprinted in the *Jewish Advocate* 9 (16 Dec. 1938): 14.

62. *Harijan*, 17 Dec. 1938: 384.

63. *Harijan*, 24 Dec. 1938: 393. Shimoni, *Gandhi*, 20, suggests that Gandhi's misinterpretation of the Hebrew Bible led him to think that the Jews believed in retributive justice and therefore sought revenge against Germany.

64. *Jewish Advocate* 9 (30 Dec. 1938): 2–3, 15.

65. Buber's letter is published in *A Land of Two Peoples*, ed. Paul Mendes-Flohr (New York, 1983), 113–26. Shimoni, *Gandhi*, 40–51.

66. *Sunday Standard* (2 Oct. 1938) as quoted in *Jewish Advocate* 9 (30 Dec. 1938): 17.

67. *Jewish Advocate* 9 (30 Dec. 1938): 17.

68. *Harijan*, 18 Feb. 1939: 24.

69. Shimoni, *Gandhi*, 53–55, quotes Gandhi as saying in the *Harijan* of 27 Apr. 1939: "In the face of such weighty contradiction [Gandhi felt he had to withdraw his remarks] without any reservation: I did not realise the importance of the rebuke, . . . I only hope that my observation has not harmed any single Jew." I cannot locate this quotation. There is no *Harijan* for 27 Apr. 1939. The dates are 22 Apr. and 29 Apr., and such a statement does not appear in them.

70. *Jewish Advocate* 10 (13 Sept. 1939): 6.

71. NAI, Home Department, F. 32/1/37 Pol. 1937. Habib ur-Rahman had placed the anti-Semitic article in the *Hindustan Standard* of Calcutta.

72. C.Z.A. File 899/55, A. E. Shohet, letters from India, 10 Sept. 1938. Shohet may have overstated the case, at least for Jinnah, who actively rebuked some Muslim leaders for their anti-Semitic remarks at the Patna meeting of the All-India Muslim League in 1938. See Stanley Wolpert, *Jinnah of Pakistan* (New York, 1984), 162–67.

73. C.Z.A. File 899/55, A. E. Shohet, letters from India, 28 Sept. 1938.

74. C.Z.A. S 25/3586, A. E. Shohet to E. Epstein, 9 Nov. 1938. Eliahu Epstein, who later changed his name to Eliahu Elath, became a great expert on Arab affairs and later served as Israel's first ambassador to the United States and then as ambassador to Great Britain (*Jewish Advocate* 9 [25 Aug. 1939]: 3).

75. NAI, Home Department, F. 31/1/36, Pol. 1936.

76. NAI, Home Department, F. 22/85/36, Pol. 1936.

77. Shertok, who had attended the London School of Economics, became head of the political department in 1933. He greatly developed the methods of Zionist diplo-

macy and became Israel's first foreign minister, Hebraicizing his name to Sharett. He played an important role in seeking to establish Israeli relations with the non-Western world and took a very liberal position on the Arabs. He was prime minister of Israel from 1953 to 1955. See Chaim Yahil, "Moshe Sharett," *EJ* 14:1309–13.

78. C.Z.A. S 25/3239, Shertok to Kallenbach, 15 July 1936.

79. Immanuel Olsvanger, a Polish-born folklorist and Hebrew translator, emigrated to Palestine in 1933. He was among the pioneers in the translation of Sanskrit and Japanese literary texts to Hebrew (Getzel Kressel, "Immanuel Olsvanger," *EJ* 12:1372). The Zionist leadership preferred to rely on foreign, rather than Indian, Jews as intermediaries with Congress leadership. Perhaps they thought the local Jews had little "clout."

80. C.Z.A. S 25/3239, Shertok to Kallenbach, 15 July 1936.

81. Ibid.; see also Shimoni, *Gandhi*, 28–29.

82. Shimoni, *Gandhi*, 28–29.

83. Ibid., 29–30. See also C.Z.A. S 25/3583, Immanuel Olsvanger's Day by Day Diary in India (in German). On Kallenbach and Polak, see also I. A. Ezekiel, "Mahatma Gandhi and his Jewish Friends," *India and Israel* 1 (Jan. 1949): 19–20.

84. C.Z.A. S 25/3583 Immanuel Olsvanger's Day by Day Diary in India (22 Sept. 1936). In May 1933 the imprisoned Nehru had written a letter to his daughter on Palestine and Transjordan, in which he outlined the background to the conflict. Although he evinced considerable admiration and sympathy for the Jews, he came down clearly on the side of the Arabs, criticizing British policy. A note he wrote in 1938 reiterates this position. See Jawaharlal Nehru, *Glimpses of World History* (London, 1949), 762–67.

85. Shimoni, *Gandhi*, 30–31.

86. *Jewish Tribune* 7 (Sept. 1936): 2.

87. C.Z.A. S 25/3583, Immanuel Olsvanger's Day by Day Diary (13 Sept., 19 Sept.). The statement about Jinnah's lack of interest in Palestine is surprising. In his presidential address at the twenty-fifth session of the All-India Muslim League at Lucknow in Oct. 1937, Jinnah spoke at length (and vehemently) against Great Britain's policy. Pirzada, *Pakistan*, 2:272.

88. C.Z.A. S 25/3583, Olsvanger to executive of the Bombay Zionist Association, 6 Nov. 1936. Percy Gourgey (personal communication, 27 Nov. 1985) says that in 1919 N. E. B. Ezra, the editor of Shanghai's *Israel's Messenger*, got the Chinese government to issue a statement favoring the Balfour Declaration and to send it to the Zionist organization. Shimoni, *Gandhi*, 31, felt that Olsvanger's political efforts were like a drop in the ocean and that while he was in India, Muslim support of the Arabs in Palestine grew, winning over Hindu politicians eager to demonstrate a common Muslim-Hindu bond.

89. *Jewish Tribune* 7 (Nov. 1936): 2. The *Tribune* rarely dealt with internal Indian politics or Indian nationalist conflicts during this period. It criticized British policy in Palestine, but never in India.

90. C.Z.A. S 5/456, A. E. Shohet, "Conditions and Scope of Work in India," Feb. 1938.

91. *Jewish Tribune* 2 (Dec. 1934): 13.

92. *Jewish Tribune* 7 (June 1936): 2.

93. C.Z.A. S 25/3583, Olsvanger's Day by Day diary (26 Aug., 28 Aug.).

94. *Jewish Minister* 2 (Dec. 1936): 9–11 (Marathi). The Bene Israel had also given many invaluable manuscripts, books, and old photos to Professor Simha Assaf of the Hebrew University, who had visited in 1934.

95. C.Z.A. S 25/3239, A. B. Salem to Leo Herrmann, 23 July 1936; Leo Herrmann to A. B. Salem, 14 Aug. 1936.

96. C.Z.A. S 24/456, *Keren Hayesod* director to E. J. Samuel, 22 June 1939; S 24/3239, Olsvanger to Shertok, 28 Aug. 1936.

97. *Jewish Tribune* 8 (Apr. 1937): 1; 8 (May 1937): 2; 8 (June 1937): 3; 8 (Jan. 1938): 1.

98. The increased Jewish immigration to Palestine between 1933 and 1936 had intensified Arab opposition. An Arab general strike launched in 1936 grew into a full-scale rebellion that lasted for three years.

99. NAI, Home Department, F. 31/1/36 Pol. 1936, telegram no. 474-S, 14 Sept. 1936.

100. NAI, Home Department, F. 32/1/37 Pol. 1937.

101. Shimoni, *Gandhi*, 32–37.

102. Great Britain, Palestine Royal Commission Report, 1937, Cmd. 5479: 282.

103. NAI, Home Department, F. 39/18/38 Pol. 1938. Weekly report of director, Intelligence Bureau, Home Department, Government of India, 27 Aug. 1938. See also Pattabhi Sitaramayya, *History of the Indian National Congress* (New Delhi, 1969), 2:69.

104. NAI, Home Department, F. 39/13/37 Pol. 1937.

105. Pirzada, *Pakistan*, 2:272.

106. Ibid., 277–78.

107. NAI, Home Department, F. 39/18/38 Pol. 1938; Intelligence Bureau of the Home Department, weekly report no. 34, 27 Aug. 1938.

108. *Jewish Tribune* 8 (Sept. 1937): 9, 11.

109. C.Z.A. S 25/3586, Shohet, Letter from India, 18 Oct. 1937; 12 Apr. 1938.

110. C.Z.A. S 5/456, A. E. Shohet, "Conditions and Scope of Work in India," Feb. 1938.

111. *Jewish Tribune* 8 (Feb. 1938): 1–2; 9 (Mar. 1938): 20; 9 (Apr. 1938): 3.

112. C.Z.A. S 5/456, extract from a letter from Dr. Benzion Shein, 27 May 1938.

113. NAI, Home Department, F. 39/18/38 Pol. 1938; Intelligence Bureau of the Home Department, weekly report no. 34, 27 Aug. 1938.

114. NAI, Home Department, F. 39/20/38 Pol. 1938; telegram no. 39/16/38, political, 22 Nov. 1938. *Jewish Advocate* 9 (21 Oct. 1938): 14.

115. C.Z.A. S 25/3586, A. E. Shohet to Eliahu Epstein, 28 Sept., 9 Nov. 1938.

116. Twenty-sixth session, Patna, 27 Dec. 1938. Pirzada, *Pakistan*, 2:315.

117. Ibid., 317.

118. *Jewish Advocate* 9 (10 Feb. 1939): 8.

119. *Harijan*, 26 Nov. 1938: 352.

120. Ibid., 353.

121. C.Z.A. S 25/3587, Epstein to Shohet, 21 Dec. 1938.

122. Shimoni, *Gandhi*, 40.

123. Ibid., 40–44, 47; Mendes-Flohr, *Two Peoples*, 117–25.

124. C.Z.A. S 25/3587, A. E. Shohet to Eliahu Epstein, 7 Mar. 1939.

125. *Jewish Advocate* 9 (4 Nov. 1938): 4; 9 (13 Jan. 1939): 4; 9 (27 Jan. 1939): 12; *Jewish Tribune* 9 (July 1938): 18.

126. *Jewish Advocate* 9 (24 Feb. 1939): 2, 4.

127. C.Z.A. S 25/3586, Shohet to Epstein, 24 Mar. 1939.

128. Ibid.

129. C.Z.A. S 25/3586, Shohet to Epstein, 8 Apr. 1939. I have not seen the "interview as recorded by Gandhi's secretary" enclosed with the letter of 8 Apr. 1939, which Shimoni, *Gandhi*, 51 n. 96, claims to have seen, although he does quote it or compare it in detail with Shohet's report. In any case, Shimoni's citation (C.Z.A. S 25, 285), differs from what I have seen. Perhaps he saw the letter and the enclosed interview in another file. After World War II Jewish terrorism prompted Gandhi to comment, "[The Jews] have erred grievously in seeking to impose themselves on Palestine with the aid of America and Britain and now with the aid of naked terrorism." Once again, he advocated nonviolence toward the Arabs, although he sympathized with the Jews' "unenviably sad plight" (*Harijan*, 21 July 1946: 229). Shimoni, *Gandhi*, 56 n. 112, points out that Gandhi was apparently not aware that the terrorism, conducted by a small number of Jews, was directed against the British.

130. Shimoni, *Gandhi*, 60.

131. C.Z.A. S 5/456, "Visit of Mr. Yehuda Nedivi to India and the Far East: Report"; Shohet to Dr. L. Lauterbach, 30 Mar. 1939; Shohet to Epstein, 13 Apr. 1939.

132. C.Z.A. S 5/456, "Visit of Mr. Yehuda Nedivi to India and the Far East: Report."

133. Edmund de Rothschild also spoke to a large Jewish crowd in Bombay, focusing on the possibilities of settlement of Jewish refugees in Guiana, Honduras, and Rhodesia, and suggesting that they could look upon Palestine as their spiritual home. The *Jewish Advocate* 10 (19 May 1939): 3–4, 14, thought his schemes were grandiose and impractical. Only Palestine would work out, it argued, and Palestine must become a political reality. The *Advocate* voiced its anger at leading British Jews who were prepared to forgo Palestine because Britain was hard-pressed by the Arabs and because Palestine could not take all the refugees.

134. Although Zionist delegates to Calcutta always complained about the lack of interest of the Ezras, Musleah, *Ganga*, 356, claims that Sir David and Lady Rachel had a "great love for Zion." Their parents had been the backbone of local philanthropic endeavors for the Holy Land, he notes, and Sir David and Lady Rachel visited there in 1920 and 1925. They were hosts to every Zionist envoy and contributed generously to the cause, Musleah notes, giving a substantial contribution toward the cost of the 1948 War of Independence. The archives show, however, that Zionist envoys thought that the Ezras' contributions were minimal compared to what they could afford and what they gave to other charities.

135. Mozelle Nathan, a wealthy Baghdadi, had accepted the presidency of the Bombay branch of WIZO, but neither she nor Sir Alwyn Ezra gave as much as the

Zionists had expected. Both had just given large contributions to the local refugee committee and other charities. C.Z.A. S 5/456, "Visit of Mr. Yehuda Nedivi to India and the Far East: Report."

136. Ibid.

137. Mandelbaum, "Jewish Way of Life in Cochin," 447.

Chapter 7. Challenges of the War
(pages 213–237)

1. Embree, *India's Search*, 115–17; Pandey, *British India*, 149–50. Wolpert, *New History*, 329–34.

2. Schermerhorn, *Ethnic Plurality*, 192.

3. *Jewish Advocate* 10 (29 Sept. 1939): 9.

4. *Jewish Advocate* 10 (16 June 1939): 13.

5. In June 1939 Britain had issued a white paper on Palestine severely curtailing Jewish immigration. The Zionists fought the white paper while supporting the British war effort.

6. *Jewish Advocate* 10 (27 Oct. 1939): 1, 3; (15 Dec. 1939): 6. On the internment see below, pp. 220–21.

7. *Jewish Advocate* 10 (12 Jan. 1940): 2; 10 (26 Jan. 1940): 8, 9; 11 (5 Apr. 1940): 6; 11 (10 May 1940): 2; *Jewish Tribune* 11 (Aug. 1940): 4.

8. *Jewish Advocate* 11 (July 1940): 2, 13; 11 (Aug. 1940): 4, 13.

9. *Jewish Advocate* 10 (27 Oct. 1939): 3; 10 (17 Nov. 1939): 2; 10 (26 Jan. 1940): 9; 11 (July 1940): 12; 11 (Sept. 1940): 11; 11 (Dec. 1940): 14; *Jewish Tribune* 11 (Sept. 1940): 4. In Sept. 1940 there were approximately thirteen rupees to a British pound and 3.2 rupees to a dollar. One million yen equaled approximately £58,500 or $234,000.

10. B. J. Israel, *Jews of India*, 22–23; interview, 21 Dec. 1977.

11. *Jewish Advocate* 10 (26 Jan. 1940): 9; *Jewish Tribune* 12 (Dec. 1941): 4.

12. *Jewish Advocate* 11 (Feb. 1942): 2; *Jewish Tribune* 12 (Dec. 1941): 4.

13. *Jewish Tribune* 12 (Dec. 1941): 3; Musleah, *Ganga*, 351. T. V., Parasuram, *Jewish Heritage*, 123, claims that the Baghdadi Jews were far less interested in military service than the "Indian Jews."

14. Anthony, *Britain's Betrayal*, 97, 132, 154–55, 171; Schermerhorn, *Ethnic Plurality*, 224, points out that often the initiative for "passing" came from Anglo-Indians who themselves wanted to escape their community through enlistment or migration to other cities in India or Commonwealth countries.

15. *Jewish Advocate* 11 (Mar. 1941): 9.

16. Ibid., 9, 11.

17. Ibid., 2

18. *Jewish Advocate* 12 (Dec. 1942): 9; 13 (Oct. 1943): 3; 12 (Jan. 1943): 3.

19. Ezra, *Turning Back*, 293–94, 390, 435–36, 587–88.

20. Pandey, *British India*, chap. 6; Wolpert, *New History*, 334–36.

21. Sam Israel, interview, 11 Jan. 1978.

22. S. R. Bandarker, interview, 16 Aug. 1978. In 1951 he helped Congress campaign in Parel, trying to get other Jews to work with him.

23. E. M. Jacob, interview, 5 Dec. 1977; Arthur Samson, interview, 29 Aug. 1980; B. J. Israel, interviews, 22 Sept., 7 Dec. 1977.

24. See Shellim Samuel, "Jews in the Indian Army," *India and Israel* 4 (Feb. 1952): 21–24.

25. *Jewish Advocate* 12 (Feb. 1943): 17; 12 (Aug. 1943): 1.

26. *Jewish Advocate* 10 (17 Nov. 1939): 2; 10 (15 Dec. 1939): 4.

27. *Jewish Advocate* 10 (15 Dec. 1939): 2.

28. NAI, Home Department, F. 10/4/43, Pub. 1943.

29. *Jewish Advocate* 12 (Apr. 1943): 6; 12 (May 1943): 3.

30. NAI, Home Department, F. 127/39 Pol. A. W. Rosenfeld, secretary of Jewish Relief Association, Bombay, "Circular," 23 Sept. 1939.

31. Ibid.

32. *Jewish Advocate* 9 (24 Feb. 1939): 14; 12 (Oct. 1942): 7, 11. Ezra, *Turning Back*, 435–37, 587, estimated that approximately twelve hundred Jews fled from Burma to Calcutta in 1942. About 25 percent of them had left Calcutta before 1945. After the war, perhaps five hundred Jews returned to Rangoon, and from 1948 on, Burmese refugees who had remained in Calcutta gradually emigrated abroad. For an account of the experience of a group of thirty Polish refugees who arrived in Calcutta in 1941, see Ezra, 579–85.

33. *Jewish Advocate* 11 (Nov. 1941): 12; 11 (July 1941): 4, 7; (Mar. 1942): 6; 12 (Apr. 1943): 15; *Jewish Tribune* 12 (Nov. 1941): 3.

34. *Jewish Tribune* 10 (Mar. 1939): 4; *Jewish Advocate* 10 (Mar. 1939): 3; 10 (16 June 1939): 14; 10 (28 July 1939): 11; 10 (25 Aug. 1939): 3, 9–10; 10 (17 Nov. 1939): 11; 10 (1 Dec. 1939): 7–8.

35. NAI, Home Department, F. 22/26/39 Pol. 1939.

36. NAI, Home Department, F. 10/130/39, Public 1939, memo from C. I. W. Lillie, deputy secretary to the government of India. Much correspondence on this issue took place in Sept. and Oct. 1939.

37. NAI, Home Department, F. 10/2/40, Public 1940; F. 10/186/39, Public 1939; F. 10/8/40, Public 1940.

38. NAI, Home Department, F. 10/130/39, Public 1939.

39. NAI, Home Department, F. 10/86/39, Public 1939.

40. NAI, Home Department, F. 10/130/39, Public, 1939, E. Conran-Smith, 6 Mar. 1940, to undersecretary of state for India.

41. Ibid., Correspondence, Mar.–May 1940.

42. NAI, Home Department, F. 10/113/40, Public 1940.

43. NAI, Home Department, F. 10/48/41, Public 1941, General Staff Branch 9/Z/7/31 Secret, case of Dr. E. W. Petzal; Home Department, F. 10/2/43, Public 1943, Captain S. P. Matzner; Home Department, F. 10/11/45, Public 1945, Captain E. Reichbaum.

44. NAI, Home Department, F. 10/15/44, Public 1944.

45. *Jewish Advocate* 12 (Oct. 1942): 7, 11.

46. *Jewish Advocate* 12 (Mar. 1943): 12.

47. F. W. Pollack, "Candid Comments," *Jewish Advocate* 12 (Apr. 1943): 3.

48. Summary tables of Jewish census figures are available in Davis, *Population*,

179. Reissner, "Statistics," 350, calculates that of this total, approximately 9 percent were Cochini, 66 percent Bene Israel, and 25 percent Baghdadi. There is no mention of European refugees.

49. *Jewish Chronicle,* 21 Aug. 1942: 1; *Jewish Advocate* 12 (Nov. 1942): 2, 14. Leonard Gordon, who has done extensive research on Bose, believes that Bose was not anti-Semitic but that he wrote some propaganda materials for Goebbels (and also for the Japanese) to satisfy their demands, making statements that he did not really believe in (personal communication, 23 Feb. 1987).

50. NAI, Home Department, F. 1/5/45, Public (c) 1945, starred question no. 202.

51. NAI, Home Department, F. 87/4487/44 Ests. of 1944. No. 104/43 Pol. Government of India, Indians Overseas Department, 23 Dec. 1943, office memorandum.

52. Central Legislative Assembly, *Debates* 1:205–6, 15 Feb. 1943, starred question no. 80.

53. Quoted in *Jewish Advocate* 12 (July 1943): 3, 4.

54. *Bombay Sentinel,* 6 July 1943, quoted in ibid., 4.

55. *Jewish Advocate* 12 (July 1943): 9.

56. Ibid.

57. Ibid., Albert J. Gubbay, letter, p. 20.

58. Central Legislative Assembly, *Debates* 4:647, 13 Nov. 1944.

59. C.Z.A. S 5/456, S. Lowy to H. Levin of Keren Keyemet L'Israel, 19 Sept. 1939; report from S. Lowy, 13 Nov. 1939.

60. *Jewish Advocate* 10 (9 Feb. 1940): 2.

61. Pirzada, *Pakistan,* 2:334.

62. *Jewish Advocate* 10 (26 Apr. 1940): 11; 11 (10 May 1940): 1.

63. *Jewish Advocate* 10 (15 Dec. 1939): 10 (23 Feb. 1940): 7; 10 (5 Apr. 1940): 4. As late as 1943, however, a *Jewish Advocate* columnist criticized *Habonim* for its lack of Zionist spirit. He claimed that Zionist delegates who had visited Bombay were always disappointed to find that *Habonim* did nothing for Zionism except sing songs. A correspondent reminded *Habonim* members that the aloofness from Zionism of Iraqi Jews did not prevent their being massacred in 1941 (*Jewish Advocate* 12 [Feb. 1943]: 11; 12 [Mar. 1943]: 14).

64. C.Z.A. S/5 726, report from Dr. Mechner, 23 Nov. 1944. *Jewish Advocate* 11 (Nov. 1941): 11; 11 (Dec. 1941): 8.

65. *Jewish Advocate* 11 (Jan. 1941): 2, 15, 16.

66. *Jewish Advocate* 11 (Mar. 1941): 10. C.Z.A. S 5/726, Norman Shohet to Leo Lauterbach, 30 May 1942; Norman Shohet to Abe Herman, 23 Nov. 1942.

67. *Jewish Tribune* 12 (Oct. 1941): 14; *Jewish Advocate* 11 (Sept. 1941): 7.

68. *Jewish Advocate* 11 (Mar. 1941): 11; 11 (May 1941): 2. The Sir Doraby Tata Trust Fund had donated 2,500 rupees in 1927 and 750 in 1929 (C.Z.A. S 5/726, report from Dr. Mechner, 23 Nov. 1977). Sir Homy Mody, director of the Tata group, may have been particularly sympathetic to Jews, his father having been a manager in the Sassoon Mills (Markovits, *Indian Business,* 210). Kulke, *Parsees,* 142 n. 40, mentions that Parsis donated more, proportionately, to the Khilafat movement than the Muslims themselves.

69. *Jewish Advocate* 11 (Dec. 1941): 2, 7.

70. C.Z.A. S 5/726, Norman Shohet to Leo Lauterbach, 29 Sept. 1942.

71. Pirzada, *Pakistan*, 2:439–40, 480.

72. *Jewish Advocate* 11 (May 1942): 2; 11 (July 1942): 4. Timberg, "Jews of Calcutta," 33, suggests that some Zionist activity in Calcutta during World War II was somewhat resisted by the community elite, who felt it a threat to the British war effort.

73. *Jewish Advocate* 12 (July 1943): 3; 12 (Aug. 1943): 1–2. When Sir Victor Sassoon returned from America, he was again approached by the Zionists but declined to add to the 1,500 pounds that Ovadia had contributed. He did come to a Zionist meeting, however, and the fact that it was attended by more than four hundred persons made some impression upon him. A Continental Jew, Mr. Starosta, after immigrating from India to Palestine, had tried to interest Moshe Shertok in a project to have Dr. Weizmann and Lord Melchett invite Sir Victor Sassoon to visit Palestine (C.Z.A. S 5/726, report from Dr. Mechner, 23 Nov. 1944). Na'im Gubbay, J. J. Gubbay's son, remembers that Sir Victor would never contribute anything for Zionism or Palestine, unless the solicitor said that the money was for orphans, and even that took some convincing (Na'im Gubbay, interview, 6 Sept. 1977).

74. C.Z.A. S 5/726, F. W. Pollack to Leo Lauterbach, 25 Aug. 1944. Pollack turned out to be right about a weak Keren Hayesod drive—but no delegate had been sent from Palestine, and the results were always better with an emissary. Maurice D. Japheth, "Zionism in India," *Shalom* (Poona), probably Sept.–Oct. 1970: 1–3, seemed to confirm Pollack's views. Japheth singled out, in addition to A. E. Shohet and J. J. Gubbay, mainly Continental Jews as the leading Zionist workers during the war years, mentioning Dr. E. Petzal, A. Leser, Mr. Starotsa, Fred Klein, F. W. Pollack, and Hans Galland.

75. C.Z.A. S 5/726, Pollack to Lauterbach, 11 Sept. 1944; Lauterbach to M. M. Epstein, 4 Feb. 1945.

76. C.Z.A. S 5/726, report from Dr. Mechner, 23 Nov. 1944; Dr. Leo Lauterbach to M. M. Epstein, 4 Feb. 1945. In 1944, one Palestinian pound equaled slightly less than thirteen rupees.

77. *Jewish Advocate* 14 (May 1945): 15.

78. Maurice Rassaby, "The Future of the Jews in India," *Jewish Advocate* 13 (Apr. 1944): 24. A. D. Shroff, a Parsi politician speaking at a Parsi nationalist conference a few days before independence, said: "Our place in the India of tomorrow should be secured on the grounds of merit and talent. Numerically we are too insignificant to merit any attention. Instead of claiming all sorts of concessions as a minority, we should completely identify ourselves with Indians and make ourselves indispensable to the country" (quoted in Kulke, *Parsees*, 264).

79. Rassaby, "Future," 24. Early in 1942, Sir Victor Sassoon had apparently made some remarks about India's political leaders and their philosophy that greatly surprised and embarrassed his coreligionists. A copy of his statement is unavailable, but in an editorial entitled "Victor Sassoon's Politics," the *Jewish Advocate* 11 (Feb. 1942): 2 deplored his lack of discretion.

80. *Jewish Advocate* 13 (June 1944): 25.

81. *Jewish Advocate* 14 (May 1945): 14.

Chapter 8. The Postwar Dilemma
(pages 238–257)

1. Cohn, *India*, 109. The Muslim League had made a separate state its price for accepting independence. Dumont, *Homo Hierarchicus*, 333–34, attributes the Muslim League's success in the elections of Jan. 1946 to two factors: (1) partition expressed the feeling of separateness among the Muslim masses and their desire to escape "from an increasingly irksome coexistence with their Hindu neighbors" and (2) religious motives inspired the idea of territorial separation. On this period see Wolpert, *New History*, 338–49, and Michael Edwardes, *The Last Years of British India* (Cleveland, 1963), part 3.

2. Schermerhorn, *Ethnic Plurality*, 327–28.

3. Ibid., 328. Many condemn reservations in recruitment to public services and even to colleges as promoting caste spirit. Dumont, *Homo Hierarchicus*, 418–19 n. 117a, has said that in default of these reservations, all civil service posts would be in the hands of the high castes, a situation that would do much more to promote caste spirit. See also Marc Galanter, *Competing Equalities: Law and the Backward Classes in India* (Berkeley, 1984).

4. Abad Ahmad, "Economic Participation," Seminar 125 (Jan. 1970): 28, quoted in Schermerhorn, *Ethnic Plurality*, 172–73.

5. Schermerhorn, *Ethnic Plurality*, 163–64, 171–73. See also Theodore P. Wright, Jr., "The Effectiveness of Muslim Representation in India," in *South Asian Politics and Religion*, ed. Donald E. Smith (Princeton, 1966); Donald E. Smith, *India as a Secular State* (Princeton, 1963); Joseph Lelyveld, "India's 55 Million Muslims Living in Rejection and Isolation," *New York Times*, 28 Oct. 1968.

6. Schermerhorn, *Ethnic Plurality*, 200–203. He is citing an informant.

7. Ibid., 224–25.

8. Ibid., 212–13, 225–28.

9. Ibid., 213, citing Gist and Wright, *Marginality and Identity*, 135, and Noel P. Gist, "Cultural vs. Social Marginality: The Anglo-Indian Case," *Phylon* 28 (Winter 1967): 365.

10. Schermerhorn, *Ethnic Plurality*, 337 n. 20. See also Rashmi Desai, *Indian Immigrants in Britain* (London, 1963).

11. Josefa Bat Orn, "Odyssey through Jewish India," *Ammi* (Shavuot, 1977), 4–5; see also Musleah, *Ganga*, 449–50.

12. Na'im Gubbay, interview, 14 Oct. 1977; A. S. Shellim, interview, 10 Nov. 1977; Walter Abraham, interview, 2 Dec. 1977. See also Ezra, *Turning Back*, 609–11, 631–32.

13. B. J. Israel, interviews, 12 Oct., 23 Nov., 21 Dec. 1977. He thinks that perhaps the British spoiled the Bene Israel by making it so easy for them to find petty jobs in government service. The educated people preferred that security to private employment or to striking out on their own, which led to a lack of ambition and an unwillingness to compete.

14. Ezra Kolet, interview, 7 Aug. 1977; B. J. Israel, interview, 12 Oct. 1977.

15. Some Bene Israel have claimed that certain Muslims who were middle-level

employers in government would say to a Bene Israel who applied, "Why don't you go to Israel?" (Lily Samson, interview, 10 Jan. 1978).

16. See Richard J. Kozicki, "India and Israel: A Problem in Asian Politics," *Middle Eastern Affairs* 9 (May 1958): 162–65; *India and Israel* 3 (Oct. 1950), India Recognition Issue.

17. Even before naming him trade commissioner, Israel had in 1948 appointed Pollack as its official liaison with the Indian Jewish community. J. J. Gubbay had expected to be named to this position; he and other Baghdadis were angered that once again the Zionists seemed to prefer to deal with Europeans (Irith Gubbay, personal communication, 4 Mar. 1987). See also *India and Israel* 3 (Aug. 1950) and 3 (Oct. 1950); Kozicki, "India and Israel," 167–68; Walter Eytan, *The First Ten Years* (New York, 1958), 181–82. See also material in the following articles in *Israel in the Third World*, ed. Michael Curtis and Susan A. Gitelson (New Brunswick, N.J., 1976): Meron Medzini, "Reflections on Israel's Asian Policy," 203; Meron Medzini, "Asian Voting Patterns on the Middle East at the UN General Assembly," 320; Benjamin Rivlin and Jacques Fomerand, "Changing Third World Perspectives and Policies towards Israel," 332. Perhaps Israel might have relented a bit instead of insisting on reciprocity. See Onkar S. Marwah, "India's Relations with the West Asian–North African countries," *Middle East Information Series* 22 (Feb. 1973): 21–36.

18. Musleah, *Ganga*, 418–20, and *India and Israel* 2 (Aug. 1949) and 5 (June 1953): 7. These rightist parties were agencies for the perpetuation and reinterpretation of Hinduism (Srinivas, *Social Change*, 146). See Kozicki, "India and Israel," 164–65. Some Bene Israel have suggested that when the Hindus suffered at the hands of the Muslims during partition, many Indians and their newspapers became pro-Israeli (E. M. Jacob, interview, 29 Dec. 1977).

19. Quoted in Mohammed Ali Kishore, *Jana Sangh and India's Foreign Policy* (New Delhi, 1969), 128.

20. *Organiser* 17 (47) 22 June 1964: 3; 18 (11) 26 Oct. 1964: 3; 18 (33) 29 Mar. 1965, as cited in ibid., 128–31.

21. *Organiser* 19 (33) 3 Apr. 1966: 5, as quoted in Kishore, *Jana Sangh*, 131. Kishore, 230, argues that since the Arab countries sympathize with Pakistan anyway, it is time for India to change her policy regarding Israel and to establish full diplomatic relations with it.

22. Bharatiya Jana Sangh, *Party Documents, 1951–1973* (New Delhi, 1973), 3:137–38, 148.

23. See Kozicki, "India and Israel," 171–72, and editorial, *Eastern Economist* 27 (2 Nov. 1956): 647.

24. Leopold Laufer, *Israel and the Developing Countries* (New York, 1967), 205.

25. Although surveys on opinions of Israel do not exist prior to 1967, 35 percent of Indians responding to a survey after the war said that their image of Israel had improved; 18 percent said it had deteriorated; another 18 percent said it had remained the same. See *Monthly Public Opinion Surveys* 10 (June–July 1965): 22–25; 12 (July 1967): 2–15; 16 (Aug.–Sept. 1971): 37–39; 17 (Apr. 1972): 7; 18 (Sept. 1973): 8; 19 (Apr. 1974): 5; 20 (Aug. 1975): 6.

26. M. D. Japheth, "Zionism in India," 4–6. Ram Jethmalani, a Congress poli-

tician, played a leading role in this league. Internecine quarrels led to the formation of a splinter group.

27. Ibid., 6–8.

28. *Shalom*, Feb. 1972: 1. Percy S. Gourgey, a Baghdadi Jew from Bombay, was a delegate to the Twenty-third Zionist Congress in 1951. See P. S. Gourgey, "Zionism in India," *Jewish Chronicle Supplement* (London), 30 Aug. 1957.

29. These immigrants do not seem to be the same Afghan Jews mentioned in chap. 6. A major famine in Afghanistan in 1944 impelled about one thousand Jews to sell their remaining possessions and leave for India, hoping eventually to reach Palestine. Hundreds lived in miserable conditions in the Magen David Synagogue courtyard. Having entered India without residence permits, they could be deported at any time. Indian Jews tried unsuccessfully to secure immigration certificates to Palestine for them. When, in the spring of 1947, the government ordered 280 Afghan Jews to leave India immediately, the World Jewish Congress interceded and persuaded it to extend their stay until the end of that year (see Schechtman, *Wings of Eagles*, 262–63).

30. M. D. Japheth, "Zionism in India," 4; E. M. Jacob, interview, 5 Dec. 1977.

31. Interviews: E. M. Jacob, 5 Dec. 1977; B. J. Israel, 12 Oct. 1977; B. B. Benjamin, 22 Dec. 1977; Sophie Corley, 15 Dec. 1977; Enoch Ezekiel, 15 Dec. 1977; Lily Samson, 10 Jan. 1978. See also Musleah, *Ganga*, 450. See Strizower, "'Bene Israel' in Israel," 132–34.

32. Na'im Gubbay, interview, 13 Sept. 1977; Nissim Ezekiel, interview, 9 Sept. 1977. At the time of Indian independence, Anglo-Indians were given opportunities to go abroad with more exchange allowance than most Indians. Jews who wanted to go to Israel had similar opportunities. Later the foreign exchange controls became tighter (Ezra Kolet, interview, 7 Aug. 1977). Weil, "Bene Israel Indian Jews in Lod," 61–62, points out that a series of laws passed by the Maharastrian government after independence eventually abolished landlords' rights and encouraged many Bene Israel to move to the cities. Life in Bombay was hard and many Bene Israel thought that they would do better in Israel.

33. Senorah Jacobs, interview, 20 July 1977; I. I. Shapurkar, interview, 20 Sept. 1977. Strizower, "'Bene Israel' in Israel," 134–37.

34. Strizower, "'Bene Israel' in Israel," 123–27, 134–41, writing about the Bene Israel of Beersheba in this period after having visited them there, felt that their conditions were not necessarily worse than those of many "oriental" immigrants resident there, but that they had suffered a tremendous loss of self-esteem. See also *India and Israel* 4 (Dec. 1951): 41; (Jan. 1952): 37, 41; 5 (Dec. 1952): 13; (June 1953): 10–11.

35. *India and Israel* during this period frequently published letters from satisfied Indian immigrants in Israel and also articles on the dignity of manual labor. Indian statistics as of 31 Dec. 1952 stated that since 1948, 2,395 Jews had emigrated from India and that 337 had returned, many apparently at their own expense (*India and Israel* 5 [June 1953]: 10; 4 [Sept. 1951]: 36). For an excellent study of the adjustment of the Bene Israel in Israel, see Weil, "Bene Israel Indian Jews in Lod."

36. Shanta Chenoy, interview, 22 July 1977; Shalom Abraham, interview, 8 Oct. 1977.

37. Meera Mahadevan, *Shulamith* (New Delhi, 1975), translated from the Hindi.

38. Shalwa Weil, "An Overview of Research on the Bene Israel," in Timberg, *Jews in India,* 20–21, suggests that the initial rejection of the Bene Israel as Jews in Israeli society was a major reason, though not the exclusive one, for their low rate of interaction with non–Bene Israel today. She points out that Bene Israel have been described as a "closed" group who have not succeeded in Israeli society politically, economically, or socially. A disproportionate percentage of Indian children are placed in special education tracks, and few Bene Israel students enter university in any given year. Even second-generation Bene Israel continue to speak Marathi with "significant others" and have difficulty learning and communicating fluently in Hebrew. Children often show signs of introversion and withdrawal, while alcoholism is a problem for many adults. She feels that Bene Israel are experiencing a marginality in Israel that they did not experience in India.

39. B. J. Israel, "The Bene Israel Struggle for Religious Equality in Israel," in Israel, *Bene Israel of India,* 89.

40. Ibid., 90. See also *Jewish Chronicle,* 16 Mar. 1962: 25; *Hindustan Times,* 12 May 1961; *Indian Express,* 11, 13 May 1961; *Truth* (The Voice of the Bene Israel Action Committee) 2 (Nov. 1961): 2; 3 (Feb.–Mar. 1962): 2.

41. B. J. Israel, "Bene Israel Struggle," 90–91; *Indo-Israel Review* 5 (20 Sept. 1962): 2, 13, 15; I. I. Shapurkar Collection, Bombay. I. I. Shapurkar to Rabbi Norman Lamm, 20 Aug. 1962.

42. B. J. Israel, "Bene Israel Struggle," 92–93; *Jewish Chronicle,* 9 Aug. 1963: 5; *Jerusalem Post,* 16 Aug. 1963: 11. B. J. Israel, letters to the secretary of the government of India, Ministry of External Affairs, 2, 3 Apr. 1963, 31 May 1963; a copy of this letter was furnished to me by B. J. Israel.

43. B. J. Israel, "Bene Israel Struggle," 93–95; *Jewish Chronicle,* 7 Aug. 1964: 28.

44. B. J. Israel, "Bene Israel Struggle," 96–97; "Statement of the Government on the 'Bene-Israel' Problem," special session of the Knesset, 17 Aug. 1964; *Jerusalem Post,* 1 Sept. 1964: 1 *Times of India,* 2 Sept. 1964: 13; 8 Sept. 1964: 6.

45. The 1951 census lists 2,623 Jews in West Bengal, of whom 1,935 were in Calcutta (India, Census, 1951, paper no. 1, Religion and Livelihood, p. 8). See also, Census, 1961, vol. 16 (West Bengal and Sikkim), part II-C (i) Social and Cultural Tables, p. 404. Na'im Gubbay, interviews, 13 Sept., 14 Oct. 1977; Musleah, *Ganga,* 416, 450. See Ezra, *Turning Back,* 295, 435–39.

46. On the Cochin Jews in Israel, see Gilbert Kushner, *Immigrants From India in Israel* (Tucson, 1973), and Mandelbaum, "Social Stratification," in Timberg, *Jews in India,* 103–8. Nathan Katz (personal communication, 30 Sept. 1987) believes that Kushner's (and Weil's) negative evaluations of the adjustment made by the Indian Jews to Israeli life were premature and overstated.

47. *Census of India,* 1951, paper no. 1, Religion and Livelihood, p. 8. *Census of India,* 1961, vol. 1, part II-c (i), Social and Cultural Tables, supplement to Table C VII, Religion, pp. 500–501. B. J. Israel, "The Jewish Population of Kulaba District of Maharastra," in *Bene Israel of India,* 99. Yehudah Weissburger, Jewish Agency representative, interview, 3 Dec. 1977.

48. *Census of India,* 1951, paper no. 1, Religion and Livelihood, p. 8. *Census of*

India, 1961, vol. 10 (Maharastra), part X (1-B), Greater Bombay Census Tables, p. 193.

49. Interviews: Mr. and Mrs. G. L. Gabriel, 22 Nov. 1977; Reginald Mathalone, 28 Nov. 1977; A. Leiser, 10 Nov. 1977.

50. Interviews: E. M. Jacob, 5 Dec. 1977; I. I. Shapurkar, 7 Oct., 22 Oct. 1977; Albert Elias, 3 Jan. 1978; E. Z. Cohen and Albert Shellim, 18 Nov. 1977.

51. B. J. Israel, interview, 19 Oct. 1977. I. I. Shapurkar (interview, 3 Dec. 1977) says that the Baghdadi synagogues initially did join the Orthodox union as a personal favor to Rabbi Norman Lamm, who had come from the United States to help promote it, but they quietly pulled out after a year or so because it was too dominated by Bene Israel. See also B. J. Israel, "Religious Evolution," 77–78.

52. Sam and Florence Halegua, interview, 6 Jan. 1977.

53. B. J. Israel, *Bene Israel of India,* 99. A. A. Shellim, interview, 18 Nov. 1977; Albert Elias, interview, 3 Jan. 1978. A similar situation prevailed in the Jewish Girls' School in Calcutta, which, by the mid 1980s, had hardly any pupils both of whose parents were Jewish (Ezra, *Turning Back,* 369).

54. Interviews: B. J. Israel, 19 Oct. 1977; Lily Samson, 10 Jan. 1979; Enoch Ezekiel, 7 Oct. 1977; Marge Gubbay, 14 Oct. 1977; Flo Japheth Hyam, 14 Oct. 1977.

55. Interviews: Moses Sultoon, 18, 20 Oct. 1977; Isaac Shabi, 10 Nov. 1977. At one point in the late 1970s, when the Jewish Agency representative went to Calcutta, the Baghdadi Jews complained that there were no Jews for their sons and daughters to marry. When the representative replied that there were hundreds of eligible Jews in Bombay, they replied, "But they're Bene Israel!"

56. Interviews: Moses Sultoon, 20 Oct. 1977; Isaac Shabi, 10 Nov. 1977.

57. Reginald Mathalone, interview, 24 Nov. 1977. Percy Gourgey, a Baghdadi Jew from Bombay and an active Zionist who moved to England in 1953, tried to intervene with the Chief Rabbinate in Jerusalem on behalf of the Bene Israel in 1964 (personal communication, 27 Nov. 1985).

58. B. J. Israel (interview, 19 Oct. 1977) says that even at this meeting, the Baghdadis spoke Arabic among themselves so that the Bene Israel would not understand.

59. Isenberg, unpublished manuscript, 199.

60. E. G. Moses, interview, 9 Sept. 1977.

61. Constitution of the National Council of Indian Jewry (Bombay, 1979), 1–3.

62. On the Jewish communities in India in the late 1970s, see Joan Roland, "The Jews of India: Communal Survival or the End of a Sojourn?" *JSS* 42 (1980): 75–90. Ezra, *Turning Back,* 9, estimates the number of Jews in Calcutta in 1985 to be 120.

Conclusion
(pages 259–265)

1. David Lelyveld, "Fissiparous Tendencies," 6–7.

2. B. J. Israel, interviews, 22 Sept., 7 Dec. 1977. Kulke, *Parsees,* 266, has pointed out that with independence, most Parsis, who until then had kept their distance from the national movement, were now forced to rethink their position: "In order to guarantee for their community a right to exist in the Indian society and in independent India, the Parsees are unconsciously reinterpreting their role in India's most recent

history. While the critical and opposing attitude of the Parsee majority to the national movement is forgotten or repressed, the active role of the Congress Parsees is mythologized."

3. Thomas Timberg, "On Indian Jews," in Timberg, *Jews in India,* 9. In pointing out that the British had offered the Bene Israel opportunities for individual mobility and a means of circumventing the caste system, Weil, "Bene Israel Indian Jews in Lod," 57, has maintained that most Bene Israel rejected coexistence in India because pluralism implied some sort of egalitarian ideology, irrespective of whether groups have equal access to resources, and India was still a hierarchical society, dominated by caste.

4. Dumont, *Homo Hierarchicus,* 331, has pointed out: "The notion of a common territory appears so necessary in the modern consciousness of political identity that it is most unlikely that things might have taken another turn. . . . [Territory] is generally considered a *sine qua non* of the realization of a nation, while other elements, a common history . . . , a common culture, a common language, are more or less frequently found, but are not indispensable."

5. B. J. Israel, manuscript, 14 Aug. 1970.

6. Ezra Kolet, interview, 4 July 1978.

7. Hugh Tinker (review of *The Children of Israel: The Bene Israel of Bombay,* by Schifra Strizower, in *Race* 14 [1972–73]: 98–99) has suggested that the Bene Israel remaining in India possess an "alternative personality, a discarded identity. . . . They remain essentially *Indian,* still warp and woof of caste and culture." Given their assimilation of certain Hindu practices in the past, he believes, they might have remained an "obscure Hindu caste with a vague folk-memory of foreign origin (like so many other castes and clans in India) had it not have been for the intrusion of the West. . . . Within the theory of national development, the transformation of a lowly rural caste within Hinduism into a self-conscious metropolitan Jewish community, is a demonstration of the pressures of modernization, urbanization, and social mobilty at work." Perhaps Tinker is overstating the case slightly in enmeshing the Bene Israel quite so deeply in Hinduism, but his observation about their changing consciousness seems appropriate.

8. Of course, the Ethiopian situation is different from that of the Bene Israel in that the Ethiopian Jews had no real alternative: their future in their homeland would have been dismal. Having initiated and organized their immigration in an operation that attracted widespread attention, the Israelis had very high motivation to absorb the Ethiopians successfully. Eventually it might be interesting to compare the integration of the Ethiopians in Israel with that of the Bene Israel.

SELECTIVE BIBLIOGRAPHY

The bibliography is arranged under the following main headings:

I. Primary Sources
   A. Official Records and Reports
   B. Private and Communal Archives
   C. Newspapers and Periodicals
   D. Other Works
II. Secondary Works

I. Primary Sources

A. Official Records and Reports

Central Legislative Assembly. Debates, 1923–44. New Delhi.

Government of India. National Archives, New Delhi: Home Department (Establishments, Judicial, Police, Political, Public), 1886–1945.

Government of Maharastra. Archives, Elphinstone College, Bombay: General Department, 1905, 1928–39; Political Department, 1922–41.

Governor's Council. *Proceedings*, Bombay, 1892–1902.

Great Britain. Palestine Royal Commission Report, 1937. Cmd. 5479.

Great Britain. Official Report, Fifth Series, Parliamentary Debates, Commons, 1934–35. Vol. 30, 29 April–17 May.

Indian Law Reports, Bombay, 1926, 1938.

Indian Statutory Commission (Simon Commission). Report, London, 1930. Cmd. 3569.

Instruments of Instructions to the Governor-General and Governors, London, 1935. Cmd. 4805.

Judgment in High Court of Judicature at Rangoon and Original Civil Jurisdiction of April 1935. Civil Regular no. 85 of 1934. J. M. Ezekiel and one vs. C. S. Joseph and others. Published in *All-India Law Reporter*, Rangoon section, 1935.

B. Private and Communal Archives

Central Jewish Board Archives, Bombay.

Central Zionist Archives, 1913–45, Jerusalem.

D. E. B. Gadkar Collection, Poona.

Gaster Papers, Mocatta Library, University College, London.

B. J. Israel Collection, Bombay.

Jacob Sassoon Charity Trusts, Ballard Estate, Bombay.

Jacob Sassoon High School, Byculla, Bombay.
Jewish Religious Union Archives, Bombay.
Jewish Welfare Association Archives, New Delhi.
I. I. Shapukar Collection, Bombay.

C. Newspapers and Periodicals

1. The following journals are available in Bombay:
"And Ye Shall Teach Them," Bombay, 1959–62.
Bene Israelite, Bombay, 1893–98.
Bengalee, Calcutta, 1921.
Bombay Chronicle, 1930.
Bombay Sentinel, 1939, 1943.
Friend of Israel, Bombay, 1898–99, 1916–21.
Illustrated Weekly of India, Bombay, 1980, 1984.
Israel Dharmadeep, Bombay, 1881–85, 1893–95.
Israelite, Bombay, 1917–26.
Jewish Minister, Bombay, 1936–37.
Maccabi, Bombay, 1959–61.
Mebasser, Bombay, 1961–62.
Satya Prakash, Bombay, 1877–82.
Shalom, Poona, 1969–73.
Statesman, Calcutta, 1938.
Times of India, 1880, 1895, 1909, 1917, 1931–39.

2. The following journals are available in Jerusalem:
The Hebrew and Voice of Sinai, Calcutta, 1904–7.
Zion's Messenger, Bombay, 1921–24.

3. The following journals are available in New York:
Bene Israel Review, Bombay, 1925–26.
Eastern Economist, New Delhi, 1956.
Harijan, Wardha, 1938–46.
India and Israel, Bombay, 1948–53.
Indo-Israel Review, Bombay, 1958–76.
Jewish Advocate, Bombay, 1931–53 (called *Jewish Bulletin* in 1930).
Jewish Chronicle, London, 1883, 1909, 1930, 1935, 1942, 1957.
Jewish Tribune, Bombay, 1933–41.
Monthly Public Opinion Surveys, New Delhi, 1965–75.
Young India, 1921.

D. Other Works

Anderson, R., and Thompson, A. *Report of the Deputation to the India Missions Made by the American Board of Commissions for Foreign Missionaries*. Boston, 1856.
Association for the Study of Jewish Religion (Poona). *First Annual Report*, 1896.
Bene Israel Conference. *Constitution and Rules*. 1919.
———. Reports, 1918–27.

Bene Israel Conference Education Fund. Reports, 1949–75.
Bharatiya Jana Sangh. *Party Documents, 1951–1973.* Vol. 3. New Delhi, 1973.
Congress and the Problem of Minorities. Resolutions adopted by the Congress Working Committee and the All-India Congress Committee since 1885 and connected matters. Allahabad, n.d. (1947?).
Council of Indian Jewry. *Constitution,* 1979.
Sir Elly Kadoorie School Building Fund Souvenir, Bombay, 1976.
Evidence, Rangoon Court Case 22, February 1935. (Obtained from Daniel Elijah Benjamin Gadkar.)
Government of India, Ministry of Information and Broadcasting. *India, 1986.* New Delhi, 1987.
Indian Friends of Israel Society. *Memorandum of Association and Rules and Regulation,* 1964.
Israelite School of the Anglo-Jewish Association. Reports, 1880–1965.
Magen Hassidim Synagogue Souvenir Programme. Bombay, 1976.
Mayor's Fund Week Souvenir. Bombay, 1960.
Proceedings of a Meeting of the Jewish Community of Bombay, 13 February 1916 at Magen David Synagogue, 1916.
Representation from Ten Bene Israel to Edwin S. Montagu, Secretary of State for India, 22 November 1917. (Obtained from B. J. Israel.)
Sassoon J. David Trust Fund. Trust Deed. Bombay, n.d.
Sha'are Rason Synagogue, 1840–1968: A Brief Retrospect. Bombay, 1975.
Thacker's India Directory. Calcutta, 1899.
Succath Shelomo Synagogue, Poona. *Golden Jubilee Souvenir, 1921–1971.*
United Synagogue of India: Decade of Community Service, 1960–1970.

II. Secondary Works

Abraham, A. S. Review of *The Children of Israel,* by Schifra Strizower. *Times of India,* 14 May 1972.
Abraham, Isaac S. *Origin and History of the Calcutta Jews.* Calcutta, c. 1970.
Anthony, Frank. *Britain's Betrayal in India: The Story of the Anglo-Indian Community.* Bombay, 1969.
Arendt, Hannah. *The Origins of Totalitarianism.* New York, 1966.
Aziz, K. K. *Muslims under Congress Rule, 1937–1939: A Documentary Record.* Vol. 1. Islamabad, 1978.
Ballhatchet, Kenneth. *Race, Sex and Class under the Raj: Imperial Attitudes and Policies and Their Critics, 1793–1905.* London, 1980.
Bat Orn, Josefa. "Odyssey through Jewish India." *Ammi* (Shavvot, 1977): 4–5.
Bayly, C. A. "The Pre-History of 'Communalism'? Religious Conflict in India, 1700–1860." *Modern Asian Studies* 19(2) (1985): 177–203.
Bayly, Susan. "Hindu Kingship and the Origin of Community: Religion, State and Society in Kerala, 1750–1850." *Modern Asian Studies* 18(2) (1984): 177–213.
Bene Israel Annual and Year Book. Bombay, 1917–19.
Benjamin, Israel J. *Un An de Séjour aux Indes Orientales (1849–50).* Trans. from Hebrew by D. L. Alger. France, 1854.

Bermant, Chaim. *The Cousinhood*. New York, 1971.

Birmingham, Stephen. *"Our Crowd": The Great Jewish Families of New York*. New York, 1967.

Braver, Erich. "The Jews of Afghanistan: An Anthropological Report." *Jewish Social Studies* 4(2) (1942): 121–38.

Cashman, Richard. *The Myth of the Lokamanya: Tilak and Mass Politics in Maharastra*. Berkeley, 1975.

Cohen, Israel. *The Journal of a Jewish Traveler*. London, 1925.

Cohn, Bernard S. *India: The Social Anthropology of a Civilization*. Englewood Cliffs, N.J., 1971.

―――. "Notes on the History of the Study of Indian Society and Culture," in *Structure and Change in Indian Society*, ed. Milton Singer and Bernard S. Cohn, 3–28. Chicago, 1968.

Cowan, Ida. *Jews in Remote Corners of the World*. New York, 1971.

Cross, J. A. *Sir Samuel Hoare: A Political Biography*. London, 1977.

Curiosities of Judaism. Bombay, c. 1887.

David, Abraham. "Sheluhei Erez Israel." *Encyclopedia Judaica* (1971) 14:1358–68.

Davis, Kingsley. *The Population of India and Pakistan*. Princeton, 1951.

Derrett, Duncan M. "The Administration of Hindu Law by the British." *Comparative Studies in Society and History* 4 (1961–62): 10–52.

Desai, Rashmi. *Indian Immigrants in Britain*. London, 1963.

Dobbin, Christine. *Urban Leadership in Western India: Politics and Communities in Bombay City, 1840–1885*. London, 1972.

Dumont, Louis. *Homo Hierarchicus*. Chicago, 1980.

―――. "Nationalism and Communalism." *Contributions to Indian Sociology* 7(1964): 30–70.

Edwardes, Michael. *The Last Years of British India*. Cleveland, 1963.

Elias, E., and Isaac, E. *Jews in India, 1963*. Ernakulam, 1963.

―――. *Jews in India, 1964*. Ernakulam, 1964.

Elias, Flower, and Cooper, Judith E. *The Jews of Calcutta*. Calcutta, 1974.

Embree, Ainslie T. *India's Search for National Identity*. New York, 1972.

Encyclopedia Judaica. Jerusalem, 1971.

Eytan, Walter. *The First Ten Years*. New York, 1958.

Ezekiel, Moses. *History and Culture of the Bene Israel in India*. Bombay, 1948.

Ezra, Esmond David. *Turning Back the Pages: A Chronicle of Calcutta Jewry*. London, 1986.

Fischel, Walter J. "Bombay in Jewish History in the Light of New Documents from the Indian Archives." *Proceedings of the American Academy for Jewish Research* 38–39 (1972): 119–44.

―――. "Cochin." *Encyclopedia Judaica* (1971) 5:621–28.

―――. "Cochin in Jewish History." *Proceedings of the American Academy for Jewish Research* 30 (1962): 37–59.

―――. "The Contributions of Cochin Jews to South Indian and Jewish Civilization." *Commemoration Volume, Cochin Synagogue Quatercentenary Celebration*, 15–64. Cochin, 1971.

————. "Early Zionism in India." Herzl Yearbook 4 (1961): 309–38.

————. "The Immigration of 'Arabian Jews' to India in the Eighteenth Century." Proceedings of the American Academy for Jewish Research 33(1965): 1–20.

————. "The Literary Activities of the Bene Israel in India." Jewish Book Annual 29(1971–72): 5–11.

————. Unknown Jews in Unknown Lands: The Travels of Rabbi David D'Beth Hillel (1824–1832). New York, 1973.

————. Ha-Yehudim be Hoddu [The Jews in India: Their Contribution to the Economic and Political Life]. Jersualem, 1960.

Fischel, Walter J., Gottlieb, Paul, and Herzog, Avigdor. "India." Encyclopedia Judaica (1971) 8:349–60.

Fischel, Walter J., Isenberg, Shirley B., and Israel, Benjamin J. "Bene Israel." Encyclopedia Judaica Yearbook (1976), 244–47.

Forrester, Duncan F. Caste and Christianity: Attitudes and Policies of Anglo-Saxon Protestant Missionaries in India. Atlantic Highlands, N.J., 1980.

Gaikwad, V. R. The Anglo-Indians: A Study in the Problems and Processes Involved in Emotional and Cultural Integration. Bombay, 1967.

Gallanter, Marc. Competing Equalities: Law and the Backward Classes in India. Berkeley, 1984.

Ghurye, G. S. Caste and Class in India. Bombay, 1950.

————. Caste and Race in India. New York, 1932.

Gordon, Leonard A. Bengal: The Nationalist Movement, 1876–1940. New York, 1974.

Gourgey, Percy S. "Zionism in India." Jewish Chronicle Supplement. London, 30 August 1957.

Griffiths, Sir Percival. The British Impact on India. Hamden, Conn., 1965.

Hasan, Mushirul. Nationalism and Communal Politics in India, 1916–1928. Manohar, 1979.

Holmes, Colin. Anti-Semitism in British Society, 1876–1939. London, 1979.

Howe, Irving. World of our Fathers. New York, 1976.

Indian Jewish Yearbook. Bombay, 1969.

Isenberg, Shirley B. India's Bene Israel: A Comprehensive Inquiry (forthcoming).

————. "Paradoxical Outcome of Meeting of Bene Israel and Christian Missionaries in Nineteenth-Century India," in Jews in India, ed. Thomas Timberg, 348–60. New York, 1986.

Israel, Benjamin J. The Bene Israel of India. New York, 1984.

————. The Jews of India. New Delhi, 1982.

————. Khan Bahadur Jacob Bapuji Israel: A Personal Sketch. Bombay, 1960.

————. Religious Evolution among the Bene Israel of India since 1750. Bombay, 1963.

Israel, Jacob B. Letters to the Bene Israel Community of British India. Bombay, 1917, 1918.

————. The Purity of the Bene Israel. Bombay, 1918.

Israel, Jacob B., Erulkar, A. S., and others. The Bene Israel Conference Imbroglio. Bombay, 1917.

Jackson, Stanley. The Sassoons. New York, 1968.

Jaffe, Benjamin. "Shemuel Tolkowsky." Encyclopedia Judaica (1971) 15:1211.

Jain, R. K. Review of *The Children of Israel: The Bene Israel of Bombay,* by Schifra Strizower. *Jewish Journal of Sociology* 15–16 (1973–74): 126–27.

Japheth, Maurice D. *Jews of India.* Bombay, 1960.

———. *Mahatma Gandhi.* Bombay, 1968.

———. *Pursuit of Truth.* Bombay, 1948.

Johnson, Barbara Cottle (Barbara Johnson Hudson). "Shingli or Jewish Cranganore in the Traditions of the Cochin Jews of India, with an Appendix on the Cochin Jewish Chronicles." M.A. thesis, Smith College, Northampton, Mass., 1975.

Joseph, Brenda. "Samaji's Synagogue: Tales and Traditions," in *Jews in India,* ed. Thomas Timberg, 361–66. New York, 1986.

Kaufmann, S. B. (Susan Bayly). "A Christian Caste in Hindu Society: Religious Leadership and Social Conflict among the Paravas of Southern Tamilnadu." *Modern Asian Studies* 15(2) (1981): 203–34.

Kehimkar, Hayeem S. *The History of the Bene Israel of India.* Ed. Immanuel Olsvanger. Tel Aviv, 1937.

Keith, Arthur Berriedale. *The King and the Imperial Crown.* London, 1936.

King, Noel Q. "A Preliminary Note on Some Jewish Anglo-Indians," in *Jewish Tradition in the Diaspora,* ed. Mishael Maswari Caspi, 191–96. Berkeley, California, 1981.

Kishore, Mohammed Ali. *Jana Sangh and India's Foreign Policy.* New Delhi, 1969.

Koder, S. S. *History of the Jews of Kerala.* Cochin, 1974.

Kozicki, Richard J. "India and Israel: A Problem in Asian Politics." *Middle Eastern Affairs* 9 (1958): 162–72.

Kressel, Getzel. "Immanuel Olsvanger." *Encyclopedia Judaica* (1971) 12:1372.

Kulke, Eckehard. *The Parsees in India.* New Delhi, 1978.

Kushner, Gilbert. *Immigrants from India in Israel.* Tucson, 1973.

Lamb, Helen. "The Indian Business Communities and Evolution of an Industrialist Class." *Pacific Affairs* 28 (June 1955): 101–16.

Laufer, Leopold. *Israel and the Developing Countries.* New York, 1967.

Laqueur, Walter. *A History of Zionism.* New York, 1972.

Lebzelter, Gisela A. *Political Anti-Semitism in England, 1918–1939.* London, 1978.

Lelyveld, David. *Aligarh's First Generation: Muslim Solidarity in British India.* Princeton, 1978.

———. "Fissiparous Tendencies and All That: Parts and Wholes in Modern India." Preliminary draft, presented at China-Harvard Seminar, J. K. Fairbanks East Asian Research Center, Harvard University, 11 April 1986.

Lelyveld, Joseph. "India's 55 Million Muslims Living in Rejection and Isolation." *New York Times,* 28 October 1968.

Lipset, S. M. "The Study of Jewish Communities in a Comparative Context." *Jewish Journal of Sociology* 5 (1963): 157–66.

Lord, J. Henry. *The Jewish Mission Field in the Bombay Diocese.* Bombay, 1894.

———. *Jews in India and the Far East.* Kolhapur, India, 1907.

MacDougall, Hugh A. *Racial Myth in English History.* Hanover, N.H., 1982.

McLane, John R. *Indian Nationalism and the Indian Congress.* Princeton, 1977.

Mahadevan, Meera. *Shulamit.* New Delhi, 1975.

Malik, Hafeez. *Sir Sayyid Ahmad Khan and Muslim Modernization in India and Pakistan.* New York, 1980.

Mandelbaum, David G. "A Case History of Judaism: The Jews of Cochin in India and in Israel," in *The Jewish Tradition in the Diaspora,* ed. Mishael Maswari Caspi, 211–30. Berkeley, 1981.

———. "The Jewish Way of Life in Cochin." *Journal of Jewish Social Studies* 1 (1939): 423–60.

———. "Social Stratification among the Jews of Cochin in India and in Israel." *Jewish Journal of Sociology* 17 (1975): 165–210.

Markovits, Claude. *Indian Business and Nationalist Politics, 1931–1939: The Indigenous Capitalist Class and the Rise of the Congress Party.* Cambridge, England, 1985.

Marwah, Onkar S. "India's Relations with the West Asian–North African Countries." *Middle East Information Series* 22 (February 1973): 21–26.

Masani, R. P. *Britain in India.* Bombay, 1960.

———. *Dadabhai Naoroji.* Delhi, 1960.

Mazgaonker, S. S. *Occasional Thoughts.* Bombay, 1917–26.

Medzini, Meron. "Asian Voting Patterns on the Middle East at the UN General Assembly," in *Israel in the Third World,* ed. Michael Curtis and Susan A. Gitelson, 318–24. New Brunswick, 1976.

———. "Reflections on Israel's Asian Policy" in *Israel in the Third World,* ed. Michael Curtis and Susan A. Gitelson, 318–24. New Brunswick, 1976.

Mendes-Flohr, Paul R., ed. *A Land of Two Peoples.* New York, 1983.

Millin, S. Gertrude. *Rhodes.* London, 1933.

Minault, Gail. *The Khilafat Movement.* New York, 1982.

Mines, Mattison. "Muslim Social Stratification in India: The Basis for Variation." *Southwestern Journal of Anthropology* 38 (1972): 334–49.

Mookerjee, Girja K. *History of Indian National Congress.* Delhi, 1974.

Morris, Morris David. *The Emergence of an Industrial Labor Force in India: A Study of the Bombay Cotton Mills, 1854–1947.* Berkeley, 1965.

Musleah, Ezekiel M. *On the Banks of the Ganga: The Sojourn of Jews in Calcutta.* North Quincy, Mass., 1975.

Nanda, B. R. *Gokhale: The Indian Moderates and the British Raj.* Princeton, 1977.

Narayanan, M. G. D. *Cultural Symbiosis in Kerala.* Trivandrum, 1972.

Nehru, Jawaharlal. *Glimpses of World History.* London, 1949.

Neuman, Robert. "Caste and the Indian Jews." *Eastern Anthropologist* 28 (1975): 195–213.

Nissim, Itzhak. *Benei Yisroel, Piskei Halakkah* [Bene Israel: Halachic Decision and the Sources for the Investigation of Their Laws and the Question of Their Origin]. Jerusalem, 1962.

Pandey, B. N. *The Break-up of British India.* New York, 1969.

Parasuram, T. V. *India's Jewish Heritage.* New Delhi, 1982.

Pirzada, Syed Sharif Uddin, ed. *Foundations of Pakistan.* All-India Muslim League Documents, Vols. 1 and 2. Karachi, 1969, 1970.

Prasad, Beni. *India's Hindu-Muslim Question.* London, 1945.

Rabinowitz, Louis. *Far East Mission.* Johannesburg, 1952.

Ranade, Ramabai. *Ranade: His Wife's Reminiscences.* Delhi, 1963.

Reissner, H. G. "Indian Jewish Statistics, 1837–1941." *Journal of Jewish Social Studies* 12 (1950): 349–66.

Reuben, Rebecca. *The Bene Israel of Bombay.* Cambridge, 1913.

Rivlin, Benjamin, and Fomerand, Jacques. "Changing Third World Perspectives and Politics towards Israel," in *Israel in the Third World,* ed. Michael Curtis and Susan A. Gitelson, 325–60. New Brunswick, 1976.

Roland, Joan G. "A Decade of Vitality: Bene Israel Communal Development (1917–1927)," in *Jews in India,* ed. Thomas Timberg, 285–347. New York, 1986.

———. "The Jews of India: Communal Survival or the End of a Sojourn?" *Journal of Jewish Social Studies* 42 (1980): 75–90.

Roth, Cecil. *The Sassoon Dynasty.* London, 1941.

Rutnagur, S. M., ed. *Bombay Industries: The Cotton Mills.* Bombay, 1927.

Sachar, Howard M. *The Course of Modern Jewish History.* New York, 1977.

Samuel, Shellim. *Treatise on the Origin and Early History of the Beni-Israel of Maharashtra State.* Bombay, 1963.

Sassoon, David S. *History of the Jews of Baghdad.* Letchworth, 1949.

Sayeed, K. B. *Pakistan: The Formative Phase.* Karachi, 1960.

Schechtman, Joseph B. *On Wings of Eagles.* New York, 1961.

Schermerhorn, R. A. *Ethnic Plurality in India.* Tucson, 1978.

Seal, Anil. *The Emergence of Indian Nationalism: Competition and Collaboration in the Late Nineteenth Century.* London, 1968.

Sharot, Stephen. "Minority Situation and Religious Acculturation: A Comparative Analysis of Jewish Communities." *Comparative Studies in Society and History* 16 (1974): 329–54.

Shimoni, Gideon. *Gandhi, Satyagraha and the Jews: A Formative Factor in India's Policy towards Israel.* Jerusalem, 1977.

Silberman, Charles. *A Certain People.* New York, 1985.

Sitaramayya, Pattabhi. *History of the Indian National Congress.* Vol. 2. New Delhi, 1969.

Smith, Donald E. *India as a Secular State.* Princeton, 1963.

Smith, Wilfred C. *Modern Islam in India.* Lahore, 1943.

Spear, Percival. *A History of India.* Middlesex, 1970.

———. *India: A Modern History.* Ann Arbor, 1961.

Srinivas, M. N. *Religion and Society among the Coorgs of Southern India.* Oxford, 1952.

———. *Social Change in Modern India.* Berkeley, 1966.

Strizower, Schifra. "The Bene Israel and the Jewish People," in *Salo Wittmayer Baron Jubilee Volume,* ed. Saul Lieberman, 859–66. New York, 1977.

———. "The 'Bene Israel' in India." *Middle Eastern Studies* 2 (1966): 123–43.

———. *The Bene Israel of Bombay.* New York, 1971.

———. *Exotic Jewish Communities.* London, 1962.

———. "Jews as an Indian Caste." *Jewish Journal of Sociology* 1 (1959): 43–57.

———. "Ten Tribes of Bombay." *Jewish Chronicle,* 1 July 1961.

Timberg, Thomas A. "Baghdadi Jews in Indian Port Cities," in *Jews in India,* ed. Thomas A. Timberg, 273–81. New York, 1986.

————. *Jews in India*. New York, 1986.

————. "The Jews of Calcutta," in *Jews in India*, ed. Thomas A. Timberg, 28–47. New York, 1986.

————. *The Marwaris: From Traders to Industrialists*. New York, 1979.

————. "On Indian Jews," in *Jews in India*, ed. Thomas A. Timberg, 3–11. New York, 1986.

Tinker, Hugh. Review of *The Children of Israel: The Bene Israel of Bombay*, by Schifra Strizower, in *Race* 14 (1972–73): 98–100.

Tucker, Richard P. *Ranade and the Roots of Indian Nationalism*. Chicago, 1972.

Vakrulkar, Solomon M. "Our Synagogues and Their Functions: An Address to the Bene Israel." Bombay, 1909.

Weil, Shalva. "Bene Israel Indian Jews in Lod, Israel: A Study in the Persistence of Ethnicity and Ethnic Identity." D.Phil. dissertation, University of Sussex, England, 1977.

————. "Contacts between the Bene Israel and the Holy Land from the Eighth Century B.C.E. until 1948: An Ethno-Historical Perspective," in *The Sephardic and Oriental Jewish Heritage*, ed. I. Ben-Ami, 165–78. Jerusalem, 1982.

————. "Names and Identity among the Bene Israel." *Ethnic Groups* 1 (1977): 201–19.

————. "An Overview of Research on the Bene Israel," in *Jews in India*, ed. Thomas A. Timberg, 12–27. New York, 1986.

Wilson, John. *Appeal for the Christian Education of the Bene Israel*. Bombay, 1866.

————. *Lands of the Bible*. Edinburgh, 1847.

Wolpert, Stanley. *Jinnah of Pakistan*. New York, 1984.

————. *A New History of India*. New York, 1977.

————. *Tilak and Gokhale: Revolution and Reform in the Making of Modern India*. Berkeley, 1962.

Yahil, Chaim. "Moshe Sharett." *Encyclopedia Judaica* (1971) 14:1309–13.

Yehudah, Zvi. "The Place of Aliyah in Moroccan Jewry's Conception of Zionism." *Studies in Zionism* 6 (1985): 199–210.

INDEX